D0344080

THE
EURO

LIBRARIES NI
WITHDRAWN FROM STOCK

ALSO BY JOSEPH E. STIGLITZ

Rewriting the Rules of the American Economy: An Agenda for Growth and Shared Prosperity

The Great Divide: Unequal Societies and What We Can Do About Them

Creating a Learning Society: A New Approach to Growth, Development, and Social Progress (with Bruce C. Greenwald)

The Price of Inequality: How Today's Divided Society Endangers Our Future

Freefall: America, Free Markets, and the Sinking of the World Economy

The Three Trillion Dollar War: The True Cost of the Iraq Conflict (with Linda J. Bilmes)

Making Globalization Work

Fair Trade for All: How Trade Can Promote Development (with Andrew Charlton)

The Roaring Nineties: A New History of the World's Most Prosperous Decade

Globalization and Its Discontents

THE
EURO

AND ITS THREAT

TO THE

FUTURE OF EUROPE

JOSEPH E. STIGLITZ

ALLEN LANE
an imprint of
PENGUIN BOOKS

ALLEN LANE

UK | USA | Canada | Ireland | Australia
India | New Zealand | South Africa

Allen Lane is part of the Penguin Random House group of companies
whose addresses can be found at global.penguinrandomhouse.com

First published in the United States of America by W. W. Norton & Company, Inc. 2016
First published in Great Britain by Allen Lane 2016
005

Copyright © Joseph E. Stiglitz, 2016

The moral right of the author has been asserted

Printed in Great Britain by Clays Ltd, St Ives plc

A CIP catalogue record for this book is available from the British Library

ISBN: 978–0–241–25815–6

www.greenpenguin.co.uk

MIX
Paper from
responsible sources
FSC
www.fsc.org   FSC® C018179

Penguin Random House is committed to a
sustainable future for our business, our readers
and our planet. This book is made from Forest
Stewardship Council® certified paper.

To the future of Europe and the European project upon which so much depends, in the hope that this book may contribute to policies ensuring its prosperity and promoting its solidarity.

CONTENTS

PART III. MISCONCEIVED POLICIES

PART IV. A WAY FORWARD?

PREFACE

The world has been bombarded with depressing news from Europe. Greece is in depression, with half of its youth unemployed. The extreme right has made large gains in France. In Catalonia, the region surrounding Barcelona, a majority of those elected to the regional parliament support independence from Spain. As this book goes to press, large parts of Europe face a lost decade, with GDP per capita lower than it was before the global financial crisis.

Even what Europe celebrates as a success signifies a failure: Spain's unemployment rate has fallen from 26 percent in 2013 to 20 percent at the beginning of 2016. But nearly one out of two youth remain unemployed,[1] and the unemployment rate would be even higher if so many of its most talented young people had not left the country to look for jobs elsewhere.

What has happened? With advances in economic science, aren't we supposed to understand better how to manage the economy? Indeed, Nobel Prize–winning economist Robert Lucas declared in his 2003 presidential address to the American Economic Association that the "central problem of depression prevention has been solved."[2] And with all the improvements in markets, shouldn't it be even easier to manage the economy? The mark of a well-functioning economy is rapid growth, the benefits of which are shared widely, with low unemployment. What has happened in Europe is the opposite.

There is a simple answer to this apparent puzzle: a fatal decision, in 1992, to adopt a single currency, without providing for the institutions that would make it work. Good currency arrangements cannot ensure prosperity, but flawed currency arrangements can lead to recessions and depressions. And among the kinds of currency arrangements that have long been associated with recessions and depressions are currency pegs, where the value of one country's currency is fixed relative to another or relative to a commodity.

America's depression at the end of the 19th century was linked to the gold standard, where every country pegged its currency's value to gold and, therefore, implicitly to each other's currencies: with no new large discoveries of gold, its scarcity was leading to the fall of prices of ordinary goods in terms of gold—to what we call today deflation.[3] In effect, money was becoming more valuable. And this was impoverishing America's farmers, who found it increasingly difficult to pay back their debts. The election of 1896 was fought on the issue of whether, in the words of Democratic candidate William Jennings Bryan, America would "crucify mankind upon a cross of gold."[4]

So, too, the gold standard is widely blamed for its role in deepening and prolonging the Great Depression. Those countries that abandoned the gold standard early recovered more quickly.[5]

In spite of this history, Europe decided to tie itself together with a single currency—creating within Europe the same kind of rigidity that the gold standard had inflicted on the world. The gold standard failed, and, other than a few people known as "gold bugs," no one wants to see it restored.

Europe need not be crucified on the cross of the euro—the euro can work. The key reforms that are needed are in the structure of the currency union itself, not in the economies of the individual countries. Whether there is enough political cohesion, enough solidarity, for these reforms to be adopted remains in question. In the absence of reform, an amicable divorce would be far preferable to the current approach of muddling through. I will show how the split-up can be best managed.

In 2015, the 28-member European Union was the second largest economy in the world—with an estimated 507.4 million citizens and a GDP of $16.2 trillion, slightly smaller than the United States.[6] (Because exchange rates can vary a great deal, so can relative country sizes. In 2014, the EU was the largest economy.) Within the European Union, 19 countries share a common currency, the euro. The "experiment" of sharing a common currency is relatively recent—euros only began circulating in 2002, though Europe had committed itself to the idea a decade earlier, with the Maastricht Treaty,[7] and three years earlier the countries of the eurozone had pegged their values relative to each other. In 2008 the region was pulled, along with the rest of the world, into recession. Today the United States has largely recovered—an anemic and belated recovery, but a recovery nonetheless—while Europe, and especially the eurozone, remains mired in stagnation.

This failure is important for the entire world, not just for those countries in what has come to be called the eurozone. Of course, it is especially dire for those living in the crisis countries, many of which remain in depression. In our globalized world, anything that leads to stagnation in such an important part of the global economy hurts everyone.

Sometimes, as the example of Alexis de Tocqueville's *Democracy in America* so clearly illustrated, an outsider can give a more accurate and dispassionate analysis of culture and politics than those who are more directly entangled in ongoing events. The same is true, to some degree, in economics. I have been traveling to Europe since 1959—in recent decades, multiple times a year—and spent six years teaching and studying there. I have worked closely with many of the European governments (mostly in the center-left, though not infrequently with the center-right). As the 2008 global financial crisis and the euro crisis brewed and broke out, I interacted closely with several of the crisis countries (serving on an advisory council for Spain's former prime minister José Luis Rodríguez Zapatero and as a long-term friend and adviser to Greece's former prime minister George Papandreou). I saw firsthand what was happening within the crisis countries and the councils of the eurozone that were forging policies in response.

As an economist, the euro experiment has been fascinating.[8] Economists don't get to do laboratory experiments. We have to test our ideas with experiments that nature—or politics—throws up. The euro, I believe, has taught us a lot. It was conceived with a mixture of flawed economics and ideologies. It was a system that could not work for long—by the time of the Great Recession, its flaws were exposed for all to see. I believe that the underlying deficiencies had been evident from the start for anyone willing to look. These deficiencies had contributed to a buildup of imbalances that played a central role in the unfolding crises and will take years to overcome.

This experiment was especially important for me, since I had been thinking and writing about economic integration for years, and especially since I had served as economic adviser to President Bill Clinton, as chairman of his Council of Economic Advisers, in the 1990s. We worked on opening up borders for trade between the United States, Canada, and Mexico through NAFTA, the North American Free Trade Agreement. We worked, too, on creating the World Trade Organization, launched in 1995, the beginning of an international rule of law governing trade. NAFTA, launched in 1994, was not as ambitious as the European Union, which allows free mobility of workers across borders. It was much less ambitious than the eurozone—none of the three countries shares a currency. But even this limited integration posed many problems. Most importantly, it became clear that the name "free trade agreement" was itself a matter of deceptive advertising: it was really a managed trade agreement, managed especially for special corporate interests, particularly in the United States. It was then that I started to become sensitive to the consequences of the disparity between economic and political integration, and to the consequences of international agreements made by leaders—as well-intentioned as they might be—in the context of far-from-perfect democratic processes.

I went from working with President Clinton to serving as chief economist of the World Bank. Here, I was confronted with a new set of issues in economic integration that was out of kilter with political integration. I saw our sister institution, the International Monetary Fund (IMF), try to impose what it (and other donors) viewed as good economic policies on the countries needing its assistance. Their views were wrong—sometimes very wrong—and the policies the IMF imposed often led to recessions and depressions. I grappled with trying to understand these failures and why the institution did what it did.[9]

As I note at several points in this book, there are close similarities to the programs that the IMF (sometimes with the World Bank) imposed on developing countries and emerging markets, and those that have been imposed on Greece and the other afflicted countries in the wake of the Great Recession. I also explain why there are marked similarities in the reasons these programs continue to disappoint, and the widespread public opposition to them in the countries they have been imposed on.

Today, the world is beset by new initiatives designed to harness globalization for the benefit of the few. These trade agreements, which reach across the Atlantic and the Pacific, called the Transatlantic Trade and Investment Partnership and the Trans-Pacific Partnership (TTIP and TPP) agreements, respectively, are once again being crafted behind closed doors by political leaders, with corporate interests at the table. The agreements evidence a persistent desire for economic integration that is out of sync with political integration. One of their most contentious features would enable corporations to threaten countries with lawsuits when their expected profits are adversely affected by any new regulation—something that no government would countenance within its own borders. The right to regulate—and to change regulations in response to changes in circumstances—is a basic aspect of the functioning of government.

The eurozone project was, however, different from these other examples in one fundamental way: behind it was a serious intent to move toward more political integration. Behind the new trade agreements, there is no intent of having harmonized regulatory standards set by a parliamentary body that reflects the citizens of all those in the trade area. The corporate agenda is simply to stop regulation, or, even better, to roll it back.

But the design of the "single-currency project" was so influenced by ideology and interests that it failed not only in its economic ambition, bringing prosperity, but also in its ambition of bringing countries closer together *politically*.

Thus, while this book is aimed at the critical question of the euro, its reach is broader: to show how even well-intentioned efforts at economic integration can backfire when questionable economic doctrines, shaped more by ideology and interests than by evidence and economic science, drive the agenda.

The story I tell here is a dramatic illustration of several themes that have preoccupied me in recent years—themes that should have global resonance: The first is the influence of ideas, in particular how ideas about the efficiency and stability of free and unfettered markets (a set of ideas sometimes referred to as "neoliberalism") have shaped not just policies but institutions over the past third of a century. I have elsewhere described the policies that dominated the development discourse, called the Washington Consensus policies, and shaped the conditions imposed on developing countries.[10] This book is about how these same ideas shaped what was viewed as the next step in the tremendously important project of European integration, the sharing of a common currency—and derailed it.

Today, the same battle of ideas is being fought in myriad skirmishes. Indeed, in some cases, even the arguments and evidence presented are fundamentally the same. The austerity battle in Europe is akin to that in the United States, where conservatives have attempted to downsize government spending, including for badly needed infrastructure, even while unemployment remains high and resources remain idle. The fights over the right budgetary framework in Europe are akin to those that I was immersed in with the IMF during my tenure at the World Bank. Indeed, understanding the global reach of these battles is one of the reasons I have written this book.

The ideas wielded in these battles are shaped by more than just economic interests. The perspective I take here is broader than narrow economic determinism: one cannot explain an individual's beliefs *simply* by knowing what will make him better off economically. But still, certain ideas do serve certain interests, and we should thus not be surprised that by and large, policies tend to serve the interests of those who make them, even if they use more abstract ideas to argue for them. This analysis leads to an inevitable conclusion: economics and politics cannot be separated—as much as some economists would like them to be. A key reason that globalization has often failed to produce benefits for large numbers in both the developed and less developed world is that economic globalization outpaced political globalization; and so, too, for the euro.

A further theme is related to my more recent research on inequality.[11] Economists, and sometimes even politicians, focus on *averages*, what is happening to GDP or GDP per capita. But GDP can be going up, and most citizens nonetheless could be worse off. That has been happening in the United States for the last third of a century, and increasingly, there are similar trends elsewhere. Economists used to argue that how the fruits of the economy were shared did not matter—that was an outcome that might be of concern to a political scientist or a sociologist but not to an economist. Robert Lucas has gone so far as to say, "Of the tendencies that are harmful to sound economics, the most seductive, and in my opinion the most poisonous, is to focus on questions of distribution."[12]

We now know that inequality affects economic performance, so that one cannot and should not just shunt these matters aside.[13] Inequality also affects how our democracies and our societies function. I believe, however, that we should be concerned about inequality not just because of these consequences: there are fundamental moral issues at stake.

The euro has led to an increase in inequality. A main argument of this book is that the euro has deepened the divide—has resulted in the weaker countries becoming weaker and the stronger countries becoming stronger: for instance, German GDP going from 10.4 times that of Greece in 2007 to 15.0 times that of Greece in 2015. But the divide has also led to an increase in inequality within the countries of the eurozone, especially in those in crisis. And this is so even in those European countries that were making progress in reducing inequality before the start of the euro.

This should not come as a surprise: high unemployment hurts those at the bottom, high unemployment puts downward pressure on wages, and the government cutbacks associated with austerity have particularly negative effects on middle- and lower-income individuals that depend on government programs. This, too, is a cross-cutting theme of our times: the neoliberal economic agenda may not have succeeded in increasing average growth rates, but of this we can be sure: it has succeeded in increasing inequality. The euro provides a detailed case study on how this has been accomplished.

Two other themes relate more directly to work on economic systems in which I have long been engaged. It is now (finally) widely recognized that markets on their own are not efficient.[14] Adam Smith's invisible hand—by which individuals' pursuit of self-interest is supposed to lead, in the aggregate, to the well-being of the entire society—is invisible because it is simply not there. And far too little attention has been paid to the *instability* of the market economy. Crises have been part of capitalism since the beginning.[15]

The standard model used by economists simply *assumes* that it is in equilibrium; in other words, if there is ever a dip in the economy, it quickly reverts to its normal path.[16] The notion that the economy quickly *converges* to equilibrium after an upset is key in understanding the construction of the eurozone. My own research has explained why economies often do not converge, and what has happened in Europe provides a wonderful if sad illustration of these ideas.

The role of the financial system is also integral to the story told here. Financial systems are obviously a necessary part of a modern economy. But in other work I have described how, if not carefully regulated, financial systems can and do lead to economic instability, with booms and busts.[17] What has happened in Europe again provides an illustration of these issues—and of how the design of the eurozone and the policies pursued in response to the crisis exacerbated problems that are ever-present in modern market economies.

A final theme with which I have been long concerned, but which I can only touch upon in this book, relates to values that go beyond economics: (a) economics is supposed to be a means to an end, increasing the well-being of individuals and society; (b) the well-being of individuals depends not just on standard conceptions of GDP, even if that concept were broadened to include economic security, but on a much wider set of values, including social solidarity and cohesion, trust in our social and political institutions, and democratic participation; (c) and the euro was supposed to be a means to an end, not an end in itself—it was supposed to increase economic performance and political and social cohesion throughout Europe. This in turn was supposed to help achieve broader goals, including enhancing the well-being and advancing the fundamental values to which I have alluded. But it should be evident that everything has gone awry. Means have become ends in themselves; the ultimate objectives have been undermined. Europe has lost its compass. This waywardness, however, is not a uniquely European phenomenon. It has happened so often in so many places: it seems almost to be a global disease of the times.

In a sense, then, the story of the eurozone is a morality play: It illustrates how leaders out of touch with their electorates can design systems that do not serve their citizens well. It shows how financial interests have too often prevailed in the advances of economic inte-

gration and how ideology and interests run amok can result in economic structures that may benefit a few, but put at risk vast parts of
the citizenry.

It is a story, too, of platitudes, uttered by politicians unschooled in
economics who create their own reality, of positions taken for short-
run political gain that have enormous long-term consequences. The
insistence that the eurozone should not be designed in such a way
that strong countries would be expected to help those having a temporary problem may have a certain appeal to selfish voters. But without a minimal degree of risk-sharing, no monetary union can possibly
function.

For most Europeans, the European project, the further integration
of the countries of the continent, is the most important political event
of the last 60 years. To see it fail, or to suggest that it might fail, or that
one aspect of the project—its currency system—might fail, is viewed
almost as heresy. But reality sometimes delivers painful messages:
the euro system is broken, and the cost of not fixing it very quickly will
be enormous. The current system, even with its recent reforms, is not
viable in the long run without imposing huge costs on large numbers
of its citizens. And the costs extend well beyond those to the economy:
I referred earlier to the disturbing changes in politics and society, the
rise of extremism and right-wing populism. While the euro's failure is
not the only reason for these trends, I believe that the huge economic
toll that has been imposed on so many of its citizens is one of the more
important causes, if not the most important one.

These costs are especially high for Europe's youth, whose future
is being put in jeopardy, whose aspirations are being destroyed. They
may not understand fully what has happened, they may not fully
understand the underlying economics, but they understand this: they
were lied to by those who tried to persuade them to support the creation of the euro and to join the eurozone, who promised that the creation of the euro would bring unprecedented prosperity and that, so
long as countries stuck to basic strictures keeping deficits and debts,

relative to GDP, low, the poorer countries of the eurozone would converge to the richer. They are now being told, often by the same politicians or politicians from the same parties: "Trust us. We have a recipe, a set of policies, which, while it may inflict some pain in the short run, will in the long run make all better off."

Despite the dismal implications of my analysis for what will happen if the eurozone is not changed—and the even worse implications if the eurozone is changed in ways that many in Germany and elsewhere are now arguing for—this book is, in the end, hopeful. It is a message of hope that is especially important for Europe's youth and for those who believe in the European project, in the idea that a more politically integrated Europe can be a stronger and more prosperous Europe. There is another way forward, different from that which is currently being pushed by Europe's leaders. Indeed, there are several ways forward, each requiring a different degree of European solidarity.

Europe made a simple and understandable mistake: it thought that the best way toward a more integrated continent was through a monetary union, sharing a single currency. The eurozone and the euro—both the structure and its policies—have to be deeply reformed if the European project is to be saved. And it can be.

The euro is a manmade construction. Its contours are not the result of inexorable laws of nature. Europe's monetary arrangements can be reconfigured; the euro can even be abandoned if necessary. In Europe as well as elsewhere, we can reset our compass, we can rewrite the rules of our economy and our polity, to achieve an economy with more and better-shared prosperity, with a strengthened democracy and stronger social cohesion.

This book is written in the hope that it provides some guidance on how Europe can do this—and that it provide some impetus to Europe's undertaking this ambitious agenda quickly. Europe must restore the vision of the noble ends it sought at the inception of the European Union. The European project is too important to be destroyed by the euro.

ACKNOWLEDGMENTS

The euro crisis has been in the making for years, and in those years, I have accumulated a large set of debts from those with whom I have been engaged in innumerable discussions on the future of the euro, academics, political leaders, those in financial markets, and citizens.

Some of the key ideas were presented at a conference, "Debt Crises: How to Manage Them, How to Ensure There Is Life after Debt," organized by the International Economic Association in Buenos Aires, August 13–14, 2012, and as the Fourteenth Angelo Costa Lecture, on May 6, 2014, at Luiss Guido Carli University, Rome.* I wish to acknowledge my debt to my discussants, Martin Guzman and Daniel Heymann, and to the other participants in these events.

Many of the ideas contained here have been discussed at conferences in recent years sponsored by the Initiative for Policy Dialogue (IPD), by

* The presentations were subsequently published as "Can the Euro Be Saved? An Analysis of the Future of the Currency Union," *Rivista di Politica Economica*, no. 3 (July–September 2014): 7–42; and "Crises: Principles and Policies: With an Application to the Eurozone Crisis," in *Life After Debt: The Origins and Resolutions of Debt Crisis*, ed. Joseph E. Stiglitz and Daniel Heymann (Houndmills, UK, and New York: Palgrave Macmillan, 2014), pp.43–79.

the Foundation for European Progressive Studies (FEPS), and by the Initiative for New Economic Thinking (INET), and at a multitude of other conferences debating the future of the euro at events in Washington, Berlin, Brussels, Rome, Madrid, New York, and elsewhere. I have particularly benefited from the discussions at the Symi Symposium organized by the Andreas G. Papandreou Foundation in Greece every summer, at which I have been a regular participant. Especially valuable was the 2015 meeting with its discussion of the crisis in Greece, with insights from Richard Parker, Robert Skidelsky, Nathan Gardels, Kemal Dervis, Leif Pagrotsky, Mats Karlsson, and Mary Kaldor, among others.

Over the years both before and after the crises, and especially in the midst of the crises, I have been fortunate enough to engage with a number of Europe's leaders, its presidents, prime ministers, central bankers, and finance ministers—with some of them quite deeply—not only in the crisis countries (Ireland, Portugal, Spain, and Greece—the one crisis country that I did not have a chance to visit was Cyprus) but also those facing difficulties (Italy, France, Finland) and some of the seemingly strong countries (Germany, Netherlands, Belgium), enabling me to get a better understanding of how they saw the future of Europe and the euro. I served on the Advisory Committee of Progressive Intellectuals for José Luis Rodríguez Zapatero (prime minister of Spain, 2004–2011). I engaged in debates and discussions with Italian prime ministers Mario Monti (2011–2013) and Matteo Renzi (2014–); presidents Nicolas Sarkozy (2007–2012) and François Hollande (2012–) in France; Enda Kenny, taoiseach of Ireland (2011–2016); José Sócrates and António Costa, prime ministers of Portugal (2005–2011 and 2015, respectively); and Alexis Tsipras, prime minister of Greece (2015–), among others. I should single out Yanis Varoufakis (Greece's finance minister during much of 2015) and James Galbraith for particularly insightful discussions in the summer of 2015 concerning the critical period surrounding the potential Grexit, and George Papandreou (Greece's prime minister, 2009–2011 and organizer of the Symi Symposium), whose insights into not only Greece but also into the entire eurozone were invaluable. His teaching stint at Columbia after he left office gave us an opportunity for even more extensive discussions. His brother Nikos, a former World Bank economist and student of mine at Princeton, provided distinctive perspectives on the interface between economics and politics and the media-banking oligarchy that had long been so influential in Greece. The IMF, one of the members of the Troika formulating the crisis policies, has been not only more open than in the past but unusually self-critical of some of the country programs, as I note later in this book. I have benefited enormously from discussions with senior officials at the IMF and want to acknowledge their openness and their willingness to discuss frankly the economics and politics behind the programs—even if I did not always agree with their conclusions.

The global financial crisis of 2008 morphed, almost seamlessly, into the euro crisis, and as the storm clouds gathered, the president of the General Assembly of the UN asked me to chair the Commission of Experts on Reforms of the International Monetary and Financial System, whose recommendations were the basis of a broad and substantive statement on the World Financial and Economic Crisis and Its Impact on Development adopted by a consensus of the 192 member states on June 26, 2009.[*] I am greatly indebted to the members and staff of the commission for their insights into crises, their causes and consequences. Though we focused much of our attention on the impacts of the crisis on emerging markets and developing countries, much of what we said has proven equally applicable to Europe.

The subject of the euro has, of course, been a fascinating one for economists. Among the numerous individuals from whom I have learned enormously, three require special note: Martin Wolf, both

---

[*] The report of the commission was published as *The Stiglitz Report: Reforming the International Monetary and Financial Systems in the Wake of the Global Crisis*, with members of the Commission of Experts on Reforms of the International Monetary and Financial System appointed by the president of the UN General Assembly (New York: The New Press, 2010).

from conversations and from his book *The Shifts and Shocks* (New York: Penguin Press, 2014); George Soros, whose deep concern for the consequences of the euro crisis and his substantial understanding of financial markets inevitably led to his immersion into the euro crisis—and again I have learned from both his writings on the subject and our innumerable discussions; and Rob Johnson, president of INET and my former student at Princeton, to whom I am grateful not only for frequent discussions on the subject but for his convening of economists from Europe and America who have attempted to come to a common understanding of the causes and responses to the crisis.

Among the most thoughtful studies on the euro crisis and reforming the eurozone have been those produced by the Bruegel think tank in Brussels, and I have found their papers, including the work of Jean Pisani-Ferry, Paul De Grauwe, and André Sapir, particularly helpful, enriched by discussions in multiple venues. At the risk of important omissions, I should also acknowledge Jean-Paul Fitoussi, Maria João Rodrigues, Stephany Griffith-Jones, Daniel Gros, Daniel Cohen, Ernst Stetter, José Antonio Ocampo, Adair Turner, Paul Krugman, Nouriel Roubini, Peter Bofinger, Heiner Flassbeck, Richard Koo, Hans-Werner Sinn, Richard Portes, George de Menil, Dennis Snower, George Akerlof, Olivier Blanchard, Jeff Sachs, Nick Stern, Dominique Strauss-Kahn, Dani Rodrik, and Thomas Piketty.

As I explain in the preface, one of the reasons that I have been so fascinated with the "euro experiment" is that it brings together so many strands of thought, so many issues, with which I have been involved: the economic integration that is at its core is central to the globalization theme, to which two of my earlier books (*Globalization and Its Discontents* and *Making Globalization Work*) were devoted. Those books set forth the great number of colleagues—both in academia and especially at the World Bank and other international institutions—to whom I am beholden. Those books, as well as *Freefall: America, Free Markets, and the Sinking of the World Economy* and *The Roaring Nineties: A New History of the World's Most Prosperous Decade*, set forth the dangers of adherence to simplistic ideas (neoliberalism, or market fundamentalism) about the functioning of markets—dangers which I saw firsthand during both my years in the Clinton administration and at the World Bank. This book builds on those insights, and thus my debts are compounding. My ideas about crises and their management were shaped by the East Asia crisis, in which I was intimately involved as chief economist of the World Bank. (Even before that, as I entered the World Bank, we had to deal with the aftermath of the Mexican crisis, which had begun at the very end of 1995, while I was serving on the Council of Economic Advisers of President Clinton.) I am especially grateful to my colleagues at the World Bank who helped shape our policies in response to that and other crises and those we recommended for preventing another occurrence—in particular, Amar Bhattacharya, Ravi Kanbur, Masood Ahmad, Gerard Caprio, Patrick Honohan, Uri Dadush, Bill Easterly, Roumeen Islam, Anupam Khanna, Guillermo Perry, Boris Pleskovic, Ajay Chhibber, Stijn Claessens, Dennis de Tray, Ishac Diwan, Isabel Guerrero, Michael Walton, Danny Kaufmann, Danny Leipziger, Homi Kharas, Mustapha Kamel Nabli,[*] Akbar Noman, John Page, Jean-Michel Severino (who served as vice president for East Asia during this critical time), Marilou Uy,[†]

---

[*] He later went on to become chair of Tunisia's central bank in the aftermath of the Arab Spring. We worked together in the years after 2011 to facilitate a smooth transition to democracy. Earlier, we had worked together as members of the High Level Group of Experts established by the secretary-general of the UN in 1993 to analyze key aspects of development policy in the light of the new thinking on economic and social issues. The results of that working group were published as Edmond Malinvaud et al., eds., *Development Strategy and the Management of the Market Economy*, vol. 1 (Oxford: Clarendon Press, 1997).

[†] Together with John Page, we had worked on an important project assessing the lessons for development from East Asia's success, subsequently published as World Bank, *The East Asian Miracle: Economic Growth and Public Policy* (New York: Oxford University Press, 1993). Marilou Uy and I also wrote more specifically on the role of the financial sector: "Financial Markets, Public Policy, and the East Asian Miracle," *World Bank Research Observer* 11, no. 2 (August 1996): 249–76.

Jason Furman, and Vinod Thomas. I have continued my involvement with the World Bank, serving on an advisory board to the chief economist. Inevitably, our discussions would turn to the global and euro crises, and the insights of the advisory board and staff of the World Bank have been very helpful. In particular, I should acknowledge discussions with the current chief economist, Kaushik Basu.[*]

For almost two decades, Columbia University has been my intellectual home. It has given me the freedom to pursue my research and provided me with bright, enthusiastic students who sought out challenges, and brilliant colleagues from whom I have learned so much, including many who have studied the euro crisis and/or the multiple other crises that have afflicted market economies, including Patrick Bolton, Charles Calomiris, Glenn Hubbard, Frederic Mishkin, and Tano Santos. Tano brought special knowledge of the Spanish crisis. The broad diversity of students from all over the world—so many of whom were keenly interested in the future of the euro—has provided an abundance of occasions for rich discussions on the topics discussed here. Most importantly, the ideas expressed in this book have been shaped by long discussions with my longtime friend and coauthor Bruce Greenwald. For many years, we have discussed the euro crisis in the course we jointly teach on globalization and markets, and these ideas have repeatedly been tested on the students in that course.

Of course, I need to make the usual disclaimer: none of those who have provided me with insights and ideas should be held responsible in any way for anything contained in this book.

The production of a book such as this entails the concerted effort of a large number of individuals. Over the years, a large number of research assistants have helped me on this project, and I wish to thank them all: Sandesh Dhungana, Jun Huang, Leo Lijun Wang, Laurence

---

[*] Together, we published a paper on a key issue in the crisis: "Sovereign Debt and Joint Liability: An Economic Theory Model for Amending the Treaty of Lisbon," *Economic Journal* 125, no. 586 (August 2015): F115–F130.

Wilse-Samson, Ruoke Yang, and Feiran Zhang. Also, a special thanks
to Hannah Assadi and Sarah Thomas for their support through the
writing process. Once again, I had the good fortune to work with
W. W. Norton and Penguin, with keen editorial contributions from
Drake McFeely and Stuart Proffitt, and especially Brendan Curry.
Debarati Ghosh and Eamon Kircher-Allen in my office not only
pushed the project through, including managing the enormous tasks
of gathering data and fact-checking, but also made important intellectual and editorial contributions.

Finally, as always, I owe my biggest debt to my wife, Anya Schiffrin,
who not only helped edit the book—bringing what would have been a
discursive tome into what I hope is a very readable volume—but constantly reminded me of the importance of the European project and
that the key question was the impact of the euro on that. This book
would not have been possible without her.

PART I

EUROPE IN CRISIS

1

THE EURO CRISIS

Europe, the source of the Enlightenment, the birthplace of modern science, is in crisis. The 2008 global financial crisis morphed seamlessly into the 2010 "euro crisis." This part of the world, which hosted the Industrial Revolution that led to the unprecedented changes in standards of living of the past two centuries, has been experiencing a long period of near-stagnation. GDP per capita (adjusted for inflation) for the eurozone[1]—the countries of Europe that share the euro as their currency—was estimated to be barely higher in 2015 than it was in 2007.[2] Some countries have been in depression for years.[3]

When the US unemployment rate hit 10 percent in October 2009 most Americans thought that was intolerable. It has since declined to 5 percent. Yet the unemployment rate in the eurozone reached 10 percent in 2009 as well, and has been stuck in the double digits ever since.[4] On average, more than one out of five youths in the labor force are unemployed, but in the worst-hit crisis countries, about one out of two looking for work can't find jobs.[5] Dry statistics about youth unemployment carry in them the dashed dreams and aspirations of millions of young Europeans, many of whom have worked and studied hard. They tell us about families split apart, as those that can leave emigrate from their country in search of work. They presage a European future with lower growth and living standards, perhaps for decades to come.

These economic facts have, in turn, deep political ramifications. The foundations of post–Cold War Europe are being shaken. Parties of the extreme right and left and others advocating the breakup of their nation-states, especially in Spain but even in Italy, are ascendant. What had seemed inevitable in the arc of history—the formation of nation-states in the 19th century—is now being questioned. Questions are arising, too, about the great achievement of post–World War II Europe—the creation of the European Union.

The events that precipitated the acute euro crisis were symptoms of deeper problems in the structure of the eurozone, not its causes: interest rates on the bonds issued by Greece and several of the eurozone countries soared, peaking in the case of Greece at 22.5 percent in 2012.[6] At times, some countries couldn't get access to finance at any terms—they couldn't obtain the money they needed to repay the debts they owed. Europe came to the rescue, providing short-term financing, with strong conditions.

After the euro crisis broke out in early 2010, Europe's leaders took a succession of actions, each of which seemed to calm markets for a while. As this book goes to press, even the Greek crisis has slipped to the background as Europe hopes that its latest agreement, in the summer of 2015, will at last work, and as other crises have come to the fore: the migrant crisis erupted to take front stage, as did that posed by the threat of Britain's exit from the EU and the terrorists' threats made so clear by the attacks in Paris and Brussels. The euro was supposed to bring about closer economic and political integration, helping Europe address whatever challenges the region faced. As we emphasize in the next chapter, the reality has been otherwise: the *failure* of the euro has made it more difficult for Europe to face these other crises. Thus, though this book is about *economics*—the economics underlying its failure and what might be done about it—

the economics is intimately intertwined with the politics. Politics make it difficult to create the economic arrangements that would enable the euro to work. And there, in turn, are grave political consequences to this failure.

This book will make clear why the actions taken so far to "solve" the euro crisis have been only temporary palliatives: more likely than not, the next episode of the euro crisis will break out in the not too distant future.

THE CENTRAL THESES

While there are many factors contributing to Europe's travails, there is one underlying *mistake*: the creation of the single currency, the euro. Or, more precisely, the creation of a single currency without creating a set of institutions that enabled a region of Europe's diversity to function effectively with a single currency.

Part II of the book (chapters 4 to 6) looks at the requirements for a successful monetary union, what Europe actually did, and how the gap between what was required to be done and what was done led to the failures of the euro, to the crises that ensued shortly after its creation, and to *divergence*, with the rich getting richer and the poor poorer—making it ever harder for the single-currency system to work. Part III (chapters 7 and 8) looks more closely at how the eurozone responded to the crises as they seemingly came to the "rescue," with programs that in fact deepened and prolonged the downturns. Part IV (chapters 9 to 12) explains what can be done to restore Europe to prosperity.

A NOTE ON THE HISTORY OF THE EURO, AND THE SCOPE OF THIS BOOK

In this book, I do not offer a detailed history of the euro, nor do I provide a detailed description of its institutions. But by way of orientation, it is useful to note a few facts about the chronology and the establishment of the euro. The common currency was an outgrowth of efforts that began in the mid-20th century, as Europe reeled from the carnage and disruption of two world wars that claimed some 100 million lives. Europe's leaders recognized that a more peaceful future would necessitate a complete reorganization of the politics, economics, and even the national identities of the continent. In 1957, this vision came closer to being a reality with the signing of the Rome Treaty, which established the European Economic Community (EEC), comprising Belgium, France, Italy, Luxembourg, the Netherlands, and West Germany. In the following decades, dominated by the Cold War, various other Western European countries joined the EEC. Step by step, restrictions were eased on work, travel, and trade between the expanding list of EEC countries.

But it was not until the end of the Cold War that European integration really gained steam. The fall of the Berlin Wall in 1989 showed that the time for much closer, stronger European bonds had grown near. The hopes for a peaceful and prosperous future were higher than ever, among both leaders and citizens. This led to the signing, in 1992, of the Maastricht Treaty, which formally established the European Union and created much of its economic structure and institutions—including setting in motion the process of adopting a common currency, which would come to be known as the euro.

Still, there was disagreement about how that greater unity should be accomplished. Today, the official history of the EU may look like a bullet-point list of events leading inevitably to the creation of an ever-expanding common market and common currency area, the eurozone. But the formation of these institutions was in fact the result of years of negotiations that were fraught with deep disagreements about the extent and form of European integration. The results were only possible because of European leaders' bargains and compromises. In the case of the euro, Helmut Kohl, the German chancellor, reportedly agreed to its creation in return for French president François Mitterrand's acceptance of the reunification of Germany. Both men were pivotal in advancing the idea of integration—and in designing many of the policies that I discuss in this book.

ALL THIS HISTORY is important, but much of it is beyond the remit of this book. The point I want to make—and which I will return to throughout—is that the euro was a political project, and in the case of any political project, politics matters.

The personalities in the politics matter, too—one thinks, for instance, of Jacques Delors, whose commission laid out the plan for the creation of the euro in 1989—though again, that is not my focus here. In describing the creation of the euro, I do not fully know what was in the minds of those who were there at its founding. They clearly thought that the system would work—or else they would not have agreed to it. They would have been naïve if they thought that problems wouldn't be exposed down the road; but presumably they believed that any such problems could and would be addressed. They believed that the single currency, the euro, and the institutions that supported it, especially the European Central Bank (ECB), would be a permanent feature of the European Union. But this book is not about that history or about the founders' individual understandings of the workings of this new system.

Instead, I am interested in the *outcomes* of that history—what we can read into them, and what we can do about them. This book is about economics and economic ideologies and their interactions with politics: it is a case study of how, even with the best of intentions, when new institutions and policies are created on the basis of oversimplified views of how economies function, the results can be not only disappointing, but even disastrous.

FLAWED AT BIRTH

The eurozone was flawed at birth. The structure of the eurozone—the rules, regulations, and institutions that govern it—is to blame for the poor performance of the region, including its multiple crises. The diversity of Europe had been its strength. But for a single currency to work over a region with enormous *economic and political* diversity is not easy. A single currency entails a *fixed* exchange rate among the countries and a single interest rate. Even if these are set to reflect the circumstances in the majority of member countries, given the economic diversity, there needs to be an array of institutions that can help those nations for which the policies are not well suited. Europe failed to create these institutions.

Moreover, there has to be sufficient flexibility in the rules to allow for adaptation to differences in circumstances, beliefs, and values. Overall, Europe has enshrined this in its principle of *subsidiarity*, which entails devolving responsibility for public policy to the *national* level, rather than the European level, for as wide a range of decisions as possible.[7] Indeed, with the budget of the European Union only about 1 percent of its GDP[8] (in contrast to the United States, where federal spending is more than 20 percent of GDP),[9] little spending occurs at the EU level. But in an arena crucially important to the well-being of individual citizens—monetary policies that are critical in determining unemployment and the bases of livelihoods—power was centralized in the European Central Bank, established in 1998. And, with strong constraints on deficit spending, the individual countries were given insufficient flexibility in the conduct of their fiscal policy (taxes and expenditure) to enable a country facing adverse circumstances to avoid a deep recession.[10]

Worse still, the structure of the eurozone itself built in certain ideas about what was required for economic success—for instance, that the central bank should focus on inflation, as opposed to the mandate of the Federal Reserve in the United States, which incorporates unemployment, growth, and stability as well.[11] It was not simply that the eurozone was not structured to accommodate Europe's economic diversity; it was that the structure of the eurozone, its rules and regulations, were not designed to promote growth, employment, and stability.

The problems with the *structure* of the eurozone have been compounded by the *policies* the region has pursued, especially in the after-math of the crisis, and within the crisis countries. Even granting the zone's flawed structure, there were choices to be made. Europe made the wrong ones. It imposed austerity—excessive cutbacks in government expenditures. It demanded certain "structural reforms," changes in how, for instance, the afflicted countries ran their labor markets and pensions. But for the most part, it failed to focus on those reforms most likely to end the deep recessions the countries faced. Even if they had been perfectly implemented, the policies pushed on the crisis countries would not have restored the afflicted countries or the eurozone to health.

Thus, the most urgent reforms needed are in the eurozone struc-ture itself—not in the individual countries—and a few, halting steps have been taken in that direction. But those steps have been too few and too slow. Germany and others have sought to blame the victims, those countries that suffered as a result of the flawed policies and the flawed structure of the eurozone. Yet without the needed reforms of the structure of the eurozone itself, Europe cannot return to growth.

DIGGING DEEPER: WHY THE FLAWED STRUCTURE AND POLICIES?

Why would well-intentioned statesmen, attempting to forge a stron-ger, more united Europe, create something that has had the opposite effect? This book is not just about this major event, the euro crisis, which is transforming Europe, and the *economics* that lay behind it. It is about the intertwining of politics and economics, and about the role of *ideas* and *beliefs*.

While the euro was a political project, the political cohesion—espe-cially around the notion of delegation of powers from the sovereign countries to the EU—was not strong enough to create the economic institutions that might have given the euro a chance to succeed.

Moreover, the founders of the euro were guided by a set of ideas, notions about how economies function, that were fashionable at the time but that were simply wrong.[12] They had faith in markets and lacked an understanding of the limitations of markets and what was required to make them work. The unwavering faith in markets is sometimes referred to as market fundamentalism, sometimes as neo-liberalism.[13] Market fundamentalists believed, for instance, that if only the government would ensure that inflation was low and stable, markets would ensure growth and prosperity for all. While in most of the world, market fundamentalism has been discredited, especially in the aftermath of the 2008 global financial crisis, those beliefs survive and flourish within the eurozone's dominant power, Germany. They are held with such conviction and certainty, immune to new contrary evidence, that these beliefs are rightly described as an *ideology*. As I note in the preface, similar ideas, pushed by the IMF and the World Bank around the world, led to a lost quarter-century in Africa, a lost decade in Latin America, and a transition from communism to the market economy in the former Soviet Union and Eastern Europe that was, to say the least, a disappointment.

The failures in the eurozone, both in its structure and policies, can thus in large part be attributed to the combination of a misguided economic ideology that was prevalent at the time of the construction of the euro and a lack of deep political solidarity. This combination led the euro to be created in a way that sowed the seeds of its own destruction.

MISCONCEPTIONS ABOUT THE PROCESS OF ECONOMIC AND POLITICAL CHANGE

Flawed beliefs about the process of reform contributed as well. Leaders knew that the eurozone project was incomplete. But the project was seen as part of a long-term process. The dynamics unleashed by the euro would force the creation of any necessary but missing institutions. This success would then further political and economic integration.

In my time as chief economist of the World Bank, I learned that one must be extremely careful in the timing and pacing of reforms.[14] An initial failure increases resistance to further reforms. This is the story of the euro.

THE WAY FORWARD

Advocates of the current policies within the eurozone, led by Germany, have essentially said *"there is no alternative"* to the current structure (the small modifications which it has been willing to accept aside) and to the policies it has imposed. This has been said so often that it has the dubious distinction of having its own acronym: TINA. Part IV (chapters 9 to 12) shows that there are alternatives to the current approach—reforms that would make the euro work (chapter 9), an amicable divorce (chapter 10), and a halfway house, but a markedly different halfway house than the current one (chapter 11), one that could easily morph into a single currency should there be sufficient resolve to make such a system work. But the current halfway house—a single currency without the minimal institutions required of a common currency area—has not worked and is not likely to do so. There either has to be "more Europe" or "less."

WORSE THAN A LOST DECADE?

From time to time—when crises hit—it takes years for economies to return to precrisis levels of growth and unemployment. What Europe faces is worse: in most of the European countries, standards of living almost surely will *never* reach the level that they would have hit had it not been for the euro crisis—or if the euro crisis had been better managed. But the failure of the euro goes even deeper.

Advocates of the euro rightly argue that the euro was not *just* an economic project that sought to improve standards of living by increasing the efficiency of resource allocations, pursuing the principles of comparative advantage, enhancing competition, taking advantage of economies of scale, and strengthening economic stability. More important, it was a political project; it was supposed to enhance the political integration of Europe, bringing the people and countries of Europe closer together and ensuring peaceful coexistence.

The euro has failed to achieve either of its two principal goals of prosperity and political integration: these goals are now more distant than they were before the creation of the eurozone. Instead of peace and harmony, European countries now view each other with distrust and anger. Old stereotypes are being revived as northern Europe decries the south as lazy and unreliable, and memories of Germany's behavior in the world wars are invoked.

DISMAL ECONOMIC PERFORMANCE

The economic performance of the countries in the eurozone has been a disappointment. The eurozone has essentially stagnated, and its economic performance has been particularly dismal since the global financial crisis. Critics of the euro always said its test would be when the countries of the eurozone faced an asymmetric shock, a change that hit some countries differently than it did others. The aftermath of the global financial crisis of 2008 has shown that these fears came true and then some: the economies of the eurozone have done more poorly than even its greatest critics had predicted. The crisis began in the United States, but the United States has recovered—albeit anemically—with real GDP[15] in 2015 some 10 percent higher than in 2007; the eurozone's GDP[16] has hardly changed since 2007—indeed, as we noted, per capita income adjusted for inflation has fallen. The eurozone even saw a double-dip recession. Some of those outside of the eurozone, such as Sweden and Norway, have been doing quite well. There is one overriding factor contributing to the eurozone's poor performance: the euro.

EVEN GERMANY IS A FAILURE

Germany holds itself out as a success, providing an example of what other countries should do. Its economy has grown by 6.8% since 2007, implying an average growth rate[17] of just 0.8 percent a year, a number which, under normal circumstances, would be considered close to failing.[18] It's also worth noting that developments in Germany *before* the crisis, in the early 2000s—when the country adopted reforms that aggressively cut into the social safety net—came at the expense of ordinary workers, especially those at the bottom. While real wages stagnated (by some accounts decreased), the gap between those at the bottom and the middle increased—by some 9 percent in a short span of less than a decade. And through the early years of the century, poverty and inequality increased, as well.[19]Germany is talked about as a "success" only by comparison with the other countries of the eurozone.

HOW THE EURO *CREATED* THE EURO CRISIS

Proponents of the euro counter that the euro *did* work, even if it worked only for a short period. Between 1999 and 2007,[20] *convergence* reigned, with the weaker countries growing rapidly as the interest rates governments and firms had to pay on their loans came down. The euro succeeded in promoting economic integration, as capital flowed toward the poorer countries. For them, the euro was the victim of an unfortunate storm coming from the other side of the Atlantic, a once-in-a-century hurricane. The fact that the hurricane resulted in devastation should not be blamed on the euro: good economic systems are built to withstand normal storms; but not even the best designed could stand up against such rare events. So the proponents claim.

It is true that the global financial crisis exposed the euro's weakest point: the way it impeded adjustments to shocks that affect parts of the eurozone differently. But the euro was not the innocent victim of a crisis created elsewhere. Markets, ever prone to irrational exuberance and pessimism, mistakenly and irrationally presumed that the elimination of exchange risk (with the single currency, there no longer was any risk associated with changes in the value of, say, the lira, Italy's currency, relative to Spain's, the peseta) meant the elimination of sovereign risk—the risk that a government could not pay back what it owed. The markets shared in the euphoria of the creation of the euro, and like the politicians who had helped create it, didn't think deeply about the economics of what had been created. They didn't realize that the way the euro was created had actually increased sovereign risk (see chapter 4).

With the creation of the euro in 1999, money rushed into the periphery countries (the smaller countries, like Greece, Spain, Portugal, and Ireland, surrounding the "core" of Europe, France, Germany, and the UK) and interest rates came down. Repeating the pattern seen around the world where markets were liberalized, the rush of money into a country was followed by a rush of money out, as markets suddenly grasped that they had been excessively euphoric. In this case, the global financial crisis was the precipitating event: suddenly, Greece, Spain, Portugal, and Ireland found themselves without access to credit, and in a crisis for which the founders of the eurozone had not planned. In the East Asia crisis a decade earlier, when sudden changes in investor sentiment reversed capital flows, exchange rates plummeted in the affected countries, helping the countries adjust. In the peripheral euro countries, this couldn't happen.[21] The leaders of the eurozone had not anticipated such an event, and as such they had no game plan.

CREATING A DIVERGENT EUROZONE

There is a large economic literature asking, what is required for a group of countries to share a common currency and have shared prosperity?[22] There was consensus among economists that for the single currency to work, what was required is that there be *sufficient* similarity among the countries.

What kind of similarity is required can be debated, but suffice it to say here that what many Europeans (Germans in particular) thought was required—a movement toward so-called fiscal prudence, low deficits and debts—was not *sufficient* to ensure that the euro would work, and possibly not even necessary.

So much importance was assigned to these fiscal concerns that they came to be called the *convergence criteria*. But the way the euro was designed led to *divergence*: when some country had an adverse "shock," stronger countries gained at the expense of the weaker. The fiscal constraints imposed as part of the convergence criteria—limits on deficits and debt relative to GDP—themselves contributed to divergence.

In particular, chapter 5 will explain how the structure of the eurozone led people—especially the most talented and highly educated—and capital to flow from the poor and poorly performing countries to the rich and well-performing. The rich and well-performing could invest in better schools and infrastructure. Their banks could lend more, making it easier for entrepreneurs to start new businesses. Even worse, EU strictures prohibited the lagging countries from undertaking certain policies that might have enabled them to catch up to the more advanced.

Rhetoric about solidarity aside, the reality is a more divided Europe with less chance to undertake the sort of policies that would restore the region to prosperity.

BLAME THE VICTIM

The adverse effects of a eurozone structure almost inevitably leading to divergence have been compounded by the *policies* that the eurozone has chosen to follow, especially in response to the euro crisis. Even within the strictures of the eurozone, alternative policies could have been pursued. That they were not is no surprise: a central theme of this book is that the same mindset that led to a flawed structure led to flawed policies.

It is perhaps natural that eurozone's leaders want to blame the victim, to blame the countries in recession or depression for bringing on this state of affairs. They do not want to blame themselves and the great institutions that they have helped create and which they now head. Blaming the victim will not solve the euro problem—and it is in large measure unfair. And with such a "blame the victim" mentality, it is no wonder that solidarity has been weakened.

As Greece went into crisis, it was easy to blame. If only Greece would reform—if only it stuck by the rules, brought its debt down, and overhauled its welfare, pension, and health systems—it would prosper and its problems would be easily resolved. There was, of course, much to complain about with the Greek policies and institutions. By most accounts, the economy was dominated by oligarchs (a relatively small group of families with large amounts of wealth who exert an enormous influence over the economy, dominating certain critical sectors, including banking and the media). Successive governments had run unconscionable deficits, exacerbated by perhaps even worse tax collection than in other countries in which small businesses play a large role. The issue was not whether Greece was perfect. These problems had plagued Greece even when it was growing faster than the rest of Europe. They were there when Europe decided to admit Greece to the European Union and the eurozone. The question was, what role did these problems play in the *crisis*? The story that it was flaws in Greece that had brought on the euro crisis *might* be convincing if Greece were the only country in the eurozone with difficulties. But it is not. Ireland, Spain, Portugal, Cyprus, and now even Finland, France, and Italy face severe difficulties. With so many countries facing problems, one cannot help but suspect that the problem lies elsewhere.

It is unfortunate that the first of the countries to go into crisis was Greece, for Greece's problem enabled Germany and others to focus on the alleged failures of Greece, and especially its fiscal profligacy, while ignoring problems afflicting other countries that did not have high debts and deficits (at least before the crisis). Before the crisis, Spain and Ireland were running surpluses—their revenues exceeded their spending—and both had a low ratio of debt to GDP. If Germany's theory that deficits and debts were the cause of crises—and thus the best crisis-prevention policy was enforcing strictures against deficits and debts—were correct, then Spain and Ireland should never have had a crisis. In the aftermath of the global financial crisis of 2008, they both saw high debts and deficits—but it was the deep crisis and its long duration that led to the debts and deficits, not the other way around.

HERBERT HOOVER FAILS AGAIN

Criticism of the euro has focused on the "programs" imposed on the crisis countries that required support—Portugal, Ireland, Greece, Spain, and, later, Cyprus. Designed by the Troika, which is the triumvirate of the International Monetary Fund, the European Central Bank, and the European Commission, these programs effectively required crisis countries to surrender large elements of economic sovereignty to their "partners" in return for the assistance. Money is lent to the crisis country (it is seldom given) but with strong conditions. The loan, together with its conditions, and the country's timetable for meeting the conditions is called the *program*.

Unlike conventional loans, where lenders typically add conditions to make it more likely that the loan will be repaid, the conditionality imposed by the eurozone branches into areas not directly related to loan repayment. It attempts to ensure that the economic practices of the country conform to what the finance ministers of the eurozone countries (dominated in particular by Germany) think the country *should* do. This coercion has backfired—the conditions imposed have often led to economic contraction, making it less likely that the money that was borrowed will be repaid.

These programs did save the banks and financial markets, but otherwise they were a failure: things that should have gone down are up, and things which should have gone up are down. Debt is up, both absolutely and relative to GDP, so it is less sustainable. In many crisis countries, inequality is up, as are suicides[23] and mass suffering, and incomes are down. As this book goes to press, *only one* of the crisis countries (Ireland) has returned to precrisis levels of GDP. The Troika's forecasts were consistently very much off the mark. They predicted that the crisis countries would return *quickly* to growth. The depth and duration of the recessions were far greater than their models had anticipated.

AUSTERITY

There were two critical parts of each of the programs—macroeconomics, focusing on cutbacks in expenditures, and structural reforms.

The dominant powers in the eurozone not only believed (wrongly) that low deficits and debts would *prevent* crises, they also believed the best way toward restoration to the health of a country in recession was a big dose of austerity—cutbacks in expenditure intended to lower the deficit. Herbert Hoover was president of the United States at the time of the 1929 stock market crash; his policies of austerity converted the crash into the Great Depression. Since Hoover, such policies have been tried repeatedly, and have repeatedly failed: the IMF tried them more recently in Argentina and East Asia. Chapter 7 will explain more fully why they failed there—and why they have failed in Europe. They fail to restore prosperity; worse, they deepen the recession. Austerity has always and everywhere had the contractionary effects observed in Europe: the greater the austerity, the greater the economic contraction. Why the Troika would have thought that this time in Europe it would be different is mystifying.

STRUCTURAL REFORMS

The second piece of each program was a mélange of changes to the economic and legal "rules of the game," called structural reforms. While the Troika thought excessive spending was at the root of the crisis, they did recognize the problem posed by the euro's rigidity.

Countries in crisis couldn't lower their exchange rate, which would boost their trade by making exports cheaper. Thus, in the view of the Troika, to regain "competitivity" they had to lower wages and prices and *restructure* their economies to be more efficient, for instance by getting rid of monopolies. Unfortunately, the Troika did a terrible job in identifying the critical structural reforms. Some of the reforms focused on trivia; others might be important for standards of living over the long run but would have little short-term effect on the current account[24] deficit. Chapter 8 will show that some of the reforms were even counterproductive, at least in the short run, as far as restoring the economies to health.

Of course, some of the Troika reforms led to lower wages directly (by weakening workers' bargaining rights) and indirectly (by increasing unemployment). The Troika hoped that the lower wages would lead to lower prices of export goods, and thus higher exports. In most cases, though, the increase in exports was disappointing.

There were, of course, alternative ways by which the eurozone could have brought about adjustment. If German wages and prices had risen, the value of the euro would have fallen, and thus the crisis countries would have become globally more competitive. This would have been a far more efficient way of adjusting—the costs imposed on Germany would have been small relative to those now being imposed on the crisis countries. But this would have put a little more of the burden of adjustment on Germany, and Germany would not have any of it. They have become the dominant country within the eurozone, and as such, they could ensure that all of the burden of adjustment rest on their poorer "partners," the countries in crisis.

Thus, both austerity and the structural reforms failed to bring the crisis countries back to prosperity. By blaming the countries and focusing on fiscal deficits, Germany and others in the eurozone had misdiagnosed the source of the problem. What is needed is not structural reform of individual countries—especially when they are so often poorly conceived, ill-timed, and even counterproductive—so much as structural reform of the eurozone. Of course, every country needs structural reforms. In the United States we should reform health care, education, energy, intellectual property, and transportation. Countries that do not make such changes in a timely way will suffer lower living standards. Such reforms are likely to be especially relevant for poorer countries—like Greece. There is obviously something holding them back. The desirability of such reforms is not the issue. However, successful reform requires careful sequencing and pacing, and citizens' buy-in—their ability to see the benefits of the policies. It does little good to say that in the long run these policies will make one better off.[25]

The Troika has done an amazingly bad job of selling the structural reforms that it has attempted to impose on the citizens of the crisis countries, because the timing and sequencing is wrong and partly because many of the reforms are, at best, questionable. No salesman, no matter how good, could have "sold" them. We'll see ample evidence in the chapters that follow.

THE PUZZLE OF COUNTERPRODUCTIVE POLICIES

One has to ask, in the case of the programs in the crisis countries, why lenders (the Troika) would impose counterproductive conditions that reduced the likelihood of repayment. Was it that the lenders really thought their programs would quickly restore prosperity? The fact that their forecasts were wrong, and repeatedly so, and by large amounts, is consistent with this hypothesis. But, given the history of failed austerity programs, one has to ask, why would anyone believe they would work in Europe when they failed elsewhere?

I have already suggested part of the answer: ideology, deeply held beliefs about how the economy functions, which change little, if at all, as evidence against these beliefs mounts. Even more technically driven "modelers," providing numerical forecasts of the economy, are influenced to some extent by such beliefs.[26]

But this may not provide a full explanation. Alternatively, there might have been a political agenda—bringing down left-wing governments, teaching electorates in other countries the consequences of electing such governments, and making it more likely that a conservative economic and social agenda would prevail more broadly within Europe. Discussions with some of Europe's leaders involved in the euro crisis leave me with the impression that this political agenda played some role.[27]

Moreover, governments are complex institutions. The arrangements underlying the European social model—Europe's economic system, which combines a market economy with strong systems of social protection and often a more active engagement of workers in economic decision-making than characterizes America's "shareholder capitalism"[28]—often have the least support from each country's finance ministry, the true architects of the programs imposed on the crisis countries. Perhaps the finance ministries see this as an opportunity to do abroad what they cannot do at home.

Finally, many have argued that there is an element of vindictiveness, almost anger—at least in the conditions imposed on Greece—at the seeming defiance of its leaders, such as when they turned to a referendum to assess popular support for the programs being imposed (see chapter 10). It is hard to believe that responsible officials in the eurozone would make an entire nation suffer simply because they disagree with a country's choice of leaders, or that they would impose conditions they believed might not be in the best interests of the country out of spite. Yet the tone of some of the discussions has left the impression that this in fact may have been the case.

SOLIDARITY AND COMMON ECONOMIC UNDERSTANDINGS

When a group of countries shares a common currency, success requires more than just good institutions. (What those institutions are will be discussed extensively in later chapters.) For reforms to work, decisions have to be made, and those decisions will reflect the understandings and values of the decision-makers. There have to be common understandings of what makes for a successful economy and a minimal level of "solidarity," or social cohesion, where countries that are in a strong position help those that are in need.

Today, there is no such understanding, no real sense of solidarity. Germany says repeatedly that the eurozone is not a "transfer union"— that is, an economic grouping in which one country transfers resources to another, even temporarily in a time of need. Indeed, just as the years since the onset of the crisis have led to economic divergence among member states, they have also led to a divergence in *beliefs*.

Of course, the leaders of the eurozone point to their repeated "successes" in reaching difficult agreements. Compromise is the essence of democracy, they rightly argue, and the process is slow. But sometimes compromises can be self-defeating, lacking the minimal level of coherence necessary to achieve economic success. What leaders of the eurozone boast about is more normally described as muddling through. It is possible that this compromise path could continue, at least for a few years. At each point, the afflicted country may say: "Having invested so much to stay in the euro, surely it will pay us to do the little more that is being asked of us—even if it prolongs and deepens the depression." In reasoning so, they fly in the face of the basic economic principle of letting bygones be bygones.[29] They compound past mistakes with further mistakes. Each of the parties grabs at straws, looking for confirmation of the success of the program.[30]

Governments in the afflicted country do not want to tell their citizens that they have suffered in vain. Those in government at the time of a decision to leave the currency know there will be turmoil, and know that there is a large chance that in the aftermath they will be thrown out of office. They know that regardless of who is actually to blame, they will bear the brunt of the criticism if things do not go well. Thus, all around, there are strong incentives not only to muddle through but also to claim victory on the basis of the weakest of evidence; a slight decrease in unemployment, a slight increase in exports: any signs of life in the economy are now grounds for claiming that austerity programs are working.

And eventually, the recessions will come to an end. They always do. But the success of an economic policy is to be judged by how deep and long the downturn before the recovery, how much suffering, and how adverse the impacts on future economic performance. In these terms, no matter how Europe's political leaders try to paint a rosy picture on the programs they have imposed on the crisis countries, *they are a failure.*

There have been some reforms in the eurozone, and they are justly celebrated. The European Stability Mechanism, a new EU institution funded by bond sales[31] and capital from eurozone countries, lends to countries in trouble and has helped recapitalize Spain's banks. But some of what has been agreed to so far is another halfway house, constructed such that it may be worse than nothing. We will explain in chapter 8 how current reforms in the banking system may actually exacerbate the problem of economic divergence noted earlier.

THE UNDERLYING PROBLEM: MARKET
FUNDAMENTALISM—IDEOLOGY RULES

The problem is not only the lack of broad consensus as to what is required to ensure the healthy functioning of an economy and the eurozone. The problem is that Germany has used its economic dominance to impose its own views, and those views are not only rejected by large parts of the eurozone but also by the majority of economists. Of course, in some areas—like seeing the coming of the 2008 crisis—the majority of economists did not do well. But later in this book, I explain why they were *especially* right about the effects of austerity.[32]

Market fundamentalism, to which we referred earlier, assumed that markets on their own are efficient and stable. Adam Smith, often viewed as the godfather of this perspective, actually argued to the contrary: that there was an important role for government. Research in economics over the past half-century has shown that not only is there a presumption that markets are *not* efficient and stable; it has also explained why that is so and what governments can do to improve societal well-being.[33]

Today, even market fundamentalists (sometimes also referred to as "neoliberals") admit that there is a need for government intervention to maintain macro-stability—though they typically argue that government interventions should be limited to a rules-based monetary policy focused on price stability—and to ensure property rights and contract enforcement. Otherwise, regulations and restrictions should be stripped away. There was no economic rationale for this conclusion—it flies in the face of a huge body of economic research showing that there is a need for a wider role for government.

The world has paid a high price for this devotion to the religion of market fundamentalism/neoliberalism, and now it's Europe's turn. In later chapters, we will see the role that these misguided ideas played in shaping the structure of the eurozone; in the design of policy responses to the crisis as it evolved and to the imbalances and distortions that arose before 2008. The eurozone embedded many of these neoliberal ideas into the currency's "constitution"—without providing for enough flexibility to respond to changing circumstances or revised understandings of how economies function. As a result, the European Central Bank focuses *only* on inflation—even in times of high unemployment.

The belief that markets are efficient and stable meant, too, that the ECB and central banks within each of the member countries studiously avoided doing anything about the real estate bubbles that were mounting in several of them in the early to mid-2000s. Indeed, a basic principle of the eurozone was that capital could move easily across borders—even when the money was being used to create real estate bubbles. But, of course, in the ideology of market fundamentalism, markets do not create bubbles.

I recall in the midst of the Spanish real estate bubble—and it should have been evident to anyone that there was a bubble—suggesting to senior people in Spain's central bank that they take actions to try to dampen it. As is now evident, the risks to the economy of the bubble breaking were enormous. The response bordered on perplexity: Was I suggesting that the government was smarter than the market?

Central bankers with a strong belief in free markets had a common mantra, beginning with the efficiency and stability of markets: one can't tell for sure whether there is a bubble. Even if there were a bubble, the only policy instruments that are available could do little about it and/or would distort the economy. And it is much better to simply clean up the mess after the bubble breaks than to distort the economy on the basis of a worry that there *might* be a bubble.

These beliefs predominated in spite of the fact that the 1990s East Asia crisis had shown that private-sector misconduct—not that of government—could bring on an economic crisis.

Beliefs about how economies function matter a great deal, and it should not be a surprise that the outcome of an economic project so influenced by flawed concepts would fall short of expectations. However flawed its origins, the euro might have worked had certain details been gotten right. But even this lack of attention to detail can partly be explained by the ideology, which held that market forces *ruled*, that they prevailed, whatever the institutional arrangements, provided that markets were given enough scope to do their magic. Ideology led to the belief that with free mobility of labor and capital, economic efficiency would be ensured. We'll see later why, without common deposit insurance in the banking system (where a single entity insures the deposits throughout the eurozone) and without some system of shared debt, free mobility of labor and capital ensure that economic efficiency will *not* be obtained.

HINTS AT A DEMOCRATIC DEFICIT

While, as we have noted, neoliberal views predominated in many finance ministries and central banks, they were far from universally shared, even within the very same countries where they had sway over finance ministries. Within all countries, there are differences in views about how the economy works, and neoliberalism is strongest in finance ministries and treasuries and weakest in labor and education ministries. Indeed, the European social model, with its strong systems of social protection, is well accepted throughout the region.

Within democracies, the particular perspectives of finance ministries and central banks should be and typically are checked and tempered; but given the structure of decision-making within supranational bodies, like the EU and the eurozone, such tempering is much less apparent. Within the current structure of the eurozone and the EU, and especially as the crisis countries' power over *economic* decision-making is increasingly circumscribed and delegated to the Troika, the perspectives of finance ministries and the ECB have come to dominate.

Both the structural reforms and macroeconomic adjustments were viewed as *economic* programs, to be designed by *experts* from finance ministries and the ECB. But these programs affected almost every aspect of society in fundamental ways. For instance, when the programs were being designed for Greece and the other crisis countries, the labor ministries were often not meaningfully involved as provisions related to labor markets and unions were being formulated. Europe might pretend that, in the end, everyone was consulted; after all, the program only went into effect if it was approved by the relevant country's parliament. But that approval was given as if a shotgun was held to their head: it was a yes or no, typically with a short deadline, and in the background hovered the reality that a no vote would plunge the country into a deep crisis.

THEORIES OF REFORM

One of the related failures of neoliberalism was the *assumption* that since the perfect markets model was the ideal toward which we should strive, any "reforms" that moved us in the direction of that model were desirable. But more than a half a century earlier, that idea had been discredited in what came to be called the theory of the second best, pioneered by Nobel Prize–winning economist James Meade, my Columbia University colleague Kelvin Lancaster, and Richard Lipsey.[34] They showed that removing one distortion, in the presence of other distortions, could even make the economy worse off. For instance, in the absence of good risk markets (where one can buy insurance for all the risks that one confronts at reasonable prices), reducing trade barriers often leads to greater risk; the greater risk induces firms to shift production to activities that yield lower returns but are safer, and the net effect is that *everyone* can be worse off, in marked contrast with situations where risk markets are perfect.[35]

Other examples of second-best economics have played an important role in the failure of Europe: Free mobility of capital might make sense if there were perfect information. Money would then flow from low-return uses to high-return uses. When a country goes into a recession, money would flow in, to help it out. Capital flows would be countercyclical—increasing in weak times, diminishing in good times, offsetting the business cycle and helping to stabilize the economy. The actual evidence is to the contrary. And the reason is that capital markets are rife with imperfections. Every banker knows that you don't lend to someone who needs the money. That's why capital market integration has often been associated with an increase in economic volatility—the flows are pro-cyclical and exacerbate economic fluctuations. More generally, around the world, capital has been flowing from poor countries, where capital is scarce, to the rich—exactly the opposite direction predicted by neoliberal theories. In chapter 5, we'll examine other reasons that free capital flows—in our second-best world—have contributed to divergence, with the rich countries in Europe getting richer at the expense of the poor.

AN ALTERNATIVE WORLD IS POSSIBLE

Europe faces a choice. There are alternatives to the current structures and policies. It could make the reforms to the eurozone structure as well as the eurozone policies suggested in this chapter (and further elaborated in chapter 9), giving the euro a fighting chance of working.

These reforms begin from the premise that the euro is a Europe-wide project, and that it requires fundamental reforms in the structure and policies of the eurozone. The problems were *collectively* created. The only solution is a collective solution.

The reforms are based on different economic understandings than those that currently underlie the structure of the eurozone. They are designed to promote convergence and include a common bank deposit system throughout the eurozone and some form of common borrowing, such as the Eurobond.

These reforms recognize that austerity on its own does not bring growth and that there are policies that could and would do so more quickly, and with less pain restore prosperity to the afflicted countries. The adoption of these policies requires a modicum of solidarity within the eurozone.

Another alternative is a carefully designed end to the euro as it exists today, perhaps with the exit of a few countries, perhaps with the breakup of the eurozone into two or more currency areas. The breakup will be costly. But so, too, will staying together—without making the necessary reforms. The current strategy, muddling through, is enormously costly. Neither is a pleasant alternative.

The euro is often described as a bad marriage, and at various places in this book I will make use of that metaphor. A bad marriage involves two people who never should have been joined together making vows that are supposedly indissoluble. The euro is more complicated: it is a union of 19 markedly different countries tying themselves together. When a couple in trouble goes for marriage counseling, old-style counselors would try to figure out how to make the marriage work, but a "modern" one begins by asking the question: Should this marriage be saved?

The costs of dissolution—both financial and emotional—may be very high. But the costs of staying together may be even higher. One of the first lessons of economics is that bygones are bygones. One should always ask: Given where we are, what should we do? In asking what Europe should do, it does little good to opine, "They should never have married." It is wrong, too, to ignore the emotional bonds that have been created in the years of marriage. But still, there are circumstances where, taking into account the history, it is better to part ways.

Many have worried that the end of the euro would mean turmoil in Europe and in global financial markets, exacerbating the problems that Europe already faces. That may in fact happen, but it is not necessary: there are ways to end this marriage smoothly, without trauma, and I lay out one such path in chapter 10.

If the eurozone chooses this path or is driven to it, dissolution does not require a Europe where each country has its own currency.

Several may share the same currency—perhaps the countries of northern Europe or perhaps the countries of southern Europe. But the 19-nation eurozone, slated for even more enlargement, perhaps should be thought of as an interesting experiment—like so many other experiments of monetary arrangements, like the European Exchange Rate Mechanism (ERM) that preceded it from 1979 to 1999, and which attempted to keep exchange rates between members of the ERM within a narrow band.[36]

There is one more alternative, which I sketch out in chapter 11, *the flexible euro*, a monetary arrangement whereby each country still trades in euros, but a Greek-euro may not exchange on par with a Cypriot-euro or with a German-euro. For those invested in keeping the flame of monetary union alive, the flexible euro provides a good way forward. It recognizes that there is not now enough political solidarity and broad consensus about economic fundamentals to undertake the reforms needed to make a single currency work; but there is enough common understanding and too much political solidarity to let the idea of a common currency simply go. A flexible euro builds on the accomplishments and successes of the eurozone, but it is based in reality.

Without using these terms, and without full consciousness of the implications of what they were doing, Europe has already partially created such a system (on a temporary basis) in Cyprus and in Greece.

The long-term ambition of the flexible euro (or of the system of multiple European exchange rates described previously) may be to *eventually* create a single currency, a full monetary union. But sequencing and pacing is crucial. In the early stages of integration, Europe seemed to have recognized this: the European Coal and Steel Community (founded in 1952) only gradually evolved into the European Union.

Europe went too fast with full monetary union, without ensuring that the changes necessary for the success of a monetary union had been made. If Europe is truly committed to monetary integration, those changes can occur, though it is likely to be years or decades before that happens. The flexible euro keeps the concept of a single currency front and center but creates a framework with sufficient flexibility that there is a prospect that it could actually *work*—that is, rather than leading to the depressions associated with the current regime, it would restore full employment[37] and high growth. When solidarity among the European partners increases and the other institutions and conditions that are required to make a single-currency system work are put into place, the bands within which the different euros fluctuate can gradually be narrowed—to the point where there is only a single currency.

URGENCY

It will not do to say, Yes, we know we need a banking union (an important reform discussed later in this book), but we must construct it carefully, and that will take years. These will be years during which suffering mounts, years during which irreversible damage occurs, years during which the promises of the European project are further dashed. In my mind, the consequences of such a course are barely distinguishable from that of muddling through, keeping open the hope of reform in the future to ensure that the euro will not fall apart, but in ways that inflict unconscionable harm on the citizens of countries in trouble.

In short, Europe should move in one of two directions: there should be "more Europe" or "less Europe." This means a choice: (a) implementing the reforms that would make the euro work *for all of Europe*. Doing so would require changes not only in how the eurozone works but in the creation of more economic integration—for instance, a common deposit insurance scheme for all of Europe. These changes are hardly revolutionary—elsewhere outside Europe they have worked—and the role of the "central" authority could still be much less than it is across the Atlantic in the United States; but it would be far more than it is today in the eurozone. Or (b) scaling down the currency project.

This could be done in a variety of ways described in later chapters. It could be done, for instance, with the exit of a just a few countries—I will explain later why the easiest, least costly way, would be for Germany to exit. Alternatively, and at a greater cost, it could be done with the exit of some of those in the "periphery." A third alternative would be the formation of two blocs using a northern- and a southern-euro. A fourth approach is the flexible euro that I suggest in chapter 11. But the current halfway house is unsustainable, and attempts to sustain it by muddling through will lead to untold economic, social, and political costs.

A persuasive case can be made that the best course *from a purely economic/technocratic perspective* is the first, creating a eurozone that works. As a political forecaster, I would, however, place my bets on a course of muddling through, doing the minimum set of reforms that prevent the collapse of the euro but do not allow for a true recovery, at least not any time soon. One might call this course the course of brinkmanship, giving the countries enough assistance to maintain their hope but not enough to support a robust recovery. But the danger of brinkmanship is that one sometimes goes over the brink.

If the analysis of this book is correct, the euro crisis is far from over. Greece will stay in depression. It will not be able to pay back its debt. Germany may pretend otherwise, saying that the debts have only to be "reprofiled"—that is, repayments stretched out over decades. But such charades are no healthier than any other hypocrisy. The eurozone will be hit by other shocks, and the weakest countries again may be thrown into crisis—there simply isn't enough flexibility within the eurozone, as currently constituted, for the eurozone to work for the weakest. And the eurozone itself is likely to have very slow growth at best.

The euro was always a means to an end, not an end in itself. Monetary arrangements come and go. The great achievement of the post–World War II era, the Bretton Woods monetary system, lasted less than three decades. First and foremost in our minds should be the ultimate objectives: shared prosperity within Europe and closer economic *and* political integration. The monetary union increasingly appears as a well-intentioned detour in the attempt to achieve those loftier goals.

There are alternative and better ways of fostering European political integration than the monetary union, which, if anything, has actually undermined the entire European project. The best way forward requires creating a shared understanding of basic economics that goes beyond the market fundamentalism that has informed the eurozone project to date. It will require greater solidarity—of a different sort than the common commitment to blindly follow poorly designed rules that virtually guarantee depression and divergence.

The current path should be viewed as unacceptable. Europe need not abandon the euro to save the European project of closer integration—a project that is so important not only for Europe but for the entire world. But at the very least, there is a need for more fundamental and deeper changes than are now under discussion. But if those deeper reforms cannot be made—if they seem politically infeasible, because there is a lack of solidarity and/or of common understanding of what is required for a common currency to work—then the more fundamental question of the euro itself will have to be revisited.

2

THE EURO: THE HOPE AND THE REALITY

The euro was founded with three hopes: (1) that it would bring Europe ever closer together, and was the next step in Europe's integration; (2) that the closer *economic* integration would lead to faster economic growth; and (3) that this greater economic integration and the consequent greater political integration would ensure a peaceful Europe.

The founders of the euro were visionaries who tried to create a new Europe. They were argonauts in uncharted waters, traveling where no one had ever been. No one had ever tried a monetary union on such a scale, among so many countries that were so disparate. So it is perhaps unsurprising that matters turned out so different from what these visionaries must have thought.

I shall argue in this chapter that even with the best-designed euro project, the benefits of a single currency would have been more limited than its advocates claimed, that its impact on overall economic integration was likely to have been ambiguous, and that one should not have been surprised that the euro was more divisive than unifying—thus setting back political integration. The very reason that the euro was an incomplete project was the reason that it was likely to prove divisive. Far from being an important step in the creation of a united Europe that would play a critical role in today's global economy, it should have been expected that the euro would have an opposite effect.

Political integration, like economic integration, was not just an end in itself but a means to broader societal objectives—among which was strengthening democracy and democratic ideals throughout Europe. I conclude this chapter by observing that the construction of the euro has instead increased the perceived democratic deficit in Europe, the gap between what Europe *does* and what its citizens want.

We have commented repeatedly on the link between politics and economics. As we have noted, one of the reasons for the failure of the eurozone is that economic integration has outpaced political integration. The hope was that the politics would catch up with the economics. But as divisiveness and the democratic deficit has grown, the likelihood that that will happen has diminished.

The euro was born with great hopes. Reality has proven otherwise.

THE CASE FOR THE EURO

Those strongly supportive of the euro make a few points—points I've encountered repeatedly in the years I have worked with European leaders, politicians, and economists.

A UNITED EUROPE WOULD BE MORE INFLUENTIAL ON THE WORLD STAGE

Euro supporters observe that successful large countries, like the United States, share a common currency. It follows, in this reasoning, that if Europe is to play a role on the global stage similar to the United States, it, too, must share a common currency. Could one imagine, they ask, an America with multiple currencies? Many Europeans, noting that if the countries of Europe were united, Europe would be one of the two largest economies,[1] worry that Europe does not pull the weight it should in the global economy, simply because it is politically divided.

But this begs several critical questions: What are the prerequisites for playing the kind of global role that the United States plays? Will having a monetary union move Europe closer to attaining those conditions? Is having a monetary union *necessary* for achieving such a goal? And how important is it for Europe to play that role?

The counterargument

In earlier centuries, the ability to exercise "power" on the global scene mattered a great deal. The wealth of nations depended to a large extent on military power. The conquest of colonies was how a relatively small island, Great Britain, became a dominant global power. Fortunately, we have a new balance of power that greatly circumscribes the exercise of military power. Even when a country wins a war, its ability to receive the spoils of war are limited. For example, American oil firms may receive slightly favorable access in Iraq because of the war, but the cost of the war far outweighed any possible benefits.[2]

Even the United States, which spends an order of magnitude more on its military than any other country in the world, cannot impose its will on others under the new rules of the game. Its attempt to do so in Iraq, against enemies with a small fraction of the population and resources of the United States, has been thwarted. It could not halt Russia's attacks against Ukraine. Whether a united Europe would have changed the picture much is arguable—and at the very least, if Europe were to pursue such influence, it would require massive increases in military spending.

If there is European consensus, Europe's influence will be heard—even without a monetary union

Conversely, if there were massive increases in military spending and agreement about military objectives, then even without full political unity, the weight of Europe would be larger, but as in the case of the United States, hardly decisive. The problem is more that it is difficult to reach a consensus about military objectives: another aspect of the diversity across Europe. With Germany so strongly dependent on Russian gas, it might be expected to be more reluctant to support strong measures against Russia.[3]

The world would not have been a better place if the UK, Poland, and others who joined the "coalition of the willing" in support of America's war against Iraq, in violation of international law, had had enough clout within a "united" Europe to force Europe as a whole to join in that war.[4] If there had been unanimity among the European countries, then of course their united view would be heard more loudly. But the lack of political integration is not the source of the problem: it is the lack of consensus. If there had been a consensus, there are already the institutions within Europe that would have allowed coordinated action and a coordinated effective "voice."

In this perspective, Europe's influence can and will be heard in those arenas where there is a European consensus.[5] The major challenge in enhancing Europe's influence is to strengthen common understandings; if, as this book argues, the euro leads to more divisiveness, then the euro is in this respect counterproductive.

The role of rules

What decisions a united Europe might take would, of course, depend on the political rules that defined the union. If there had to be unanimity among the countries within Europe, then in the absence of a broad consensus about policies, the likely result is gridlock. If the political system gave disproportionate power to Europe's corporate interests, what Europe would "bargain" for in trade agreements would be rules that advance those corporate interests. While those interests would like to see a more united and powerful Europe, it is not obvious that the potential outcomes would serve the interests of the citizens well.

Greater power for a united Europe would translate into greater well-being for European citizens only if the political system was truly democratic. There are good reasons to be concerned about this, given the current political structure of Europe.

THE EURO AND PEACE

The second argument for more political integration focuses on the role that the EU has played in sustaining peace within the core of Europe. Given the destruction of the two world wars of the previous century, it is understandable why this should be of paramount importance. Some observe the absence of war within the core of Europe over the past 70 years and give the European Union credit. That may well be the case, though there are many other changes that have occurred as well—the creation of the UN, nuclear deterrence, and changes in attitudes toward war. Our question, though, is a narrower one: There is no evidence that sharing a single currency, or the closer integration resulting from sharing a single currency (if that actually happened), would reduce the probability of conflict; no evidence to suggest that it would make a difference either directly or indirectly. Even supposing that adopting a common currency promotes integration, it's not clear that, where economic integration and increasing peace coincide, the former is the cause of the latter. This book will argue that the currency union may actually run counter to the cause of greater economic integration.[6]

THE EURO AND EUROPEAN IDENTIFICATION

There is a quite different set of arguments for a single currency, perhaps better reflecting the political drive for it: Every day when individuals use the currency, they are reminded of their identity as Europeans. As this identity gets fostered and strengthened, further political and economic integration might be possible. The importance of this has almost surely been diminished as we have moved to electronic money and the use of debit and credit cards. Young people seldom make use of those funny pieces of paper we call cash.

But it should have been clear at the onset that such psychological benefits, if they exist, would be overwhelmed if the euro failed to deliver on its *main* promise of furthering prosperity. Indeed, if it actually led to worsened economic performance, one might have anticipated a backlash, not just against the euro but against the entire European project.

ECONOMIC INTEGRATION

The previous section explained why the simplistic arguments for the euro—that it would lead to a more powerful and influential Europe through a more united Europe and that it would enhance the ability to sustain peace—are unpersuasive. Here I take a broad perspective on economic integration, explaining why the euro (by itself) was unlikely to have promoted the kind of economic integration that would enhance growth and societal welfare, and why it should have been expected that the euro might actually impede further economic and political integration.

TRADITIONAL ARGUMENTS FOR THE BENEFITS OF ECONOMIC INTEGRATION

There is a long-standing argument that closer economic integration would lead to faster economic growth, based on the idea that larger markets lead to increases in standards of living as a result of economies of scale (that is, unit costs of production decrease as the scale of production increases) and taking advantage of comparative advantage (that is, there are efficiency gains from having each country specialize in the country's *relative* strengths).

These notions date back to the late 18th and early 19th centuries, in the works of two of the great classical economists, Adam Smith[7] and

David Ricardo.[8] But there are several flaws in applying Smith's and Ricardo's analyses of largely agrarian 18th- and early 19th-century economies to Europe at the beginning of the 21st century. First, tariff and trade barriers are already low; the law of diminishing returns suggests that the relative benefits of further reductions may be fairly small. Most importantly, there is already free movement of goods, labor, and capital within the EU: the euro is irrelevant for this analysis.

Secondly, Smith and Ricardo ignored the benefits of tailoring policies, including regulations and the provision of public goods,[9] to local differences in tastes and preferences. Some societies may prefer more stability and better systems of social protection, and greater expenditures on public education and health; others may be more committed to preserving existing inequalities.

Greater economic integration—or, I should say, certain forms of economic integration—may, as we shall see later, impede the ability of different countries to realize societal well-being by advancing their own conceptions of what the state should do and how it should do it.[10] In the days of Adam Smith and David Ricardo, the economic role of the state was very limited; today, it is far more important—partly because of changes in the structure of the economy itself, and partly because increases in standard of living have led some societies to demand more of these *collective* goods provided by government.

Indeed, advances in our standards of living largely result from our creation of a learning society[11]—of advances in technology and knowledge—which themselves are in the nature of public goods, goods that have to be collectively provided: all individuals can benefit from such advances.[12] Markets by themselves will not result in efficient levels of investment in research and learning; they may not even result in learning and research going in the right direction. There will be too little basic research and too much research figuring out how to increase the market power, including that derived from patents.

I stress these changes in our economy and our economic understanding partly because they are at the root of the failure of the euro experiment, which was influenced by ideas about the functioning of the economy that, even as the euro was being designed, were being discredited and were badly out of date. In the world of Smith and Ricardo, there was little role for the state—though, as I have said, even Smith recognized that there was a far greater role than his latter-day devotees. In their world, since there was little need for collective action, it would have made little difference whether the collective action that was undertaken was done at the level of the nation-state or the European-wide level. Differences in views about what the government should do or how it should do it, too, would not have mattered much. Today, they matter a great deal. That's why today, those in one part of the eurozone, such as Greece, are so unhappy about being told what to do by others with different views of the nature of society and the role of government; and with close economic integration, they can even be significantly affected by what the governments of other eurozone countries do—especially when, as in the case of Germany, government decisions have major effects on smaller countries. As we shall see in later chapters, Germany's decision to constrain wages was a form of competitive devaluation that disadvantaged other countries in the eurozone, especially those with less pliant workers.

BENEFITS AND COSTS OF INTEGRATION
WITH COLLECTIVE ACTION

If collective action is, today, far more important than it was in Smith's and Ricardo's day, differences in *views* about what the state should do can be, in turn, of first-order importance. This has two important implications—one that Europe has recognized, the other which it has not. The first is the *principle of subsidiarity* discussed earlier: public decisions should be taken by the lowest level of authority possible. Decisions about local highways, local schools, local police and fire departments, even the local environment should be made by local communities, not by national or supranational authorities. The problem is that there are often spillovers from the action of one local community (or one national government) to others, in which case there needs to be at least some coordination and some actions taken by higher-level authorities.

At the creation of the euro, there were worries that with the euro, there would be significant externalities—instances in particular where the action of one country had adverse effects on others. In setting the rules and regulations governing the euro, they had thought that they had focused on constraining the most important spillovers. They had not.

The externalities upon which the euro's designers focused arose when countries borrowed excessively. If such borrowing was somehow "monetized" (converted to money by the central bank), there would be inflation, and Germany had had a long-standing concern about inflation. They took pride that the Bundesbank (their central bank) had maintained tight control over their money supply, and that Germany for decades had not faced high inflation.[13] They were worried that in giving up their own central bank and joining others, some of whom had not demonstrated such discipline, that would no longer be true. That is why the countries that belonged to the euro had to commit themselves to low levels of deficits and debts.

The obsession with deficits was, however, largely a matter of pure ideology: there is little if any evidence that such deficits and debts (at least at moderate levels—levels still substantially higher than the 3 percent deficit/GDP limit to which Europe agreed) would have significant spillover effects to *others*.

On the other hand, wage policies such as that of Germany, where until recently there was no minimum wage and in which there was a concerted effort to lower wage levels in the 1990s to make the economy "more competitive," do have significant spillover effects. Such policies are, as I explain in chapter 4, another version of competitive devaluation, or "beggar-thy-neighbor" policies that played out so disastrously in the Great Depression. With the "fixed exchange rate" of the euro,

Germany couldn't lower the value of its currency. But it could lower its cost of production by enacting policies that lowered wages. For a variety of reasons, these are policies that Germany could undertake much more easily than could other countries of the euro, which made them particularly attractive to German policymakers as instruments for gaining an advantage relative to the country's neighbors. Sadly, the creators of the euro paid absolutely no attention to this far more important externality.

The second implication was that if there were significant differences in economic structures, values across countries, or views about the functioning of the economy, the scope for welfare-increasing collective action at the European-wide level would be limited. Consider the simplest task of a central bank—setting interest rates to balance the risk of inflation versus unemployment. If the circumstances of the countries for which the central bank is responsible are different, then a policy that might be appropriate for a country fighting inflation would be totally inappropriate for one worried about unemployment. Sharing a common currency and a central bank—a shared public good—could be a disaster. A democratic compromise might be bad for both: unacceptable inflation in one, coupled with unacceptable unemployment in the other.

But even if the economic structures across countries were the same, views about the appropriate policy course could differ absent a broad agreement about how the economy functions. People in one country might believe that if the unemployment rate drops below some threshold, inflation would break out. Such a country would want the unemployment rate to be pushed down to that level but no further. Other countries might hold that one could push the unemployment rate down further. To put a floor on the unemployment rate would impose unacceptable costs on workers. To force countries with such differing perspectives to accept the same policy would be foolish. Again, compromise would leave both unhappy.

Finally, even if the economic structures were the same, and their understandings of how the economy behaves were the same, as we've seen, different countries could have different values. One might be more concerned about inflation and its effects on bondholders, the other about unemployment and its effects on workers. These different sets of values would imply quite different monetary policies.

In each of these instances, unless one could show a compelling reason for the countries to have the *same* policies—to have the shared currency—it would seem to make little sense to do so. There are large costs, and these costs have to be compared to the benefits.

THE MULTIPLE ASPECTS OF ECONOMIC INTEGRATION

The benefits of integration depend on the form of integration—and there are many different forms of economic and political integration. This multiplicity is already evident in Europe. There is free migration among many but not all of the European countries. Within the Schengen area, individuals can move freely practically as if there were no borders at all.[14] The Schengen area includes most of the EU countries, but not the UK and Ireland, and includes some countries that are not part of the EU, namely Iceland, Norway, and Switzerland.[15] With the migrant crisis, the boundaries across which free migration should be allowed are being debated—and even what should be meant by free migration.

There is a free trade area. Switzerland, Norway, Lichtenstein, and Iceland are part of the European Free Trade Association but not of the EU. There are courts that address disputes between, say, Iceland on the one hand and EU members (like Netherlands and the UK) on the other. This court, the European Free Trade Association Court, ruled that Iceland did not have to compensate UK and Dutch savers after the Icelandic banks in which they had put their money went bankrupt, beyond the amount that was in the deposit insurance fund. There are courts, too, that rule on human rights issues anywhere in

Europe (for example, the European Court of Human Rights). The EU is unusual in having taken some forms of integration quite far—and yet gone slowly in others. For instance, as we have noted, the EU central budget—analogous to the federal budget of the United States—is *very* limited, only about 1 percent of EU GDP, with the largest share of the funds going to provide agricultural subsidies.[16]

There is a rich agenda of programs that could enhance economic and political integration. The Erasmus program, which facilitates students studying in other European countries, is an example of a program that strengthens the identity and integration of the continent. An EU-wide tax on high incomes, to be used for redistribution, would be another important step in furthering economic integration and enhancing EU economic performance by addressing the region's increasing inequality. (We will discuss this further in later chapters.)

The European integration project saw integration being accomplished in a step-by-step fashion, gradually, over a long period of time. This book is about only one such step—what I have described as a misstep: the creation of the euro, a single currency, done prematurely before the requisite conditions were satisfied, and in ways that have pulled Europe apart.

DOES SHARING A COMMON CURRENCY IMPROVE WELL-BEING AND PROMOTE FURTHER INTEGRATION?

The previous section explained that there are many different forms of economic integration, and that in some instances, closer integration, of at least some forms, may not be desirable.

Close economic integration can be achieved without sharing a currency. The United States and Canada have had a free trade agreement since 1988. Canada, too, has, I believe, benefited from not sharing a common currency with its southern neighbor. Currency flexibility strengthened its ability to adapt to the multitude of shocks that a natural resource–based economy inevitably faces. The flexibility of its currency played an important role in enabling exports to substitute for government spending as Canada put its fiscal house in order in the early 1990s.

Some of the countries in the EU are members of the eurozone, but many (Denmark, Sweden, UK, Bulgaria, Croatia, the Czech Republic, Hungary, Poland, and Romania) are not. Sweden, for instance, has grown faster than almost all the countries of the eurozone, and later chapters will argue that its success is because Sweden is *outside* the eurozone. Chapter 3 will explain that the eurozone as a whole has been performing more poorly than those countries in the EU that are not part of the eurozone—and I believe that the single currency is one of the important reasons that this is so.

HOW THE EURO MAY DIRECTLY IMPEDE ECONOMIC DIVERSIFICATION

Among the architects of the euro, there appeared to be simply a *presumption* that sharing a common currency would promote every aspect of economic integration. There was no general theory upon which the advocates of monetary union could draw, not even historical experiences that they could cite. There had never been an experiment quite like this.

Having a common currency eliminates one major source of economic risk—the risk of changes in the exchange rate.[17] Exchange-rate risk is one of the important risks that firms have to manage. How they manage that risk—both through decisions in financial markets and about the structure of production—can in theory have important effects on the extent of *real* economic integration, including diversification of production throughout the region. It turns out that the establishment of a currency area (such as the euro) *may* actually lead to greater concentration of economic production in a few countries within the area. The hope, of course, was otherwise: that having eliminated one important source of risk, firms would be *more* willing to produce in different countries.

To understand the effects of changes in an exchange-rate regime, one has to understand the variety of ways that firms cope with exchange-rate risks. One of the ways that firms manage such risks in the short-term is through buying and selling foreign exchange forward, trading in futures markets, "locking in" the exchange rate at the time a transaction is made. Thus, if a firm in the United States is producing widgets to export to Canada in six months' time, it does not know what the value of the Canadian dollar (relative to the US dollar) *then* will be. But it doesn't really have to worry: it can sign a contract to deliver the goods in six months' time with payment in Canadian dollars, and it can convert those *future* Canadian dollars now into US dollars. There is, of course, a cost to this financial transaction (which can be viewed as a kind of insurance against exchange-rate fluctuations). In well-functioning markets, however, the cost of such insurance is relatively low.

But these mechanisms do not work very well for long-term investments, partly because the necessary markets do not exist or have high transactions costs.

There is an alternative way of managing such risks: diversifying production across the markets in which one transacts, in which one buys and sells. The American firm might set up part of its production process in Canada, and as it does so, America's and Canada's real economy becomes more integrated. When a firm does that, the variability in its costs of production and in its profits is reduced.

However, once there is a currency union, this argument for diversification of production no longer applies. If there are advantages in concentrating production in one or a few locales, as is often the case, then production may get more concentrated. It may move, for instance, to a country with better infrastructure, enabling the richer country with better infrastructure to get an increasing share of production, enhancing their tax base and allowing them to invest in even better infrastructure.

INTELLECTUAL INCOHERENCE WITHIN
THE EUROPEAN PROJECT

In analyzing the benefits of a single currency, one cannot escape a fundamental incoherence in the European project: The design of the euro was predicated on a belief in well-functioning markets. But with well-functioning markets, the costs of managing exchange-rate risks should be low. With well-functioning markets, the realignments in exchange rates would reflect only changes in fundamental information, information that is typically revealed gradually. Thus exchange-rate adjustments would be slow and gradual. Adjustments in exchange rates (prices) are, in turn, an important mechanism by which well-functioning economies adjust to events that may affect one country differently than they affect another (economists refer to such events as "shocks," with no intimation that they are cataclysmic in nature). For instance, an increase in the demand by China of the goods produced by Germany and a decrease in demand for goods produced by Italy could easily be managed by an increase in Germany's exchange rate and a decrease in that of Italy. This will enable Italy to sell more, bolstering its economy.

There is a strong presumption then that taking away price adjustment mechanisms leads to a more poorly performing economic system. When a group of countries choose to have a single currency, they effectively *fix* their exchange rates. They take away this adjustment mechanism. That should imply a more poorly performing economy.

What *should* have underlain the design of the euro was a recognition of market failures and imperfections; an acknowledgement of the lack of robustness of the standard competitive model discussed earlier, which played such an important role in the "conception" of the euro—slight market imperfections can lead to the system behaving differently than the way it would with "perfect markets"; and an understanding of the theory of the second best discussed in the previous chapter. Much of the high level of volatility we observe in exchange rates is evidence of market irrationality and imperfections. At one moment, there may be euphoria about the prospect of, say, America's economy; shortly later, sentiment changes.

Had there been a recognition of the limitations of markets, perhaps the founders of the euro would have been more cautious in its creation, paid more attention to the details, and put more emphasis on ensuring that the institutions that would have enabled it to work were simultaneously put into place.

THE EURO: SOME ADVANTAGES EVEN IN WELL-FUNCTIONING MARKETS, BUT A MAJOR RISK

There was, of course, a certain popular appeal to having a single currency. People could travel from one country to another without exchanging currency. Exchanging currencies was a bother—and often expensive. The fact that it was expensive should have said something about the functioning of financial markets: the costs of exchanging currencies should be extremely small, if markets actually functioned efficiently, as hypothesized in the standard models.

But while transactions costs are an annoyance for travelers today, they are not economically significant. Most transactions (both in numbers and value) are mediated electronically—through bank transfers and debit and credit cards. The costs for computers to move from one currency to another is negligible. (The prices charged by banks may be significantly larger, again testimony to market failures that are pervasive in the financial system. But the appropriate response is not to reconfigure entire currency arrangements but to regulate and reform the financial sector.)

There is another kind of transaction cost that sharing a currency may reduce: the exchange-rate risk going forward of longer-term investments that we discussed earlier in the chapter. But these costs have had at best a second-order effect in major production and supply chain decisions. China, for instance, has become integrally incorporated into the global supply chain, in spite of exchange-rate risk as well as political and supply-side risks. Of course, if the benefits of integration were small, then these costs might be an impediment; but by the same token, the welfare losses (for instance, from increased costs of production) arising from the lack of integration would also likely be small.

One economic risk totally overwhelms these small benefits. With flexible—fully or "managed" flexible exchange rates—exchange rates can be realigned as circumstances change. The adjustments may be daily or hourly or more infrequent. But they occur and are typically small, and firms and individuals have learned how to cope easily with them—sometimes with the assistance of financial markets.

But in the *absence* of these adjustments, the exchange rate eventually gets so far out of alignment that it cannot function.[18] In the case of Argentina, which had fixed its exchange rate in 1990 to the dollar, the misalignment became intolerable by 2001—there were interlinked currency, financial, and debt crises that were very costly; but after the country abandoned the dollar peg, letting its exchange rate fall by some 75 percent, and discharged the debt that had accumulated in the era of its overvalued currency, it grew impressively: at the fastest rate, next to China, in the world.[19] So far, all the countries within the euro have stayed in but at a great cost.

In short, the *economic* argument for having a single currency is far from compelling. The savings in transactions costs are not likely to be significant. The EU countries with differing currencies had already experienced significant economic integration with the formation of the European Union; we have seen how a single currency might, in some respects, even impede integration, say, of production across the region. The modest benefits that do exist are overwhelmed by the costs of the crises that so frequently arise as *real* exchange-rate misalignments emerge.

ECONOMIC INTEGRATION OUTPACING
POLITICAL INTEGRATION

Those outside of Europe have been deeply interested in its "experiment" in integration. Europe's earlier success as it eliminated barriers to the movement of goods, services, and capital served as an example to be followed; its current problems arising from the euro serve as a warning of integration gone awry. More broadly, Europe's integration provides insights for globalization in general. Globalization is nothing more than the closer integration of the countries of the world—and nowhere has that integration been taken further than in Europe. There is an ongoing debate: What is required for globalization to succeed? What happens if globalization does not work well? What are the benefits and costs, and who receives those benefits? Who bears the costs? The successes and failures of Europe are seen as lessons for both regional integration and globalization. The problems in achieving a successful monetary union in Europe have dampened enthusiasm elsewhere, for instance in both Africa and Asia, for this form of economic integration.

The fundamental insight to glean is that economic integration—globalization—will fail if it outpaces political integration. The reason is simple: When countries become more integrated, they become more interdependent. When they become more interdependent, the actions of one country have effects on others. There is thus greater need for collective action—to ensure that each does more of those things that benefit the other countries in the union and less of those things that hurt others.

Moreover, most policies have ambiguous effects: some individuals are made better off, others worse off. With sufficient political integration, some of the gains of the winners can be transferred to the losers, so that all are made better off, or at least no one is much worse off. With sufficient political integration, those who lose in one policy reform can have the confidence that in the next they will win, and thus in the long run, all will be better off.

There are thus two problems: in the absence of sufficient political integration, an economic union lacks the institutions to undertake the requisite collective action to make the integration work for all; and in the absence of sufficient solidarity, certain groups will almost surely be made worse off than they would be in the absence of integration. Indeed, part of the objection to globalization has been that in some countries most citizens have actually been made worse off, even if it has led to better overall performance as measured by GDP.[20]

In chapter 4, we will explain the economic conditions necessary for a monetary union to work. In focusing, however, on the *economic conditions*, economists have neglected the far more important issues of the political and social conditions necessary for success. We note the failure to put in place the institutions that would have enabled the monetary union to work. But the failure to establish these institutions was not an accident. It was the result of a lack of sufficient political commitment to the European project. In the absence of solidarity, it is hard to have political integration, precisely because no one is confident that the system will work for them.

Conversely, when there is a high level of solidarity, then there will be more confidence in collective decision-making. With this higher level of solidarity, there will be a greater willingness to give up more degrees of political sovereignty and to have greater political integration. One is more likely to accept losses for oneself, if it contributes, in some way, to the general well-being.

In the list of economic conditions necessary for success of a monetary union, perhaps the most important is that there be enough economic similarity among the countries. When the countries are *economically* very similar, it is also the case that political differences are likely to be smaller and the policies will affect them all similarly. In such circumstances, creating common political institutions—political integration—is easier.[21] But when economic circumstances differ

markedly—when some countries are debtors and others creditors—
then political integration, including creating the political institutions
necessary to make economic integration work, becomes more difficult.

Having similar economic structures may make it *more likely* that
two countries share common beliefs, but it far from guarantees it.
There is ample evidence that countries with similar economic systems and at similar standards of living, at least today, can have quite
different beliefs (though many economic historians trace these differences back to differences in economic structures in earlier times).
Understanding the nature of these differences is critical for assessing the kind of economic and political integration that is desirable, or
even feasible.

What is required then is not only that they have similar economic
structures but *also similar belief systems*—beliefs about social justice
and how the economic system works.

In the discussion in the following chapters, several sets of beliefs
will play an important role—including some of the beliefs that we
discussed earlier in this chapter concerning what makes for a good
economy.

CONCEPTIONS ABOUT HOW THE ECONOMY WORKS

It is hard for an economic federation to work if the different members
of the federation have different views of the laws of economics—and
there are fundamental differences in conceptions about how the
economy works among the countries of the eurozone that were present even at the time of the creation of the euro, but which were then
papered over. These differences have impeded not just the formulation of appropriate programs in response to the euro crisis but have
meant that programs designed by (or acceptable to) Germany, the
country that has become the dominant power in the eurozone, have
often been viewed as *imposed* on those accepting them.

Of course, the crisis country has "voluntarily" accepted the terms, but it has accepted the terms not because it believes that the "program" will solve the problems but because *not accepting* the terms would lead to intolerable consequences—including the possible departure from the eurozone. And those in the eurozone, as well as many economic pundits, have been successful in convincing the crisis countries that the departure from the euro would be extraordinarily costly.

That those in the crisis country do not believe in the economic theory underlying the "voluntary" programs has two consequences: the programs are unlikely to be effectively implemented, and they are likely not to be politically sustainable—especially if the programs are less successful than promised. In chapter 3, we will show that that has in fact been the case—not only less successful than promised but even worse than some of the harshest critics of the euro anticipated.

Perhaps the most obvious instance of such differences in conceptions of how the economy functions is "austerity," the belief that by cutting spending or raising taxes a country in recession experiencing a fiscal deficit (an excess of spending over revenues) could be brought back to health. Modern scientific economics has refuted the Hooverite economics I discussed in the last chapter. The point I make here, though, is different: it is difficult for a group of countries to share a common currency and to work together when there is such a disparity in the views of the laws of economics. Decisions are going to have to be made in response to a myriad of unforeseen circumstances. There will never be unanimity, but when there are large disparities, it is inevitable that there will be considerable disgruntlement with whatever decision is taken.

There are a myriad of detailed issues in which different conceptions of how the economy functions play out, not just the macroeconomic issues of austerity and inflation previously discussed. One aspect of the neoliberal agenda entails privatization. There are strong arguments that governments should focus their attention on those areas where they have a comparative advantage, leaving the private sector to run the rest. Though this principle makes theoretical sense, in practice determining where the government has a comparative advantage is difficult.

Experiences around the world have shown a variety of outcomes. Perhaps the most efficient steel companies in the world in the 1990s were the government-run firms in Korea and Taiwan, and there is little evidence that the privatization of the Korean company, POSCO (demanded by the IMF in its 1997 financial rescue), led to improved efficiency. In Canada, there is scant evidence that the major national private railroad company is more efficient than the large public one; in Chile, little evidence that private copper mines are more efficient than public mines. In Latin America, the privatization of telecoms did not lead to greater productivity, at least in those instances where investments had not been overly squeezed by government budget constraints.[22]

Many of the government-run enterprises are in sectors where there are *natural monopolies* (for instance, because the economies of scale are so large that there should be only one firm), and with such monopolies, the issue is not whether there will be government intervention but the form that it will take. Both as a matter of theory and practice, well-run government monopolies may do just as well as government-regulated private monopolies.[23]

Thus, the demand of the Troika for privatization of certain Greek government-owned assets is dictated as much by ideology as by evidence and theory.

Again, our point here is simple: it is that there are deep divides across Europe about what gives rise to a well-functioning economy. So long as each country is allowed to choose for itself, matters are fine. But it is not so fine if economic integration entails giving one country (or group of countries) the power to dictate to others what they should do. That has happened across the eurozone, in matters concerning both macroeconomics and microeconomics, and especially in countries that are in crisis. It is especially troublesome when the policies foisted on the country don't work—for the very reasons that the citizens of the country thought; the costs of the mistake, of course, are borne by the country upon whom they are imposed, not by those imposing them. This is the story of the eurozone.

Later chapters will explain why the policies being imposed on these other countries by the Troika are wrong, based on a flawed understanding of economics. But even if they were correct, one has to ask: Are the gains from this aspect of economic integration, the euro, great enough to justify the loss of self-determination? This chapter has argued that the benefits are *at best* questionable, and if that is the case, the answer to whether the benefits of the euro are worth the costs is unambiguous.

VALUES: SOCIAL JUSTICE AND THE IMPORTANCE OF COLLECTIVE ACTION

Some of the privatizations, such as those involving basic services, raise questions of values: a society may feel that there is a basic right to minimal access to water or electricity, rights and values that might be undermined by a profit-maximizing monopolist.

Labor rights and worker protections illustrate other aspects of the struggle over values. Some have questioned whether the programs that have been imposed on the countries in crisis have gone beyond those designed to increase economic performance. Not content with an approximately one-fifth decline in labor costs in Greece,[24] it appears that the Troika wants to weaken workers' bargaining rights, which would lead to still lower wages. The language of the programs is sometimes ambiguous and may obfuscate what is really being asked within the negotiations.[25] There is a concern that what was being asked, say of Greece, may have violated the International Labor Organization's core labor standards, to which almost all countries have agreed.[26] But there is also a concern that, given the evidence that unionization may actually increase productivity, these measures will be counterproductive.[27]

Different societies have different values, different conceptions about how the economy works, and indeed, even different conceptions about democracy and what constitutes a well-functioning society. Germany's finance minister, Wolfgang Schäuble, has repeatedly emphasized the importance of *rules*, and if there are rules, they must be obeyed. Of course, many of the most heinous crimes have been committed by those who simply said they were just obeying rules. For a society to function well, there must be the right rules, and the right degree of flexibility to deviate from the rules when appropriate. Given our limited knowledge, we can never be sure whether our model of the economy is right; there is always the possibility that rules that might have made sense were our model right are very wrong if our model is wrong. And when we discover that our model is wrong—even *possibly* wrong—perhaps because the world itself has changed, we have to have the flexibility of changing what we do. Different societies may, of course, come down with different views on striking the right balance between rules and discretion.[28]

Again, the key issue is the extent to which economic integration entails surrendering important aspects of a country's ability to make its own decisions. If there is a broad consensus on these matters of values, there may be limited differences about what policies to undertake. But if some countries think minimal access to water or electricity is a basic right, or that workers should have certain basic rights to collective action, then they will be deeply unhappy if contrary policies are imposed on them—and they should be.

A DEMOCRATIC DEFICIT

The European project was ambitiously aimed at bringing the countries together, but together in a political union that would reflect basic European values. Some of these values, however, are obviously not universally agreed to or respected, especially in certain countries or in certain parts of certain countries. A basic liberal value is respect for a diversity of views. There will and should be less tolerance for views that do not respect some of the core values. Far more problematic, though, is the right of one country to impose its values on others. Doing so can undermine another core European value, democracy—and this is of especial concern when what is being touched upon affects basic principles of social justice. Among the core values are the core labor standards—which, as we noted, some suggest were being undermined in at least one of the Troika programs. Again, the question is, are the benefits of this aspect of economic integration and monetary integration worth the costs? And this time, what is at stake is more than judgments about economic performance; it's about more fundamental issues of social justice and democracy.

From the very start, the European project was afflicted with a democratic deficit. It was a top-down project, conceived by foresighted leaders, who were less successful as salesmen. In some countries—especially those emerging from fascism and communism—there was enthusiasm about being part of Europe. Indeed, the prospect of joining the EU provided a major impetus for institutional reforms that played an important role in the success of the countries in eastern and central Europe as they made a transition from communism to a market economy.[29] But repeatedly, when various aspects of the European project were subjected to referendum—Denmark's and Sweden's referendums on the euro, France's and Netherlands's on the European Constitution, Norway's referendum on joining the EU—anti-EU sentiments prevailed.[30] Even when pro-EU forces won, there were significant votes on the other side.

One of the reasons is the construction of the EU itself—with the laws and regulations promulgated by a commission that is not *directly* elected. Not even the head of the European Commission is elected. Devising rules and regulations that worked for the entirety of the diverse region inevitably led to complexity. Of course, Europe has recognized this, and it has slowly but steadily been moving toward greater democratic accountability—except on one front: the monetary union.

If the euro is to be successful, it has to be an economic project that is consistent with, and even reinforces, other fundamental values. It has to strengthen democracy. But the euro has done the opposite.

The most powerful institution in the eurozone is the European Central Bank, which was constructed to be independent—not answerable to or guided by elected leaders—another neoliberal idea that was fashionable at the time of the construction of the euro. Though it remains fashionable in some quarters, it is increasingly being questioned. As we will see in chapter 6, the countries that performed best during the global financial crisis were those with more accountable central banks.

The actions of any central bank have large political and distributive consequences—seen most clearly in times of crises. Central banks are good at cloaking their decisions in jargon suggesting that they are simply implementing their mandate. But there are choices in how they implement that mandate. Though they would almost surely deny it, the ECB's decision to shut off funds to the Greek banking system in the summer of 2015 was an intensely political act.

The growing democratic deficit is seen most obviously in the fact that when given the opportunity, the countries of Europe have repeatedly rejected the policies being imposed on them. In 2015, 61 percent of the electorate in Greece voted to reject the conditions imposed, and in Portugal and Spain similar proportions supported candidates opposed to austerity. But opposition is evident, too, in numerous other elections, including in Italy, where voters turned out the party supporting austerity; they elected parties calling for an alternative course.

In spite of these elections, the policies remained effectively unchanged. In Portugal, matters were even worse: the president initially refused to install the antiausterity coalition on the grounds that it contained anti-euro parties, even though, having won 62 percent of the votes, the coalition controlled the parliament.

In each country, the newly elected government was told in effect that they had no choice: accept the conditions or your banking system will be destroyed, your economy will be devastated, and you will have to leave the euro. What does it mean to be a democracy, where the citizens seemingly have no say over the issues about which they care the most, or the way their economy is run? This democratic deficit destroys confidence in democratic processes—and encourages the growth of extremist parties that promise an alternative.

But the lack of commitment to democracy has become increasingly evident as the programs that have been imposed on the countries in distress have evolved. This was seen most clearly in Greece. Early on, there were suggestions from Germany that Greece give up its vote as a member of the eurozone until it had been rehabilitated, until it was out of the "program." It was reminiscent of the United States, unusual among democracies, where in most states those in prison cannot vote, and in others, people once convicted of a felony lose their right to vote forever. Greece had, evidently, in the eyes of Germany committed the crime of getting overindebted; and while it wasn't being asked to permanently give up its vote, until its debt was at the level where Greece could manage on its own, it was suggested that Greece should be deprived of its voting rights.

The programs demanded of Greece have illustrated this profound lack of commitment to democracy in other ways. One demand was that Greece not submit any bill for public consultation until after it had been reviewed by the Troika.

When George Papandreou, prime minister of Greece, proposed a referendum in 2011 to get the support of his people for the program that was being demanded, the leaders of the Troika were genuinely offended. They acted as if they felt betrayed. What, ask the people? Ironically, Papandreou believed he would win support of the population for the program—so committed were the Greeks to the euro that they were willing to suffer the pain and indignities of the program in order to stay within Europe. He believed that with this affirmation, there would be more "country ownership" of the program, and with that greater commitment it would be easier to implement the program effectively. I agreed. As chief economist of the World Bank, I saw the big difference that it made when there was country ownership, and at the Bank, we worked hard to achieve this while I was there. We engaged with civil society, we explained the development strategies, we had seminars. By contrast, when the program is viewed as imposed from outside, there are widespread attempts to circumvent it.

Perhaps the worst instance of this "nondemocratic" stance became evident after Greece elected a leftist government in January 2015, headed by 41-year-old Alexis Tsipras, that had run on an antiausterity platform—not a surprise given five years of failed prior programs, with GDP falling by a quarter and youth unemployment peaking above 60 percent. Conditions and terms that had been proposed to the previous center-right government of Antonis Samaras (from the New Democracy Party, closely linked to the oligarchs, and a party that had been engaged in some of the deceptive budgetary practices that brought on the Greek crisis) were withdrawn. Harsher conditions were imposed. As support for Tsipras and his unconventional finance minister, Yanis Varoufakis (who is an excellent economist, having come from a teaching stint at the University of Texas at Austin), grew, if anything the eurozone negotiators took a still harder stance. It perhaps didn't make things easier that he was probably the *only* economist among the finance ministers with whom he was supposed to "negotiate."

In the end, Greece knuckled under. Germany refused to restructure Greek debt—even after the IMF said that that would have to be done. They refused to back off from a required primary fiscal surplus of 3.5 percent (the amount revenues would have to exceed expenditures, net of interest payments) for 2018—a number virtually guaranteed to continue depression.[31]

The Greek people had wanted two things and they could not have both: they wanted an end to austerity and the restoration of growth and prosperity; and they wanted to stay in the eurozone. Tsipras knew that the latter was, for the moment, more important than the former, and that's what he opted for, as he acquiesced to the demands of the eurozone. For the moment, they have stayed inside the eurozone, and the eurozone has been kept whole—but at a great cost to European democracy (not to mention the cost to the Greek people, which we will discuss at greater length below).

When he turned, once again, to the Greek people for confirmation, they again resoundingly supported him. The Greeks had survived another assault from Berlin, but the government, and the Greek people, had had to sacrifice their economic agenda. As I have suggested repeatedly, no issue is of more concern to a nation and its people than the conduct of economic policy.

Within the EU and eurozone, governments were supposed to have retained large domains of sovereignty. What happened in Greece and what was happening elsewhere within the eurozone gave the lie to this idea. At least in some circumstances, economic sovereignty had been surrendered. In still others, key elements had been given up.

The eurozone institutions, such as the ECB, to which that economic sovereignty had been given up, were a far cry from democratic. The democratic deficit that had been apparent at the birth of the eurozone has grown ever larger. The deepest hopes of the euro—that it would bring stronger political integration based on a strengthening of democratic values—are thus just that: still hopes. The reality is otherwise.

The political and social costs of the euro are apparent. The question is, what have been the benefits? The statistics that lay bare the economic disappointment of the European project are presented in the next chapter.

3

EUROPE'S DISMAL PERFORMANCE

I t is too soon to tell whether the hopes and dreams of the founders of the euro will *eventually* be borne out. Today, however, it is plain to see that Europe—or more accurately, the eurozone—has been performing dismally.

Nothing conveys how bad things are in Europe as their impression of when things are going well. The slightest signs of growth or a reduction in unemployment are trumpeted as the harbinger of the long-awaited recovery—only to be followed by disappointment as the economy stagnates. As noted in the preface, it is good that Spain's unemployment fell from 26 percent in 2013 to 20 percent at the beginning of 2016. But even this "improvement" is partly because so many young Spaniards have left the country, and even with Spain's alleged growth, GDP per capita is 5.7 percent below its peak in 2007.

The eurozone's downturn has lasted now for eight years, and it is unlikely that Europe will return to robust growth anytime soon. While already it is clear that Europe is facing a lost decade, there is a risk that in a few years' time we will be speaking of Europe's lost quarter-century. Of this we can be sure: Eurozone output will *forever* be lower than it would have been without the crisis, *forever* be lower than it would have been had the crisis been better managed. Moreover, growth rates going forward will be lower than they would have been without the crisis, lower than they would have been had the crisis been better managed.

As those, for instance, in Ireland celebrate the return to growth (in 2015 it was Europe's fastest growing economy),[1] they need to remember: every (or almost every) economy recovers from a downturn. The test then of a policy is not *whether* there was eventually a recovery. As we said earlier, the success of an economic policy is to be judged by how deep and long the downturn before the recovery, how much suffering, and how adverse the impacts on future economic performance. The great success of Keynesian economics was that it led to *much* shorter downturns (and longer booms) than in the pre-Keynesian era. With downturns nearly a decade long—with GDP in most of the crisis countries slated to be lower in 2017 than a decade earlier—the management of this crisis can hardly be called a success. Some, like Ireland, should commend themselves on doing better than others, such as Portugal and Greece. But, each, in their own way, except when graded against their other failing peers, are an abject failure.

While GDP is the standard measure of economic performance,[2] there are other indicators, and in virtually every one, the eurozone's overall performance is dismal, and that of the crisis countries, disastrous: unemployment is very high; youth unemployment is very, very high; and output per capita is lower than before the crisis for the eurozone as a whole, much lower for some of the crisis countries.

If the decline in GDP per capita or work in the crisis countries were equally shared across the population, that would be one thing. But it is not. Certain individuals can't find a job as the unemployment rate soars, while others hold on to theirs. Not surprisingly, especially in the crisis countries, inequality has also increased.

The eurozone's performance on all accounts has been worse than those countries in Europe that do not belong to the eurozone, and worse than in the United States—the country from which the global financial crisis originated and therefore the country which one would have expected to suffer the most.

In this chapter, we lay out a few key statistics that hopefully will make clear how poorly the eurozone has been performing. Indeed, as we noted in chapter 1, even Germany, often held up as the paradigm of success, has been performing poorly.

These data speak for themselves. They show how badly things are going. The fact that the eurozone is doing so much more poorly than countries elsewhere, including countries seemingly similar, suggests that there is common cause for the eurozone's travails: the euro. Much of the rest of the book attempts to link the eurozone's poor performance to the euro and the structure of the eurozone itself. The concluding section of this chapter explains succinctly why the eurozone's poor performance has to be blamed on the euro.

THE EUROZONE AND THE CRISIS

We begin our analysis by describing the economic conditions in the eurozone today, and what has happened since the onset of the crisis.[3] We observed in chapter 1 the widely shared fear that the real test of the euro would occur when the eurozone faced a shock—with the shock affecting different countries differently. The rigidities of the euro and the eurozone's rules, it was thought, would not enable the region to respond. Those fears proved warranted.

STAGNANT GDP

Eurozone GDP adjusted for inflation has been stagnating now for almost a decade. GDP in 2015 was merely 0.6% above that in 2007 (see figure 1).[4]

FIGURE 1

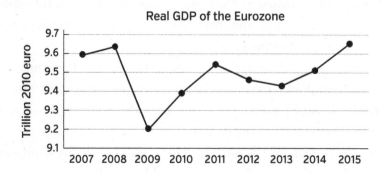

Real GDP of the Eurozone

But looking within the eurozone, we see the pattern of divergence anticipated in chapter 1. While on average, eurozone countries have not done well, some have grown modestly, while others, like Greece, have had calamitous declines (see figure 2). Germany, the so-called champion, has grown by 6.8 percent over the eight years since 2007, but at an average annual rate of just 0.8 percent adjusted for inflation, a rate that under normal conditions would have been described as *near-stagnation*. It only looks good by comparison with its neighbors in the eurozone.

FIGURE 2

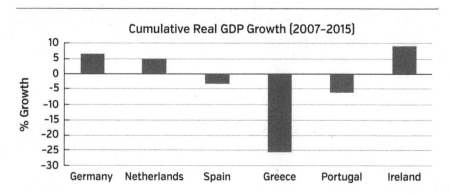

Cumulative Real GDP Growth (2007–2015)

Comparison with the Great Depression

The downturns facing some of the eurozone countries are comparable to or deeper than in the Great Depression. Figure 3 compares the current crisis to the Great Depression for several countries.

FIGURE 3[5]

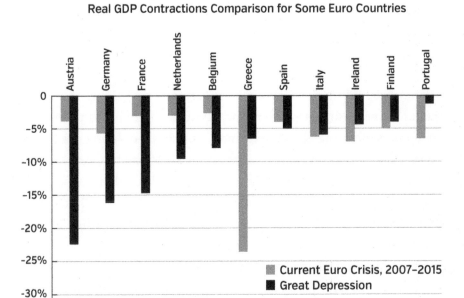

Real GDP Contractions Comparison for Some Euro Countries

Comparison with non-eurozone European countries[6]

The structure and policies of the eurozone have had an especially negative effect in impeding adjustment to shocks—in particular the shock of the global financial crisis. We can see that by comparing growth in the eurozone with non-eurozone Europe (excluding the transition countries of eastern and central Europe). By 2015, non-eurozone Europe had a GDP some 8.1 percent higher than in 2007, in comparison to the 0.6 percent increase within the eurozone.[7] And if we consider some of the transition countries of eastern and central Europe that also did not "suffer" from having the euro, there is an even starker difference: no country using the euro came near the success of Poland (28 percent growth) or Romania (12 percent growth).

Comparison with the United States

As we noted earlier, the crisis, of course, began in the United States, yet the United States' recovery, though anemic, is much stronger than that of the eurozone. From 2007 to 2015, while eurozone output stagnated, US output grew by almost 10 percent.

STANDARDS OF LIVING

A long-accepted mark of economic progress is that living standards should be increasing year after year. Because different countries have populations growing at different rates, standards of living are better captured by looking at GDP *per capita* than GDP itself. Figure 4 shows per capita GDP between 2007 and 2015 for the United States, the EU, eurozone, and non-eurozone European countries: a more than 3 percent increase for the United States and a 1.8 percent decline for the eurozone.

These numbers, as bad as they are, do not fully capture the magnitude of the declines in the standard of living in the crisis countries, for several reasons. An important element of well-being is economic security, and the crisis countries have been marked by significant increases in insecurity, reflected by astounding increases in unemployment and cutbacks in systems of social protection.

Another important element of well-being is "connectedness," especially ties with members of one's family. Here again, there is great suffering in the worst-afflicted countries, as large numbers of young people have had to migrate to London or Berlin or Sydney to obtain jobs. Ireland experienced a nearly 75 percent increase in the number of long-term emigrants from 2007 to 2013. Hundreds of thousands of Greeks have emigrated since the start of the crisis; the number of annual emigrants increased by more than two and

FIGURE 4

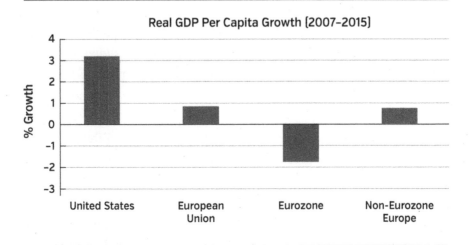

Real GDP Per Capita Growth (2007–2015)

European Union is all EU members in 2007, a total of 27 countries; eurozone refers to the 13 countries using the euro in 2007; non-eurozone Europe refers to Norway, Sweden, Switzerland, and the UK. In each case, growth refers to increase in per capita real GDP, using the countries own price deflator.

a half times from 2008 to 2013.[8] Many of these are likely never to return. Partly because of emigration, the total population of Greece has declined.[9] Not surprisingly, the emigrants were disproportionately those of working age, including many of Greece's most talented workers—implying likely lower future growth and a lower ability to repay its debts.[10]

Government spending and austerity

In the crisis countries, especially in Greece, there was one more source of erosion in living standards: the Troika forced large decreases in government spending, including in public programs providing education and other basic services. Cutbacks in social programs have heightened insecurity. In Greece, for instance, government expenditure fell by some 22 percent between 2007 and 2015.[11] This was especially painful for lower- and middle-income Greeks.

PRODUCTIVITY

As we've seen, the EU and the eurozone, by creating a single currency and promoting the free flow of labor and capital, was *supposed* to create a more productive Europe. So, too, the structural reforms imposed on Greece and Spain and the other crisis countries were supposed to increase productivity.

Because working-age populations (ages 15 to 64) in different countries have grown at different rates—Japan's working-age population has been shrinking at the rate of around 1 percent a year while the United States' has been increasing at 0.7 percent a year, and Germany's has been decreasing at 0.3 percent a year[12]—it is perhaps more meaningful to compare real (inflation-adjusted) growth per person of working-age GDP than just GDP. One *expects* Japan's growth to be lower than that of the United States', simply because there are fewer workers. If Japan's growth *per working-age population* is higher, it tells us something important: it is either finding more jobs for those of working age or it is increasing their productivity.

The eurozone has not been doing well when viewed from this perspective—for the eurozone as a whole, GDP per working-age person has increased by just 0.6 percent during 2007–2015, while for non-eurozone European countries, there has been a 3.9 percent increase.[13] The comparison with the United States looks even more unfavorable: while by 2011, US growth in GDP per working-age population had largely returned to precrisis levels, the eurozone area's number was markedly below—in fact, well below not only that of the United States but of the world and high-income countries.[14]

In the crisis countries, performance has predictably been even worse. If there has been any increase in productivity, that effect has been overwhelmed by the increase in unemployment. In Greece, output per working-age person has decreased by about 23 percent since 2007. Of course, one of the reasons that Greece has performed so badly is that unemployment is so high. So it's worth looking at what has happened to output per *employed* worker. Here, even the best-performing countries of the eurozone do not look very good. While Greece's productivity (output per *employed* worker) has declined by 6.5 percent from 2007 to 2015, even Germany has seen a decline (of 0.7 percent), while the United States has had a 7.9 percent increase over the same period.[15]

UNEMPLOYMENT

Unemployment is important both because it represents a waste of resources—perhaps the most important inefficiency in the market economy, with millions who would like gainful work not being able to obtain it—but also because of the pain it inflicts on those out of work and their families. Unemployment insurance is supposed to help the unemployed, but it is only a partial palliative.

Unemployment is an area where the eurozone performance has been particularly dismal, with average unemployment reaching almost 11 percent in 2015, close to record highs. In the crisis countries, unemployment has been twice that: in Greece, the jobless rate reached a record of 27.8 percent in 2013, and 2015 saw only small reductions from these peaks.[16]

Youth unemployment

Even more disturbing is the increase in youth unemployment—twice the level of the overall unemployment. The persistence of high unemployment, especially among youth, will have long-lasting effects: these young people will never achieve the incomes that they would have achieved if job prospects were better upon graduation from school.[17]

Hours worked

In the eurozone, across-the-board average hours worked per worker have declined—implying an even worse performance: fewer people are working, and those who are working are working fewer hours. Even in the so-called star performer, Germany, hours worked per worker fell by almost 4 percent between 2007 and 2014. (It's worth noting that the allegedly lazy Greeks worked almost 50 percent more hours than the allegedly hard-working Germans in 2014.)[18]

INEQUALITY

We have focused so far on *overall* economic performance. But crises are especially hard on those in the middle and bottom of the economic spectrum. They face a high risk of unemployment. Many are at risk of losing their homes. When the unemployment rate increases, wages are cut back, or at least do not increase at the rate they otherwise would. Hours worked are cut back. And as we have noted, those in the middle and bottom are more dependent on public services, and especially in the worst-afflicted countries (but even in those not in crisis) public expenditures have suffered from enormous cutbacks.

We don't have good data to see how these citizens are faring, but for a few countries, we do have data on what has been happening to inequality. These data suggest that indeed, many are facing hardship. In Spain, for instance, in the years before the crisis, inequality had been coming down, but by 2014, the Gini coefficient, a standard measure of income inequality, was about 9 percent over its 2007 level. In the case of Greece, the Gini coefficient increased by 5 percent from just 2010 to 2014. It usually takes years and years to move the Gini coefficient by a few percentage points.

Data on poverty reinforce the conjecture that those in the middle and bottom have suffered particularly from the crisis. In virtually every country in the eurozone there has been an increase in poverty, especially childhood poverty. By 2012, according to Oxfam, a third of Greeks were below the poverty line and 17.5 percent of the population, more than one million, of those between 18 and 60 lived in households with no income at all.[19] From 2008 to 2012, according to a UNICEF measure, the proportion of Greek children in poverty increased from 23 percent to 40.5 percent.[20]

THE EURO, THE EURO CRISIS, AND LONGER-TERM PERFORMANCE

It is now abundantly clear that Europe's economy has not been performing well—and has not been performing well at least since the onset of the crisis. But what about its performance *before* the crisis, and what are the prospects going forward?

To answer that, figure 5 plots the growth of the eurozone for the two decades before the creation of the euro on January 1, 1999, and extrapolates that growth forward (the solid line in the figure). For the period 1999 to 2008, the extrapolation represents an estimate of what would have happened *but for the euro*. For the period after 2008, the extrapolation represents an estimate of what would have happened but for the euro *and* the financial crisis. The figure also shows the actual output, the dotted line. Before the euro, there were periods when output was slightly above the trend, others when it was slightly below, but the deviations are relatively small. By comparing the solid line with the dotted line, we can see how the economy performed relative to the simple extrapolation.

There are three striking observations. First, *there is not even an overall euro-area growth spurt after the formation of the eurozone.* The euro may have helped create bubbles in Spain and Ireland, but it didn't seem to increase growth for the eurozone as a whole.

Secondly, incomes now are far below the trend that GDP had followed in the years before the euro. By the end of 2015, the gap between that number and the eurozone's actual GDP was 18 percent—for a loss of some €2.1 trillion ($2.3 trillion dollars at the 2015 average exchange rate of 1.1 dollar per euro). If we add up the gaps year by year, by 2015, the cumulative loss was in excess of €11 trillion, or $12.1 trillion.

Thirdly, the gap is still increasing—and I believe it will continue

FIGURE 5[21]

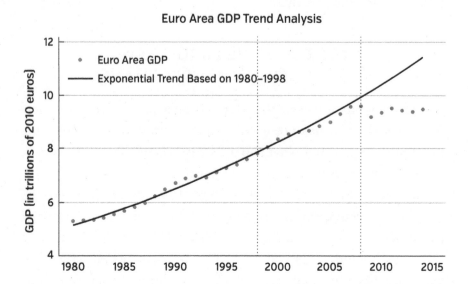

Euro Area GDP Trend Analysis

to increase so long as the eurozone continues with its current policies. But assume, optimistically, that somehow it managed to return
growth to its prior level (unlikely, in the best of scenarios, for the reasons that I have already laid out). Then the total value of the lost output is almost €200 trillion ($220 trillion).[22]

If one believes that this performance is even partly due to the introduction of the euro, then there is a heavy burden on the currency's
advocates to show that the economic and political benefits exceed
these very hefty numbers.

THE EURO AND INDIVIDUAL
COUNTRY PERFORMANCE

Germany and those who are doing relatively well now blame the
crisis on fundamental flaws in the structure of the crisis countries.

They have rigid labor markets, are prone to corruption, are nations of tax avoiders and lazy spendthrifts. While one might not be able to do anything about the culture of these countries, at least one can do something about the structure of their economy by weakening their unions, changing their labor and tax laws, and so forth. These "reforms" would enable them to grow once again. The hypothesis of this book is quite different and simple: the euro has impeded their adjustment to the changing circumstances of the world economy, especially the 2008 global financial crisis and the rise of China. Neither their national character nor the institutional and legal frameworks changed in 2008, so if that was what was causing the problem today, one should have seen consistently bad performance, both before 2008 and after. Figure 6 shows the growth rates of Finland and the five crisis countries before (average growth of real GDP, 2000–2007) and after (2007–2015). It shows that each performed remarkably well in the earlier period—in some cases better than the average for the eurozone. It is clear that there is nothing about the structure of these economies that prevents growth. The data are consistent with our hypothesis that there is something that impedes

FIGURE 6

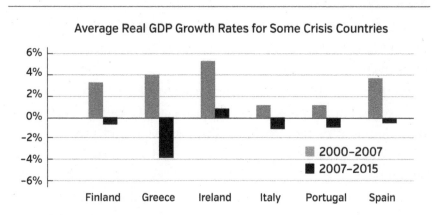

Average Real GDP Growth Rates for Some Crisis Countries

2000–2007
2007–2015

adjustment—the euro. (Finland, as we will explain shortly, though not in a crisis, has been hit by several significant adverse shocks.)

Of course, as we have noted, there are many differences, such as education levels, location, prior investment, etc., that might lead each to have different standards of living. But, as we have already noted, even some of the cultural stereotyping is not supported by the data.

FUTURE PROSPECTS

When there is a short and shallow economic downturn, economies often bounce back and make up for the lost time. After the recessions of 1980–1981 in the United States, there was a strong recovery, with growth in excess of 7 percent in 1984. Output in subsequent years was still below what it would have been had there been no recession, but the bounce back was significant.

By contrast, when downturns are long lasting, there is little or no bounce back. The recession eventually comes to an end, but growth after recovery does not make up for what has been lost in the interim. Indeed, there is a high probability that future growth rates will be lower than normal. The *human, physical, and intellectual capital* of the country is destroyed, or at the very least, does not increase as much as it otherwise would. Not surprisingly, this results in output, output per hour (productivity) and rates of productivity growth being lower than they otherwise would be. Data presented earlier in the chapter are consistent with this: the euro crisis has been deep and long, with deep and persistent consequences.

But there is a further mystery: Because of lower investment during a recession or crisis, we expect productivity (output per worker) to be lower after the recession. But the decline in productivity is *greater* than we can easily account for. We get less output for any level of inputs, taking account, for instance, of the smaller capital stock.[23] We can estimate the predicted effect of the smaller capital and other observable inputs on productivity. The difference between this and the actually observed decline in productivity is the result of missing "dark matter." Something *hard to observe* is missing.

Even if we can't precisely parse out the components of this dark matter, it's real and needs to be taken into account. There are many components of this missing capital. In their twenties, individuals accumulate skills that increase their productivity over a lifetime. But those skills are gained largely through on-the-job training. When there are no jobs—and youth unemployment in the worse-afflicted countries exceeded 50 percent—there is no on-the-job learning. Indeed, there is even attrition of the skills (including the minimal skills related to being productive members of the labor force).

Microdata confirm these observations: Those who enter the labor force in a bad (recession) year have a significantly lower lifetime income, and this is especially true of those who remain unemployed for extended periods. We also know that those who lose their job in a recession face a significant loss in future income, especially if they face protracted unemployment.

Similarly, firms increase their productivity over time both by learning in the process of production (what is called learning by doing)[24] and by spending on research and development. But when economies go into a recession, even a mild one, cutbacks in production mean less learning; and when there is a deep downturn, firms typically face severe budgetary constraints. Firms save where they can, and even though it is bad for the firm's long-run prospects, R&D expenditures typically are among the areas where there are the greatest cutbacks. And such cutbacks have become even worse as markets have shifted to a greater emphasis on quarterly returns: short-termism has become rampant.[25] So, too, firms tend to cut back on other forms of long-term investments. Workers get fired to improve the cash flow of the firm, but this undermines worker loyalty. Bankruptcies increase, and as firms go bankrupt, the organizational and informational capital in firms is destroyed.

There has been a destruction of societal capital, which is not well reflected in our standard metrics, which focus on *physical* capital, such as machines and equipment. This is seen most dramatically in Greece, the country with the deepest depression. The Troika has forced the tearing up of the social contract, the bonds which existed among members of society. Those who had, for instance, worked hard, on the assumption that they would be paid a modest but livable pension, are now being told that their pension would be cut to levels below subsistence. It is inevitable that such destruction of social capital would have important consequences not just for the functioning of society but for the economy.

This analysis has strong policy implications: there are significant *long-term* consequences of not taking strong countercyclical policies to ensure a quick restoration of the economy toward full employment. Taking account of these long-term effects implies that the eurozone's performance since the creation of the euro is even worse—there has been *destruction* of human and organizational "capital," and at the minimum, human and knowledge capital has not increased as much as would normally have been the case.

GERMANY

Germany is sometimes held out as a counterexample to the crisis afflicting the rest of the eurozone. Its leaders have seemed to argue that others should follow its examples: if you play by the rules, keeping deficits and debts low, you will prosper.

But Germany only looks successful by comparison to others in the eurozone. If we weren't grading on the curve—judging on the basis of *relative* performance—Germany would get a grade of perhaps D-.

As we noted earlier, Germany has grown at an average annual rate of just 0.8 percent from 2007 to 2015 adjusted for inflation, a rate that is about the same as that of Japan during 2001–2010 while it was still in its famous twenty-year malaise. Its performance is especially weak, once account is taken of the rate of growth of its working-age population, which we noted earlier was shrinking at only 0.3 percent a year, compared to a 1 percent decrease a year for Japan.

But, as the International Commission on the Measurement of Economic Performance and Social Progress has emphasized, GDP provides an inadequate measure of overall economic performance. It does not, for instance, take into account the distribution of the benefits of growth: even in Germany, large fractions of the population have seen stagnation or even decreases in their incomes.[26] From 1992 to 2010, the income share of the top 1 percent increased by about 24 percent;[27] and from the mid-1980s until the mid-2000s, Germany's Gini coefficient and poverty rates climbed steadily—the latter ultimately exceeding the average for the OECD countries.[28] Germany's success in achieving competitiveness came partly at the expense of those at the bottom, though it does a much better job of protecting those at the bottom than the United States does.[29]

While Germany is hardly the success that it would like to claim for itself, its modest success does not even provide a template for others. Its growth is based in part on strong trade surpluses, which are not achievable for all countries: A basic identity has it that the sum of trade deficits must equal trade surpluses. If some country has a trade surplus, some other country *has* to have a trade deficit.

CONCLUDING REMARKS

A single currency was supposed to enhance economic performance for the members of the eurozone. In the years before the crisis, it's hard to detect any beneficial effect. Critics said the test would come with a crisis: there would then be large losses, as the euro impeded adjustment. This chapter has presented overwhelming evidence that the critics were right. On every criterion by which performance is usually measured, the eurozone has been failing. Its performance has been poor relative to the United States, from which the crisis originated, and relative to non-eurozone Europe. Even Germany could not escape.

COUNTERFACTUALS

Supporters of the euro can't deny these statistics. They can only give them a different spin. Some might claim that yes, things are bad, but if not for the euro, they would have been even worse. Economists call such thought experiments—analyzing what the world would have been like if it were different in some particular way—*counterfactuals*.

Here, theory and evidence are totally on the side of the critics of the euro—and much of the rest of this book is devoted to explaining why that is so. The basic idea, though, is simple. If Greece, for instance, had not been tethered to the euro, when the crisis struck, it could have devalued its currency. Tourists, deciding where to take a vacation, would have found Greece so much cheaper and would have flocked to the country. Its income would thus have increased, helping it to recover quickly. Even more, its central bank, realizing the depth of its economic downturn, would have given a further boost to its economy by quickly cutting interest rates—in contrast to the ECB, which even raised interest rates in 2011. At the time of the crisis, Greece suffered from a balance-of-payments problem—importing more than it exported. The adjustments in exchange rates, too, would have done much to correct that, discouraging imports as it encouraged exports and tourism. Even more compelling stories could be told for the other crisis countries.

Supporters of the euro might respond by pointing out that *if* Greece owed money to, say, Germany in Germany's currency, the weakening of Greece's exchange rate would increase the *real* indebtedness of Greece. True—but that is precisely what is happening now, as Troika policies have lowered Greek incomes by more than a quarter. More relevant, Greece would likely not have borrowed in German currency, precisely because it (and presumably its lenders) should have been aware of the risk that that entailed.[30]

CORRELATION AND CAUSATION

The poor performance of the eurozone, both absolutely and relative to others, might, of course, be due to some factor other than the euro. And there have been changes in the global economy that have affected the eurozone and, more particularly, one group of countries within the eurozone relative to others. That's why Germany's suggestion that the failures of the countries in the eurozone are due to their profligacy seems so out of touch with economic reality, so demonstrative of a total lack of analysis. As we pointed out, only Greece could be tarred with profligacy. Finland has been doing poorly in recent years, with incomes 5 percent below 2007, not because of profligacy but because it has been struck thrice by bad fortune: its leading company, Nokia, has lost ground to other hi-tech companies, like Apple; another leading industry, forestry, has been facing weakening demand; and a major trading partner, Russia, has gone into recession (from low oil prices), and then was hit by Western sanctions. Even Germany's claim that its success is a result of its own is not so obvious: it had the good fortune for many years of producing goods that were in high demand by China, the engine of global economic growth, while some of the other countries in the eurozone that were not doing so well were producing goods that were competing with Chinese goods.

Later chapters will show clearly the link between the euro and the eurozone's weak performance; the timing of the eurozone's weakness is not a coincidence. It is causation, not just correlation. The above analysis has illustrated how the euro impeded adjustment. But the euro also contributed to the crisis itself, as it facilitated trade deficits in Greece, Spain, and other afflicted countries, and these imbalances led to increases in prices in those countries relative to those in Germany. Those imbalances were not sustainable—and were not sustained. But undoing them and dealing with their consequences has proven extraordinarily painful, with costs far greater than the miniscule benefits the countries received in the short period in which they were building up.

THE REAL COSTS OF THE EURO

No economist has a perfect crystal ball. Advocates for the euro might claim that the euro will enable a strong comeback. Such an argument might have been more persuasive a few years ago. As the crisis, recession, and near-recession has dragged on, while elsewhere, more robust recoveries have set in, it appears just the opposite: as we have observed, the eurozone is slated for a lost decade, at best. I have explained why even the rate of growth of GDP is likely to be lower in the future than it has been.

But the cold economic statistics of this chapter do not capture the true failure of the eurozone. Other statistics—a marked increase in suicides[31]—may give a better sense of the stress ordinary individuals are feeling. Newspaper articles have graphically depicted the *social costs* of the crisis—pictures of large numbers of citizens picking through garbage and begging, closed stores, social unrest manifested in violent protests. It is the effects of the euro and the eurozone on the lives of the citizens of Europe, including those in the crisis countries, that we should keep in mind as we discuss the sometimes complex issues of monetary arrangements and their effects on economic performance in the following chapters. We need to keep remembering: monetary arrangements are a means to an end, not an end in themselves.

PART II

FLAWED FROM THE START

4

WHEN CAN A SINGLE CURRENCY *EVER* WORK?

B.E.: before the euro. A world where you traveled from one European country to another, from France to Germany to the Netherlands, constantly changing currencies—from the franc to the deutsche mark to the guilder. The arrival of the euro simplified the life of a traveler. It has replaced 19 different currencies in 19 different countries with a single currency.[1]

Creating a single currency involved, however, not just a change in the pieces of paper that are used to buy goods. It involved creating a central bank, the European Central Bank, for the entire eurozone. The ECB determines the interest rates that prevail throughout the area and acts as a lender of last resort to the banks in the eurozone—providing money that banks may need, for instance, as depositors withdraw funds, *even when no one else will provide those funds*. The central bank sets interest rates and can buy and sell foreign exchange. Both of these affect the exchange rate between the euro and other currencies, such as the dollar.[2] (The exchange rate specifies how many units of one currency trade for another. Thus, at the start of 2016, the dollar/euro exchange rate was 0.92, meaning if an American went to Europe with $100, he would get back €92.) A higher interest rate leads to a higher demand for euros, and thus a higher exchange rate. Monetary policy is one of the most important instruments in a government's economic toolkit. When the central bank wants to stimulate the economy, it lowers interest rates and makes credit more available.[3] And lowering interest rates leads to a lower exchange rate, making exports more competitive and discouraging imports. On both accounts, the economy is strengthened.

Markets on their own don't ensure full employment or financial and economic stability. All countries engage in some form of public action, intervening in the market to promote macro-stability. Today, except among a lunatic fringe, the question is not *whether* there should be government intervention but how and where the government should act, *taking account of market imperfections.*

When two countries (or 19 of them) join together in a single-currency union, each cedes control over their interest rate. Because they are using the *same* currency, there is *no* exchange rate, no way that by adjusting their exchange rate they can make their goods cheaper and more attractive. Since adjustments in interest rates and exchange rates are among the most important ways that economies adjust to maintain full employment, the formation of the euro took away two of the most important instruments for ensuring that.

Because using a common currency took away the ability to use the exchange rate to adjust exports and imports, the obvious symptom that something was wrong—that some adjustment which *should* have occurred wasn't happening—was a persistent disparity between the country's imports and exports. Normally, if there is an excess of imports, the exchange rate falls, making imports more expensive and exports more attractive. If, for instance, Greece imported more than it exported, the imbalance could and would be corrected by making the value of its currency weaken; that would make exports more attractive, imports less so. With fixed exchange rates, this can't happen. An excess of imports has to be financed, and if the country with the trade deficit can't borrow the money to finance it, there will be a problem.

Ceding control over exchange and interest rates can be *very* costly for a country. There will be enormous problems unless something else is done. The magnitude of the costs and the nature of that "something else" depends on a number of factors, among which the most important is how similar the countries are. Given the diversity of Europe, the "something else" that needed to be done was much larger than what Europe did *or is likely to do.*

If countries with a shared currency are sufficiently similar, of course, all of the countries will be hit by the same shocks—an increase or decrease in the demand for their products by China, for example. In the same way, the responses that are appropriate for one country are appropriate for all. In such a situation, the cost of forming a currency union may be low. Economist Robert Mundell, my colleague, received a Nobel Prize for asking and answering the question, what are the conditions in which a group of countries can easily share the same currency?[4] His analysis made clear that the countries of the euro are too diverse to easily share a common currency.

The founders of the eurozone worried about these differences. The 1992 Maastricht Treaty creating the euro required that those joining the eurozone satisfy so-called *convergence criteria*—intended to ensure that the countries would in fact converge. Governments joining the euro had to limit their deficits (the annual amount by which their revenues fell short of expenditures) and debts (the cumulative amounts they owed). They were required to have deficits less than 3 percent of GDP and debts less than 60 percent of GDP.[5] Subsequently, all the countries of the EU (and not just those within the eurozone) reinforced their commitment to these deficit and debt constraints, in what was called the Growth and Stability Pact.[6]

It made sense that the countries of the eurozone worried about being too disparate. They understood excessive disparities would put strains on the euro: one part could be facing deep recessions and another inflation, one part could have a large trade surplus, another a large trade deficit. Any interest rate that worked for one part would exacerbate the problems of another. Somehow, they seemed to believe that, in the absence of excessive government deficits and debts, these disparities would miraculously not arise and there would be growth and stability throughout the eurozone; somehow they believed that trade imbalances would not be a problem so long as there were not government imbalances.

The evidence is now all too apparent. Even countries with no government deficits and low public debt (like Spain and Ireland) had crises. Many countries without large government deficits or debts have had large trade deficits. Many of the countries of the eurozone did not—and still have not—adjusted well to the shock of the 2008 global financial crisis and its reverberations. There has been neither growth nor stability, and the countries of the eurozone have *diverged* rather than converged.

The previous chapter showed that the euro had failed on its promise of European prosperity. This chapter begins the explanation of why. After explaining how it is that the 50 diverse states of the United States can share a common currency, I show that the *necessary conditions*—in terms of the institutional arrangements and conditions—for success were missing in Europe. I explain, too, why sharing a common currency is so difficult—how in the absence of the requisite institutions it can lead to sustained high levels of unemployment, to current account deficits (where countries persistently import more than they export), and, even worse, to crises. These are not just theoretical possibilities: these concerns have played out with a vengeance in Europe.

A natural question is, should the founders of the euro have imposed other conditions—for instance, not just on fiscal deficits but on current account deficits—to have ensured convergence? Would these conditions have ensured growth and stability? Later in this chapter we will explain why the obvious additional stricture—on current account deficits—simply wouldn't work. There are a set of rules for countries, combined with a set of institutions for the eurozone, that could make a single currency work for even a diverse set of countries. In chapter

9 I will describe one such set of rules, applying not just to countries with trade deficits but also to those with trade surpluses. As we shall see, those rules and institutions are markedly different from those in place in the eurozone today.

As we have noted, this book is not only about *events*, about what has been happening in Europe, but about *ideas*, about the role of ideology in shaping the construction of the eurozone. The founders of the euro seemed to believe that satisfying the convergence criteria was key in ensuring the viability of the euro. They were obviously wrong. In this chapter, we also attempt to explain how neoliberalism (market fundamentalism) led them astray.

THE UNITED STATES AS A CURRENCY AREA

Many Europeans look at the United States and ask, if the 50 states of the United States can all share the dollar, why can't the 19 states of the eurozone share a currency? We noted above that if the constituent states were similar enough, then whatever monetary policy was correct for one, would work for the others. But the individual US states differ markedly—there are agricultural states and industrial ones; there are those that are helped by a fall in oil prices and those that are hurt; there are states that are chronically borrowing from others and some that are net lenders. These differences give rise to major differences in perspectives about economic policy: states that are net debtors and in which manufacturing is important typically argue for low interest rates, while the creditor states, with a large financial sector, argue for high interest rates. There is a long-standing distinction between Wall Street and Main Street. So while similarity might be sufficient for the success of a currency area, it is hardly necessary.

There are three important adjustment mechanisms within the United States that enable the single-currency system to work. Unfortunately, as we will see, none of them are present within Europe—or at least present in sufficient strength to make the eurozone work.

When, say, South Dakota faces an adverse shock, people move out. Because English is the nation's common language, and because many key programs, like Social Security and Medicare, are national programs, migration is relatively easy. There are, of course, costs of moving, and in some professions, like law, licensing serves as a barrier. Still, there is little comparison with Europe: while in principle there is free migration in the EU, there are still large linguistic and cultural barriers, and even licensing differences. Americans are used to moving from one region to another; Europeans are not.

There is another problem: Few Americans in other states worry about, say, South Dakota becoming depopulated.[7] But Greece does care if most Greeks, or even most talented young Greeks, leave the country. And it should care. In the United States, it makes little difference, in the larger scheme of things, whether people move to the jobs or the jobs move to the people.[8] In Europe, the Greeks and Estonians want to be sure that enough jobs move to these relatively small countries to preserve their economy, culture, and identity.[9]

Another big difference is that South Dakotans think of themselves first and foremost as Americans, and that identity is unchanged as they move. A South Dakotan is not in California as a "guest" but as a right, a right the revocation of which is unimaginable. After a very short period, he has full voting rights and rights to all the benefits extended to those living in California. There is no distinction between a native Californian and an "immigrant" from South Dakota. Both are "Californians." Recent European debates about how many years an immigrant has to live in his new country before he obtains certain welfare rights show that the same is not true in Europe. Despite the ease of working in the new location, a Pole in Ireland is still fundamentally a guest. Further, his political and cultural identity—and hopes for the future—will more than likely continue to be Polish.

There is another important adjustment mechanism in the United States: After a shock, South Dakota will receive financial support from the federal government in one way or another. Some of this support is automatic: with an economic downturn, many people will turn more to *national* welfare programs, to Medicaid (the national program that provides health care for the indigent, which is locally adminis-tered but largely federally financed), Medicare (the national program for health care benefits for the aged), Social Security (the national program for retirement for the aged), the Supplemental Nutrition Assistance Program (or SNAP, the national program that provides food-purchasing assistance for the poor), etc. In deep downturns, the federal government picks up much of the tab for unemployment insurance. In Europe, each of these programs is financed by national governments, so if Greece has a crisis, its government has to cover the increased welfare payments—at precisely the time when government revenues are falling.

Beyond these automatic programs, the federal government can use discretionary powers to support states in difficulty. If California is in recession, more military money can be spent in that state, in an attempt to resuscitate it. But Europe's federal budget is, as we have noted, miniscule. There is simply little discretionary money that can be used in a countercyclical way.

In the United States, there is a third source of shared support in the event of an adverse shock: the banking system is, to a large extent, a *national* banking system. If any bank runs into a severe problem (as happened to many a bank in 2008), the institution is bailed out not by the individual state but by a federal agency (the Federal Deposit Insur-ance Corporation, or FDIC). If the state of Washington had been forced to bail out Washington Mutual, the country's largest bank that failed in the financial crisis, it couldn't have done it—it would have been simi-lar to Iceland trying to bail out banks ten times bigger than the coun-try's GDP.[10] Similarly, California might have had a hard time dealing with the problems posed by the failure of Countrywide Financial (the largest mortgage company, other than Fannie Mae and Freddie Mac).

Again—up until now—each country within Europe has been respon-sible for its own banks. And as we shall comment in the next chapter, this contributes to a downward vicious cycle: weak banks lead to the government's fiscal position worsening, and that in turn weakens banks further.

Some of the reforms in the design of the eurozone that we suggest later attempt to move Europe *toward* the American model, to a system where a single interest rate and a single exchange rate are consistent with shared prosperity—to move the eurozone *enough* in this direction to make the prospects reasonable for the euro to work.

WHY SHARING A COMMON CURRENCY AMONG COUNTRIES WITH MAJOR DIFFERENCES IS A PROBLEM AND HOW THE EUROZONE FAILED TO DO WHAT WAS NEEDED

Even at the founding of the euro, most realized that differences among the countries of the eurozone were large and that the union lacked the type of institutional arrangements which would allow disparate economic entities to share a common currency. There were huge differences even in the beginning—between, say, Portugal with a GDP per capita of about 57 percent of Germany's, similar to the differences among the US states, where Mississippi's GDP per capita is 48 percent of Connecticut's. Later entrants, though, included countries that were much poorer: Latvia, which joined in 2014, has a GDP per capita just 31 percent of Germany's.[11]

The hope was that the countries could converge, that over time, they could become *more* similar, and with sufficient convergence, it could become a currency area that would work reasonably well. But in many cases this failed to materialize. For example, by 2015, not only had Portugal and Germany not converged, but Portugal had actually fallen further behind—its GDP per capita is now estimated at just 49 percent of Germany's. As our discussion about the United States made clear, more than just "enough similarity" would be required: no matter how close they converged, there would remain enough differences that *additional* institutions would be required, such as America's common banking system. Apparently, many didn't grasp this, and those that did simply assumed that those institutions would arise as they were needed. The eurozone would supply the institutions that were needed as they were demanded. The political momentum created by the euro, it was hoped, would be strong enough to accomplish this.

There were two key challenges in making a single-currency area (like the eurozone) work: how to ensure that *all* of the countries can maintain full employment and that *none* of the countries has persistent trade imbalances, with imports exceeding exports year after year.

The problem with a common interest and exchange rate is simple: if different countries are in different situations, they ideally want different interest rates to maintain macroeconomic balance and different exchange rates to attain a balance of trade. If Germany is overheated and facing inflation, it might want the interest rate to rise, but if Greece is facing a recession and high unemployment, it wants the interest rate to fall. The monetary union makes this impossible. (We noted that for the United States, if there are enough *other* ways of adjusting, enough *other* institutions that can help in such a situation, then the disadvantage of not being able to set different interest rates can be overcome. There's the rub: Europe didn't pay attention to the necessary complementary institutions.)

It should be obvious that there are myriad shocks that would have different effects on different countries. A country that imports more oil will be more adversely affected by an increase in the oil price. A country that imports more gas from Russia will be more adversely affected by an increase in the price for gas that Russia charges. These differences are a result of the *structure of the economy* in each country. No matter how much countries converge in terms of deficits and debts, there will continue to exist large differences in structure.

Differences in debts and deficits, of course, also matter. But deficits and debts matter in the corporate and household sector as well as in the public sector. A country where households and firms borrow heavily abroad will be hurt by an increase in global interest rates, and conversely one that lends will be helped. The impacts may be more limited if borrowing takes the form of long-term bonds, so that what it pays only increases gradually, as old bonds are replaced by new. If it borrows short-term, then the borrower may immediately face a problem: if it is the government, it confronts a fiscal deficit, as the interest rate it has to pay for funds increases immediately. Highly indebted households and firms can go bankrupt, because they cannot meet their debt obligations.

The countries within Europe differed in these and other ways, implying that it was virtually impossible for them all to attain full employment and external balance simultaneously, in the absence of other institutional arrangements of the kind found in the United States. The eurozone failed to put into place these institutional arrangements.

MAINTAINING FULL EMPLOYMENT

An economy facing an economic slump has three primary mechanisms to restore full employment: lower interest rates, to stimulate consumption and investment; lower exchange rates, to stimulate exports; or use fiscal policy—increasing spending or decreasing taxes. The *common currency* eliminated the first two mechanisms, but then the convergence criteria effectively eliminated the use of fiscal policy. Worse, in many places it forces countries to do just the opposite, cutting back expenditures and raising taxes in a recession, just when they should be increasing expenditures and cutting taxes.

In an economic slowdown such as 2008–2009, tax revenues plummet and expenditures for unemployment and welfare soar, so deficits rise. As we have noted, the convergence criteria require that countries limit their deficits to 3 percent of GDP, and almost all of the eurozone countries exceeded that limit at one time or another, when they went into recession. Between 2009 and 2014, for instance, all but Luxembourg exceeded the 3 percent deficit limit at least once.[12] Countries that exceeded the limit were required to increase taxes or lower spending, weakening total demand. These *austerity* policies weakened the European economies further.

THE EUROZONE "THEORY"

I have just described the standard Keynesian theory on economic downturns. Seemingly, behind the founding of the eurozone were alternative hypotheses about how an economy with high unemployment could get back to prosperity *without* increasing government spending and without the flexibility afforded by having its own exchange and interest rate: (a) cutting the government deficits would restore confidence, which would increase investment; and (b) markets by themselves would adjust, to restore full employment.

The confidence theory dates back to Herbert Hoover and his secretary of the Treasury, Andrew Mellon, and it has become a staple among financiers. How this happens has never been explained. Out in the real world, the confidence theory has been repeatedly tested and failed. Paul Krugman has coined the term *confidence fairy* in response.

When Hoover tried to reduce the deficit in the years after the 1929 stock market crash, he didn't restore confidence; he simply converted a stock market crash into the Great Depression. When the IMF forcibly made the countries under its programs—in East Asia, Latin America, and Africa—reduce their deficits, it, too, converted downturns into recessions, and recessions into depressions.

No serious macroeconomic model, not even those employed by the most neoliberal central banks, embraces this theory in the models they use to predict GDP.

A few economists have nonetheless put forward the seemingly contradictory notion of "expansionary contractions." Closer examination of the alleged instances shows that what happened was that a few countries had extraordinarily good luck. Just as they cut back on government spending, their neighbors started going through a boom, so increased exports to their neighbors more than filled the vacuum left by the reduced government spending. Canada in the early 1990s provides an instance. Today, even the IMF recognizes that austerity hurts the economy—and in doing so, even hurts confidence.[13]

I have often referred to the obsession with the debt and deficits as deficit fetishism. This does not mean that governments can run as large a deficit or debt as they might like. It just means that simplistic rules, such as those embedded in the convergence criteria, are indeed simplistic and do not provide a basis of good policy. It may be necessary to impose some constraints, but the constraints have to be carefully and thoughtfully designed—for example, taking into account the state of the business cycle and the uses to which the funds are being put. For instance, rather than focusing on the deficit, the designers of the euro should have focused on structural deficit—what the deficit would have been had the country been at full employment.

As it is, the convergence criteria not only prevented a country from responding to a downturn but created a built-in mechanism for deepening it. As GDP went down, say, because the market for the country's exports diminished, its tax revenues went down. Under the convergence criteria, it would be forced to cut back expenditures or raise tax rates, both of which would lead to a still weaker economy. Economists refer to such provisions as "built-in destabilizers." Well-designed economic systems have built-in stabilizers, not destabilizers.

One of the economic victories of the Clinton administration while I served as a member of the Council of Economic Advisers was on precisely this issue: Republicans wanted to pass a constitutional amendment that would have limited deficits, just as the convergence criteria did. While we were in a period of prosperity—so great that eventually the federal government ran surpluses—we knew that market economies were volatile. If we hit a bump, and we did hit a big bump in 2008, it would be important to be able to stimulate the economy. We correctly assessed that other mechanisms, like monetary policy, would not suffice. Had such a constitutional amendment passed, in 2009 the recession would have been *much* deeper.

The irony is that while the convergence criteria were intended to help the countries converge, and the austerity imposed was intended to reduce the fiscal deficit, typically, the effects were just the opposite. At best, the magnitude of the reduction in the deficit was far less than hoped, simply because the cutbacks led to an economic slowdown—and that in turn led to reduced tax revenues and increased expenditure on unemployment benefits and welfare.

THE ECB MANDATE EXACERBATES THE PROBLEMS: A BIAS TOWARD UNEMPLOYMENT

The previous discussion explained how, even if the ECB set interest rates in the interests of the eurozone as a whole, the weakest economies would be left facing unacceptable levels of unemployment. Had they not been in the eurozone, these countries could have lowered their interest rates.

But as we observed in chapter 1, the mandate of the ECB is to focus on inflation, not unemployment. As long as there is inflation for Europe as a whole, and especially Germany, the ECB pays not only little attention to the plight of countries suffering with high unemployment but even to the *average* unemployment rate. That could be high—the eurozone would need a rate cut to restore the average unemployment rate to a reasonable level—but under the ECB mandate, that may not occur. Indeed, as we have already noted, twice in 2011 (in April *and* July) the bank raised interest rates despite the euro crisis.

INTERNAL DEVALUATIONS AND EXTERNAL IMBALANCES

The second problem posed by a single-currency area relates to *external imbalances*—where imports persistently exceed exports, requiring the country to borrow to finance the difference. Such borrowing, as we shall see, is often problematic and exposes countries to the risk of a crisis. When exchange rates can adjust, a devaluation (a decrease

in the value of one currency relative to another) makes that country's goods cheaper and imports more expensive, reducing imports
and increasing exports. This is the market mechanism for correcting external imbalances. This mechanism is short-circuited in a currency area.

We observed earlier that when two countries decide to share the
same currency, one can't make its products more competitive *relative*
to the other by adjusting the exchange rate. But if prices in the country decline relative to the other, then the *real* exchange rate changes,
and its goods become more competitive—both relative to goods from
other countries within the eurozone and relative to other countries
in the world.[14] This alternative adjustment mechanism is referred to
as internal devaluation—and those who believe in the euro have put
their faith in it. Indeed, one can see austerity policies as *facilitating*
this adjustment process. The greater the weakness in the economy,
the greater the shortfall in aggregate demand, the more the downward
pressure on prices, and, therefore, the stronger the forces for adjustment. The advocates of the euro thought that this would be the mechanism that would eliminate external imbalances—if only government
doesn't short-circuit this mechanism by maintaining an excessively
strong economy.

As curious as it may seem, the neoliberal advocates of the euro
thought that in some ways unemployment was a good thing. Consider a country exporting shoes, which suddenly finds the demand for
its products diminished (for example, because of Chinese competition). It has simultaneously an unemployment problem and a trade-
balance problem. The notion was that if only one let nature take its
course, both problems would self-correct. The unemployment would
lead to lower wages, lower wages would lead to lower prices, exports
would then increase, imports decrease, to the point where imports
and exports were in balance. Meanwhile, the increased demand for
exports would help restore the economy to full employment. Admit-
tedly, the adjustment process could be painful—none of this would

happen overnight. In the meanwhile, families would suffer from unemployment; children's lives would be ruined, as a result of lack of nutrition or access to health. Humanitarian versions of these "tough" policies emphasized the importance of a safety net; but, of course, the convergence criteria—and the absence of help from others in Europe—meant that increased expenditures on such assistance had to come out of somewhere else in the budget, like public investment, hurting the country's future growth. In practice, safety nets always proved inadequate, and, as we shall see in later chapters, the suffering was enormous.

Still, the neoliberal proponents of the euro would argue that perseverance pays: there is redemption through pain. Interfering in this natural market process might reduce unemployment today, but it only extends the period of adjustment.

INTERNAL DEVALUATION HAS NOT WORKED

There has been considerable internal devaluation among European countries. Prices in crisis countries have on the average been increasing less than most elsewhere in the eurozone.[15] But this internal devaluation has not worked—or at least not worked fast enough to quickly restore the economies to full employment. In some countries, such as Finland, low inflation has not been enough even to restore exports of goods and services to the levels before the crisis. In some of the crisis countries, Troika policies may not only have had adverse effects on demand but even on supply. In other countries, exports did not grow in the way that had been hoped—they did not grow enough to offset the adverse effects on the nontraded sector.[16]

If exports had grown at healthier rates, that would have stimulated the economy and helped restore full employment. But there is another, less healthy way of reducing a trade deficit. Imports fall when incomes plummet: one can achieve a current account balance by strangulating the economy. And that, not internal devaluation, was at the heart of the success that the eurozone achieved in getting trade balance. Even Greece had achieved close to trade balance by 2015. But most of the reduction in trade deficit came from a reduction in imports.[17]

WHY WE SHOULD NOT HAVE EXPECTED INTERNAL DEVALUATION TO WORK

If internal devaluation were an effective substitute for exchange-rate adjustment, then the gold standard would not have been a problem in the Great Depression. Yet most scholars believe that the gold standard was a major problem—some going so far as to place much of the onus for the Great Depression on the gold standard.[18] By the same token, if internal devaluations were an effective substitute for exchange rate adjustments, Argentina's fixing its exchange rate with the dollar prior to 2001 would not have been a problem. As that country's unemployment increased—exceeding 20 percent—prices within its borders did fall, but again, not enough to restore the country to full employment, especially as in those years the dollar was strengthening.

EXPLAINING THE FAILURE OF INTERNAL DEVALUATION

There are several reasons that internal devaluations might not work: wages may not fall; the fall in wages may not lead to a fall in the price of export goods—or at least not enough of a decline; and the fall in prices may not lead to an increase in exports—or at least enough of an increase. Each of these elements has played out in the euro crisis.

Slow wage adjustments: blaming the victim

There are many in Europe (including Jean-Claude Trichet, head of the ECB from 2003 to 2011, and thus at the helm in the run-up to the crisis and in its first years) who blame the failure of the internal devaluation mechanism on wage rigidities—on the failure of wages to fall even in the presence of high unemployment. They believe that markets on their own, in the absence of unions and government intervention, would be flexible. In their attempts to blame the victim—workers are to blame for their own unemployment because they've demanded too high wages and too many job protections—these critics focus on constraints imposed by government and unions. But across Europe, and around the world, one can see high unemployment rates with little adjustment in wages in economies with weak unions and without government constraints.

Market rigidities

This "puzzle" of why wages in market economies often don't decline in the presence of even high unemployment motivated my research, along with that of many others, into wage rigidities. The theory that I developed, called the efficiency wage theory, focused on the well-documented fact that cutting wages undermines worker productivity. It hurts workers' morale, especially when they become distracted about their ability to keep their home; it weakens loyalty to the firm; firms worry about workers looking for better paying jobs, increasing turnover costs; it hurts firms' ability to recruit especially good workers; and it weakens workers' incentives.[19] Given the magnitude of these effects, I have been more surprised at the magnitude of the wage decreases, especially in Greece, and I have not been surprised at the countervailing decreases in productivity noted in chapter 3.[20]

Why internal devaluations often lead to large decreases in GDP

Internal devaluations were seen, as we have noted, both as a way of correcting an external imbalance and of supporting a weak macro-economy, for as exports increased, the economy would grow. The Troika has been consistently disappointed: the growth in exports has been smaller than expected (as we have just observed), but the decrease in GDP has been *much* larger than they expected—even larger than can be accounted for by the disappointing performance of exports.

Their analyses made two crucial mistakes. First, they paid insufficient attention to what would happen to the large and important
nontraded goods sector, which includes everything from restau-
rants and haircuts to doctors and teachers, and typically amounts
to something something like two-thirds of GDP. (By contrast, manufactured goods, such as textiles and cars, are called "traded" goods.)
The contraction in demand and output in the nontraded sectors outpaced the slow response in the export sector—explaining the large
decreases in GDP.

When countries (or firms and households within a country) are
indebted in euros (or in a foreign currency), an internal devaluation
increases leverage, or the ratio of what households, corporations, and
even governments owe relative to their (nominal) income. High leverage is widely viewed to have been critical in bringing on the Great
Recession. Internal devaluation increases economic fragility by bringing more households and firms to the brink of bankruptcy. Inevitably,
they cut back spending on *everything*. The cutbacks in imports were
one reason that trade balance was improved; the cutbacks in domestically produced goods is one reason that GDP declined so much.

The multiple consequences and manifestations of this fragility
were apparent in the East Asia crisis. As their exchange rate fell, many
firms and households simply couldn't repay what they owed in foreign
currencies. Defaults and bankruptcies soared. Compounding this
problem were strategic defaults by households and firms that might
have repaid their debts at great cost. They took advantage of the confusion surrounding mass foreclosures and bankruptcies to attempt to
renegotiate their own debts.

This then had follow-on effects. First, lenders suffered. Their balance sheets deteriorated as defaults mounted. Their ability and willingness to make loans decreased. In the economic turmoil following
wage cuts and the other economic changes associated with crises, risk
increased, and this, too, discouraged lending.[21]

In the euro crisis, the exchange rate (of one country within the
eurozone relative to others) couldn't change, but internal devaluation,

attempting a *real* devaluation, had exactly the same effects, with all the consequences noted here.

One of the consequences was to the banking system, and the failure to take adequate account of these was the second major reason that the Troika underestimated the magnitude of the adverse effects of internal devaluation. And they should have been aware that these effects were likely to be worse in Europe than in East Asia: as the banks weakened as a result of defaults and bankruptcies, money could easily move out of the banks in the weak countries to those in the strong *within the eurozone.* This in turn would lead to further decreases in lending and further decreases in GDP.

Explaining the disappointing performance of exports
All of this helps explain the disappointing performance of exports. First, even when wages fell, firms often didn't pass on the wage cuts to prices. They were worried. They knew that if they needed funds, they couldn't turn to the banks. It became imperative for them to build up their balance sheets—and for many of them, the crisis itself had done marked damage to their net worth. Firms operating simultaneously in both trade and nontraded sectors might be especially affected, because even if exports had remained strong, domestic sales declined. One of the few ways that firms have to strengthen their balance sheet is to maintain prices. Sure, there is a long-run cost of keeping prices high—but the short-run benefits in the world of austerity and tight finance that the eurozone had created in the crisis countries outweighed those costs. We see this reluctance to pass on wage cuts in the form of lower prices dramatically in the data. If wage cuts were fully passed on, real wages (wages adjusted for inflation) would have remained constant; prices would have fallen in line with the reduction in labor costs. In fact, as we noted earlier, unit labor costs decreased by about 16 percent from 2008 to 2014 in Greece. While nominal wages and labor costs were thus plummeting, prices continued to rise, albeit at a slower rate than in the rest of the eurozone.

This was not the only unintended but important *supply-side* effect of the eurozone reliance on internal devaluation. Earlier, I described the impact on the financial system. One of the most important costs of firms is the cost of capital. While eurozone leaders were preaching about the importance of the restoration of *competitiveness* in the crisis countries, they were actually undermining competitiveness—for both the structure of the eurozone and its policies led to a higher cost of capital, as banks were weakened and money fled the crisis countries.

Ironically, the "tough love" that was partly built into the structure of the eurozone, partly as a matter of policy choice, while *intended* to help exports (by driving down wages), hurt them in still another way. As small enterprises faced an increasing risk of bankruptcy, foreigners who might have bought their goods shied away, worried that when the time came for delivery, the companies would be unable to do so. They worried that before that date, they might be forced into bankruptcy. A retail outlet needed to be sure that the goods would be in the store in time for Christmas. A missed delivery could represent a massive loss of profits. Thus, again, demand and supply were intertwined.[22] The failure to ensure an adequate supply of capital and the increasing risk of bankruptcy made it even more difficult for the crisis countries to export.

Not only was the euro structure and policy bad in the short run: it was bad in the long run. The increase in risk meant that firms were less willing to undertake investments or even increase employment *at any interest rate.*

So once again, internal devaluation, while intended to increase competitiveness, restore external balance, and promote employment, had just the opposite effect—not just in the short run but even in the long.

Imbalances within Europe: competitive devaluations
Because wage flexibility differed among the countries of the eurozone, simply leaving it to the markets to adjust meant that, at least in the short run, trade imbalances could even grow. Those with more

flexible wages and prices got a competitive advantage over their neighbors. Germany had even managed to get its workers to agree to lowering wages and benefits in the 1990s. But what matters more often is how effective unions are in just keeping up with inflation and getting a share of increased productivity. Such differences arise as a result of institutional arrangements (for instance, the way wages get bargained—in some countries, wages are bargained at the national level, in others at the sectoral level, in still others at the level of the firm or even of a production unit), cultural differences (German workers seemed more willing to accept wage cuts than workers in other countries), and structural differences (German households were less indebted than in other countries, so the adverse effects of increased leverage on households from wage cuts were much smaller).

Of course, these differences wouldn't have mattered that much if the countries had not joined together to share a single currency. Then countries with more wage rigidities could have compensated by lowering their exchange rate. They could have sustained their economy by lowering interest rates. By joining the eurozone, they had given up these options.

In a world in which countries can set their exchange rate (the value of their currency, say, relative to the dollar), when a country lowers its exchange rate to get a competitive advantage over others—for instance, to help restore its economy to full employment—we say it has engaged in a *competitive devaluation*. It is a form of beggar-thy-neighbor policy: one country gains at the expense of its trading partners. Beggar-thy-neighbor policies marked the Great Depression, and one of the reasons for the founding of the International Monetary Fund was to discourage such competitive devaluations. Within a currency area, such as the eurozone, countries obviously can't engage in the traditional form of competitive devaluation. But what we have just described is another form of competitive devaluation—where wages are suppressed so that the *real exchange rate* is lowered relative to one's neighbors. And this form of competitive devaluation is just as much a beggar-thy-neighbor policy but even more onerous: the burden of the invidious policy is placed on the workers in the country engaging in the policy.

A bias toward unemployment

There was one more aspect of the design of the eurozone that made matters even worse. As we observed in chapter 1, the European Central Bank is required to focus on inflation. In effect, the eurozone, in its very construction, was *biased* toward having higher unemployment—toward having a more poorly performing macroeconomy *on average* than would have been the case had it had a more balanced mandate like that of the United States. And that simply exacerbated the problem of unemployment in the crisis countries.

Zero lower bound

But then, even the stronger countries came to be affected. The EU had succeeded in making Europe more economically integrated. A large fraction of each country's trade is with other countries within Europe (close to two-thirds of exported goods and services by value go to other EU member states).[23] Weaknesses, not just in the crisis countries but in France and Italy, ricochet back on the stronger, especially so when some of the stronger countries—like Germany—suffer from deficit fetishism, and so maintain austerity, even when they can easily access funds. The "old" doctrines had it, don't worry: even if a country can't use fiscal policy, monetary policy can stimulate the economy. If Germany should get weak, clearly, the ECB would come to the rescue by lowering interest rates.

But at the time of the construction of the eurozone, no one conceived that interest rates would ever reach the point where they couldn't be lowered—that they would hit the zero lower bound.[24] Once that happened, the adverse effects of its neighbors' slowdown couldn't be offset by monetary policy. No wonder that German growth has been so anemic, as we saw in chapter 3.

THE TWIN DEFICITS

The discussion in this section—and even more so in the next, where I explain how persistent trade deficits often lead to crises—poses a puzzle. It should have been expected that taking away the ability to adjust the exchange rate could lead to trade deficits, and that trade deficits would put at risk the stability of the eurozone. Why didn't those constructing the eurozone focus on these trade deficits? Instead, attention was centered on *fiscal deficits*.

To understand why they might have done this, one has to go back in time. The idea that government deficits and trade deficits were closely linked was very popular in the early 1990s when the eurozone was founded. It found its way into standard textbooks under the title "the twin deficits." The reasoning was simple: If government increases spending *and nothing else changes*, aggregate demand will increase. *If the economy is at full employment*, that increase in aggregate demand can only be satisfied by increasing imports. *If exports don't change* (say, because the exchange rate doesn't change), then there necessarily must be an increase in the trade deficit. The italicized phrases show the critical assumptions in the reasoning, and subsequent research showed that those assumptions are often not true.

We *now* understand that trade deficits are often not caused by government profligacy but by private sector excesses, and that accordingly curbing government profligacy—as the convergence criteria attempt to do—won't necessarily prevent large and persistent trade deficits.

In the United States, for instance, the government deficit came down dramatically during the Clinton administration—by the end of Clinton's term, there was a surplus—and yet the trade deficit continued to grow. Investment increased, replacing government spending.

In fact, even the *causal* relationship between the trade deficit and government spending, to the extent that there is such a relationship, has been questioned. When a country experiences a trade deficit, perhaps as a result of a sudden decrease in its exports because of a down-turn in a trading partner, unemployment will normally increase as a result of the deficiency in aggregate demand. But since Keynes, democratic governments tend to respond to such increases in unemployment by increasing government spending. Thus, it is not the increase in government spending that causes the increase in trade deficit, but the increase in the trade deficit that causes the government spending.[25]

What has happened in Europe under the euro has confirmed these insights. Only in Greece was government spending a substantial source of the country's trade deficit.

There was another reason why many of the founders of the eurozone may have been less worried about trade deficits caused by the private sector. They believed that if that ever happened, it would not be a problem: in their ideology, the private sector could do no wrong. So if there was a trade deficit, it was a good thing. It meant, for instance, that firms were borrowing for productive investments that would yield a return more than enough to offset the debt required to finance it.

That they believed this was testimony to their *faith* in markets: there is a long history of market excesses, to which Spain and Ireland's housing bubbles (not to mention that of the United States) add but further examples.

WAS THERE AN ALTERNATIVE?

While some in Europe, and especially in Germany, are in denial—they continue to believe, in the face of overwhelming evidence to the contrary, that if one controls government deficits, one can manage trade deficits—others are more realistic. They believe that the problem of trade deficits has to be addressed head-on, demanding even stronger macroeconomic strictures: not only budgetary discipline but also other conditions, such as those associated with current account deficits (gaps between imports and exports).

Proposals to expand the list of requirements have a problem (besides the obvious political one, of how the eurozone could be brought to agree on an expanded set of rules): any such strictures run counter to the euro's neoliberal architecture. How can one distinguish between a "good" trade deficit—one which is the natural consequence of economic forces—and a "bad" deficit? After the fact, it is clear that the Spanish deficits were "bad." The funds flowing into the country were used to finance a real estate bubble. That was a mistake. But it was a private sector mistake, just as the tech bubble and the housing bubble in the United States were private sector mistakes. But beforehand, it is hard to tell good investments from those that are part of a wave of irrational exuberance. Market fundamentalists could never tolerate government even attempting to make such a distinction. That would imply relying on the judgment of some government bureaucrat over that of a businessman who presumably was putting his own money and that of his investors at stake. Indeed, even as it seemed obvious that the market had gone awry, with the real estate bubbles in Spain and Ireland, the eurozone's neoliberal economic leaders were waxing poetic about the wonders of the market. When I said that government might want to tame such excesses, the notion was met with horror: Was I suggesting that government bureaucrats were wiser than the private sector?

Thus, the euro is caught between a rock and a hard place: Markets by themselves can't do the adjustments necessary to ensure full employment and external balance. Internal devaluations don't work. And simply regulating fiscal deficits won't suffice either: it makes ensuring full employment *more* difficult and does little to ensure trade balance. Regulating the economy in other ways, to ensure that imports are in line with exports, would require interventions in the market economy that would be intolerable, at least from the perspective of the neoliberal ideology that underlies the euro. There are other institutional developments, entailing further economic integration—moving in directions that has enabled a single currency to work in the diverse United States—that might enable the euro to work. We discuss these later in the book. But first, we need to understand more fully the dangers of *not* correcting current account deficits.

WHY CURRENCY AREAS ARE PRONE TO CRISIS

Countries that try to fix their exchange rate relative to others face not only protracted periods of unemployment, because they lack the instruments to return to full employment when they are hit by an adverse shock, but are prone to crises. The same is true of countries within a currency area; they, too, cannot adjust their exchange rates. The economic costs of these crises are enormous; they are felt not only in the high unemployment and lost output today but in lower growth for years—in some cases, decades.

Such crises have happened repeatedly, with the euro crisis being only the most recent and worst example. In chapter 2, for instance, I described the Argentine crisis in 2001–2002.

It is easy to understand why such crises are so common with currency pegs. If somehow the exchange rate becomes too high, there will be a trade deficit, with imports exceeding exports. This deficit has to be financed somehow, offset by what are called *capital inflows.* These can take the form of debt or direct investments. The problems posed by debt are most obvious: eventually the debt reaches so high a level that creditors' sentiments begin to change. They worry that they will not be repaid. These sentiment changes can occur gradually or rapidly. Surprisingly—again testimony to market irrationality—the changes often happen suddenly, and not in response to any real "news." The mystery then is often not that the lenders are pessimistic, but why weren't they more pessimistic earlier. Such changes have been called "sudden stops":[26] the flow of money into a country suddenly halts and the country goes into crisis.

It is when sentiments change quickly that a debt crisis is likely to follow, as lenders refuse to roll over their debt as it becomes due, and the country can't find *anyone* willing to lend. The country's choices are then limited: it either defaults, or goes to the IMF for a rescue package, accepting the loss of its economic sovereignty with a loan accompanied by strong conditions.[27]

Typically, when there are private excesses leading to a trade deficit, what is borrowed abroad, say by households or firms, is intermediated by domestic banks, who borrow, say, dollars from abroad and lend them to, say, consumers to buy cars (as in Iceland) or other consumer goods. If the foreign lenders demand repayment from the banks, and the banks can't come up with the money, we then have a *financial crisis.*[28]

The trade deficit itself creates another problem. A high level of imports weakens domestic aggregate demand. Unless there is an investment boom—such as a real estate bubble—to sustain full employment, the government has to spend more.[29] In this case, the capital inflows go to finance the resulting government debt. But unless the government spends the money wisely, for instance, on public investments that increase the country's productivity and output, eventually, the creditors' sentiments will change.

Again there is a debt crisis: the government can't roll over its debt, if the debt is short-term. But even if there is no rollover problem, because the debt is long-term, the country suddenly can't finance its *fiscal* deficit. If it doesn't want to finance its spending by printing money, with the possible resulting inflation, it has to cut back on spending, plunging the economy into a downturn.[30]

Banking and financial crises more generally are associated with *economic crises,* as aggregate demand and output fall and unemployment soars. In the case of a financial or debt crisis, banks can no longer lend, and firms and households whose spending depends on borrowing have to cut back.

In the case of the euro, of course, there was no option of the exchange rate, say, for Greece or Spain, falling *to correct* a trade imbalance. This made the *economic, debt, and financial* crises even worse. As we shall see, to bring back a semblance of "balance," those in the crisis countries are being sacrificed. With a big enough recession or depression, imports are brought into alignment with exports.

In each of those instances where a crisis emerged, one might well ask, why didn't the lenders see that the country was getting overindebted? How could they let the situation arise? There are two answers. The first is that financial markets are short sighted. They often can't see or understand what is going on in their own backyard, as the US 2008 financial crisis demonstrated. Seeing and understanding what is going on elsewhere is even more difficult. Markets get caught up in fads and fashions—lending to Latin America in the 1970s and to East Asia in the early '90s, for example, which eventually resulted in the Latin American and East Asian crises.

Of course, the bankers don't like to blame themselves; they blame the borrower. But these loans are voluntary transactions. If there is an irresponsible borrower, it means at a minimum that there is an irresponsible lender, who has not done due diligence. The reality is worse. Lenders are supposed to be experts in risk management. And in many cases, they take advantage of inherent political problems:[31] governments are easily induced to borrow excessively. The current government benefits from the increased spending, and the prosperity that results, while costs are borne by some future government.

The interaction between shortsighted financial markets—with incentive structures that encourage reckless lending—and short-sighted governments creates a potentially explosive mix, which, when combined with fixed exchange rates, is almost sure to explode. These problems arise within honest governments, who are simply obeying natural incentives. But obviously, corruption can make matters worse, with a corrupt financial sector paying kickbacks in one form or another to corrupt politicians or their political parties.

The second reason countries get overly indebted is that lenders are regularly bailed out—by the IMF, by the European Central Bank, and by governments. With losses thus socialized, there are especially perverse incentives to engage in excessive lending abroad. What happened in the eurozone is again only the latest of a long string of such bailouts. (These bailouts typically have names of countries, like the Mexican, Korean, Argentinean, Brazilian, Indonesian, and Thai bailouts. But in each instance, the bailout is really just a bailout of Western banks.)

Of course, some observers in Europe have recognized this. That is why they have demanded what has euphemistically been called *private sector involvement* (which has its own acronym, *psi*) or *bail-ins*. Private sector lenders too have to bear losses. But too often, these demands come too late, after the smart short-term money had had a chance to pull out. This places the burden on those who made longer-term loans. (Of course, these were *partially* to blame for the crisis as a result of their overlending; but the short-term lenders were also to blame—indeed in some cases more so. The long-term loans may have been made in a time where the prospects of the country looked great. The impending problems should have been more apparent to the short-term lenders.) And often, bail-in demands are imposed on the wrong parties. In 2012–2013, Europe demanded that ordinary depositors in Cyprus take a haircut—that is, a write-down in the value of their deposits. The eurozone authorities thought that by forcing depositors to take a bigger loss, they would reduce the amount of money that they would have to fork over.[32] Until then, it was assumed that when banks went through restructuring, depositors would be protected. The possibility that depositors could take a loss has undermined confidence in banks throughout the weaker countries of the eurozone and contributed to funds leaving these banks, thereby contributing to Europe's malaise.[33]

THE ROLE OF MARKETS—AND THE EURO—IN CREATING EXCHANGE-RATE MISALIGNMENTS

The role of the single currency in creating crises is greater than this discussion suggests. We began with the assumption that somehow, the exchange rate had gotten misaligned—some countries had too high of an exchange rate. As countries entered the eurozone, there was an attempt to ensure that the exchange rate was "right"—that is, the conversion from the old currency to the euro was done correctly.

Even when they got the initial conditions right, however, the euro itself led to a misalignment—to a real exchange rate (taking account of *local* prices) that was too high in several countries, so that their imports systematically exceeded exports. Money, for instance, rushed into Spain and Ireland in the years after the start of the euro in 1999, and especially in the years preceding the 2008 crisis. Lenders somehow thought that the elimination of exchange-rate risk meant the elimination of all risk. This was reflected in the low interest rates that these countries had to pay to borrow. By 2005, the risk premium on Greek bonds (relative to German bonds—that is, the amount *extra* that had to be paid to compensate for market participants' perception of the higher risk of Greek bonds) fell to a miniscule 0.2 percent; on Italian bonds, it also dropped to 0.2 percent; on Spanish bonds, to 0.001 percent.[34]

The low interest rates at which funds were available in Spain (combined with the euro-euphoria, the belief that the euro had opened up a new era of prosperity and stability) helped create a real estate bubble; in the years before the 2008 crisis, more homes were constructed in Spain than in France, Germany, and Ireland combined.[35] The real estate bubble distorted the Spanish economy. Private sector irrational exuberance, not government spending, put the Spanish economy off-kilter. Indeed, some in the government were worried, and worked hard to diversify the economy, so that if it turned out that there was a real estate bubble, other sectors (in Spain, for instance, green energy and new knowledge sectors) could pick up the slack when it burst. The bubble broke before these efforts were fully successful.

In the absence of the eurozone, a country flooded with speculative money could have raised interest rates to dampen the real estate bubble. But being part of the euro made this impossible. A country like Spain and Ireland facing a real estate bubble could and should have imposed capital gains taxes or imposed restrictions in lending by local banks. But the market fundamentalist ideology dominant in the eurozone ruled these measures out.

The government could, alternatively, have cut back on its spending and allowed wasteful private investment to crowd out more productive public investments. But the governments of Spain and Ireland were flush with tax revenues generated by the boom, and they felt no need to do so. Both countries were in surplus. Managing inflation was the job of the ECB, not their job. Their job was to stick within the budget constraints demanded by the Maastricht Treaty and spend money well; and they were doing that. According to the convergence criteria—and the ideology of the time—everything was fine. In short, the constraints imposed by the eurozone, combined with irrational markets and neoliberal ideology framework *created* the overvalued euro exchange rate that in turn led to the crises.

BORROWING IN A FOREIGN CURRENCY

The euro created crises for another reason, one that appears to have been largely unanticipated, partly because it created a situation that had never occurred before. Debt crises typically do not occur in countries that have borrowed in their own currency. They can at least meet the promises they made by printing more of their own money. The United States will never have a Greek-style crisis, simply because it can print the money that it owes.[36]

In the past, countries had a choice: issue debt in a foreign currency, and face the risks of owing more—in domestic terms—if the exchange rate falls, and the even worse risk of default if it falls too much; or issue debt in one's own currency, and pay a higher interest rate. Of course, if markets worked well, the higher interest rate did nothing but compensate foreign lenders for the exchange-rate risk—the money they were repaid might be worth much less than at the time they lent it.[37] But shortsighted governments (often egged on by international financiers and even the IMF) encouraged borrowing in foreign currency, because the impact on *today's* budget was less, simply because the *nominal* interest payments were lower.

After the rash of crises in the 1990s and early 2000s, though, many governments had learned their lesson. They began to borrow in local currency, and put pressure on firms and households in their country to borrow in local currency,[38] and local currency markets developed.

The eurozone created a new situation. Countries and firms and households within countries borrowed in euros. But though they were borrowing in the currency they *used*, it was a currency that they did not control.

Europe unwittingly created the familiar problem faced by highly indebted developing countries and emerging markets. Greece does not control the printing presses of the currency in which it has borrowed. They owe money in euros. Their creditors are not willing to roll over their debts. Their earnings of euros from exports are insufficient to pay what is owed. They simply can't meet their obligations.

Markets should have recognized the new risky situation that the eurozone had created, and limited their lending in response. But as so often happens, they were caught up in another episode of irrational exuberance—euro-euphoria. They focused on the benefits of the elimination of exchange-rate risk, not the costs associated with an increased default risk, especially of government bonds. Many saw the large flows of funds as a sign of success for the eurozone. Having watched analogous instances of capital flowing across borders as restrictions on capital flows were brought down, especially from my perch at the World Bank, I was not so sanguine.

To avoid this situation, Europe as a whole could have borrowed in euros, on-lending the proceeds to the different countries, who would then be responsible for repayment of the money. But it chose not to centralize lending in that way. In making this choice, the eurozone leaders enhanced the likelihood of a debt crisis.

Not only did those countries signing up to the eurozone not fully realize the consequences of borrowing in a currency out of one's control, they also didn't realize the implications for their national sovereignty: a transfer of power had occurred that could be—and was—abused. When lenders wouldn't lend to, say, Spain, the only recourse the country had was to turn to their partners in the eurozone, to get money through the European Central Bank or through some other mechanism.[39] It was a fateful development.

Without access to funds, the country would careen toward bankruptcy. But there is no good international legal framework for dealing with the bankruptcies of countries, as Argentina and many other countries have learned to their chagrin. In the absence of such a framework, defaults can be very costly. Creditors have an incentive to scare the country at risk—to make them believe that the costs of default will be very high, far higher than knuckling under to the creditors' demands.[40]

As soon as some of the countries in the eurozone owed money to other member countries, the currency union had changed: rather than a partnership of equals striving to adopt policies that benefit each other, the ECB and eurozone authorities have become credit collection agencies for the lender nations, with Germany particularly influential. Though this was never the intent when the eurozone was created, that this is what happened should have been expected. It is simply a reflection of the old adage "He who pays the piper calls the tune." Germany had the money. The German parliament had to approve any significant new program. It became clear that their parliament would only approve these new programs if there were sufficient "conditions" imposed on the crisis countries. The Germans have repeatedly even challenged the constitutionality of the actions the ECB designed to help the crisis countries.

The power to withhold credit becomes the power to force a country to effectively cede its economic sovereignty, and that is precisely what the Troika, including the ECB, have done, most visibly to Greece and its banks, but to a lesser extent to the other crisis countries. They have imposed policies not designed to promote full employment and growth but to create surpluses that in principle might enable the debtor countries to repay what is owed.

WHY EVEN TRADE SURPLUSES MATTER

I have explained why, with fixed exchange rates, countries may wind up with large trade deficits, and how a sudden stop in the willingness of others to finance that deficit can precipitate a crisis. The way Europe has chosen to get rid of trade deficits is to put the economy into depression. When the country is in a depression, it no longer buys goods from abroad. Imports are reduced. The "cure" is as bad as or worse than the disease.

But even trade surpluses are a problem. Germany has been running huge trade surpluses—consistently larger than China's as a percentage of GDP, and in many years, even larger in dollar terms. Indeed, in recent years, its surpluses as a percentage of its GDP have been almost twice that of China's.[41] The United States has criticized China's surpluses, saying they represented a risk to global stability. The reason is simple: over the entire world, the sum of the surpluses has to equal the sum of the deficits. If some country is running a surplus, exporting more than it is importing, other countries *must* be running a deficit, that is, importing more than they are exporting. So if deficits are a problem, so too for surpluses. If China's surpluses are a global problem, so too are Germany's.[42]

Similarly, if the exchange rate is set so that the eurozone as a whole has a trade balance, which it roughly did in the years before the crisis, and Germany has a surplus, that means the rest of the eurozone *must* have a deficit.

In some respects, surpluses are an even bigger problem than deficits, as Keynes argued,[43] because they contribute to a shortfall in global demand. These countries are producing more than they are buying and thus not spending all of their income. Of course, the deficit countries would *like* to buy more. But if no one is willing to lend to them, they can't, or if they are under an IMF or Troika program that *prevents* them from spending more, they can't. When there are large imbalances (such as associated with Germany's trade surplus), the not-spending of the surplus countries is not fully compensated for by overspending in the deficit countries. The result is that overall *global* demand is weakened.

Before the crisis, Germany recycled its surpluses, in effect, lending them to the periphery countries, like Spain and Ireland, which allowed them to run deficits.[44] But in doing so, it helped create the euro crisis and enhanced *divergence* within Europe. The periphery countries became debtors, with Germany as the great creditor. As we have noted, there is no greater divide than the one between creditors and debtors.

Our discussion here has focused on borrowing and lending *by the country*. The analysis does not distinguish between private and public borrowing. That's important: trade imbalances can be a problem whether they originate in the public sector (as in Greece) or in the private (as in Spain and Ireland). The convergence criteria only focused on the public sector problem. Historically, private sector borrowing has been as or more important.

SURPLUSES: VICE OR VIRTUE?

The countries in surplus often look at their trade surplus—not buying as much from abroad as they are getting from selling goods and services—and the associated savings as a badge of honor. Savings is a virtue. Germany says that all countries should imitate what it does. But Germany's virtue is a peculiar one: as we've seen, *by definition* not all countries can run surpluses, and anything Germany does to create its surpluses is, in effect, increasing some other country's deficit. The country with a deficit, in turn, is likely to face weak demand, and possibly even high unemployment and a crisis. If exports create jobs, then imports destroy them. It is hardly a virtue if one can only obtain it by forcing someone else to be a sinner—if one's actions inevitably lead to problems in some other country.

Modern economics, beginning with Keynes, has explained that in a world of unemployment there is the *paradox of thrift*. If everyone tries to save more, but investment is fixed, all that happens is that incomes fall. Ironically, total savings is not increased. The reasoning is simple: In equilibrium, savings *must* equal investment. Thus, if investment does not change, savings *cannot* change. If individuals insist, say, on saving a higher fraction of their income, the only way that the *level* of savings can be changed is if the *level of income* is reduced.

Today the world is in this precise situation, with a deficiency of aggregate demand leading to slow growth and some 200 million unemployed around the world. This deficiency of aggregate demand is the cause of what many have referred to as global secular stagnation. (The term *secular* just means that it is *long-term* as opposed to *cyclical*, temporary slow growth that is part of recurrent business cycles.) The jobs "gap" has increased enormously since the onset of the Great Recession, with some 60 million fewer jobs in existence than what would have been expected if there had been no crisis.[45]

There is another reason that surpluses are particularly problematic. Typically, it is easier for the surplus country to deal with its surplus than it is for the deficit country to do something about its deficit. There is ample scope, for instance, for both Germany and China to increase wages, especially at the bottom. Until recently, Germany hasn't even had a minimum wage, and even now, its minimum wage is only €8.50 an hour (which at 2015 average exchange rates was equivalent to $9.35),[46] as compared to €9.47 (roughly $10.42) in France. If German workers' incomes increased, they would buy more, including more imported goods.

By and large, the countries in crisis, and even France and Italy, have managed to reduce their current account deficits; with Germany not only having maintained but actually increased its surplus, the eurozone now has a large overall surplus estimated to be $452 billion in 2015.[47] But by the basic arithmetic of global deficits and surpluses, this has been accomplished only by increasing deficits in the rest of the world. It will be hard, if not impossible, for the eurozone to maintain this surplus indefinitely without problems appearing in the rest of the world. Something will have to give.

EXTERNALITIES, AND THE EURO AND GLOBAL GOVERNANCE

When individuals, firms,, or countries impose costs on others—which they do not themselves have to pay—economists say that there is an *externality*. The analysis above explained how German trade surpluses impose externalities on the rest of the world, including on its partners within the eurozone. A well-designed global economic system—and a well-designed eurozone—would have adopted measures to deal with this externality. Currently, at the global level, we have no way of inducing countries not to run surpluses.[48] The G-20—the group of the 20 largest economies, which sees its role as helping coordinate global economic policies—attempts to cajole countries not to do so. Ironically, it has focused its attention on China, whose surpluses have been coming down, instead of Germany.

Within the eurozone, too, nothing has been done to curb surpluses. As we have noted, the focus of attention has been on *government* activities, and only on deficits. The mistaken presumption has been that government deficits are the main source of externalities, the main aspect of a country's behavior that impinges on the well-being of others and the functioning of the economic system.

CONCLUDING COMMENTS

The founders of the euro knew that making a single currency work for a diverse set of countries would not be easy. But their analysis of what it would take was deeply flawed: the convergence criteria that they formulated, limiting public (fiscal) deficits and debts, made the task of achieving full employment throughout Europe even more difficult. Adding to the difficulty was the task of limiting trade deficits, the creation of which the euro itself was at least partially responsible. Persistent trade deficits set the scene for crises: the predictable and predicted crises emerged just a decade after the beginning of the euro.

THE RESPONSE

Seeing how things were turning out so differently from what had been promised—crises and depressions rather than a new era of prosperity—one might have hoped that Europe's leaders would have realized both that the economic analysis underlying the euro was flawed and that, if the euro was to work, the "incomplete project" needed to be completed, and in a hurry. They had to put into place the institutional arrangements required to make up for the loss of countries' ability to use the interest and exchange rate to maintain full employment and to keep imports in line with exports.

Instead, Germany has tried to blame the euro crisis on failures to enforce budgetary discipline. Our analysis has argued otherwise: it is the very structure of the eurozone itself, not even the failings of the individual countries, that is to blame. Market mechanisms (internal devaluation) are not an adequate substitute for the loss of the ability to adjust interest and exchange rates. The euro created the euro crisis.

That the narrative blaming the euro crisis on fiscal deficits was wrong should have been obvious: several countries in Europe had maintained fiscal discipline and yet have been facing severe unemployment, even crises—not just the allegedly profligate countries of Europe's south, but even the more responsible countries of the north, Ireland and Finland. Market economies can suffer from crises simply as a result of the dynamics of capitalism; in the absence of adequate regulation, there are often credit bubbles. But the ideology of neoliberalism ignored these sources of volatility—the source of the Great Recession itself as well as the East Asia crisis—as it conveniently focused on the budgetary failures in Greece, which were easier to understand, and excoriate.

This failure to diagnose the source of the eurozone's problem was inevitably linked to the failure to take actions that would address those problems. Instead of correcting the underlying problem, they continued implementing policies based an obviously flawed theory. As the crisis unfolded, they renewed their commitment to the convergence criteria, binding themselves to stricter enforcement.

That they did so suggests one thing: it was a matter of ideology, not economic science. It was a *willful* failure not to look at the evidence. It may not have been in Germany's interest to understand the failures, for that might have called upon it to do more than just lecture its partners.

A LOOK FORWARD

Although the convergence criteria were supposed to foster convergence, the structure of the eurozone has increased differences among the countries of the region in fundamental ways—exacerbating the large differences that already existed when the eurozone was formed. Most importantly, it increased the divide between creditor and debtor countries. The next chapter explains the ways in which the current eurozone structure results in the stronger countries within the eurozone becoming stronger, and the weak weaker. The creditor countries become richer; the debtor countries, poorer. And a hoped-for convergence has transformed into divergence.

5

THE EURO:
A DIVERGENT SYSTEM

The eurozone was a beautiful edifice erected on weak foundations. The cracks were clear from the beginning, but after the 2008 crisis, those cracks became fissures. By the summer of 2015, 16 years after the euro was launched, it looked as if Greece would have to exit. A huge creditor/debtor schism had opened up, and political power within the eurozone rested with the creditors, and Germany in particular. The crisis countries were forced into deep recessions and depressions. Europe had created a divergent system even as it thought it was putting together a convergent one.

Several features of the eurozone that were thought of as *essential* to its success were actually central to its divergence. Standard economics is based on the gravity principle: money moves from capital-rich countries with low returns to countries with capital shortage. The presumption was that the risk-adjusted returns in such countries would be high. But in Europe under the euro, movements of not just capital but also labor seem to defy the principles of gravity. Money flowed upward.[1] In this chapter, I explain how Europe created this gravity-defying system. Understanding the sources of the divergence is essential to creating a eurozone that works.

DIVERGENCE IN CAPITAL AND FINANCIAL MARKETS AND THE SINGLE-MARKET PRINCIPLE

One of the strengths of the eurozone was that capital and labor could move freely throughout the region. This is sometimes called the "single-market principle." Free mobility was supposed to lead to the efficient allocation of labor and capital, thereby strengthening Europe's prosperity. Each would go to that place where returns were highest.

As capital left the rich (capital abundant) countries to go to the poor (capital scarce), so the theory went, incomes across the eurozone would become more similar and the whole eurozone would work better. Natural market forces would result in convergence; if governments did their part—keeping low deficits and debts—the market would do the rest. The leaders of Europe should have known that there was a significant body of economic analysis—theory and evidence—showing that those expectations were wrong.

In fact, there was a real world example in plain sight: conditions in Italy were quite different from textbook economics. There are no government-imposed barriers to the movement of capital and labor between the north and south of Italy. There is the same legal framework. Yet, the south of Italy has had a persistently lower income than the north. Though there have been periods in which there was some convergence, in recent decades, it has not occurred.[2]

THE SINGLE MARKET TOGETHER WITH THE EUROZONE AND MARKET IRRATIONALITY CREATED THE EURO CRISIS

The previous chapter explained how a free flow of capital, combined with the creation of the eurozone, led to the euro crisis. Ever-foolish capital markets thought the elimination of exchange-rate risk meant the elimination of *all* risk and rushed into the periphery countries.

In some cases, they created real estate bubbles. In all cases, they created upward pressure on prices and current account deficits that were not sustainable. One country after another went into crisis, as markets eventually realized that the current account deficits were unsustainable, and as real estate bubbles broke. But by then it was too late: money that should have gone into making these economies more productive went instead to financing consumption and real estate bubbles (in Spain and Ireland) and government deficits (Greece).

The previous chapter also explained how as prices in these countries increased relative, say, to those in Germany, imports increased relative to exports. Trade deficits became a regular feature of these countries' lives. Internal devaluation was supposed to undo the damage that had been done.[3] But as we saw, internal devaluation works, at best, slowly and can be very costly: Increasing wages and prices is far easier than the reverse.

The same irrational money that had created the euro crisis, realizing the enormous mistake that had been made, did what finance always does in such situations: it leaves.

Of course, this analysis does not describe all of the countries facing economic recession and large trade deficits. As we noted earlier, Finland has suffered from problems in a couple of its leading export sectors and from weaknesses in some of its major export markets. But even here, the euro is to blame for the prolonged downturn, because it has taken away the standard instruments by which it might return quickly to full employment with trade balance—and has put nothing in their place.

CAPITAL FLIGHT

As the euro crisis emerged, money left the banking systems of the weak countries, going to those of the strong countries. As money flowed out of their banking systems, the banks in weak countries had to contract their lending. I refer to this contraction in lending as *private auster-*

ity. The magnitude of this contraction is enormous and affects especially small and medium-size enterprises. Not surprisingly, countries where such businesses play a more important role are more adversely affected. (Large multinationals can borrow in international markets and thus are not as dependent on what happens within any particular country.) By 2013, the volume of small loans of less than €1 million—a proxy for lending to small and medium-size enterprises (SMEs)—was still far below its precrisis peak in all of the crisis countries: nearly halved in Portugal, down by two-thirds in Greece and Spain, and down by more than 80 percent in Ireland. But the decline was large even in many near-crisis countries: a decrease of a fifth in Italy, for example.[4]

By 2015, the European Commission was celebrating "green shoots" for the continent's SMEs, which account for 67 percent of employment in the European Union.[5] To many, the upbeat tone seemed premature, particularly in crisis countries. SMEs haven't recovered in Greece, where more than a third continue to report "access to finance" as the single largest obstacle to doing business.[6] Later, we shall see how the European Central Bank, headed by Mario Draghi, took forceful actions to restore confidence in the market for bonds, especially the bonds of the crisis countries; but while he may have saved the bond markets and the wealthy players in *that* game, back on Main Street, what he did seemed to have little effect.

EXPLAINING THE FLOW AGAINST GRAVITY

The flow of money out of the crisis countries' banking systems is understandable. Confidence in any country's banking system rests partially on the confidence in the ability and willingness of the bank's government to bail out banks in trouble. This in turn depends in part on the existence of (1) institutional frameworks that reduce the likelihood that a bailout will be necessary, (2) special funds set aside should a bailout be necessary, and (3) procedures in place to ensure that depositors will be made whole.[7]

Typically, banks benefit from an implicit subsidy in jurisdictions where governments possess greater bailout capacity. The link between confidence in banks and confidence in the governments under whose authority the banks operate can be seen in the close relationship between risk premiums on government debt and bank debt from the same country.[8]

Money flowed into the United States after the 2008 global crisis even though the crisis had been precipitated by failures in the United States' financial system. Why? It was not that investors thought that American banks were better managed or that that they managed risks better. It was simply that there was more confidence in the willingness and ability of the United States to bail out its banks. (The government, with bipartisan support, had quickly put together a $700 billion bailout package in 2008, and it was clear that more money would be forthcoming if needed. The influence of Wall Street on the American government was palpable.)[9]

Similarly, today in Europe, what rational wealthy Spaniard or Greek would keep all his money in a local bank, when there is (almost) equal convenience and greater safety putting it in a German bank?[10]

The effects of capital leaving the crisis countries are significant: only by paying higher interest rates can banks in those countries compete, but higher rates puts these countries and their firms at a competitive disadvantage. A downward spiral ensues: as capital leaves, the country's banks have to restrict lending, the economy weakens; as the economy weakens, so too does the perceived ability of the country to bail out banks in trouble; and that increases the interest rate banks have to pay, so the banks weaken further and capital is further incentivized to leave.[11]

DIVERGENCE IN THE ABSENCE OF A CRISIS

The euro crisis has highlighted how the structure of the eurozone itself created divergence, but there would be divergence even in the absence of a crisis. The ECB sets a *single* interest rate for the entire region. But the interest rate set on, say, German government bonds, is not the interest rate that firms in France or Italy, let alone Greece, pay—or even that the governments in these countries pay. There is a spread in interest rates, reflecting differences in the market's judgment of risk and the ability of the banks in each country to provide credit to the country's companies. The poorer and more poorly performing economies, and the countries with greater inherited debt, will have to pay higher interest rates, and, especially because of the intertwining of banks and governments *in the current eurozone structure*, so, too, will companies in these countries. This gives the country and its companies a distinctive competitive disadvantage, again leading to divergence.

Fixing the problem

There is an easy solution to this particular problem: common comprehensive deposit insurance for all banks in the eurozone. With such common insurance, no one would worry about the loss of money in their bank account; there would be no incentive for money to flow from the weak countries to the strong.[12]

A banking union

Germany is worried that with common insurance, there would be a net transfer from strong countries (like Germany) to the weak, and as Germany constantly insists, the eurozone is not a transfer union—a federation in which money is transferred from one country or region within the federation to another. That's why it insists, too, that if there is common deposit insurance, there has to be a common regulatory framework. And to ensure fair treatment of banks across the eurozone in the event of a default, there has to be a common procedure for "resolution," that is, for dealing with banks in distress, where depositors are demanding back more money than the bank has liquid funds to pay.[13]

These three provisions—deposit insurance, common regulations, and a resolution procedure—together are called a "banking union." And by 2014, there *seemed* to be broad consensus within the eurozone on the necessity to move forward with such a banking union if Europe was to prevent the increasing divergence that was emerging. But, Germany argued that one should proceed carefully and gradually. It demanded, before there can be common deposit insurance, there must be common supervision (that is, regulation). Subsequently, Germany seems to have backed off being willing to have common deposit insurance, at least anytime soon, *even with common supervision and common resolution.*

But the halfway house with common supervision and no common deposit insurance would be worse than no house at all. Common supervision would introduce a new kind of rigidity into Europe. Yet, as I explained in the last chapter, the eurozone's lack of flexibility and ability to adapt to the specific circumstances of different countries presents one of the region's key problems. Managing the banking system of any country is a delicate matter, especially in an economic downturn. Shutting down banks hurts not just the shareholders and bondholders of the banks but also borrowers—they may not be able to easily find another source of finance—and, in the absence of deposit insurance, depositors.

Forbearance—a slight easing of regulations in times of economic downturn, allowing banks that would have been normally shut down because of their weak balance sheet to continue operating—has been part of traditional central bank practice. Of course, had there been better regulation of banks *before* the downturn, there would have been less need for forbearance. But central bankers and regulators have to deal with the hand that they have been dealt.

For the eurozone, the worry is that the rigid application of rules will make forbearance more difficult. Decisions made in Brussels and Frankfurt may not be those best suited for the economies around the eurozone. Banks may be shut down, at great cost to their country's economy. Bank regulators are typically not economists. They are just following rules. But this rigid application of rules, in the absence of common deposit insurance, may make it even riskier for depositors to keep their money in the banks of a weak country: it may exacerbate the problem of divergence.

REGULATORY RACES TO THE BOTTOM

Europe not only allowed *capital* to flow freely within its borders but also financial firms and products—no matter how poorly they are regulated at home.

The single-market principle for financial institutions and capital, in the absence of adequate EU regulation, led to a regulatory race to the bottom, with at least some of the costs of the failures borne by other jurisdictions. The failure of a financial institution imposes costs on others (evidenced so clearly in the crisis of 2008), and governments will not typically take into account these "cross-border costs."

Indeed, especially before the 2008 global financial crisis, each country faced pressures to reduce regulations. Financial firms threatened that they would leave unless regulations were reduced.[14]

This regulatory race to the bottom would have existed within Europe even without the euro. Indeed, the winners in the pre-2008 contest were Iceland and the UK, neither of which belong to the eurozone (and Iceland doesn't even belong to the EU). The UK prided itself on its system of light regulation, which meant essentially self-regulation, an oxymoron. The bank managers put their own interests over those of shareholders and bondholders, and the banks as institutions put their interests over those of their clients. The UK's Barclays bank confessed to having manipulated the market for LIBOR, the London interbank lending rate upon which some $350 *trillion* of derivatives and other financial products are based.[15]

Still, the eurozone was *designed* with the potential to make all of this worse. The advocates of the euro said that it would enable financial products to move more freely, since the exchange rate risk had been eliminated. In their mind, financial innovation meant designing better products to meet the needs of consumers and firms. That's the standard neoliberal theory. More modern theories emphasize imperfectly informed and often irrational consumers and firms operating in markets with imperfect and asymmetric information, where profits can typically be enhanced more by exploiting these market imperfections than in any other way. Nobel Prize–winning economists George Akerlof and Rob Shiller document this widespread behavior in their brilliant book *Phishing for Phools*—using the term for Internet scammers who systematically "fish for fools."[16] With financial products moving ever more easily throughout Europe, the opportunity to take advantage of a whole continent of people who might be duped into buying financial products that were not suitable for them proved irresistible.

Difficulties in regulation

Attempts to regulate the financial sector around the world have made it clear that such regulation is not easy. Well-paid lobbyists from the financial sector approach any or all with as large a gift or campaign contribution as the antibribery and electoral laws of that country allow.[17] Not surprisingly, the financial sector exercises enormous political influence and is enormously successful in persuading politicians that they should not "overregulate." Excessive regulation, these opponents claim, could stifle the financial system and thus prevent it from fulfilling the important functions that it must fulfill if an economy is to prosper. The result is that in most countries, the financial sector is underregulated.

Somehow, the banks' money makes their arguments seem more cogent, in spite of the historical record showing the adverse consequences of underregulated banks—up to and including the 2008 crisis.[18]

This political influence on regulatory reform in Europe and the United States has meant that the reforms have almost surely not been sufficient to prevent another crisis; in certain areas, such as the shadow banking system, there has been little progress, and in other areas, such as derivatives, what progress there has been has been significantly reversed, at least in the United States.[19]

Fixing the problem

The threat of a regulatory race to the bottom is why there has to be strong regulation at the European level. But under Europe's current governance structure, this will prove even more difficult than getting good regulation within a country. The UK has been vigorously defending its system of light regulation. It may have cost its taxpayers hundreds of billions of pounds, yet today policymakers focus on the potential loss of profits, taxes, and jobs from downsizing (or rightsizing) the financial sector. The losses of a few years ago seem ancient history, not to be mentioned in any polite conversation of regulatory reform.

There is a second problem with Europe-wide financial regulation and supervision—can it be sufficiently sensitive to the circumstances of the different countries? Earlier, we suggested that it was unlikely that banking supervision could or would be.

In the absence of an adequate system of financial regulation and supervision at the European or eurozone level, each country has a responsibility to its own citizens, to make sure that they are not taken advantage of by others selling flawed financial products. There is great inefficiency in having duplicative regulatory regimes. But the costs pale in comparison with the harm from inadequate financial sector regulation.

The principle of financial market liberalization—allowing financial firms and products to move freely across Europe—has to be replaced with a more subtle condition: no country can discriminate against the financial products and firms from another member country, but each could demand that banks be adequately regulated in any way it saw fit; it could demand that the banks operating in its jurisdiction be adequately capitalized in a separate legal entity (subsidiary) within its country—so that its citizens would be paid off in the event of a financial collapse, or if a suit was brought claiming deceptive practices, the firm had adequate net worth to pay off the claim. The country would have the right to ensure that its financial sector is stable, that it does what it is supposed to do and not do what it should not.[20]

DIVERGENCE AND FREE LABOR MOBILITY

An economic framework that combines free mobility of labor with country (place-based) debt[21] creates divergence, just as we saw that free mobility of capital does. It also leads to the inefficient allocation of labor.[22]

This may sound surprising. After all, in standard theory, free mobility is supposed to ensure that workers move to where their (marginal) returns are highest. This would be true if wages were equal to the (marginal) productivity of a worker, for, by and large, workers will gravitate toward where wages are highest.

But individuals care about their wages *after tax*, and this depends not only on their (marginal) productivity but also on taxes. Taxes, in turn, depend in part on the burden imposed by *inherited debt*. This can be seen in the cases of Ireland, Greece, and Spain. All three countries are facing towering levels of inherited debt, a debt that had swollen through financial and macroeconomic mismanagement. In the case of Ireland, the European Central Bank *forced* the government to take on some of the debts of the private banks, to socialize losses, even though earlier profits had been privatized.[23]

When marginal productivities are the same, this implies migration away from highly indebted countries to those with less indebtedness, and the more individuals move out, the greater the tax burden on the remainder becomes, accelerating the movement of labor away from an efficient allocation.[24]

The fact that skilled labor is more mobile than unskilled creates another driver of divergence and inequality. When skilled workers leave, a country is said to be hollowing out: their departure lowers incomes and future growth prospects. Hollowing out robs these countries of the potential entrepreneurs who will start new businesses and the academics who will train a new generation of researchers. It impedes a country's capacity to catch up. The poorest workers, who are stuck at home, wind up paying for the mistakes of their parents—or more accurately, of the bankers and politicians of an earlier era. They pay doubly if there is complementarity between skilled and unskilled workers (that is, if the productivity of unskilled workers increases when they have more skilled workers to work with). In this case, fewer skilled workers results in less pay for unskilled workers. This is undoubtedly happening in Greece and some of the other crisis countries.

And matters are further worsened by the interaction between capital flows and labor flows: decreased availability of loans to small and medium-size enterprises further diminishes opportunity in the crisis and near-crisis countries, encouraging even more migration, especially of those talented and more educated individuals who can get jobs elsewhere in the EU.

Of course, in the short run, emigration may bring benefits to the crisis country: it reduces the burden of unemployment insurance, and domestic purchasing power increases as remittances from abroad (sent by the emigrants) roll in.[25] But the outward migration also hides the severity of the underlying downturn, since it means that the unemployment rate is less, possibly far less, than it otherwise would be.[26]

These tax induced "distortions" in migration patterns are exacerbated by differences in government spending. Individuals care not just about their after-tax wages but also about publicly provided amenities. Countries with large inherited debts have limited public revenues to spend in providing these amenities; and this is even more true in the crisis countries where the Troika is forcing deep cutbacks in government spending.

Indeed, free migration, stoked by debt obligations inherited from the past and Troika policies imposed to ensure repayment, may result in depopulation of certain countries, in some cases exacerbating natural market forces trending in that direction. As we noted in the last chapter, one of the important adjustment mechanisms in the United States (which shares a common currency) is internal migration. If such migration leads to the depopulation of an entire state, there is some limited concern, but this pales in comparison to the justifiable worries of Greece and Ireland about the depopulation of their homelands, with its risk to their culture and identity.

Fixing the Problem

There is a partial *economic* fix to these problems, one that would also address some of the key macroeconomic issues raised in the last chapter. Eliminate place-based debt by creating eurobonds—bonds that are a common obligation.[27] Germany has been adamantly against this and similar ideas, but it has never proposed an alternative way to cope with the inefficiencies in eurozone labor movement.

The reform would improve matters in several ways. Interest payments in the crisis countries would be much lower. Lower spending on debt service would allow these countries both to lower taxes and to undertake more expansionary fiscal policies, increasing incomes. All of this would reduce the magnitude of the forces for divergence—both outmigration of especially skilled labor and capital flight.

OTHER SOURCES OF DIVERGENCE

I have described perhaps the two most importance sources of divergence—capital flight and labor migration. But there are three more that deserve brief note.

DIVERGENCES IN PUBLIC INVESTMENT

As economies weaken, because of the fiscal constraints imposed by the convergence criteria,[28] the governments of those countries are unable to make competitive investments in infrastructure, technology, and education. This is true even if the return on these investments exceeds by a considerable amount the interest rate the country has to pay to get funds. As a result, the gap between the strong countries and the weak in the level of these public services and investment, often complementary with private investment, increases.

This then interacts with the two forms of divergence already discussed: if these public investments are complementary with labor and capital—that is, they raise their productivities—then rich countries will have higher *private* returns to capital, even though they have a superabundance of private capital. If these countries have a more educated workforce (as a result of more investments by the public in human capital), the same results hold.

There is a long-standing anomaly in development economics: Why does capital seem to move from developing countries to those that are developed?[29] Part of the answer lies in these complementary public investments, which increase the return to private investments.

Fixing the Problem

European-wide investment, financed by the European Investment Bank (EIB), Europe's region-wide development bank, is a partial fix. But even though the EIB is the world's largest multilateral lending institution, its resources are limited. What is needed is a further recapitalization of the EIB.

Some propose a related second fix: creating national development banks, whose lending for investment is off the country's balance sheet and therefore outside the convergence criteria. But by pooling the risks of the different member countries, the EIB can obtain funds almost certainly at a lower rate than a development bank within a crisis country, and this is a major advantage. Indeed, some multinational development banks can borrow money at a rate lower than the rates at which any of their member countries can borrow.[30] On the other hand, a national development bank may be able to discern among alternative

SME borrowers, and thus be more effective in lending to SMEs. Some countries (such as Brazil) have found it useful to have both national and state development banks.

More broadly, limits on deficits should be revised to distinguish between consumption and investment expenditures, and to allow countries to borrow beyond the 3 percent limit for investment.[31] After all, we have noted, such investments increase the economic strength of the country.

DIVERGENCES IN TECHNOLOGY

Contrary to the presumption in standard theory, countries do not necessarily naturally converge in technology (knowledge).[32] The leading countries remain the leaders. East Asia is the exception, but countries in this region achieved convergence through active government policies, called *industrial policies*. They realized that what separates more advanced countries from the less advanced is a gap in knowledge, and knowledge does not, on its own, flow freely.[33] Markets in knowledge are not well described by the standard economic model; economies in which knowledge is important are not, in general, efficient: markets invest too little, and often in the wrong direction.[34] And, markets, on their own, do not necessarily eliminate the knowledge gap.

Indeed, it has been well known that increasing returns to scale associated with innovation (an investment in R&D yields disproportionately greater expected returns the greater the sales) gives big firms an advantage over small firms. There can be economies of scope, where research in one area has benefits for others and spillover from one firm to another, reflected in clustering. The consequence of such economies in scale and scope is that countries with technological advantages often maintain those advantages, unless there are countervailing forces brought about by government policies.

Policies aimed at closing the technology gap are, as we have noted, called industrial policies—even when they apply to other sectors of the economy, like the service sector. But European competition laws prevent, or at least inhibit, such policies.[35] The rationale for such a law is understandable *if one believed that markets on their own converged*: one would not want to give a leg up to one firm from one country through the artificial prop of government support.[36]

If natural market forces do not lead to convergence, but instead to divergence or at least the sustaining of advantages, then the prohibition against industrial policies simply preserves and exacerbates differences. A cynic might say that this was the intent of the law: to preserve power relations. But I am convinced that the rule in Europe was driven more by ideology and misguided economic beliefs than narrow self-interest. The predominant view in neoliberal policy circles at the time the euro was founded—a view since largely discredited—was that market forces would on their own lead to convergence; industrial policies were neither needed nor effective.

Of course, technological divergences in turn exacerbate all the other divergences noted earlier. If German technology is better than that of Portugal, capital will flow from the capital-scarce country to the capital-rich, and so, too, will skilled labor.

Fixing the problem

Again, there is an easy fix to this problem of divergence: rather than discourage industrial policies, the eurozone should actively encourage such policies, especially for countries that are lagging behind. Such active policies hold out the promise of *real* convergence.

DIVERGENCE IN WEALTH

Finally, there is a divergence in *wealth*. I described in the last chapter how, when the exchange rate is set for the eurozone as a whole to have balance, Germany runs a trade surplus and the periphery runs a deficit. Running a trade surplus simply means lending to the rest of the world; running a trade deficit means borrowing. This is perhaps the most disturbing aspect of the eurozone's divergence: some countries, most notably Germany, have increasingly become creditor countries, some debtors. This creates a divergence in economic interests and perspectives: it makes it all the more difficult for a common currency to work for the benefit of all.

THE CRISIS POLICIES EXACERBATE DIVERGENCE

Chapter 3 showed the magnitude of the divergences that have opened up in Europe. Some of these, as I have explained, are the natural result of the eurozone as it was constructed. But some are a result of the policies that the eurozone has adopted in response to the crisis.

For instance, we noted the outflow of more talented people from a country with a high level of place-based debt. Austerity has exacerbated the outmigration from the poor countries of both capital and labor: austerity, as I explain in later chapters at greater length, leads to deeper and longer recessions, and investors don't like to invest in countries in a recession, so money flows to where economic conditions are better. So, too, high unemployment induces outmigration, leaving a greater debt burden per capita on those who remain behind. So, too, cutbacks in public services associated with austerity and the underinvestment by the government—for example, in infrastructure, technology, and education—make living and investing in the afflicted countries less attractive.

Making matters even worse, the policies of the Troika in Cyprus and Greece have encouraged the further capital flight out of the banking systems of those countries—or any seriously afflicted country. The Troika has shown that, no matter what an individual government says about deposit guarantees, even for small depositors, the Troika is at least willing to consider significant haircuts (where depositors will get back only a fraction of the value of their deposits), if it can't figure out a better way of saving the banks. It has also shown that to enforce its wishes, the Troika is willing to take actions that *force* the temporary shutdown of a country's banks—obviously making the retention of money in the country's banks even more risky, and encouraging money to move to stronger banks in Germany and elsewhere.

Recent efforts to resuscitate the eurozone economy have created potential new sources of divergence, the significance of which we will be able to ascertain only over time. Under policies announced in early 2016, the ECB can buy corporate bonds, but the corporate bonds that it can and is likely to buy are those of large German and French corporations, again giving them an advantage over companies in other countries.

HOW ONGOING "REFORMS" MAY LEAD TO MORE INSTABILITY AND DIVERGENCE

That the eurozone has not been working as planned seems clear. Not surprisingly, this has spurred reforms. They have created a €500 billion (about $550 billion) eurozone-wide safety net for countries and banks in difficulty.[37] We have discussed, too, the proposed banking union—and explained why the current halfway house may be worse than nothing.

There are two other reforms, one eurozone wide, one part of the most recent program for a crisis-afflicted country, which are worse—large movements in the wrong direction.

First, we noted earlier how Germany misdiagnosed why the eurozone wasn't working the way it was supposed to: they blamed fiscal profligacy, so they doubled down on that theory, requiring even more binding commitments of the eurozone members on their deficits and debts, with stringent penalties for those that didn't comply. This was called the Fiscal Compact, and portends an era of even weaker eurozone performance.

The second was part of the new program introduced for Greece in the summer of 2015. We noted that the Troika consistently underestimated the magnitude of the downturn that the policies they had imposed generated, and thus overestimated the improvement in the fiscal position. In effect, the actual austerity imposed was somewhat softened by the realities within Greece.[38]

The bad news is that the Troika is headed toward a policy which insists that the budget numbers they set out actually be realized: if expenditures turn out larger or tax revenues smaller than originally anticipated—say, because a downturn was greater than originally anticipated—expenditures have to be cut back further and taxes raised further. This will be a strong automatic *destabilizer*. As the economy weakens, tax revenues will be less than anticipated, and so Greece will be forced to increase taxes even more, further weakening the economy.[39]

How free mobility encourages "reforms" that lead to greater instability and inequality

We've focused on the changes to the stability of the European economy arising from the creation of the eurozone and the policies that the eurozone has adopted in response to the crisis. But there are other factors at play in Europe, and they are resulting in an economic system that may be still less stable. Most importantly, progressive taxes and broad welfare benefits act as strong *automatic* stabilizers; as tax systems have become less progressive through much of Europe and welfare benefits have been trimmed, one would expect more economic volatility.

Free mobility of labor and capital have contributed to this untoward trend. Just as we noted earlier that there was a regulatory race to the bottom, so, too, for taxes. Countries compete to attract firms, capital, and highly skilled workers, and one way that they do so is through lower taxes. With such easy mobility, it is similarly hard to have very progressive taxes. Rich individuals threaten to leave and locate themselves and their businesses elsewhere.

Luxembourg and Ireland provided the worst examples, effectively giving some of the largest multinationals a free pass on taxes—a legal way of avoiding paying the taxes that they should have paid.[40] With free movement of goods, firms can locate in a low tax jurisdiction within the EU but sell their goods anywhere in the EU.

The resulting reduction in progressivity in the tax-and-transfer system meant that inequalities of income and wealth *within* most of the eurozone countries increased[41]—compounding the effect of the divergence among countries to which the structure of the eurozone has contributed in so many ways.

CONCLUDING COMMENTS

Tinkering with an economic system can be dangerous, unless one really knows how it works. And since economic systems are constantly evolving, knowing how they work is truly difficult. The founders of the euro changed the rules of the game. They fixed the exchange rate and they centralized the determination of the interest rate. They created new rules governing deficits and new rules governing the banking system. Hubris led them to believe that they understood how the economic system worked, and that they could tinker with it in these major ways and make it perform better.

Europe thought it had a better understanding of markets, and that markets were increasingly sophisticated—witness the "advances" and "innovation" in financial markets—and the two together would result in a better working economic system. A larger market, with better rules, and a single currency would lead to an even better economic system. It hasn't worked out that way. I have explained how, with the best of intentions, Europe created a more unstable and divergent economic system—one in which the wealthier countries get wealthier and the poorer countries poorer, and in which there is greater inequality within each country.

Details matter. One can't simply say, free capital movements lead to increased efficiency. One has to know what happens when a bank goes bankrupt. Who picks up the tab? One can't simply say, free labor movements lead to increased efficiency. One has to know something about the design of the tax system, and who pays for a country's past debts.

And above all, one has to know about monetary policy and central banking. Well-designed central banks can lead to increased stability and a better-performing economy. A poorly designed central bank can lead to higher levels of unemployment and lower levels of growth. The next chapter looks at the mistakes the eurozone made in the construction of its central and most important institution, the European Central Bank.

6

MONETARY POLICY AND THE EUROPEAN CENTRAL BANK

At the heart of the monetary union is the European Central Bank (ECB), an institution that has proven itself to be the strongest and most effective institution within the eurozone, and perhaps within the broader European Union. Indeed, Mario Draghi, head of the European Central Bank since 2011, may have saved the eurozone, with his famous speech that the ECB would do *whatever it takes* to preserve the euro[1]—and in saying that, restoring confidence in the bonds of the countries under attack.

While in that instance the ECB played a constructive role in preserving the eurozone, the mandate, governance, and actions of the ECB have, over the decade and a half of its existence, raised questions about whether the ECB, as presently constituted, is "fit for purpose": Can and will it conduct monetary policy that ensures growth, stability, and shared prosperity for the entire eurozone? The bank has a mandate to focus only on inflation—even when today, as we've seen, the critical problem facing Europe is unemployment and many are worried about deflation or falling prices. More broadly, its behavior sometimes seems to manifest what critics view as its basic defect—flawed governance, evidencing the democratic deficit that, as we noted in chapter 2, has been undermining the greater European project.

What it does seems often more consonant with the interests and perceptions of bankers than of the citizens of the countries that it is supposed to serve.

This chapter argues that critics of the ECB are fundamentally correct. Like the euro itself, the ECB was flawed at birth. Its construction was based on certain ideological propositions that were fashionable at the time. These beliefs, however, are increasingly questioned, especially in the aftermath of the 2008 global financial crisis. While other central banks, most notably the US Federal Reserve, have reformed, focusing much more on unemployment and the stability of the financial market—and even beginning to talk about how their policies affect inequality—the ECB's mandate is limited by the Treaty of Maastricht of 1992 to a single-minded focus on inflation.

The deeper problem of the ECB is the absence of democratic accountability. Conservatives have tried to frame monetary policy as a technocratic skill. Hire the best technocrats, and one will get the best monetary policy. The euro crisis and the global financial crisis, in which central banks played such a central role, revealed that central banks were making intensely political decisions. But central banks always have made political decisions—even when limited to assessing the risks of inflation; they simply made a pretense of just being technocratic. The decision to make the ECB independent, without adequate political accountability, and to focus only on inflation, were themselves political decisions, with strong distributive consequences.

In this chapter I will describe the structural flaws in the ECB and how these flaws have translated into policy decisions, some of which have worked well, but others of which have weakened the eurozone economy and increased the divides within it.

THE INFLATION MANDATE

When the ECB was established in 1998 as part of the process that created the euro, it was constructed expressly to limit what it could do. It was given a single, clear mandate: to maintain price stability.[2] This is markedly different from the mandate of the US Federal Reserve, which is supposed to not only control inflation but also promote growth and full employment. In the aftermath of the 2008 crisis, the Fed was given a further mandate—maintaining financial stability. It was ironic that this had to be added to the list, for the Federal Reserve was founded in 1913 to protect the integrity of the financial system after the panic of 1907. Indeed, in the decades before its founding, the problem facing the American economy was deflation.

Over time a belief developed within large parts of the economics profession (especially conservatives, espousing what we referred to earlier as "neoliberalism" or "market fundamentalism") that for good macroeconomic performance it is necessary, and almost sufficient by itself, to have low and stable inflation maintained by the monetary authorities. Of course, now we know that is wrong: the damage done by the financial crisis is far greater than any damage that might be inflicted by all but rampant inflation. In chapter 3, I explained how in Europe alone, the cumulative loss in GDP from the financial crisis is in the trillions of dollars. No one, not even the most ardent advocate of the ECB focusing on inflation, ever thought the cost of inflation would be even close to that. The bank's priorities were wrong, but it wasn't the ECB's fault: inflation had been its mandate; it was simply doing what it was told to do.

This belief that the central bank should focus on inflation was based on a simplistic ideology, supported by simplistic macroeconomic models that assumed efficient markets.[3] This ideology was essentially incorporated into the charter of the European Central Bank,[4] where it was mandated to "act in accordance with the principle of an open market economy with free competition, favouring an efficient allocation of resources."[5] Europe seemed to be saying that an open-market economy with free competition resulted in an efficient allocation of resources, in spite of the massive body of economic research, theory, and empirical evidence showing that that was not the case *in the absence of adequate government regulation.*

In this view underlying the ECB, then, government was the problem, and government had to be constrained. The gold standard had done this, but under the gold standard, the supply of money was essentially random, determined by the luck of finding new sources of gold (or other precious metals, if they became part of the monetary system). The result of this "system" was a period of high inflation when the supply of gold increased enormously—for example, after the discovery of the New World—and periods of deflation, such as the end of the 19th century in the United States, when there was a shortage of gold.[6] In the 20th century, the world moved off gold-backed currencies to fiat money—paper bills and nonprecious coins backed only by the guarantee of the government; it was this guarantee that gave these pieces of paper their value. The risk with paper money was that the government could print too much, and prices would spiral out of control, interfering with the smooth workings of the market. Thus, the only thing that one needed to worry about was inflation. The job of the central bank was to prevent this, by regulating the amount of money.

There was a contrasting view that developed in the aftermath of the Great Depression. Government intervention could help restore the economy to full employment faster than the market would on its own. Monetary and fiscal policy (changes in taxation and expenditure) were both required—with the relative role of each varying with the circumstance. In the United States, these views were incorporated in legislation by the Employment Act of 1946, which gave responsibility for maintaining stability in inflation *and employment* to the federal government.[7]

The worst fluctuations in output and employment were, moreover, created by the market themselves; they were not just acts of nature. This was made especially evident in 2008: a man-made housing bubble brought the global economy down. But the 2008 crisis was itself only the most recent manifestation of issues that have plagued capitalism from its origins.[8] Over the past 40 years, economists have come to understand the "market failures" that give rise to bubbles, booms, panics, and recessions. Market failures are particularly prevalent in financial markets. Good financial market regulation can at least reduce the frequency and depth of crises brought on by the excesses of the financial market players: the regulations introduced after the Great Depression prevented a recurrence for almost a half-century. Interestingly, while some central bankers recognized that "irrational exuberance"[9] might drive markets to behave irrationally, they still refused to intervene to dampen the bubbles. Their devotion to the ideology of free markets was simply too strong.

On both sides of the Atlantic, central bankers overestimated the rationality of markets and underestimated the costs that underregulated markets could impose on the rest of society. Fundamental to these failures, in turn, were others: a failure to understand the linkages among financial institutions and between financial institutions and the "real" economy, and a failure to grasp the incentives confronting decision-makers in the financial industry; these naturally led market participants to act in a shortsighted way that embraced excessive risk-taking—including actions creating systemic risk, which made the entire economic and financial system more unstable.[10]

CONSEQUENCES OF THE FIXATION ON INFLATION

While the most obvious, and most costly, consequence of the fixation on inflation was that insufficient attention was paid to financial stability, even without the crisis Europe has paid a high price for imposing too narrow a mandate on the ECB. It was virtually inevitable that with no focus on unemployment at the ECB, the average unemployment rate would be higher—higher than it would have been had full employment been among its principal mandates, regardless of whether there were a crisis or not. There would always be a greater gap between actual and potential output.

An inflation mandate also can lead to a counterproductive response to a crisis, especially one accompanied by cost-push inflation arising from, say, high energy or food prices. In such situations, workers suffer from inflation due to high oil prices. But then they are told, "You should suffer doubly": higher interest rates (raised to fight inflation) will dampen demand, leading to lower employment and wages.[11]

The single-minded focus on inflation was particularly unsuited for a global environment in which other central banks had more flexible mandates. While the Fed lowered interest rates in response to the crisis, the continuing inflationary concerns in Europe meant that the Fed's actions were not matched by reductions there.[12] The upshot was an appreciating euro (as the higher *relative* interest rates increased demand for European bonds) with downward effects on European output. Had the ECB taken actions to lower the euro's exchange value, it would have stimulated the economy, partially offsetting the effects of austerity. As it was, it allowed the United States to engage in competitive devaluation against it.[13]

There were those in America who celebrated Europe's flaws—at least in a shortsighted, selfish way. Europe was giving us a big gift, allowing us to export more at the expense of their exports and to import less from Europe. This was one of the reasons that the United States recovered more strongly than Europe; and one of the reasons that Europe languished.

In short, the result of the ECB's focus on inflation is that growth and stability are lower than they otherwise would have been—ironic, since the alleged purpose of the economic framework of the eurozone was to promote growth and stability. But the eurozone's framework for the ECB was worse, as we shall see: other constraints imposed on the ECB further limited its ability to promote stability and growth; and the way it conducted monetary policy meant that whatever growth occurred benefited those at the top disproportionately. The ECB played a role in exacerbating Europe's increasing inequality.

CONSTRAINING MONETARY AUTHORITIES

Long-standing battles over monetary policy center on what constraints should be imposed on monetary authorities. The mandate to
focus *just* on inflation is an example of a major constraint. Conservatives don't trust government—and the central bank is part of government. Some, such as archconservative Milton Friedman, even believe
that central banks caused the Great Depression by restricting the
supply of money.[14] Monetary policy during the 2008 crisis did much
to disprove his theory: central banks everywhere massively increased
the money supply. In Friedman's theory, the economy would have
quickly been back to full employment and even would have faced
inflation. Instead, economic growth in Japan, Europe, and the United
States was anemic, and many countries even faced deflation.

Standard wisdom among conservative bankers, including at the
ECB, constrained what central banks did even more. Conservative
economists like Friedman believed that central banks should exercise no discretion, simply increasing the money supply at a fixed rate;[15]
or when that theory failed to stabilize the economy, to increase or
decrease the money supply according to a simple formula, dictated by
the inflation rate.

So, too, the set of instruments, it was argued, should be limited:
central banks should only buy and sell short-term government bonds.
German members of the ECB Board resisted quantitative easing
(QE)—entailing the buying of long-term bonds, some of which might
not even be government bonds—long after policymakers in the United
States and Japan had augmented their tool kit with QE.[16] (QE was supposed to stimulate the economy by lowering the cost of long-term borrowing, lowering the exchange rate, and increasing the value of the
stock market. In practice, these effects turned out to be small.)

These limitations greatly weakened the scope of what the ECB
could do—even beyond the limitations imposed by the inflation mandate. Especially after the crisis, the ECB, the most important eco-

nomic institution in the eurozone, had an impossible task: to restore *all* of the countries of the zone to full employment with its hands tied behind its back.

The lack of fiscal policy—with limited spending by the EU as a whole and debt constraints facing each of the countries—put a special burden on monetary policy. Even with no constraints, the ECB's powers, its ability to maintain growth and employment throughout the eurozone, were limited. But rather than asking how to *maximize* what it could do, the economic conservatives dominating the construction of the ECB focused on imposing limitations on it. They fixated on the downside risk of an excessively exuberant ECB leading to inflation, not the upside potential of higher growth and employment.

Broadening the ECB's instruments to include regulatory policies (like capital requirements and capital adequacy standards for banks) might be used to create a more nuanced financial policy, sensitive to differences in the economic situation in different countries. Discretionary regulatory policies could have allowed the ECB to influence lending in individual countries in different ways. While with the euro, there is a single euro interest rate for effectively riskless bonds throughout the region, I have explained how firms borrowing in different countries can face markedly different costs of capital. Those in weak countries face a higher interest rate—when they really need a lower one. At least by providing scope for the banks in weak countries to lend more, one can reduce the magnitude of the tilt in the playing field so that credit in weak countries would not contract as much as it otherwise would.[17]

Faith in markets by neoliberals not only meant that monetary policy was less needed to keep the economy at full employment; it also meant that financial regulations were less needed to prevent "excesses." To conservatives, the ideal was "free banking," the absence of *all* regulations. Milton Friedman persuaded Chile's oppressive dictator Augusto Pinochet to try it beginning around 1975. The disastrous results were predictable and predicted: banks recklessly created credit, and when the credit bubble eventually broke, Chile entered a deep recession. It would not be until long after, more than a quarter-century, that the debt Chile undertook to get out of this mess was finally repaid. More recently, the Great Recession was a textbook example of the dangers of underregulated markets.

Central banks can play an important role not only in preventing the financial sector from imposing harms on the rest of society ("negative externalities," such as credit card abuses and excessive risk-taking) but in helping ensure that the sector does what it is supposed to: providing credit, for instance, to small businesses.[18]

To be fair, there are disagreements among economists about these issues. Keynesians are especially sensitive to the waste of resources, the human suffering, the long-term costs of lower growth, all of which result from unnecessarily high unemployment. Both in its structure and its functioning, the ECB made a political choice that reflected the views of economic conservatives.

THE POLITICAL NATURE OF MONETARY POLICY

As we noted in the preface, monetary policy, as technical as it may seem, has long been recognized as being political: inflation reduces the real value of what debtors owe, helping them at the expense of creditors. No wonder, then, that bankers and bond market investors rail so strongly against inflation. On the other hand, the fight against inflation typically entails raising interest rates, which lowers growth and hurts employment and workers. Balancing inflation and unemployment is, or should be, a political decision.

In the 2008 crisis, hundreds of billions of dollars were effectively given (or lent at below-market interest rates) by central banks in the advanced countries to commercial banks, in the most massive government-assistance program to the private sector ever conceived. This program of corporate welfare for the suffering banks was greater by an order of magnitude than any welfare program constructed by any government to alleviate the suffering of ordinary individuals. Much of the money was provided through central banks, not appropriated by parliaments or national congresses—again, an intensely political act, without democratic accountability.[19]

If monetary policy were simply a technocratic matter, it might be left to technocrats. But it is not. There are large distributive consequences. Indeed, central banks may have played an important role in increasing inequality.

INCREASING INEQUALITY

Today, in most countries around the world, inequality is viewed as one of the greatest threats to future prosperity. At Davos, where the world's economic leaders come together every January, recent surveys of global risks have consistently placed inequality at or toward the top of the list.[20] Inequality is important because divided societies don't function well; it leads to a lack of cohesiveness that has political, economic, and social consequences. In my book *The Price of Inequality*, I explained the mechanisms by which greater inequality leads to poorer economic performance—lower growth and more instability. Since then, a wealth of studies at the IMF and elsewhere has corroborated this perspective.[21]

Unfortunately, central banks everywhere, and especially the ECB, have largely ignored their role in creating inequality. Their excessive focus on inflation—even when their mandates are nominally broader—has led to higher unemployment, which has increased inequality. Central bank policies have helped ratchet wages down. In recessions, real wages typically fall, but then, in the recovery, just as they start to increase, inflation hawks scream about the risks of inflation, interest rates rise, and unemployment increases to a level making further wage increases difficult.[22]

But the role of the ECB in increasing inequality was worse. Central bankers have enormous influence that goes beyond monetary policy narrowly defined—for instance, to setting interest rates and the money supply. The head of the ECB is looked to for setting the economic agenda, and, not surprisingly, there is a tendency to focus on their narrow remit, inflation, thinking that by controlling inflation, growth and prosperity will be advanced. Jean-Claude Trichet, the ECB governor during the run-up to the crisis, perhaps in his pursuit of the ECB's mandate of stable prices, used his influence to push for policies that increased inequality. In the early days of the crisis (from 2008 to 2011) he repeatedly argued that there should be more wage flexibility (a euphemism for saying that wages should be cut—part of the "blame the victim" approach to unemployment discussed in chapter 4, in which workers are blamed for their unemployment, for asking for wages that are too high and for employment contracts with a modicum of security). Of course, wage cuts were in the short-run interests of corporations and their owners: I say short-run interests because he should have realized postcrisis Europe faced a lack of demand and that cutting wages would weaken demand and deepen the recession.

Trichet went so far, in a secret letter to Spain's prime minister, José Luis Rodríguez Zapatero (which Zapatero published in his memoirs),[23] to hint—actually, more than hint—that he would be willing to help Spanish banks if and only if they agreed to enact labor market reforms that would lead to lower wages and less job protection.[24] Zapatero apparently refused but, interestingly, introduced reforms that had much the same effect; and the assistance was forthcoming.[25]

DISTRIBUTION, POLITICS, AND THE CRISIS

The political nature of the ECB became especially apparent with the euro crisis—who was blamed, who was saved, and under what conditions. Most dramatically, the bank decided *not* to act as a lender of last resort for Greece in the summer of 2015. As Greece negotiated with the Troika, the country's banks were forced to shut down, and behind the scenes, the ECB threatened to impose further costs on Greece if it didn't knuckle down to the Troika's demands. The ECB had become Europe's sledgehammer, the tool by which Greece was forced to accede to what the Troika wanted.

More generally, as the ECB decides on what collateral to accept, and with what haircut (for example, to provide a loan of €70 against the collateral of a €100 bond), it may be deciding on the life and death of a financial institution; and when a country is in a crisis, with many precarious banks, the ECB effectively decides on the life and death of the country's banking system. No decision could be more political. There is no technical manual available; such decisions are a matter of a judgment—of the future viability of the institution—but in reality, it is a judgment strongly colored by the political consequences of alternatives.[26]

The prioritization of banks over citizens was as evident in Europe as it was in the United States during the crisis,[27] and at times almost as evident in his successor, Draghi, as it was in Trichet. As Ireland's crisis emerged in 2010, Trichet demanded that Ireland assume the liabilities of its bankrupt banks[28]—and the cost of restructuring the banks led to an increase in Ireland's debt-to-GDP ratio from 24 percent in 2007 to an estimated 95.2 percent in 2015. While there is some debate about whether Ireland would have assumed some of these debts without intervention, there is little question that some of the debt was assumed only because the ECB made it a condition for getting assistance. (Indeed, the Troika was divided on the matter: the IMF believed that the government should not have had to bear all of these liabilities; there should have been deep debt restructuring, with bank shareholders and bondholders bearing more losses. Ordinary laws of capitalism require the government should not have assumed any liabilities until shareholders and bondholders had been entirely wiped out.)[29]

The ECB apparently worried about the effect that forcing shareholders and bondholders to bear more of the costs in Ireland might have had on other European banks. But they should have worried about this before the crisis, ensuring that European banks were adequately capitalized and had not engaged in excessive risk-taking.

The critical issue is this: the Troika was asking ordinary Irish citizens to pick up the tab for regulatory failures of the ECB and other regulatory authorities within the eurozone. To me, this is unconscionable—as it seems to most Irish people with whom I have discussed the matter. But evidently not to the bankers in the ECB.

GOVERNANCE

Among the critical decisions any society has to make are those related to *governance*, who makes the decisions and to whom are those who make decisions accountable? And how transparent is the decision making process? Many of the criticisms of the European Union, in its current form, relate to governance. But in the case of the eurozone, and its most important institution, the European Central Bank, the problems of governance are especially severe. This is partly because financial markets have successfully sold the idea that independent central banks lead to better economic performance. Europe has taken this mantra to an extreme.[30]

The central question of governance is the extent of accountability of the ECB to democratic processes. There is, in fact, a wide range of degrees of de facto and de jure independence. In the UK, for instance, the government every year sets the inflation target, but that country's central bank, the Bank of England, has independence in implementing the target. While in principle, the US Federal Reserve is independent, in fact, some of its central bankers have understood very much the limits of that independence: as Paul Volcker put it, "Congress created us, and Congress can uncreate us."[31]

The crisis of 2008 provides perhaps the best test of the hypothesis of the virtues of central bank independence—and those countries without independent central banks performed far better than those with.

CAPTURE

The main reason for this difference in performance is simple: there is no such thing as a truly "independent" institution. All institutions are "captured" to some extent or another by some group or another. We would like a central bank to reflect the broad interests of society. But central banks in most countries—including the European Central Bank—are captured by a small group, the financial market.[32] Both the interests and beliefs of the financial market differ from those in the rest of society. Although for a long time, both in the United States and Europe, those at Goldman Sachs and other large banks have been trying to sell the idea that what is good for Goldman Sachs and the other big banks is good for *all*, it simply isn't true. And anyone who subscribed to this idea was surely disabused of it by the Great Recession and the abuses of the financial sector.

Many, if not most, of the central bankers came from and/or went to the financial sector after they finished their tenure. (Draghi himself had spent years at Goldman Sachs before moving on to the Bank of Italy.) In many ways, this is natural: one needs and wants expertise in finance, and much of that expertise resides in those who have worked in the financial sector.[33] While even then most didn't buy into the idea that what was good for Goldman Sachs was good for the economy, it was not that difficult for these democratically unaccountable central bankers to go along with ideas such as "self regulation." It appealed especially to those who believed in meritocracy and technocracy. Running a central bank was (in this view) like running a mine: put a good engineer (or economist) in charge and all will be well.

But our earlier discussion made clear that the decisions central bankers make are *not* just technocratic: there are potentially large distributive consequences, and so long as that is the case, there cannot be full delegation to technocrats. Moreover, the one thing economists agree on is that incentives matter. The revolving door meant that it was in the interest of central bankers to do what they could to help their friends in the financial sector, from whence they came and to which they would go.[34] Helping friends in banks needn't even be a conscious decision—though it surely has been in some cases. Rather, the mere proximity and entanglement of central bank leadership and staff with the private financial markets—an inescapable symptom of the revolving door—ensures a convergence of priorities and perspectives. (This is sometimes referred to as *cognitive capture*.)

Self-regulation turned out to be a joke: those in the financial sector did not have the incentives (and in many cases, even the skills) for self-regulation. Even in the best of cases, the banks would have no incentives to take into account the externalities that their actions (or their failures) would have on others. But it should have been obvious that the incentives of banks and bankers were to engage in excessive risk-taking and socially unproductive—and in some cases destructive—activities. It was willful neglect that central bankers, in Europe and America, failed to take this into account.[35]

CONSEQUENCES OF CAPTURE

Every aspect of central bank policy, both in Europe and America, in the run-up to the global financial and the euro crises, and in their aftermath, reflected the capture of the central bank by the financial sector—with perhaps the most dramatic manifestations occurring in the midst of the crises themselves. In 2012, Greece needed to restructure its bonds. Prudent banks had bought credit default swaps (CDSs) as insurance against a default in the bonds they owned. A CDS can provide the bondholder with a payment equal to the loss he would otherwise face if there is a default. When bonds are restructured, new bonds are issued in exchange for the old. The new bonds typically stretch out the repayment period, but there is also a write-down, with the nominal value of the new bonds markedly lower than that of the old.[36] If this happened, the CDSs would make up for the losses.

There are some ways of restructuring that "trigger" the CDSs—that is, which result in a payout. Of course, a bank that bought a CDS as insurance would want the restructuring to be done in a way that the insurance policy paid off. And a *good* regulator would want the banks who hold risky bonds in their portfolio to have insurance *and* that the insurance pay off.

The ECB, however, insisted that the restructuring be done in such a way as *not* to trigger the CDSs. Their position was unfathomable— until one realized that (1) while some banks had bought insurance (CDSs) against the loss of the value of their bonds, other banks (typically big banks) had sold CDSs. (When someone buys insurance, there has to be someone else on the other side of the market, selling insurance. Obviously, when the insured against event occurs, the firm/bank selling the insurance is worse off.) These banks had sold CDSs as nontransparent gambling instruments. And (2) the ECB was more interested in the big banks that were engaged in selling insurance— essentially gambling and speculating on whether Greece could pay off its debts—than in the ordinary banks that had bought insurance.[37]

CENTRAL BANKS AS POLITICAL INSTITUTIONS

These examples, as well as our earlier discussions about monetary policy decisions about inflation versus unemployment, make it clear that central banks—including the ECB—make political decisions. They face trade-offs. There are large distributive consequences of their decisions. There are different risks associated with different policy choices. In the United States, when they gave money to the banks, they could have imposed conditions, such as that the banks lend to small and medium-size businesses. In Europe, they could have demanded that Ireland not bail out its banks, rather than that it do so.[38] They could have demanded that the Greek restructuring be done in a way that the CDSs paid off.

Not even the leaders of the ECB would deny that they face such choices. But if trade-offs exist, the people making them need to be politically accountable. In Europe, the governance is even worse than in the United States. Europe pretended that it could get around the problem of governance by giving the ECB a simple mandate—ensuring price stability (also known as fighting inflation). Inevitably, there are going to be judgments about what price stability means (zero inflation or 2 percent or 4 percent), and in making those judgments policymakers will have to consider the consequences of different targets. If pursuing a 2 percent inflation target versus a 4 percent target were to lead to much slower growth, I doubt that many voters would support that target given the chance.

There are winners and losers in most economic policies. In making their decisions, policymakers in the ECB have to make judgments *with distributional consequences.* These are not merely technocratic issues, like the best design of a bridge. Slightly higher inflation might lead to lower bond prices, even as it led to higher employment and wages. Bondholders would be unhappy, even if the rest of society celebrated. But central banks that are not democratically accountable almost always pay more attention to the views of the bondholders and other financiers than to the workers.

At one point, the European Commission thought that if Spain's unemployment were to fall below 25 percent, there would be an increase in inflation. Later, they revised that number down to 18.6 percent. Others think these conjectures absurd.[39] But here again there are trade-offs, this time in who bears the risks. By acting *as if* the critical threshold is a high number, like 25 percent, or even 18.6 percent, when it is in fact lower, one condemns unnecessarily large numbers of people to unemployment, and the higher unemployment results in lower wages for many workers. Those in the financial market and business sector might welcome these lower wages; workers obviously do not.

There is a political agenda in pretending that setting monetary policy is a technocratic matter best left to experts from the financial sector. Reflecting the mindset of those in the financial sector, these "experts" respond to the apparent tradeoffs in a markedly different

way than would ordinary workers. Removing central banking from
political accountability, at least in the way that it has been done in the
United States and Europe, effectively transfers decision-making to
the financial sector, with its interests and ideology.

The crises themselves should have shown that it was not expertise
and wisdom that the wizards of the financial market brought to the
table. The deregulation agenda that financiers pushed in Europe and
America was really about rewriting the rules and regulations of the
financial market in ways that advantaged those in the financial markets at the expense of the rest of society. It was *not* about creating a
financial market that would lead to faster and more stable growth,
and that was why what emerged was lower growth and increased
instability.[40]

THE NEOLIBERAL ARGUMENT FOR
CENTRAL BANK INDEPENDENCE

The neoliberal argument for central bank independence—the argument that prevailed at the time the ECB was established—seemed to
be predicated on three critically flawed assumptions: first, that all that
mattered was inflation; secondly, that fighting inflation through monetary policy was a purely technocratic matter; and thirdly, that central bank independence would strengthen the fight against inflation.

I have already explained what was wrong with the first two hypotheses. The third hypothesis was based on a deep distrust of democracy.
It was feared that democratic governments would be tempted to inflate
the economy before an election. A stronger economy would help get
the government reelected—with the price of inflation paid afterward.
Only by taking monetary policy out of the hands of politicians could
this kind of inflationary pattern be broken; and with confidence that
the technocrats assigned to limit inflation would fulfill their mandate,
inflationary expectations would be brought down, and thus economic
stability ensured. Democratic electorates are, however, more intel-

ligent than this hypothesis gives them credit. Indeed, governments have the same incentive to spend before an election. No one has proposed taking away the spending power from government, to ensure that they don't "misbehave." And in fact, democratic electorates have strongly punished governments that overspent. Fiscal responsibility—in some cases *excessive fiscal responsibility*, with a focus on deficits that exceeds practical sense—regularly features in elections.[41]

BEYOND INDEPENDENCE

Even if one believed that an independent central bank would result in better monetary policy, one could have constructed a European Central Bank that was more *representative*, that is, which viewed the inherent policy trade-offs, including the hidden trade-offs, in a more balanced way. Some countries have recognized this—for instance, forbidding those from the financial sector from being on the board of the central bank, since they have a vested interest and particular perspectives on monetary policy. Some countries require that there be representatives of labor—since they often see the world through a different lens than do those in the financial sector. The eurozone has done neither. This tilts the balance, *even given the ECB's inflation mandate*: a more hawkish concern over inflation, an insufficient concern over the consequences for growth and employment.

CONCLUDING COMMENTS: ECONOMIC MODELS, INTERESTS, AND IDEOLOGY

A central thesis of this book is that certain ideas—certain economic models—shaped the construction of the eurozone; these ideas are at best questionable, at worst wrong. In computer science, there is an old adage: garbage in, garbage out. So, too, in the construction of institutions: institutions built on faulty ideology are not going to work well; economic institutions built on flawed economic foundations are going to serve the economy poorly. This chapter has amply illustrated this in the context of monetary policy and the central institution of the eurozone, the ECB.

While the single mandate and the narrow view of the instruments at their disposal may have narrowed the set of actions that the ECB could undertake, the ECB has been, to say the least, controversial. It has been charged, especially within Germany, with acting beyond its mandate, and acting improperly. Even though in its construction, conservative ideas predominated, since the crisis it has used new instruments and undertaken new responsibilities, which conservatives say go beyond its remit. It has been sued for its program of buying government bonds, for engaging in quantitative easing, and for its new supervisory roles. The ECB is governed by a board, the members of which have views about what the bank can do and what the bank should do that markedly differ. The Germans have consistently argued for a narrow construction, and in spite of common wisdom that they enjoy hegemony in the eurozone, the ECB has on a number of times—most notably with the undertaking of QE—taken actions vehemently opposed by Germany, both on grounds of policy and that the actions are beyond those allowed to it.

Institutions evolve. The problems confronting Europe and the world today are different than what they were when the eurozone was designed. Even when the eurozone was founded, inflation was not the issue. The world had moved into a new era, with inexpensive Chinese goods helping to dampen prices. It was clear that growth and employment would be among the issues of the future. The 2008 crisis reminded everyone why some central banks were created in the first place—to maintain financial stability—a responsibility that had been almost forgotten in the years when an obsession with inflation dominated the scene. The strong restraints on the ECB clearly limit its ability to adapt in ways that it could and should. The ECB's narrow mandate and narrow set of instruments puts Europe in a distinct disadvantage.

The ECB has had three heads in its short history, each with a distinctive style, each leaving his mark. Trichet will be remembered for his colossal misjudgments, in particular raising interest rates at moments where the economy was contracting. He demonstrated a commitment to fulfilling the ECB's mandate, fighting inflation, come what may. The costs of these mistakes were palpable. He played a disastrous role in the development of the euro crisis, forcing the Irish government to assume the liabilities of its banks. The Irish people were unjustly forced to pay the price for others' mistakes—a double injustice, because it was in effect a transfer of money from the poor to the rich. But Trichet knew where he stood: he was an ally of the bankers against ordinary workers, constantly demanding wage cuts that would lower their standards of living.

If Trichet did much to undermine the eurozone—could it have survived if he had remained in office?—Mario Draghi is given credit for its survival, with his famous 2012 speech promising "whatever it takes." Few speeches in history have had such impact—bringing down interest rates on sovereign bonds throughout the region.

The speech was magical in another way as well: no one knew whether the ECB had the authority and resources to do "whatever it takes." A few academics and pundits worried, what would happen if the promise was tested? If there was a run against Italian bonds? If suddenly, there was a shift in mood, and investors came to believe that the ECB did not have the resources to sustain high prices for the enormous numbers of outstanding Italian bonds? What would happen if Germany successfully opposed the ECB doing "whatever it takes"? In short, no one knew whether Draghi was an emperor with or without clothes. It was, of course, in no one's interest to find out, or at least not at the time. And so long as it was not shown that the emperor had no clothes, remarkably, the market acted as if he did, whether he did or didn't.

THERE ARE CHOICES

Quantitative easing, which was grudgingly adopted, with strong opposition from some members of the ECB Board, has not restored

Europe to robust growth. Neither has it resulted in massive inflation, as its critics once feared. Over the nearly two decades since its creation, the ECB has not been able to assure full employment and economic stability for *all* of Europe. That might be asking too much: given the diversity among the countries, critics of the eurozone would say that that was an impossible task. But it has not even achieved reasonable growth, employment, and economic stability *on average*. Chapter 3 vividly described the eurozone's dismal performance: it has had a double-dip recession and repeatedly faced threats of deflation, with an unacceptably high level of eurozone unemployment.

In the brief history of the ECB, we have seen costly misjudgments and the use of its enormous power to obtain outcomes that benefit the banks and the major powers within the European Union at the expense of citizens and the weaker countries. This should be deeply troubling.

The main point of this chapter is a simple one: there are alternative ways of structuring central banks—with different mandates, different instruments, and, more importantly, different governance—that are more likely to lead to better economic performance, especially from the perspective of the majority of citizens. Doing this should be high on the agenda of reform for the eurozone. It is one of the essential tasks if the eurozone is to be restored to growth and prosperity.

AFTERWORD: DEVELOPMENTS IN MONETARY THEORY AND POLICY OVER THE PAST THIRD OF A CENTURY

The eurozone is a *monetary* union, so it is important to understand the ideas concerning money and monetary policy that prevailed at the time the eurozone was created and subsequently. This section describes the evolution of the dominant doctrines over the past third of a century. Ideas that were fashionable at the time the eurozone was founded—such that *all* that a central bank had to do was to focus on inflation and that would ensure growth and stability—are now widely discredited among both academic economists and policymakers, including those at the IMF. Yet these ideas are set in stone in the ECB, and still widely held within powerful groups inside the eurozone. This puts the ECB in a difficult position: following its mandate puts it on a course that is opposed by large fractions of European democracy. It is important to have rules, but having the wrong rules, as we noted earlier, can be a disaster.

In recent decades, central banking has been dominated by a succession of beliefs—one might call them religious beliefs, for they are held with firm conviction, even passion. And this is so, even though the empirical evidence underlying them is at best weak. The good news concerning central bankers is that their religions evolve, even if they change their beliefs very slowly in response to evidence against the currently fashionable doctrines.

MONETARISM

At one point, the religion was called *monetarism*—all central bankers believed that one should increase the monetary supply at a fixed rate and, accordingly, monetary authorities should keep their eye on the money supply.

Monetarism was never really a theory; it was based on an alleged empirical regularity—that the ratio of the money supply to the volume of transactions (called the velocity of circulation) was fixed. There was no theoretical reason that this should be so. No sooner had Milton Friedman announced this new law of nature than nature played a trick on him, and on the countries that followed his dicta: the velocity of circulation started changing. Those of us who had studied more deeply the nature of financial markets understood and predicted these changes. New forms of financial instruments, like money market funds that we now take for granted, were coming into play, and there were changes in the regulations governing financial markets.

Monetarism swept the world of central bankers as the cult of the day. It was based on a simplistic model. It could be grasped easily by central bankers with limited abstract capacities, and it provided rich opportunities for empirical testing. There was enough ambiguity in the theory to lead to heated discussions: What was the right definition of money? How should it best be measured? What was the right measure of GDP? How should it be measured?

Interestingly, conservative central bankers following such doctrines actually exposed the economies for which they were responsible to real risk. At the time the experiment with monetarism began, its full implications were not known. At the time (the late 1970s) the United States faced what was widely viewed as an unacceptably high inflation rate, Paul Volcker, newly chosen to head the Federal Reserve, responded with this new tool. Interest rates shot up beyond anything that had happened before, and beyond what most had expected—the Fed fund rate eventually reaching 19 percent. But while this new "theory" seemed to work in bringing down inflation, from 13.5 percent in 1980 to 3.5 percent in 1983, the medicine had serious side effects. America's deepest recession since the Great Depression, with unemployment reaching 10.8 percent in 1982, in spite of a massive stimulus from fiscal policy with the large 1981 Reagan tax cut; and debt crises throughout the world in countries that had borrowed in the 1970s to offset the effects of the oil price rise, in the perhaps-reasonable belief that so long as interest rates remained within the realm of what had happened in the past, they could manage things. The result was the lost decade of the 1980s in Latin America.

INFLATION TARGETING

As this monetarism religion waned in the onslaught of overwhelming evidence that it did not provide good guidance—even ignoring its noxious side effects—a new religion took its place, inflation targeting.[42] If inflation was the only thing that central banks should care about, it made sense for them to target their policies to inflation. Never mind about unemployment or growth—that was the responsibility of someone else. Countries around the world adopted this philosophy, and with conservatives loving rules, there developed a rule, named after John Taylor, with whom I taught at Princeton and Stanford, and who was to go on to be the under secretary of the Treasury for International Affairs in the Bush administration. His rule (the "Taylor rule") prescribed by how much the central bank should raise interest rates in response to a level of inflation in excess of its target. One didn't really need a board to set interest rates, just a technician, who would calculate the inflation rate (government statistical offices do that) and then plug the number into the formula. The interest rate would pop right out. The money supply should be increased or decreased until that target was reached. One didn't have to ask why inflation was high or whether the disturbance to the economy was temporary or permanent. Those judgments, made by mortal government appointees, would inevitably be more fallible than the infallible rule.

Countries following such a simplistic policy also had disastrous results. When food prices rose very rapidly in 2007, inflation—especially in developing countries where food is such an important part of the market basket—rose, too; but it made no sense to raise interest rates: raising interest rates would not lower food prices. The problem of food prices was global, but even in a moderately sized country, raising interest rates would have a negligible effect on global food prices. The only way the monetary authority could have an effect on inflation was to drive down other prices—have *deflation* in the nontraded goods in the economy. And the only way to achieve that was to cause those sectors to go into depression, by raising interest rates very high. No matter how important one thought that inflation was, the cure was worse than the disease.

The European Central Bank never went so far as to go to either the extreme of monetarism or the Taylor rule, but it did something almost as bad. It focused exclusively on inflation—after all, that was its single mandate—and for a long time it continued to use as an indicator of its monetary stance (whether monetary policy was loose or tight) the rate of growth of the money supply, a holdover from the days when monetarism reigned king.

QUANTITATIVE EASING

When the Federal Reserve put interest rates down to zero—and still the economy did not recover—it felt it could and should do more. One idea was to purchase long-term bonds, driving down the long-term interest rates and providing more liquidity to the economy. This was called *quantitative easing*. The ECB was slow to introduce quantitative easing. It did so long after the United States, and even after Japan. Even as it undertook QE, the ECB may not have grasped why quantitative easing had such a limited effect in the United States—and why therefore the benefits would likely be still weaker in Europe. The problem in quantitative easing in the United States from 2009 to 2011 was that the money that was created wasn't going where it was needed and where the Fed wanted it to go—to increase spending in the United States on goods and services. Important credit channels, especially to small and medium-size businesses were clogged. So the money naturally flowed to foreign countries, especially economies that were already growing strongly and beginning to face inflation; they didn't want the extra money, and they created barriers to these flows—imperfect, but still somewhat effective. The three main channels through which quantitative easing helped the economy were all weak: a slight weakening of the value of the dollar helped exports— but these effects were eventually countervailed by America's trading partners; mortgage rates were reduced as long-term interest rates fell, but the monopolistic banks—and bank concentration after the crisis was greater than before—took much of the lower interest rates and simply enjoyed it as extra profits; and the stock market bubble led the very rich to consume a little more, especially of luxury goods, many of which were made abroad. What the economy really needed was more lending to businesses, but big businesses were already sitting on $2 trillion of cash and were essentially unaffected by QE. And because the Fed and the Obama administration had fixed their attention on the big New York banks and other international banks, the ability of the smaller regional and community banks to make loans remained impaired.[43] The result was that years after the crisis such lending remained before its precrisis level.

By the time that the ECB considered undertaking quantitative easing, it was known that it was a weak instrument. The ECB could and should have realized that the benefit it would get from the exchange rate was likely smaller than what the United States had gotten. First, because everyone was now doing it, Europe wouldn't get the benefit of competitive devaluation. Secondly, the emerging markets had set up controls to ensure that they were not disadvantaged. Thirdly, and most importantly, little domestic demand would be created unless the credit channels were fixed, and in this respect, Europe was much worse off than the United States, as we saw in the last chapter, with dramatic decreases in SME lending and a shrinking of the banks in the periphery countries. The ECB could have taken more aggressive measures to ensure that the money didn't go into credit bubbles, and that more of the money went into supporting new businesses and expanding old businesses. Their philosophy of "trusting the market" may have made them hesitant to do so.

Some were worried that QE would result in inflation. But massive QE had not resulted in inflation in the United States, and there was even more of a reason not to be worried about incipient inflation in Europe. Much of the money was held by banks. The problem was that the banks were not lending out money. Much of the money that the Fed and the ECB helped create simply stayed within the Fed and the ECB, or in any case, didn't lead to more lending. Since the additional liquidity was not leading to more spending, it could not lead to more inflation.

There were, however, other risks associated with this massive expansion of central bank balance sheets. One was that it could lead to asset price bubbles—just as the earlier easy-money policies had contributed to the real estate bubble. The breaking of those bubbles, in turn, might lead to economic volatility. The Fed at least had tools to deal with such a problem. It could raise margin requirements (the amount that investors had to put down when they made an investment in, say, a stock or commodities). And in the aftermath of the crisis, it even had a mandate to do so—it was required to ensure not just low inflation, high growth, and full employment but also financial stability. Unfortunately, the European Central Bank, with its mandate formulated in the period of neoliberal ascendancy, focused just on inflation, leaving it to others to worry about the stability of the financial system.

THE NATURAL RATE HYPOTHESIS

Monetary policy, in the way it has been managed in Europe and the United States, has proven of limited effectiveness in the restoration of robust growth. Long ago, Keynes had argued that when the economy was in a recession, or worse, depression, that was likely to be the case. But there has been a strand in economics which has questioned more broadly the effectiveness and desirability of an *active* monetary policy, one directed at maintaining the economy at full employment, more broadly; and these ideas have been especially influential among conservatives.

Critics of an active monetary policy argue that if one tried to get the unemployment rate below a critical level, called the *natural rate*, and hold it there, there would be ever-increasing inflation.[44] This theory greatly narrowed what central banks should do: if one was committed to avoiding superinflation, at most one could have a short period of unemployment below this threshold, to be offset by another period while it was above. In this view, central bankers faced no trade-offs. Their job was simply to keep the unemployment at the "natural rate."

This theory has been increasingly questioned.[45] If one looks at the data, one can't see a systematic relationship between inflation, or the increase in inflation, and unemployment. *If* there is a natural rate, it is a movable target, and we almost never know where it is. Thus, policymakers have to guess, and in making that guess, there are big trade-offs: a risk of much higher unemployment than necessary versus a risk of somewhat higher inflation than we might desire.

Thus, even if the simplistic models that say there is no trade-off between unemployment and inflation were correct, once we take account of the fact that we don't know what the natural rate of unemployment is, there are trade-offs. The risks of underestimating the natural rate and overestimating it are borne by different people. Central bankers—in Europe and America—have managed these risks focusing more on financial markets than on workers, and in doing so there has been an unambiguous loss in output and an increase in inequality from what otherwise would have been the case.

PART III

MISCONCEIVED POLICIES

7

CRISES POLICIES: HOW TROIKA POLICIES COMPOUNDED THE FLAWED EUROZONE STRUCTURE, ENSURING DEPRESSION

Those outside of Europe—and many in Europe—have been appalled at the unfolding drama in the crisis countries, especially Greece, Spain, Portugal, and Cyprus. Pictures abound of middle-class individuals suddenly in jeopardy: retirees whose pensions have been cut to the bone; and young people, college graduates, who have looked and looked for a job and can't find one, living in homeless shelters. These stories tell us that something is wrong. So, too, do youth unemployment rates of 30 percent or more. It wasn't this way before the euro.

My wife and I gently tried to confront the prime minister of one of the northern European countries at a private meeting in 2013. Was he aware of how bad things had become? News articles that fall and winter had described formerly middle-class families in Spain and Greece scavenging for survival, unable to afford to heat their homes in winter, even eating out of garbage cans.[1]

His cold reply, delivered with a gentle smile, was that they should have reformed their economy *earlier*; they should not have been so profligate. But, of course, it was not these individuals who had been profligate, who had failed to reform. Innocent citizens were being asked, forced actually, to bear the consequences of decisions that had been made by politicians—ironically, often politicians from the same political party of the right that the Troika seemed so fond of.

The lack of empathy on display at that dinner—the lack of European solidarity—has been in evidence repeatedly. Bad enough was the scolding and flippancy of those like the prime minister we spoke to, as the guiltless citizens of the worst hit countries suffered real privation. Yet the biggest display of callousness has not been in any politician's comments, public or private, but in the actual policies that the Troika has foisted on these countries in their moments of desperation. These policies have compounded the crises, weakened the hard-fought bonds of European unity, and magnified the in-built frailties and flaws of the eurozone's structure.

Astonishingly, even with the avalanche of evidence that the Troika's programs have failed the people of the countries they were supposed to help, its leaders have been claiming success for their austerity. This stretch of imagination—that Spain, Portugal, and Ireland were success stories—could only be achieved by wearing blinders that hid all but the most limited economic indicators from view. Yes, the Troika's 2010–2013 Economic Adjustment Programme for Ireland had brought the country's financial sector and government back from the brink of total economic collapse.[2] But the austerity the Troika imposed helped ensure that Ireland's unemployment rate remained in double digits for five years, until the beginning of 2015, causing untold suffering for the Irish people and a world of lost opportunities that can never be regained. (For comparison, the United States' unemployment rate peaked at 10 percent for just one month in 2009 during the Great Recession.)

And Ireland was one of the *best* cases. In 2011, the IMF bailed out the Portuguese government as it faced spiraling borrowing costs in the wake of the global financial crisis. Its cash injection of €78 billion came with strings attached, of course. The government was required to lower its deficit from nearly 10 percent of GDP in 2010 to 3 percent in 2013.[3] Barring strong economic growth, the only way to achieve that reduction was austerity—reductions in government spending, such as lowered wages for public servants, and increases in taxes. (Without such assistance, of course, Portugal would have had to have even more drastic cutbacks, because it, too, was cut out from capital markets.) The IMF has also claimed its Portugal program as a success. And indeed, if all one cares about is the lending rate for the government, the bailout achieved its aims. Portugal went from paying 13 percent on its 10-year bonds at the end of 2011 to paying less than 3 percent by the end of 2014 (when the program ended),[4] among other improvements to the government's fiscal position and borrowing abilities.[5] Yet austerity kept the fundamentals of the economy feeble. By 2015, GDP per capita was still down an estimated 4.3 percent from before the crisis.[6] Unemployment was still above 12 percent in early 2016. Growth predictions in the next years are sluggish: the IMF estimates that GDP will not expand more than 1.4 percent annually at any point in the next several years. The government might be borrowing with more ease, but the Portuguese people never experienced a real recovery.

Although Spain's 2012 bank bailout didn't come with direct conditions requiring reduced government spending or higher taxes, after 2008 the country still swallowed the austerity snake oil being hard-sold on the continent. A commonsense look at the data—and the hundreds of thousands of *indignados* who marched in the streets in 2011—showed that these policies' legacy of evictions, wage cuts, and unemployment was anything but a triumph. Yet in mid-2015, with nearly a quarter of the Spanish workforce still unemployed, the German Council of Economic Experts (along with many other austerity boosters) was claiming Spain as the prime example of the virtues of austerity.[7]

It was with these fundamental perversions of the definition of economic success that the Troika blundered forward to its worst misadventure yet, in Greece. There, its program has been wrong, destructive, and almost unbelievably narrow-minded. More than that, it has bordered on inhumane. Still, in 2015 the Troika doubled down on its manmade disaster.

For instance, as Greece entered its third "program" in the fall of

2015, Europe demanded that Greece end a program of "forbearance" against those who owed money on their mortgages: in order to save great swaths of its population from homelessness and deeper destitution, Greece had implemented a temporary ban on home foreclosures when the crisis set in.[8] The ban was still in effect in 2015, but with many amendments that had reduced the scope of loans it covered. (The Troika often masquerades its "demands" as simply "proposals," things that the crisis country should *consider*. But they are more than proposals—Greece *had* to accede to them. There are "negotiations," but as the story of the "foreclosure proposal" illustrates, in the end typically what is "agreed" is little different from what was originally proposed, though there may be a few cosmetic changes, a face-saving gesture to enable the crisis-country government to swallow the bitter medicine.)

The leaders of the Troika appear to believe that those not paying their mortgages are deadbeats who are exploiting the foreclosure ban to take a holiday from their bills. Be tough, and the deadbeats will pay. The reality, though, is otherwise. With the depression, with hundreds of thousands out of a job, hundreds of thousands more having to take massive pay cuts of 40 percent or more, most of those not paying *can't* pay. Europe was betting that toughness would yield a bonanza for the banks, and the amount Europe would need to recapitalize them would be reduced accordingly. More likely, though, is that thousands of poor Greeks would join the homeless, and the banks would be saddled with homes that they could not sell.[9]

Greece pleaded with the Troika to soften its draconian demands. But the Troika held fast, ordering severely watered-down protections: only those with an income below €23,000 a year would still be fully protected.[10] Of course, families with such a low income typically don't own a home, so the exemption meant little. Greek officials capitulated and wanly claimed that the majority of Greeks would be eligible for some protection—a claim that seemed thin. What was unambiguous was that many on the brink of destitution had been pushed a few more inches toward the edge.

The technocrats of the eurozone were not focused on the statistics that captured this suffering. Nor did they see that beneath the cold statistics were real people, whose lives were being ruined. Like the airplane bombing from 50,000 feet, success is measured by targets hit, not by lives destroyed.

The technocrats were interested in different statistics: interest rates and bond spreads (how much extra those in the crisis countries have to pay to borrow money), budget and current account deficits. Unemployment rates sometimes seemed just a measure of collateral damage, or, more positively, a harbinger of better times ahead: the high unemployment rate would drive down wages, making the country more competitive and correcting the current account deficit.

Perhaps the one advantage of the Troika's Greek tragedy is that it provides a paradigmatic example of the problems with the eurozone's policy response to the global financial crisis and its aftermath. While in this chapter and the next I discuss the case of Greece in special detail, it should be kept in mind throughout that the policy mistakes the Troika forced on Athens in its time of need are simply amplified versions of those it established through pressure, cajoling, and loan conditions in other crisis-hit countries.

THE IMPERATIVE TO DO SOMETHING

As the crisis in the eurozone unfolded in early 2010, the leaders of the currency union had to do *something*. Bond yields were soaring—long-term Greek interest rates started the year at 6 percent and reached 12 percent by December.[11] The real crunch, however, arrived when it came time for Greece to borrow more, to finance its huge fiscal deficit (10.8 percent of GDP in 2010) and to repay loans coming due. No one would lend. And if the government couldn't borrow, they couldn't repay what was owed. Default was the next step. But if Greece defaulted on its bonds, those who owned the bonds would be put into a more precarious position. German and French banks, let alone Greek

banks, that held significant amounts of these bonds might themselves become insolvent. Worse, because of the lack of transparency
in the financial market, no one knew exactly how each bank would be
affected. Some banks that had not lent to Greece may have lent money
to other banks that had, so they, too, might be at risk. Some banks had
bought insurance against losses, but some banks had gambled, taking
bets that Greece would not default. It was a mess. And it was a mess
that could spread. The world had just experienced a dose of this kind
of contagion: in the aftermath of the collapse of Lehman Brothers, the
entire world went into an economic recession, as financial markets
froze. It was not clear whether Greece was small or large relative to
Lehman Brothers; most importantly, it was not clear whether it was
systemically significant.

In chapter 1, I described how as each country went into crisis,
the Troika formulated a program *supposedly* designed to bring the
country back to health, and for the countries that had lost access to
international credit markets, to regain access. Here was the critical
flaw: a focus on access to capital markets and the repayment of debts
owed, rather than the restoration of growth and an increase of living
standards of the people of the country. Not a surprise: finance ministers naturally focus on financial markets. But the European project
was not supposed to be about financial markets—they were simply a
means to an end. The means became an end in itself.

As one program after another unfolded, as one country after another
went into crisis, two things stood out: (1) each country that undertook
one of the programs went into a deep downturn, sometimes a recession, sometimes a depression, from which recovery was at best slow;
and (2) these outcomes were *always* a surprise to the Troika, which
would forecast a quick recovery after an initial drop, and when the
predicted recovery didn't occur, Troika proponents would argue that
it was still just around the corner. Figure 7 shows, for instance, in the
case of Greece what the Troika thought would happen as a result of
their initial program in May 2010 and what actually happened. They

realized that there would be a downturn, but they predicted a quick turnaround.[12] By 2015, just four years later, the economy was nearly 20 percent below where they thought it would be.[13]

These dismal forecasts made it clear: the Troika's grasp of the underlying economics was abysmal. While the Troika now might want to shift blame—the country had not done what it was told to do—the truth is otherwise: Greece's depression wasn't because Greece didn't do what it was supposed to; it was because it did. So, too, for the other crisis countries. Their downturns were largely because the countries had faithfully followed the Troika's instructions.

This and the next chapter explore more closely what Europe did to achieve such adverse results. I look at the programs imposed on the crisis countries and show that these programs would *inevitably* lead to deep recessions and depressions. I also explain why the negative effects were even larger than what most of the standard economic models had predicted.

FIGURE 7

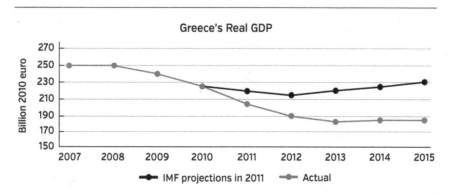

There were alternative policies that would have set these countries on the road to recovery—a growth policy rather than austerity, and a deep debt restructuring. This chapter will focus on the *macroeconomic policies*—those aimed directly at the budget, at deficits and debt.

It is the macroeconomic policies that have resulted in the downturns, recessions, and depressions plaguing Europe.

The next chapter continues the discussion of the programs, focusing on the structural policies that were imposed on the countries, policies directed at reforming particular markets, in an attempt to make the crisis countries more competitive.

Much of the discussion of this and the next chapter focuses on the Greek program, simply because that program highlights more clearly than any of the others the problems of *all* of the programs imposed on the crisis countries and because it illustrates most clearly the mindset of the Troika.

THE MACROECONOMIC FRAMEWORK OF THE CRISIS PROGRAMS

The leaders of Europe like to think of the crisis programs as providing both symptomatic relief—getting over the immediate problem—and creating the basis for long-term adjustment. More accurately, one can think of the programs as mechanisms to ensure that debtors pay the costs of adjustment and creditors get repaid.

Added to the mix is a large dose of politics: some of the creditor countries, particularly Germany, did not want its taxpayers to know the costs that might be imposed on them; they wanted their citizens to *believe* that they were going to be repaid, even if that was essentially impossible. There is a high price associated with such a charade, with most of the costs borne by Greek citizens, for instance. But even Germany is likely to bear some of the costs, because of the reduced probability of repayment.

Politics affects creditors and debtors alike, and Greece provides the best example of this interplay. Germany and the Troika imposed harsh conditions on the government of George Papandreou[14] after it had uncovered and transparently disclosed budgetary chicanery by the previous Greek government. The punishment paved the way for the return of the Samaras right-wing government that had actually put Greece in its impossible position.[15]

In effect, rather than punishing the party that had acted badly, the Troika had rewarded it. It was even worse: when in power, the Papandreou government had begun a process of curtailing the power of the Greek oligarchs, who had a controlling interest in banks and the media and were exploiting the linkages between the two. But the New Democracy party of Samaras was closely linked with the same oligarchs, and it was no surprise that upon his return to office, the Papandreou reforms were reversed, without a peep out of the Troika. Thus the Troika programs were counterproductive when it came to encouraging the most fundamental reforms that were widely seen as necessary for long-term shared prosperity in Greece.

Fiscal balance can be restored by cutting expenditures and raising revenues. The social and economic consequences depend greatly on which expenditures are cut and how revenues are raised. Under Troika programs not only was there too much emphasis on restoring fiscal balance, but they also went about restoring balance the wrong way: the programs resulted in more adverse effects on output, employment, and societal well-being than was necessary. The IMF especially should have known that poorly designed tax measures can backfire—tax revenues can fall, and so, too, can economic output.

In the sections that follow, we take up different aspects of the macroeconomic policies imposed on the crisis countries.

AUSTERITY: THE MYTH OF THE SWABIAN HOUSEWIFE

At the center of the macroeconomic programs was austerity—a contraction in government spending and an increase in revenues. While the authorities in Europe seemed surprised by the strongly adverse outcomes that were so much worse than their models predicted, I was surprised that they were surprised. As we have noted in earlier chapters, austerity has *never* worked.

THINKING ABOUT AUSTERITY

In some ways, it was not a surprise that the leaders of the eurozone would demand that Greece cut its deficit. The crisis in Greece seemed to stem from the fact that the government couldn't borrow more, and the country had had a very large and unsustainable deficit for years. This logic though did not apply to Spain, for instance, where the crisis arose from the banking sector, and where, as we have repeatedly noted, the country had had a surplus before the crisis—the crisis had caused the deficit, not the other way around.[16]

The obvious immediate goal was to make it so the countries wouldn't need to borrow more, and that's where the austerity programs fit in: cut expenditures and raise taxes enough, and there would be no need for outside finance. But such matters are not so simple. Austerity leads to economic slowdowns, lowering revenues and increasing social expenditures on items like unemployment insurance and welfare; any improvement in the country's fiscal position is much less than expected, and the suffering is much greater than expected.

This is the fundamental difference between the Swabian housewife, which Germany's chancellor Angela Merkel so famously talks about, and a country: the Swabian housewife has to live within her budget, yes, but when she cuts back on her spending, her husband doesn't lose his job. If he did, the family would obviously be in much worse shape. Yet that's exactly what happens when austerity is imposed on a country: the government cuts spending, and people lose their jobs.

There is a better analogy than the Swabian housewife, and that is between a country and a *firm*. In the case of firms, we focus on the balance sheet. No one would ask about the size of the liabilities; they want to know what the assets are and what the net worth is. If a firm borrows to buy assets that increase its net worth, it's a good move. Countries that borrow to finance investments in, say, infrastructure, education, and technology can be better off, and especially so if there are underutilized resources (unemployment). Austerity is then bad both in the short run—it leads to higher unemployment—and in the long—it leads to lower growth.

PRIMARY SURPLUSES

The Troika focused its attention on the size of the primary surplus in the crisis countries, the excess of revenues over expenditure *net* of interest payments. This was understandable, given the interests of creditor countries like Germany. They wanted to be paid back, naturally enough. But obviously, a country that is borrowing can't repay. The only way the government can repay what is owed is if it runs a surplus. That such a surplus would normally lead to a weak economy is obvious: when the government has a surplus, it is taking away from the purchasing power of its citizens more than it is adding back through its spending. Thus, it is contributing to a lack of demand.

Sometimes, something else can make up for the shortfall. The United States had a primary surplus in the latter part of the 20th century, under President Clinton, but it had an economic boom driven by the tech bubble. The high level of investment sustained the economy. But when the tech bubble broke, the country quickly went into recession.

Germany, of all countries, should understand this. At the end of World War I, Germany was made to pay reparations by the Treaty of Versailles. To finance the reparations, it would have to run a surplus. Keynes correctly predicted that German reparations and the resulting German surplus would cause a German recession or worse. The depression in Germany that followed had disastrous political consequences not just for Germany but for the entire world. For a while, Germany avoided the depression by borrowing from the United States to sustain demand. But with the Great Depression in the United States, this source of funds was cut off, and Germany, too, went into depression.

Given the history, it is shocking that Germany and the Troika have demanded that Greece and other crisis countries maintain large primary surpluses. In the case of Greece, it insisted that the primary surplus reach 3.5 percent by 2018.[17] Even the IMF knows that such a target will only extend and deepen the country's ongoing depression. The current program allows easier targets for 2015–2017, but if Greece complies with the agreement's primary surplus target for 2018, no matter how faithfully it fulfills the structural reforms, no matter how successful it is in raising revenues or cutting back on pensions, no matter how many are left to die in underfinanced hospitals, the depression will continue.

THE DESIGN OF THE AUSTERITY PROGRAMS

The basic design of the program sets fiscal targets, scaling down the primary deficit and eventually reaching a primary surplus. In the earlier agreements between Greece and its "partners," the fiscal targets were almost never met—simply because the Troika was using fictional forecasts.[18]

Now, in the "memorandum" of August 19, 2015, if the targets are not met, as they almost surely won't be, additional doses of austerity become automatic. While previously, austerity led to contraction, there was always the hope that the Troika would relent as it saw the magnitude of the contraction induced. Now it's a *built-in destabilizer*, which *guarantees* a deep downturn. As the economy weakens and tax revenues fall, tax rates will have to increase—and this will depress the economy still further. (Even conservatives in the United States have argued that when the economy weakens, tax rates should be reduced, not increased.) And as the market comes to realize this, the adverse effects will be all the larger.

HIDDEN AGENDAS

Even if one were fixated on the fiscal deficit, there are fiscal policies that could stimulate the economy without increasing current deficits. These deploy the principle of the balanced-budget multiplier. If one imposes a tax and spends the resulting revenue—so the deficit is absolutely unchanged today—the economy expands. The expansionary effect of the spending outweighs the contractionary effect of the tax. And if the expenditures are well chosen—say, on teachers rather than wars—and so, too, the taxes—say, on the wealthy—then the "balanced-budget multiplier" can be large: a dollar of increased spending can induce much more than a dollar of increase in GDP. Furthermore, if the money is spent on long-lived investment goods, increasing productivity, the resulting increase in *future* tax revenues puts the government's long-run fiscal position in a better shape.

Some eurozone countries have done the opposite. France, for instance, has lowered the corporate income tax, and to offset the decrease in revenues, cut spending. The balanced-budget multiplier predicts that the result will be a contraction in the economy. What France has been betting on is that the lowered corporate income tax will lead to more investment, improving aggregate supply and demand. But what is holding back investment in France and elsewhere in Europe among large corporations is lack of demand for their products. Without demand for their products, firms will not invest, even if the tax rate were close to zero.

Moreover, even if there were demand for the company's products, both theory and evidence questions the importance of the corporate tax rates as a driver for investment. The reason is simple. Most investment is financed largely by debt. What firms care about is the *after-tax* cost of these funds. If they have to pay 10 percent interest, but the tax rate is 50 percent, since they can deduct all of their interest payments, the after-tax cost is only 5 percent. In effect, the cost of the investment is shared with the government, which picks up half the tab in the form of reduced taxes. *The higher the tax rate, the lower the cost of funds to the firm.* By itself, this would suggest that the higher the tax rate, the *more* investment; but, of course, higher taxes also reduce the returns from the investment. What matters is the balance between these two effects—and a close look at that shows that there is little effect on investment.

If France wanted to stimulate its economy, it should have lowered taxes on corporations that invested in its country and created jobs, and increased them on those that did not.[19]

That the balanced-budget multiplier was virtually never even discussed with respect to the eurozone crisis implies a hidden agenda: downsizing government, decreasing its role in the economy. This conclusion is reinforced as we look more closely at the details of the austerity programs.

INCREASING REVENUES

The programs had two key ways of raising revenues: taxation and privatization.

DESIGNING TAX INCREASES

Normally, the IMF warns of the dangers of high taxation. They worry about the disincentive effect, the discouragement to work and savings. Yet in Greece, the Troika has insisted on high effective tax rates even at very low income levels. For instance, they insisted on (and secured) a value-added tax of 23 percent on a large number of products and services, which, combined with an income tax that even at very low levels of income is at around 22 percent, made for an effective tax rate close to 40 percent.

All recent Greek governments recognized the importance of increasing tax revenues, but mistaken tax policy can hasten an economy's destruction. In an economy where the financial system is not functioning well, where small and medium-size enterprises can't get access to credit, the Troika demanded that Greek firms, including mom-and-pop operations, pay all of their taxes ahead of time, at the beginning of the year, before they have earned any money and before they even know what their income is going to be.

The requirement is intended to reduce tax evasion, but in the circumstances in which Greece finds itself, it destroys small businesses. While the Troika has talked about structural reforms with *positive* supply-side effects, this measure alone probably has a stronger negative supply-side effect than *all* of their structural reforms put together. Such draconian measures inevitably lead to more tax evasion—again seemingly in contradiction to another major thrust of the Troika programs.[20]

This new tax requirement seems at odds, too, with another of the demands Greece has confronted: that it eliminate its withholding tax on money sent from Greece to foreign investors. Such withholding taxes are a feature of good tax systems in countries like Canada, and are a critical part of tax collection. Evidently, it is less important to ensure that foreigners pay their taxes than Greeks do. This measure takes on special meaning when it is noted that allegedly one of the largest nonpayers of taxes is the German company that managed Athens airport until 2013. According to some, this company is hundreds of millions of euros in arrears.[21] Obviously, if one thinks that the government is not good at collecting taxes, an irresponsible foreign investor will try to get his money out of the country without paying taxes. Possession is nine-tenths of the law. In this case, it may be ten-tenths. It then becomes very difficult for the government to recover such amounts.[22]

There is among economists broad agreement about the central ingredients of a good tax system. A good tax system should not "distort" the economy any more than is necessary. That's why taxes on land and natural resources are desirable—the amount of land doesn't change no matter what the tax imposed. More generally, a good tax system levies taxes on items where impacts on demand or supply are limited. With high and increasing inequality, a good tax system has to be sensitive to who bears the burden: it should be disproportionately on the rich, not the poor. Finally, well-targeted taxes can help restructure the economy, for instance, by promoting renewable energy and by discouraging polluting activities.

The Troika's tax demands—say, in the case of Greece—violate these principles. Tourism provides another instance where the Troika's tax demands are likely to be counterproductive. Especially in the niche in which Greece competes, tourists comparison shop. Greece was concerned about a higher value-added tax's impact on tourism, especially in the country's islands, which face high transport costs. High taxes would lower demand for Greek tourism, simultaneously hurting employment, GDP, and Greece's current account—and tax revenues might actually decrease. But the Troika would hear none of this.

Many of Greece's problems in tax compliance are similar to those among small businesses everywhere, especially so in a *cash* economy. Yet, Troika policies effectively encouraged those in countries with financially precarious governments to move their money out of banks.[23]

The Troika undermined tax collection in other ways: when taxes are viewed as imposed by outsiders at high levels, in ways that make no sense (for example, exempting foreign transfers from withholding taxes, forcing small businesses to pay taxes a year ahead of time), resentment builds, and trust and voluntary compliance erode. The taxes are not viewed as the product of democratic consensus but as the imposition of foreigners—hypocritical foreigners who do not even pay the taxes they owe.[24] And then when the numbers and pay of tax collectors are cut—along with their job security—there is inevitably demoralization of those responsible for tax collection.

There were alternative taxes, more consistent with the basic premises of a good tax system. Property taxes can be a good thing—a key part of a good tax program—but the Troika couldn't even get that one right. The one asset in a country that is not movable is its land. Not only is land not movable but it is inelastically supplied: the amount of land does not decrease when one taxes it more. There has long been a strong presumption in favor of land taxes.[25]

Under the Troika programs, Greece had adopted a new property tax, but with their small property the only thing separating many ordinary Greeks from outright poverty, the tax was deeply resented. The strict enforcement of the tax against unemployed people with no source of income would mean the loss of their major asset. What should have been deployed was a *progressive property tax*, on all *large* property holdings.

A problem which the Troika should have recognized early on was the absence of a comprehensive *national* property register. But this gap could easily have been remedied: individuals could have been asked to declare all of their property holdings, with a description—for example, the number of rooms, whether there is a pool, and a value. Modern technology, including satellite imagery, allows the verification of at least some aspects of the description. Individuals who do not report accurately their holdings could be threatened with the loss of their property, and a special tax could be levied on large houses and on pools (but not so large that it would pay people to fill in their pools). The government could be given the right to purchase the property at, say, 125 percent of the declared value—providing a clear incentive for honest reporting. The law also could require that the beneficial owner of all properties be declared.

Well-considered tax policy can correct for market failures, generating a double benefit—tax revenue as well as improved economic efficiency. Perhaps the most important market failure the world faces today concerns climate change—we do not price carbon. Greece has a rich potential abundance of renewable energy, both solar and wind. Besides, developing these industries would reduce its consumption of oil. One of the country's industries is oil refining, so if Greece consumed less, there would be more to export. Thus, a high tax on nonrenewable energy would simultaneously generate revenues and improve Greece's balance of payments.[26]

We have repeatedly observed that one of the problems of the eurozone was that it eliminated the power to adjust the nominal exchange rate. But, again, in the absence of that power, tax policy *could* have been deployed—because Greece produces relatively few goods, consumption taxes, especially on luxury goods like high-price cars, which have to be registered in the country and are imported, would have been progressive, could have raised substantial revenues, and would have gone some way in correcting the trade deficit.

PRIVATIZATIONS

There is an alternative way of raising revenues, and that is selling state assets—i.e., privatization. Of course, such sales do not directly or necessarily improve the balance sheet of the country and its government.

Earlier in this chapter, we emphasized the importance of not just looking at a country's debt but at its balance sheet—liabilities in relationship to its assets. The Troika and the eurozone more broadly didn't do this. In the case of privatizations, too often they looked only at *cash flow*, without regard to the long-run consequences. When a country sells its assets in a fire sale, its "net worth" is decreased with long-run consequences—either less revenues for the government, because it doesn't own an asset that yields returns, or greater costs, because it now must, for instance, pay rent for office space, having sold its own buildings.[27]

The best case for privatization is when the government has proven itself incapable of managing an asset well and where there are several competitors for the asset, each of which would improve the efficiency of management. The worst case for privatization is when the asset is sold to a monopolist, who uses his market power (his power to raise price above the cost of production) to exploit consumers—with consumers and firms even worse off under even an efficient monopoly than under an inefficient government operator.

Moreover, privatization gives rise to an unhealthy political dynamic: the monopolist uses its profits to buy political influence, which extends and enhances its market power. Privatization can thus result in increased corruption in addition to a less competitive and overall less efficient economy. (In Europe, corruption is more likely to take the more sophisticated form of campaign contributions rather than cash-stuffed paper envelopes, but it is corruption nonetheless.)[28]

When the privatization results in foreign ownership, further problems arise. First, changing taxes and regulatory structures that affect the profitability of the foreign enterprise may generate enormous political pressure from the governments of its home country. What would otherwise have been a domestic matter becomes an international affair. When the new owner of the asset or its government has political power over the country—as the Troika does over the crisis countries—the interests of the citizens may not be well served, as the provision on tax withholding of cross-border flows dramatically illustrates.[29]

Moreover, the flow of profits out of the country can even have an adverse effect on the balance of payments. Especially if there is a fire sale, the benefits of the inflow in the short run are more than offset by the long-term capital outflows from the repatriation of profits.

There is one special case of privatization that is particularly problematic: when the enterprise buying the asset is partially or totally owned by a foreign government. One has to ask, in what sense is it a *privatization* if the purchaser is a public entity? It is hard to simultaneously argue that governments *necessarily* are less efficient and that one should sell one's assets to another government.

In the case of Greece, the problems with privatization have already become evident. Some of the privatizations, past and proposed, have been to enterprises owned in part by the German government (at the subnational level). As I have noted, a German company held a significant stake in the management of the Athens airport until 2013, and the proposed privatization of regional airports is to a company in which German public entities are a major partner—the German state of Hesse, the largest shareholder, owns some 34 percent of the company.

There is another unsavory aspect of at least one of the privatizations that have occurred under the Greek programs, that of the regional airports referred to earlier: one of the partners in the privatization is one of the oligarchs—anomalous since one of the main structural reforms in the Greek program *should* be weakening the oligarchs' power.[30]

That the Troika faces conflicts of interest should be obvious. So, too, it should be obvious that neither these conflicts of interest nor the public relations issues that result have been well managed—these failures undermine confidence in the entire Troika program, not just in Greece but in all of the crisis countries, and raise troubling questions about whose interests are being served by the programs.

CUTTING SPENDING

The second part of restoring fiscal balance, after raising revenue, is cutting spending. As we noted earlier, the debts of Ireland and Spain increased not so much through *ordinary* spending as through bank bailouts. These two cases are so important that we will focus on them in the next section of this chapter.

The spending cuts that the Troika has imposed in the crisis countries, like the tax increases, have not been well designed. Like the tax cuts, the Troika *should* have focused on cuts that would have had the least adverse effects on GDP and on societal well-being. Ordinary citizens are the most dependent on public expenditures like schools, publicly provided medical care, social programs, and welfare benefits. The rich can take care of themselves. (Of course, in any country and in any program, there are inefficiencies, but the Troika programs went well beyond squeezing out such inefficiencies.) And there are other obvious options for cuts, if there were the political will to pursue them.

In the 21st century, military conflicts in the heart of Europe have been rare. This may have a little to do with the European Union itself, a lot to do with the United Nations and changed attitudes toward war, and some to do with NATO. In any case, most of the countries' defense posture would be little affected by major cutbacks in defense expenditures: in any real attack, they would have to rely on NATO.[31]

There exists also a massive set of inefficient subsidies (some hidden within the tax code), often to well-off business groups, the elimination of which would lead to a more efficient economy and more equal society. Most countries (including the crisis countries), for instance, have large energy subsidies, and in particular for fossil fuels.

The irony is that a very large fraction of spending at the EU level (more than 40 percent of the EU budget) goes to distortionary agricultural subsidies, much of which goes not to small farmers but to large agribusinesses.

PENSIONS

In the case of Greece, the Troika has focused on cutting public sector pensions, which it views as outsized. It appears that this is true for *some* Greek pensions; others are not even enough for survival. One cannot retire in dignity with a monthly pension of under the poverty line of €665—yet 45 percent of Greece's retirees are attempting to do that.[32]

Indeed, a higher fraction of older Greeks were at risk of poverty in 2013 (some 15 percent) than the eurozone average, and in early 2012— well before the demands of 2015 that almost led to the Greek exit (or "Grexit," as it is called)—Greece was actually spending less per person 65 and over than were Germany and most other eurozone countries.[33] But pensions are rightly thought of as a form of deferred compensation. The individual performed work, for which he is paid in two ways: wages today and a pension in the future. The pension is part of the contract.

Both before and after the Greek crisis of the summer of 2015, the Germans argued that Greece's debt should not be restructured— a contract is a contract—even though it was patently clear that the debt would *have* to be restructured. Somehow this belief in the sanctity of contracts did not extend to pensions. Not paying a promised pension fully is, in effect, tearing up the contract.[34] Worse still, cutting pensions affects the most vulnerable members of society—in contrast with a debt contract, where the lenders are financially sophisticated and understand the risks of default.

Today, around the world, there is a great deal of concern over wage theft—after the worker has performed his work, the employer doesn't pay what is promised. The worker can't, of course, get back his time and effort. That is why wage theft is viewed as an egregious crime. But reducing pensions from their promised level *is* wage theft, merely in a different form.[35]

Greece's Council of State, its highest administrative court, recognized the illegality of the proposed pension cuts.[36] To the Troika, the violation of these individuals' basic rights seemed an annoyance. Its response was to demand other reforms that would "fully compensate for the fiscal impact of the Constitutional Court ruling."[37]

Future pensions are, of course, different from past commitments. The level of such pensions should be seen as part of appropriate compensation packages—what is required to attract talented people to perform the important business of the public sector. Again, the Troika hasn't framed the matter this way. If those in the public sector are not appropriately compensated, then the public sector won't be able to fulfill its necessary tasks. Citizens will then feel, justifiably, that they are not getting their money's worth out of their taxes, and tax compliance will decrease. Another vicious circle begins, where the Troika is clearly more a part of the problem than of the solution.

SAVING THE BANKS

The financial sector was at the center of the Great Recession, and it has been at the center of the euro crisis. As we've seen, a real estate bubble fueled by excess housing credit brought down Spain. And as is typical after the bursting of such a bubble, many who had taken out loans couldn't repay, and the weakened banks curtailed lending. The cessation of a major engine of economic growth—real estate investment—combined with the curtailed lending ensured that recession would follow. In turn, government attempts to prop up the banks, combined with falling tax revenues and increased social expenditure as the economy went into recession, put the government in a precarious fiscal position.

The eurozone had been constructed on the premise that each government was responsible for its own banks. Consider the case of Spain. As Spanish banks weakened, they had to pay very high interest rates. The banks faced a crisis—they might not even be able to borrow, depositors might withdraw their funds, and the high interest rates might drive them into insolvency. The banks and the government were intimately intertwined, as we noted in chapter 5. What gave depositors in banks some confidence that they could have their money when they wanted it was the backing of the government. But the weakening of the fiscal position of the government weakened confidence in the banks. At the same time, the weakening of the government's fiscal position meant it could only borrow at a high interest rate. Many investors were not willing to lend at all. To keep interest rates on government bonds from soaring even further, Spanish banks had to buy and hold on to large amounts of government debt. The decline in the price of Spanish government bonds then meant a worsening of Spanish banks' balance sheets.

To an outsider, it was apparent that what was going on was a bootstrap operation: banks lent the government money (typically, by buying government bonds), and the government guaranteed the banks, allowing them to get access to money from markets at lower rates—so long as the government guarantee had much worth—and to lend some of that money to the government.

Eurozone policy toward Spain (and some other crisis countries) was in many ways predicated on this bootstrap operation, wherein lending to the government would help bail out the banks, and lending to the banks would help bail out the governments, as the banks bought government bonds when no one else was willing to do so.[38]

The eurozone stepped in with a variety of measures to help Spanish banks, though the Spanish government was ultimately supposed to bear the downside risk. But if the Spanish government could have borne the downside risk, it could have rescued the banks on its own. It was precisely because of the interlinking of the two that outside help was needed. Not surprisingly, the effect of such measures was at best temporary.

A "CONFIDENCE" GAME?

What finally restored stability (but not strong growth) to Europe was Draghi's promise in 2012 to do whatever it takes to support the European sovereign (government) bond market. Sovereign spreads—the higher interest rates that Greece, Spain, and other crisis countries had to pay relative to Germany—came down. Even Greece's spread fell from 27.3 percentage points in February 2012 to 12.0 by the end of the year. Italy, Portugal, and Spain, though never experiencing a spread as large as Greece's, fell as well—to 3.2, 6.0, and 4.0, respectively.[39] The increase in bond values improved the balance sheet of banks. It was a confidence game that was seemingly costless and has worked—at least for a while. As we noted earlier, no one knows, of course, whether the ECB in fact can and will do "whatever it takes" if that day of reckoning arrives when a periphery country, in the face of a sudden loss in confidence in that country's bonds, needs ECB support.[40]

Any existing confidence in the ECB's promise would, of course, be greatly eroded were Greece or some other member to leave the eurozone precisely because the ECB had not done whatever it takes. In the Greek crisis of the summer of 2015, the ECB showed itself resolutely unwilling to back Greece unless its government acceded to the demands of the Troika. As the negotiations ground on, the ECB went so far as to stop acting as a lender of last supply, forcing Greece's banks to shut down for three weeks—hardly evidence of a willingness to do whatever it takes, more evidence of the *political* role of the ECB discussed in chapter 6.

If there is an exit from the euro of one or more members, the knowledge that the euro is *not* a binding commitment among its members—a commitment that will *never* be broken—will make the Draghi confidence trick far less likely to work the next time. Bond yields could spike, and no amount of reassurance from the ECB and Europe's leaders would suffice to bring them down from stratospheric levels.

Even if the ECB were willing to do *whatever it takes*, it is not clear, short of a massive debt restructuring that the ECB could save the day. The IMF is consistently brought in to provide liquidity when there is a lack of confidence by markets. In a very large fraction of cases, the IMF fails to restore the economy to health, for two reasons: First, the IMF is a senior creditor—that is, it gets paid back before anyone else does. Thus, loans by the IMF worsen the risk profile of all other creditors; they stand further down the queue. The IMF "rescue" therefore makes these bonds even riskier.[41] Secondly, the IMF typically supplies the funds with a long list of "conditionalities," just as the Troika has done with its other members. Usually, these conditionalities are misconceived—both the macroeconomic/fiscal conditions and the structural ones. As in Greece, they almost guarantee a bigger economic downturn. And, of course, as the economy's prospects grow dimmer, there is little reason that market confidence will be restored.[42]

BAILOUTS AND DEBT RESTRUCTURINGS: WHO IS REALLY BEING HELPED?

The first symptom of the crisis was the high interest rates paid by Greece on government debt (sometimes referred to as sovereign debt), followed by Greece being closed out of the market—no one would buy any new bonds that the Greek government might try to issue.

The leaders of the eurozone realized they had to do something, for if Greece didn't pay back the loans that were due, it could spell troubles not just for Greece but for the rest of Europe. Many of the Greek bonds were held by German and French banks. The eurozone's immediate response was to provide credit, not so much to help Greece but to help their own banks. But at what interest rate? To demonstrate to German taxpayers that they would not be subsidizing Greeks, the Troika demanded a high interest rate—so high that it was clear from the outset that Greece's ability to repay the debts was low. If they had chosen a lower rate, that might not have been the case. At the time the crisis broke out, Greek debt was around 109 percent of GDP—lower than US debt at the end of World War II (118 percent), much lower than Japan's debt now (246 percent) and the UK's debt at the end of World War II (which reached some 250 percent).[43] If one manages to "grow" the economy, increase GDP, and keep interest rates low, this debt-to-GDP ratio can be brought down, and dramatically so, as both the history of the United States and the UK demonstrated. But if one imposes stifling conditions and charges high interest rates, then the economy will stagnate, and the debt-to-GDP ratio will increase.

Some in Germany (and elsewhere) claim high interest rates were necessary to discourage moral hazard, the risk that governments would spend recklessly and then turn to Europe for assistance. But no government would willingly put itself through the torture that Greece has endured. Moreover, whatever mistakes in lending occurred earlier—punishing Greece today doesn't rectify yesterday's mistakes.

The real moral hazard problem arises for banks, who have an incentive to induce countries to borrow excessively, knowing that current politicians benefit from the increased spending and future politicians pay the price. Repeated bank bailouts encourage this kind of behavior: the Mexican, Latin American, and East Asian bailouts, each of which bears the name of a country, are really bailouts of the European and American banks that lent recklessly.

These bailouts, of course, not only distort incentives but are expensive. They are, in fact, just one of the many forms of subsidy to the financial sector, especially the big banks,[44] sometimes hidden in the lower interest rate they pay to those who provide them funds because of anticipation of the bailouts. If instead of just bailing out failing banks, the governments took shares in those banks, then the country's fiscal position would be that much stronger when the banks rebounded, and perhaps the banks would be more prudent in their lending.[45]

True to history, Germany and the Troika did little to address the banks' moral hazard in the case of Greece and some of the other European bailouts. Indeed, as we saw in the case of Ireland, the ECB demanded (secretly) that Ireland bail out its banks.

Whatever the reason, Germany's demand for high interest rates was well in excess of those at which Germany could borrow. This dealt a blow to any notion of European solidarity: What does solidarity mean if one country is able and willing to make a profit off its neighbor in its time of need?[46]

As it became obvious that Greece could not make the repayments, new loans were needed, with new conditions—ever more onerous. Of the total lent to Greece, less than 10 percent ever got to the Greek people. The rest went to pay back creditors, including German and French banks.[47] It may be nice that the German and other European governments bailed out their banks (though whether that is good policy is another matter), but the Greeks rightly asked why it should be done so much on their backs.

A FRESH START: AN ALTERNATIVE TO DEPRESSION-GENERATING AUSTERITY

Debt restructurings are an essential part of capitalism. If a country (or a firm or a family) is temporarily facing difficulty in servicing its debt,[48] then a short-term loan to help it through the troubled period makes sense. But if there is a long-term problem, the loan needs to be written down. The individual needs a fresh start. Typically, a country has a bankruptcy law to allow this fresh start. The same principle applies to nations. But there is no international law for restructuring debt—though as we noted earlier there is now a move within the United Nations to create such a framework, and a resolution establishing a set of principles for debt restructuring was overwhelmingly passed in September 2015.

Debt restructuring improves a country's fiscal position, because the government doesn't have to spend as much servicing the debt. The money not transferred abroad can be used to stimulate the economy. Of course, of the array of possible actions, restructuring is most disliked by the creditor countries' governments—and even more so when the debt is owed to "official" bodies.[49]

The severe austerity (and the other features of the Troika programs) makes little sense even from the perspective of the creditors. It's like a 19th-century debtors' prison. Imprisoned debtors cannot make the income to repay. So, too, the deepening depression in Greece will make it less and less able to repay. Debt restructurings are not a panacea—they do not resolve all of a country's problems. But without a debt restructuring, a write-down of what is owed, overindebted countries *can't* return to health. In the case of Greece, the IMF has recognized the need for a debt restructuring; but even with a restructuring, unless there is relief from the extreme austerity measures now in place, the prospects for the country remain bleak.

One shouldn't feel too sorry for the private sector creditors: typically they have been well compensated for their risk, in terms of interest rates well in excess of the safe interest rate—for example, the rate on US Treasury bills.[50] If they have not been well paid, it reflects a lack of due diligence on the part of the creditors or a bout of irrational optimism.[51] Of course, creditor governments don't like admitting to their citizens that they or their country's banks have to take a loss. There are strong incentives for "pretend and extend"—pretend that the debtor is only having a temporary problem and extend the loan, so as not to "recognize" the loss. But the costs of this charade are usually high, especially to the indebted country, and that has proven to be the case particularly in Greece.

Germany has been insisting that there be no restructuring of Greece's debt—only that there be another bout of pretend and extend. The problem with pretend and extend is that it provides no framework for a resumption of growth; it condemns the debtor country to never-ending misery; there is no fresh start. Moreover, Germany's refusal to restructure put Greece in the impossible situation of having to agree to a program that it knew would not and could not work. The Troika program was incoherent: the Germans simultaneously said there must be no debt write-off and that the IMF must be part of the program. But the IMF cannot participate in a program where debt levels are unsustainable, and the IMF *had already* determined that this was the case for Greece's debts.[52]

COULD GREECE PROCEED IN A RESTRUCTURING ON ITS OWN?

There is an argument that Greece should begin the process of debt restructuring on its own, if Germany doesn't accede: even the IMF says that debt restructuring is absolutely necessary. Whether or not the current program is well implemented, it will lead to unsustainable levels of debt. The Greeks might take a page from Argentina, exchanging current bonds for GDP-linked bonds, where payments increase with Greece's prosperity. Such bonds align the incentives of debtors and creditors.[53]

As we saw in earlier chapters, after Argentina restructured its debt and devalued, it grew rapidly—the fastest rate of growth around the world except for China's—from its crisis until the global financial crisis of 2008. Of course Greece and Argentina are different economies. Argentina benefited from both a debt restructuring and a devaluation; if Greece only had a debt restructuring, would that be enough?[54] Argentina benefited, moreover, from a large increase in exports as a result of the commodity boom. There are, however, some striking similarities: Both countries were being strangled by austerity. Both countries under IMF programs saw rising unemployment, poverty, and immense suffering. Had Argentina continued with austerity, there would have just been more of the same. The Argentine people rose up and said no. Greece is in a similar situation: if conditions continue as is, it will mean depression without end.

CONCLUDING COMMENTS

This chapter has focused on the macroeconomic and financial sector dimensions of the programs that have been imposed on the crisis countries. It is these that have predominantly determined the fate of the crisis countries; it is macroeconomic austerity that has led to the dismal performances.

And while in some respects, Greece was not typical of the crisis countries—in most, it was private sector misconduct, not public sector profligacy that brought on the crisis—Greece exemplifies the failures on the all-important macroeconomic front. Greece had the biggest and fastest fiscal consolidation among the advanced European economies in the aftermath of the global financial crisis, ruthlessly cutting back expenditures and raising new revenues.[55]

In the summer of 2011, as the first signs of the failure of the austerity policy emerged, Europe's leaders recognized that they needed a growth strategy. They promised Greece one. They didn't deliver. There was only more of the same. The bailouts of Spain, Greece, and the other countries in crisis appeared aimed more at saving the European banks that had lent these countries money than at restoring the crisis countries to health; it seemed aimed more at saving the euro than at preserving the well-being and economy of the crisis countries.

In the end, then, it was not so much European solidarity that engendered the "help" that Germany provided to its neighbors as self-interest. A restructuring of Greek debt might have been the most economically sensible thing to do when the crisis broke out in 2010, with Germany providing direct help to its own inadequately regulated banks. But for German politicians, it was easier to vilify Greece and provide indirect assistance to German banks through a bailout loan, called a "Greek bailout," and then impose policy conditions on Greece that would seemingly force it to repay what was borrowed.

In the end, the economic policy didn't work. It didn't work for the debtor countries or for the creditor. It didn't work for the eurozone as a whole. Greece couldn't repay. And the Greeks paid an enormous price for Germany's political gambit. With the ongoing euro crisis, it is too soon to tell whether it worked for Germany's politics, for Merkel and her government.

It would have been easy to restore Greece to growth: deep debt restructuring (simply recognizing that money that can't be repaid won't be repaid); a primary surplus of 1 percent by 2018, not the 3.5 percent Europe has demanded; and reasonable structural reform focused on the central issues facing the economy today (which I will describe in greater detail in the next chapter).

The short-run economic consequences of the misguided programs in Greece and elsewhere are already evident. The longer-term consequences in terms of slower growth and lower GDP will only be seen over time. The best evidence is that a country that goes through a deep downturn never bounces back to make up for what is lost. What is lost is lost forever.

The social and political consequences not just in Greece but throughout the eurozone are also almost inevitable—and potentially disastrous. Indeed, already some of these are evident, with the growth of more extreme parties: the centrist parties, both the center-left and the center-right, that had staked their reputation on the success of the Troika programs and on the idea that the euro would bring prosperity for all have been discredited. More than 60 percent of voters in Spain, Greece, and Portugal have rejected the austerity parties. The Irish government was all but turned out. While these effects are felt most strongly in the crisis countries, they are also present elsewhere in the eurozone, most notably in France and Italy. And the failures in the eurozone almost surely have contributed to broader skepticism about the value of European integration, evidenced most starkly in the strong support for leaving the EU in the UK. In Spain and elsewhere, separatist parties, calling for the breakup of long-established nation-states, are in the ascendancy, reversing a 200-year trend of national political integration within Europe.

While this chapter set forth the Troika's macroeconomic policies, the next outlines the structural reforms they imposed on the crisis countries, explaining why they, too, failed and how there were alternatives that would have worked so much better.

ACADEMICS FOR AUSTERITY: AN ASIDE

While the austerity programs described in this chapter have largely been driven by politics and politicians, not surprisingly, academic economists have raised their voices.

The vast majority have sided with the views expressed here: austerity has never worked. When the government reduces demand, output falls, unless something else fills the gap. It's that simple. And because it is so simple, we haven't spent much time in the text explaining why, exactly, austerity has never worked. Here, we consider how austerity doctrines have sometimes garnered support—outside of ideologues and those special interests who might benefit from austerity—and why the IMF and the Troika could have repeatedly gotten it so wrong in predicting its effects.

In the immediate aftermath of the financial crisis, three economists championed the seemingly paradoxical notion of "expansionary contractions."[56] (The academy rewards counterintuitive analyses.) They argued that there were important instances where when governments had contracted government spending, the result was that the overall economy grew.

The notion that there could be expansionary contractions was a chimera. A series of papers showed major flaws in their analysis.[57] The IMF, which had supported austerity-style policies in the past, in fact reversed itself. It pointed out that when governments contract spending, the economy contracts.[58]

The big flaw in the pro-austerity study was confusing correlation with causation. There were a few countries, small economies with flexible exchange rates, where a contraction in government spending was associated with growth; but in these cases the hole in demand created by the government contraction was filled in with exports. Canada in the early 1990s was lucky because the United States was going through a rapid expansion, the recovery from the 1991 recession. Canada benefited, too from a flexible exchange rate that enabled it to sell its goods more cheaply to the United States. There is a moral to the story: if you are in a recession, and you want to recover, choose your neighbors carefully. If they are having a boom, you can use that to restart your economy.

But for the European crisis countries in the aftermath of 2008, such "contractionary expansions" were not an option: Europe as a whole—the main trading partner of each of the crisis countries—was experiencing slow growth, if not a recession. Because each of the crisis countries was part of the eurozone, none could lower its exchange rate; and because of the flawed policies of the ECB, the euro exchange rate with the rest of the world was actually very strong. In this context, austerity would produce what it usually does: a slowdown, if not a recession or depression.

The fact that in a few instances austerity was associated with economic expansion only meant this: in these instances, but for the austerity, the expansion would have been even stronger. In some cases, in spite of the expansion of trade, the economy remained below full employment. In such cases, austerity had *worsened* the level of unemployment; the austerity had not *caused* the reduction in the unemployment.

An analogy might be useful: When Ronald Reagan became president of the United States, the government undertook two policies almost simultaneously, a large tax cut and very tight monetary policy. The economy went into the deepest economic downturn, the worst, up to that point, since the Great Depression. It would be wrong to infer that the tax cut caused the economic downturn. It simply made the economic downturn less bad than it otherwise would have been.

Before the 2008 crisis, some argued that increased government spending did not increase GDP. The empirical work leading to this conclusion focused on years in which the economy was at or near full employment. When the economy is at or near full employment, there is no room for GDP to increase. Thus, an increase in government spending necessarily "crowds" out other forms for spending. But such analyses have no bearing in a postcrisis world experiencing massive unemployment—in the eurozone, unemployment stands at 10.2 percent as this book goes to press.[59] In fact, when there is already a high level of unemployment, there is a "multiplier"—that is, reductions in government spending can lead to reductions in GDP that are a multiple of the cutbacks.[60]

Another strand of academic work cited by austerity advocates focuses on the consequences of the debt that arises when government spending is financed by borrowing. Kenneth Rogoff and Carmen Reinhardt argued that countries with debt-to-GDP ratios in excess of 80 percent would grow more slowly.[61] Upon closer scrutiny, there were major "spreadsheet" and other technical mistakes in their work. More significantly, however, Rogoff and Reinhart failed to test whether growth was lower at higher debt ratios in a way that was statistically significant, and whether this was true *always* or only under certain conditions. Such a test would have helped to identify the different conditions under which an increase in debt might make a significant difference. There was a further statistical problem—they had failed to show causality: whether low growth had *caused* the deficits and debts (as was the case after 2008) or, as they claimed, the deficits or debts had caused low growth.[62]

By itself, the debt-to-GDP ratio does not tell us much about debt sustainability. The ratio may not even be a good measure of a country's resilience, its ability to withstand shocks, or its overall economic strength. As noted earlier, the United States had a debt-to-GDP ratio of 122 percent after World War II. In the succeeding decades, the country experienced its most rapid growth—this in spite of the fact that war spending does not provide the foundations for future growth as well as does other types of investment. A country that borrows to make productive investment—in education, technology, or infrastructure—enhances its future potential: for most countries, the returns on these public investments far exceed the cost of capital. Thus, such investments, even when debt financed, strengthen the country's balance sheet and make it more capable of withstanding shocks.

EXPLAINING THE MAGNITUDE OF THE DOWNTURN

Olivier Blanchard, when he was chief economist at the IMF, observed that the economic downturn in Greece was greater than could be accounted for by the amount of austerity that had been imposed. He was of course correct in the sense that Troika models had very badly estimated the effects of their policies. He was saying something more, though: "normal" multipliers—which translate a change in government spending into a change in GDP—would have predicted a much smaller decline in GDP than had actually occurred.

Yet, when the depth of the economic downturn was plotted against the level of austerity imposed, the Greek case did not appear unusual. Yes, the amount of austerity imposed on Greece was greater than that imposed on any other country. But given the magnitude of the austerity, the magnitude of the downturn was much as one would have expected.

While there were many limitations in the standard models[63] that help explain why they did so badly in predicting the *magnitude* of the multiplier—and why Blanchard and others were surprised at the depth of the downturns—the most significant were (1) the failure to analyze carefully the financial sector, and (2) the failure to analyze carefully the distributive consequences of the policies.

The models typically had no banks; this was an especially curious omission, for if there were no banks, there would be no central bank. And how then could we have had the banking crisis of 2008? The focus in the standard models was on the money supply, not on credit. The euro crisis and the way it was managed, however, led, as we saw in chapter 5, to a massive contraction of the supply of credit, especially to small and medium-size enterprises, and this "private austerity" compounded the effects of the public austerity.

Inequality and distribution

The standard models also ignored how increasing inequality affects macroeconomic performance. Indeed, some economists were positively hostile to even discussing the distribution of income.[64]

The crises, and how they have been managed, have had adverse effects on inequality. In Spain, as we observed earlier, inequality before the crisis had been going down; in the aftermath of the crisis it increased. Inevitably, unemployment increases inequality both directly and indirectly, as wages fall and as government services, upon which ordinary citizens depend, decrease.

Since those at the top spend a smaller percentage of their income than the rest, an increase in inequality lowers aggregate demand, and thus economic performance. This is especially so when, as now, monetary policy is unable to stimulate the economy. In recent years, the IMF has stressed how inequality weakens growth.[65]

Thus, while the IMF had begun to recognize the importance of inequality for economic performance, and while its own research had provided convincing evidence that government cutbacks would lead to significant contraction, even its research department had failed to ascertain fully the effects of the austerity programs, because their models did not adequately incorporate the dramatic weakening of the financial sectors in the crisis countries and the increase in inequality, and had overestimated the growth in exports and underestimated the impact of the decrease in demand for nontraded goods. But the IMF was only one member of the Troika. And worse, the Troika programs did not seem to consider the possibility of these untoward effects being as large as they turned out to be, even as they were unfolding— and seemed reluctant to reconsider their programs, even as evidence mounted that they were not working in the way anticipated.

8

STRUCTURAL REFORMS THAT FURTHER COMPOUNDED FAILURE

The Troika program imposed *structural reforms* on the crisis countries as a condition for providing assistance. Structural reforms simply refer to changes in the structure of the economy and in the individual markets within—for instance, labor markets and financial markets. All countries are constantly in need of structural reform and transformation as the economic situations that they confront change. After the financial crisis of 2008, there was a broad consensus that there was a need for *deep* structural reforms in financial markets throughout the advanced countries.

In the crisis countries, the Troika demanded, as a condition for providing assistance, a mélange of reforms, ranging from the trivial to the counterproductive, with little focus on the truly important. The most demanding reforms were those imposed on Greece, and they were remarkably ineffective, sometimes even destructive.

There is an old adage about Nero fiddling while Rome burned. Greece was in a depression. Its people were starving. Surely, there should have been a sense of urgency. Doctors triage at the hospital, first looking to the death-threatening problems; later attending to less important matters. But not only did the Troika fail to prioritize, many of the most important changes that *should* have been on the reform list were not.

BLAMING THE SUPPLY SIDE

The Troika has argued that the crisis is, in no small measure, the consequence of structural problems, and as such they had to be attended to right away. But structural problems don't suddenly arise. There were no changes in the structure of the afflicted countries that could account for their going from near full employment precrisis to massive unemployment after 2010.[1] As we noted in chapter 3, some of the crisis countries had, before the crisis, even grown faster than the average for Europe as a whole. Without any of these structural reforms, Greece grew at a faster rate (3.9 percent) than the EU (2.6 percent) from 1995 to 2007, until the global crisis, and so did Spain (3.8 percent).[2]

The Troika might claim that, even if the structural problems didn't cause the crises, reforms would help the economies recover. It is not, however, "structural impediments" that are holding the crisis countries back—it is, as we have seen, the eurozone itself. Because structural problems thus cannot be (and are not) the *cause* of the crisis, structural reforms *within the individual countries* cannot and will not be the cure.

The eurozone's leaders disingenuously pretended such reforms would make the citizens of the crisis countries better off.[3] It is now obvious that they did not do that—and it should have been obvious at the time that the Troika imposed these demands that they would not.

Some of the reforms seemed intended at increasing the likelihood that creditors would be repaid, by reducing the current account deficit—what countries had to borrow—and converting the deficit into a surplus so that the country had the euros to repay. In the absence of flexible exchange rates, as we noted in chapter 4, the only way to correct current account deficits is to have a *real exchange* adjustment—

that is, to lower the prices of the goods that the country sells abroad. But as we shall see, some of the reforms seem as motivated by advancing the business interests within the dominant countries in the euro-zone as anything else. And, ironically, the reforms as a whole—the combination of structural and macro-economic reforms—turned out to be counterproductive, in particular, weakening Greece to the point where it could not pay back what was owed.

THE TROIKA'S STRUCTURAL REFORMS: FROM THE TRIVIAL TO THE COUNTERPRODUCTIVE

As we have noted, the structural reforms were a grab bag, ranging from the trivial to the counterproductive.

FOCUSING ON THE WRONG THING

While some of the reforms might be justified as helping correct the unsustainable trade deficit of the individual crisis countries, many could not be. To correct the trade deficit, it should have been obvious that the Troika should have focused on "tradable" goods—exports and imports. Too often, however, the Troika did not do so; it did not even focus on nontraded inputs into the traded sector. Instead, much of its attention was centered on nontraded consumer goods (like taxicabs and bread). Lower prices in the nontraded sector, especially of certain consumer goods, may have affected the living standards of Greeks, though as we shall see even that might not be true, once one includes all the effects, including that on employment; but such changes only have a negligible effect on the current account. In some cases, the "reforms" may have even worsened the trade deficit.[4]

Trade deficits can be reduced by improving the *real* exchange rate, by lowering the price of the goods the country exports. There are three ways of doing this: (1) lowering wages, and hoping that the lower wages get translated into lower prices; (2) lowering the cost of other inputs, in particular nontraded intermediate inputs (like electricity), by increasing competition in those sectors; or (3) improving technology and competition in traded goods.

TECHNOLOGY

Improving technology is important, but typically cannot be done overnight—and the Troika policies probably set back the agenda. Firms in economies on the verge of collapse are thinking about survival, not about investing in R&D. And government investments in infrastructure, education, job training, or even technology—all of which might have increased productivity—had to be curtailed under the onslaught of austerity. All of these compounded the adverse effects of the eurozone structure itself discussed in chapter 5: The migration out of the crisis countries of some of their most talented young people hurt productivity not only in the short run but also in the long; and the flow of capital out of the crisis countries meant that the cost of capital facing firms in these countries soared—if they could get finance at all—making productivity-enhancing investments even harder. And prohibitions against industrial policies—policies by which lagging countries might hope to catch up to the more advanced partners in the eurozone—made closing the technology gap all the more difficult.

THE TRIVIAL

When it came to promoting competition, the Troika mysteriously focused on nontraded consumer goods rather than on traded goods or nontraded that might possibly have had an effect on trade. But even then, their choice of what to focus on was most peculiar. No one has fully articulated how many of the seemingly trivial reforms struck the fancy of the Troika—how they entered the "hit list."[5] Here, I describe a few of the more controversial ones in the Greek program.[6]

Fresh milk

Somehow, if one believed that the worst problem facing Greece was the definition of fresh milk, Greece would really have been in good shape. Greeks enjoy their fresh milk, produced locally and delivered quickly. But Dutch and other European milk producers would like to increase sales by having their milk, transported over long distances, appear to be as fresh as the local product. In 2014 the Troika forced Greece to drop the label "fresh" on its truly fresh milk and extend allowable shelf life. Under these conditions, large-scale producers elsewhere in Europe seem to believe they can trounce Greece's small-scale producers. In theory, Greek consumers would benefit from the lower prices, even though the lower prices might mean lower quality. In practice, the new retail market is far from competitive, and early indications are that the lower prices were largely not passed on to consumers.

The size of a loaf of bread

Or consider another seemingly strange debate in the middle of a depression: the Troika demanded that Greece change its regulations concerning the size of bread loaves. In the past, loaves could only be sold in specified sizes: .5 kilo, 1 kilo, 1.5 kilos, and 2 kilos. There is a long-standing literature explaining how such standards actually increase competition, because they facilitate comparison shopping. But the Troika wants stores to be able to sell any size loaf. Somehow they see this as a competitive restriction.[7] (I have never heard a good rationale for the Troika's position on this matter.) But even if one couldn't defend Greece's previous regulations, it is preposterous that the Troika held an entire country hostage over things like this.

Pharmacies

There are some restrictions on competition that the elimination of which, if done well and sold well, might have been beneficial. But again, the Troika botched it. A major complaint of the Troika concerned restrictions on drugstores (pharmacies). For instance, Greece required that each pharmacy be owned by a pharmacist and did not allow over-the-counter drugs to be sold outside of pharmacies. The Troika claimed that Greek regulations led to high drug prices. Again, it was somewhat mysterious why the Troika would get so exercised over this, when there were so many more profound problems. Allegedly, the drugstore reform was intended to help consumers by increasing competition, thereby lowering prices. But why was the Troika suddenly so concerned about ordinary Greeks—as they pushed policies that led real incomes to fall by a quarter and forced even very poor Greeks out into the streets? The sudden and seemingly isolated concern for the ordinary Greek citizen seemed out of sync with other aspects of what the Troika was doing. Nor would lower prices for over-the-counter drugs do anything for Greece's balance of payments.

Perhaps doubts about the Troika's motives fed into resistance to the reform. The widespread perception in Greece is that many of the drugstores are mom-and-pop stores, owned by someone in their neighborhood, eking out a basic living, not living high off monopoly pricing. They saw the large number of pharmacies as evidence of competition, and were befuddled by charges of lack of competition. Many Greeks felt some solidarity with their neighborhood pharmacy; they were willing to pay a slightly higher price and even to support the regulatory system which allowed that. They may have understood that allowing others to sell over-the-counter drugs might have lowered profits, that the reduced profitability of running a pharmacy might lead to fewer pharmacies and thus to even higher prices for prescription drugs and less accessibility to medicines when they were needed.[8]

For people with this view, the Troika seemed to have another agenda, akin to that in the fresh milk case: opening up Greece to multinational chains and strengthening grocery stores (including chains) that could now sell these products, which might provide lower prices, but at the same time would be destroying the livelihood of thousands of Greeks.

The Troika could have taken steps to reassure the Greek people that the true agenda behind pharmacy reform was simply to lower prices for consumers. The fact that the Troika failed to convince most Greeks of these aims showed the deep popular distrust about their motives. No one gave the Troika the benefit of the doubt.[9]

Contributing to the distrust was the fact that many of the regulations the Troika was so vehemently demanding that Greece change, such as on closing hours, were similar to those elsewhere in Europe, *including Germany.* When Germany's finance minister, Wolfgang Schäuble, was confronted with this fact, his response was, in effect, that Greece was in dire straits—it couldn't afford these inefficiencies; Germany could. But he never explained how more trading hours would lead to a smaller trade deficit or even a higher GDP. These were regulations affecting a nontraded sector, and so were irrelevant for its exports. Money not spent on Sunday will be spent some other time— there is no evidence that these restrictions have any effect on national savings rates.[10]

Making Greeks even more suspicious that the Troika had another agenda than just increasing the well-being of the Greek people was the fact that they failed to sustain an even more important reform, one that brought down drug prices even more: the e-government drug-price initiative of Prime Minister George Papandreou (which would have resulted in lower prices by increasing market transparency) went by the wayside once he was forced from office.

WEAKENING LABOR

The alternative to increasing competitiveness through improved productivity was lowering wages. I suspect that while many were horrified at the increased unemployment in the crisis countries, secretly, many in the Troika thought of this as almost a necessary means to the long-run end of making the euro work: as we noted in chapter 4, higher unemployment would lead to lower wages, lower wages would lead to lower prices, and this process of "internal devaluation" would *eventually* restore equilibrium to the current account and bring the economy back to full employment. It was a very costly way of achieving what flexible exchange rates would have accomplished.

Not satisfied with the huge decreases in labor costs (in the case of Greece, reductions of about 20 percent) that the market had brought about on its own, just through the high unemployment that the Troika policies had engendered, the Troika demanded reform to labor institutions, in the euphemism of the day, to create more flexible labor markets; in the reality of the day, the reforms would weaken workers' bargaining power, lower wages still further, and increase profits. The Troika even put into question their commitment to the basic right of collective bargaining, the core labor standards that have been agreed to by almost all of the countries around the world.

The language in which European authorities shrouded their demands was often obscure, but the intention seemed clear, so clear that in 2011 one of Papandreou's loyalists, a bright and devoted economist, resigned from the government rather than be a party to this abnegation of basic workers' rights.

Here is what the Troika demanded of the Tsipras government (to which it reluctantly agreed), with the interpretation of Yannis Varoufakis, Greece's former finance minister, in brackets. The Greek government agreed to

> undertake rigorous reviews and modernization of collective bargaining [i.e. to make sure that no collective bargaining is allowed], industrial action [i.e. that must be banned] and, in line with the relevant EU directive and best practice, collective dismissals [i.e. that should be allowed at the employers' whim], along the timetable and the approach agreed with the Institutions [i.e. the Troika decides.]
>
> On the basis of these reviews, labour market policies should be aligned with international and European best practices, and should not involve a return to past policy settings which are not

compatible with the goals of promoting sustainable and inclusive growth [i.e. there should be no mechanisms that wage labour can use to extract better conditions from employers.][11]

But there was something strange as the Troika continued to make these demands on "labor market" reform on Greece: By 2015, the current account deficit had largely been eliminated. Indeed, according to the ECB, its competitiveness was above the average for the eurozone. Any further cuts seemed punitive, and as we shall shortly explain, even counterproductive. Almost surely, they would lead to even further decreases in GDP.

The Troika policies highlight general principles: (1) the rules of the game (the terms under which unions can bargain) matter, and they matter a lot; and (2) who sets the rules matters, and can matter a lot. If the finance ministers are setting labor laws—within any country— one will wind up with different labor laws than if labor ministers set the rules. No country should want the finance ministry to set its labor laws; our democracies are designed to make sure that weight is given not just to the interests and perspectives of the financial markets, and thankfully so. And even more so, no country would want its labor laws to be written by the parliament of another country—let alone the finance ministry of another country.

While, as we have noted, the government of the crisis country always *accedes* to the demands, they do so with effectively a gun at the head: the feared consequences of not doing so are simply too great *not* to accede.

COUNTERPRODUCTIVE REFORMS

The Troika sold the reforms on the grounds that they would help the economy grow. Greece showed dramatically that they had the opposite effect. Some of the structural reforms, including those we discussed earlier in this chapter, had an even worse outcome: local firms would be displaced by large European multinationals, in which case the "reform" would increase the profits of the multinational, lowering the income of those within the country. While consumers still benefited from the lower prices, this time there was another adverse effect: the transfer of profits from within the country to outside meant that spending on nontraded goods decreased, with a multiplier on national income and jobs—that is, income in the crisis country went down by a *multiple* of the profits that were effectively transferred abroad.[12] Consumers who had jobs benefited slightly from the lower prices, but if, as to be expected, tax revenues fell alongside GDP, they were worse off as a result of the cutback in government services and systems of social protection.[13] On net, many, especially in the lower rungs of society, were worse off, some much worse off. Of course, those individuals who lost their jobs suffered enormously—twice over, both from the loss of their job and the decrease in public services.

Many of the structural reforms demanded by the Troika could, especially in the aggregate, have an adverse effect *even narrowly on the current account.* If Greeks start buying Dutch milk, imports are increased and the trade balance worsens. And similarly for many other so-called structural reforms.[14]

REFORMS THAT WOULD HAVE MATTERED

In each of the crisis countries, there are reforms that might have led to a stronger economy, both in the short run and the long.

INDUSTRIAL POLICIES

Most advanced countries are in need of a structural transformation of their economy, from the sectors (mostly manufacturing) that were dominant in the past to those that will define the 21st century. Because the pace of productivity increase in manufacturing is greater than that of demand, global manufacturing employment will be decreasing, and because of globalization, the share of this global employment that will be captured by the advanced countries, including those in Europe, will be diminishing. A few countries, like Germany, may be able to maintain a niche, at least for a while, especially if they can manage to have an undervalued currency. Germany has benefited from being wedded to the "weaker" countries of the eurozone, for the net effect is that the euro, the currency today, is weaker than say the German mark would have been. But most of the advanced countries will have to restructure themselves away from manufacturing toward new sectors, like the more dynamic service sectors. And even those that continue to have significant presence within manufacturing will have to restructure: from low-skilled to high-skilled manufacturing.

Markets, on their own, are not very good at restructuring themselves. The move from agriculture to industry in the late 19th and early 20th centuries was often traumatic.[15] Those in the older sectors saw their incomes and wealth evaporate, and had little access to capital markets; they couldn't make the investments required to shift from the old economy to the new. But much the same is true as the economy moves from manufacturing to the service sector, and especially as it moves toward an innovation and knowledge economy. Creating a learning economy is not easy, and the government needs to play a central role.[16] At the center of America's knowledge economy are its first-rate higher educational institutions, many of which were established more than a hundred years ago, some hundreds of years ago. And even they achieved much of their greatness as a result of migration from Europe around World War II, and with massive government support in the war and afterward for research. So, too, the culture and "ecology" of Silicon Valley—with its venture capital firms and close nexus between universities and enterprises—was created over a span of decades.

Without a concerted government effort, those countries that are behind will remain behind.[17] There is a range of government policies, called industrial policies, discussed briefly in chapter 5, which have proven effective in pushing economic restructuring. In the case of the United States' move from agriculture to an industrial/manufacturing economy, the war effort itself was *the* industrial policy. It pulled people out of the rural sector to fight the war, and to urban areas to make armaments required for the war. After the war, the government provided free higher education to all who had fought (which was essentially every young person)—to ensure that they had the skills required for the "new economy." In the last half-century, the US government has once more played a central role, with its major investments in technology.[18] But again as we saw in chapter 5, the kinds of industrial policies that have worked so well around the world[19] are largely precluded within the eurozone; and the austerity measures imposed by the Troika have forced a scaling back in public expenditures that might have facilitated such a structural transformation.

PROMOTING EQUALITY

Markets, on their own, often produce excessively high levels of inequality—levels that are, or should be, socially unacceptable, and actually undermine economic performance. Sometimes this is because governments do too little to offset the intergenerational transmission of advantage.[20] Sometimes this is because governments do too little to offset the agglomerations of political and economic power that can be self-perpetuating: economic inequality leads to political inequality, which leads to writing the rules of the market economy in ways that perpetuate and extend economic inequality in a vicious circle.[21] Some of the crisis countries emerged from long periods of fascism, with relatively high levels of inequality, and it would take a concerted effort on the part of the government to create a more inclusive society.

But again, many of the Troika policies lead to more inequality and a less inclusive economy.[22] Before the crisis, Spain was one of the success stories in bringing down wage inequality; since the crisis, inequality and poverty have been growing there as they have in the other crisis countries.[23]

In Greece, the Troika emphasized that the "fiscal adjustment is fairly distributed across the society, and protects the most vulnerable," and that the "lowest-income and lowest-pension earners, as well as the most vulnerable and those requiring family support, will all be protected and compensated for the adverse impact of the adjustment policies."[24] Yet, as we have seen, well-being indicators have all pointed downward since the adoption of the program that was so confidently predicted to restore growth. By the end of 2014, some 36 percent of Greeks were "at risk of poverty or social exclusion." The rate is the highest in the eurozone and some 10 percentage points higher than currency union's average. The proportion of Greeks below the poverty line (50 percent of the median income) has also increased, from 12.2 percent in 2009 to 15.8 percent in 2014. This may not sound so dramatic until you remember that median incomes also decreased significantly; thus, the increase in the poverty rate shows the disproportionate burden of the Troika programs on those at the bottom.[25]

But the Troika not only did too little to help those at the bottom; they did too little to prevent the concentration of wealth and income at the top. There were alternative policies in which the burden of adjustment would have been more fairly shared, and in which the increase in poverty would have been smaller.[26]

REBALANCING POWER

In Greece and elsewhere, the Troika should have focused on the *major* concentrations of economic and political power and sources of economic rents, which in turn contribute so much to inequality.[27] Instead, the important reforms that would curb the Greek oligarchs were largely left off the agenda. The Troika was quiescent as proposals were put forward to roll back initiatives of the Papandreou government on transparency and e-government, which would have dramatically lowered drug prices, put a damper on nepotism, and curbed the ability of banks to lend to media that they or their friends owned, money that distorted the political process.

So, too, the Troika could have pushed for the progressive property tax aimed at the oligarchs that I discussed in the last chapter, rather than the tax they insisted upon, a nonprogressive one that hurt so many who were already suffering so much.

Such a comprehensive and progressive property tax would, of course, have been resisted by the oligarchs who own so much of Greece's wealth, and that makes it precisely the kind of issue on which the Troika should have weighed in. But often, as one looked at the details of the Troika programs, one wondered what side the Troika was on: Was it just an accident, a slip, that they opted for a property tax that would have inflicted pain on ordinary Greeks, rather than one that would have hit the oligarchs?

The Troika made token measures to *seem* as if they were equally tough on the rich, measures that they surely knew would be ineffective: for example, they insisted on the elimination of all preferences for the shipping industry. Greece's constitution provides favorable treatment for shipping, testimony both to the importance of the industry and to the political influence of the rich shipowners. But there are special problems in taxing shipping, and the Troika's insistence that shipping be taxed at *normal* rates seemed insensitive to these complexities; so it was virtually guaranteed to raise little revenue.[28] If there were ever an industry that was *movable*, this was it: shipping can easily relocate to a low-tax jurisdiction. The absence of international cooperation in taxation of corporations that operate across boundaries has, in fact, made tax avoidance a central part of the business model of every multinational.[29] While the Troika has criticized tax avoidance in Greece, dominant countries in the eurozone have been among those most adamant *against* changing the international framework for taxation in ways that would reduce tax avoidance, and the head of the European

Commission, Jean-Claude Juncker, in his role as premier of Luxem-bourg, perfected that country's role as a center for tax avoidance.[30]

While the tax on shipping that they are demanding—which is unlikely to raise much revenue but *is* likely to hurt Greece's GDP, sim-ply because much of it may move out of Greece to other jurisdictions—is being presented as an example of the Troika's strong anti-oligarchic stance, what they are doing to small businesses in Greece is hard to fathom: they are forcing small businesses, which can't move, to pay a year's tax in advance.[31]

REFORMING THE FINANCIAL SECTOR

The fourth structural reform that the crisis countries needed was reform of the financial sector—noncrisis countries needed such reforms themselves. The financial sector had failed before the crisis to perform the basic services that it is supposed to provide—allocating capital, providing funds to small and medium-size enterprises, and managing risk. Rather than serving society, it had harmed society. Europe might take pride that such abuses were less than in the United States, that the financial sector hadn't taken so much from the rest (in the United States, they took close to 8 percent of GDP in the years before the crisis, as opposed to Europe, where the share remained under about 6 per-cent), and given back so little. But it is not much to crow about.

In Greece, for instance, the banks remained largely in the hands of the Greek oligarchs. These have continued in their practice of "con-nected" lending, lending to their other business interests and those of their friends and family. Particularly invidious was their lending to the media that they owned—which often lost money but enhanced their political influence. In doing so, they enriched and empowered themselves economically and politically.

As it became clear during the crisis that the Greek banks would have to be recapitalized, it made sense to demand voting shares for the government. This was necessary to ensure that connected lending, including to the oligarchic media, be stopped. But when the Papandreou government proposed this, the Troika resisted. He nonetheless persisted, but when he left office—after the Troika adamantly opposed his initiative to put the program to a referendum—these efforts were undone.[32]

Rather than a *restructuring*, though, what happened was a *weakening* of the financial sector in the crisis countries—as we have noted, an almost inevitable consequence of the structure of the eurozone itself. Had the eurozone recognized this problem, they could have undertaken countervailing measures. They could have created a fund for lending to small and medium-size enterprises, and at various times, there were discussions about establishing such a fund.

But the Troika undertook actions that weakened the banks in the crisis countries *even further*, as we have noted repeatedly. The shutdown of the Greek banks was the most obvious case of this. And by repeatedly discussing a haircut for depositors, they convinced those depositors to move their money out of the crisis-country banks. In practice, this was not only a counterproductive policy—at least from the perspective of increasing GDP—but it was also an inequalitarian policy, for large corporations could easily heed the warning and move their money out. Small businesses and ordinary individuals that could not easily access banks abroad were left behind.

CLIMATE CHANGE

A fifth structural reform that is needed in the crisis countries, as it is needed everywhere in the world, is responding to the reality of climate change. Especially in the absence of a price for carbon, the market on its own won't do this. Before the crisis, several European countries had embarked on strategies to move toward renewable energy. Countries like Greece and Spain had the potential to produce solar and wind power that they could export to the rest of Europe.

The private sector, on its own, won't make these investments, not now, without an adequate carbon price. Europe could have helped countries to restructure their energy sectors to be less dependent on fossil fuels, but that would have required spending that was beyond the budget envelope of these countries. It was investment spending that would have yielded high social, and perhaps even private, returns. Europe could have underwritten these investments. And in making these investments, it would have stimulated economies—the opposite of the ineffective structural reforms on which the Troika focused. These investments also would have improved current accounts by lowering the cost of energy (increasing export competitiveness) and reducing the need for countries to import oil and gas.[33]

CONCLUDING COMMENTS

In many ways the programs imposed on Greece and the other crisis countries reminded me of the programs, marked by excessive austerity and a myriad of structural reforms, imposed on Indonesia and other emerging markets in crises in earlier decades. In the case of Indonesia, for instance, there were dozens and dozens of conditions, each with precise timelines. Many seemed, at first blush, strange: Why in the midst of a depression, where the unemployment rate in the main island of Java was reaching 40 percent, was the IMF discussing the clove monopoly; so, too, why in the midst of Greece's unemployment, with youth unemployment peaking above 60 percent, was the Troika talking about how old milk can still be called fresh, or how bread should be sold?

In both cases, the conditions were, at best, not well explained, and this undermined confidence in the program and the political will to ensure that it was effectively implemented. Sometimes, it turned out that the conditions reflected special interests who had successfully bent the ear of the authorities imposing the conditions. While there has been no disaster on par with the IMF's unforgivable destruction of Indonesia's private banking sector, the destruction of the Greek banking system was almost comparable:[34] in 2011 alone, 17 percent of the deposits fled, and by the end of 2015 the assets of Greek banks were down nearly 30 percent from their 2010 peak.[35] The flight was facilitated, of course, as we noted in chapter 5, by the single-market principle in the absence of a banking union, but it was aggravated by Troika policies.

The eurozone claims Spain is a success, simply because growth has returned, even as youth unemployment remains high. It is not a success if one looks at the country's balance sheets, its investments in infrastructure and human capital, even its GDP, which in 2015 was still more than 2 percent below what it was in 2007, eight years earlier. It is not a success if one assesses the human suffering. Similar stories can be told about the other crisis countries. Even Ireland, which is held up as proof that the Troika programs *can* work, and had strong growth in 2015 (7.8 percent), is *not* a success when measured by these broader gauges. GDP per capita adjusted for inflation in 2015 was only 3.4 percent higher than in 2007. And this for the *best*-performing country.

Even looking narrowly at the sustainability of their debt, *all* of the crisis countries have done poorly—and are far worse off than they were before the crisis. From 2007 to 2015, Spain's (gross) debt-to-GDP ratio has increased from 36 percent to an estimated 99 percent, Greece's from 103 percent to 178 percent—and is expected to explode to over 200 percent, Cyprus's debt-to-GDP ratio has increased from 54 percent to 109 percent, and even the star performer Ireland has seen its debt-to-GDP ratio *almost quadruple*, from 24 percent to 95 percent.

But the eurozone programs have been a success, in the sense that the German and French banks have been repaid—some may have even been saved from an early demise—and current account balance has been achieved, necessary if there is to be a transfer of resources from the crisis countries to those that they owe money. Perhaps the real goals of Germany and the other creditor countries have indeed been achieved.

THE NEED FOR GROWTH

European leaders have recognized that Europe's problems will not be solved without growth. But they have failed to explain how growth can be achieved with austerity and with the ill-conceived and often counterproductive structural reform measures they have been pushing. Instead, they argue for restoring confidence, and that the restoration of confidence will bring about a restoration of growth. However, because austerity has destroyed growth and lowered standards of living, it has also destroyed confidence, no matter how many speeches are given about the importance of confidence and growth.

Confidence will only be restored when there are fundamental reforms in the structure of the eurozone itself and in the policies that it has imposed on those partners in the eurozone in crisis. But that, I suspect, will only happen when there is a greater sense of political cohesion and social solidarity than is evident today.

Europe, and especially Germany, which has played a central role in the formulation of these policies, has a quite different take on these policies. Like medieval bloodletters, Germany and its associates in the eurozone argue to stay the course. What is needed, they say, is more austerity and structural reform. This course will only bring a continuation of the current suffering. Things may improve slightly. But by any standard—other than a comparison with the bottom of the downturn—Europe's performance has been dismal, and there is only more in store. Many in the crisis countries have survived only by drawing on their savings, some by selling the family silver, others by selling the family home. But it is a strategy of mere survival, without hope.

We presented in this and the previous chapter an alternative to what Europe has done, *even within the confines of most of its current rules*. Even within its strictures, there were policy choices that could have been made; those that were made exacerbated the downturns, making them longer and deeper, with far more suffering. These rules didn't dictate the speed with which fiscal balance had to be restored. Just as Greece has become the poster child for bad behavior by a eurozone member, the Greek program has become the poster child for the mistakes of the Troika. The eurozone rules didn't dictate that Greece would be instructed to go from its huge fiscal deficit to an unconscionably high 4.5 percent surplus in *very* few years. Nor did they dictate the harsh foreclosure policies, pushing an increasing fraction of Greece into poverty. So, too, for the structural reforms. As an alternative to the trivial, distracting, and counterproductive reforms pushed by the Troika, there were meaningful reforms that might have set Greece on the path toward shared prosperity. It would still not be as rich as Germany, but it would not be facing the abject poverty and depression it faces now.

There is nothing in this alternative program that required a Nobel Prize to construct, nothing based on information not already available to the eurozone authorities at the time they designed their programs.

Rereading the successive Memorandum of Agreement between Greece and the Troika, one is bewildered: their forecasts were consistently so wrong, but made with such conviction. In the first and succeeding memorandum, they would write, "the design of the programme makes it robust to a number of unfavourable developments.... The fiscal programme is based on conservative assumptions.... The fiscal adjustment is fairly distributed across the society, and protects the most vulnerable.... The recovery strategy takes into account the need for social justice and fairness, both across and within generations.... The Greek programme rests upon very strong foundations." Was it irrational optimism, a belief that things would really work out that way? Or bureaucrat hypocrisy—they knew what they were supposed to say, and the incongruence between the world and these words was of little moment. Call it cognitive dissonance run wild, or dishonesty, as you will.

There is something in the last memorandum, signed soon after the

Greek voters had rejected essentially the same program by an over-whelming vote of 61 percent, a vote supported by the Greek govern-ment, which provides more than a hint that it was sheer hypocrisy: the agreement begins by affirming, "Success requires ownership of the reform agenda programme by the Greek authorities," and suggest-ing that there is that ownership.

As I looked at these programs, I saw the same two forces that had constructed the failed IMF programs in so many of the countries around the world that I described in *Globalization and Its Discontents*—corporate and financial interests in alignment with and supported by ideology; but this time it is playing out within the very borders of Europe.

While the Troika could have crafted a program that worked—or at least one that failed less badly—the structure of the eurozone itself made the tasks difficult at best.

This, then, is the situation facing the eurozone: they have con-structed a monetary arrangement characterized by divergence rather than convergence, where crises are likely not to be rare occurrences—not once in a lifetime events to be studied in history courses, but frequent events that have to be constantly dealt with. And the interests and ideology of the dominant powers have propa-gated policies that are extraordinarily painful for those within the crisis countries. The first crises were fomenting within the euro's first decade. Even then, there was a mixture of causes, reflecting the eurozone's diversity, associated with public sector profligacy in only one (Greece), but private sector misdeeds and misallocations in oth-ers, and bad luck, with economic fortunes turning against them, in still others. While some in northern Europe like to blame the prob-lems of those in the south, Ireland and Finland are reminders that culture and geography are not the driving forces. Finland, with one of its leading firms, Nokia, facing problems—and with a recession in its neighboring country Russia—is expected to have a GDP per capita in 2017 that is less than 93 percent of that a decade earlier. The eurozone system does not even work for the hardworking, well-educated, highly disciplined Finns.

And since the countries of Europe are all tied together, even the well-performing economies will be dragged down. The double-dip recessions are no surprise. It is not a pretty picture. And of this we can be sure: the reforms made since the beginning of the euro crisis do not suffice; some, in the half-finished state that they are likely to remain for years, may make matters worse.

THE COUNTERFACTUAL

Even defenders of the eurozone's austerity and misconceived structural reform policies have to admit that things have not gone as had been anticipated. In the discussions prior to the euro, it was thought there was a trade-off: a single currency would bring higher growth (for instance, by lowering interest rates, because of the reduction of exchange rate risk), but there would be slower adjustment to a disturbance. Chapter 3 showed that for the eurozone as a whole there was no burst of growth after the launch of the euro, but that after the crisis, performance was dismal. The evidence suggests that the benefits were nil, but the costs—as the crisis was managed—were palpable.

Still, some ask: Wouldn't things have been even worse for Greece and the other crisis countries were it not for the euro and the help that these countries got from their eurozone partners? Economists refer to such matters as counterfactual history: We know what has happened. We can only speculate about what might have been.

Of course, in the years preceding the creation of the euro, not everything had gone smoothly. There was exchange-rate volatility. Some countries faced bouts of high inflation. Post-fascist Spain had had high unemployment. Many were buffeted by the same global forces that led to episodic recessions. Still, none suffered as they have suffered in the euro crisis. Take Greece, the poster child for what has gone wrong. Looking at the IMF database since 1980 (the last 35 years), its deepest downturns prior to the euro were in 1981–1983, when the economy shrank almost 4 percent, and 1987 and 1993, when it shrank by 2.3 and 1.6 percent, respectively. But in the euro crisis, in a single year, the economy shrank by 8.9 percent (2011), and that was followed by year after year of continued contraction. Greece had had bouts of unemployment—it reached 12.1 percent in 1999. But that was less than half of its peak above 27 percent in 2013.

The cost-benefit ratio as the euro has been managed for the crisis countries is clear: slight benefits during the short span of time between the establishment of the euro and the 2008 crisis as they benefited from the flood of money coming in, creating the imbalances from which they would subsequently suffer so much, but far outweighed by the costs in the years after the crisis.

Had they known back in 1992, when they signed up for the euro, what they know now—and had the people of Europe been given a chance to vote on joining the euro—it is hard to see how they could have supported it. But that is a different question from that confronting Europe today. That question is, having created the euro, where do they go from here?

The next four chapters describe *what has to be done.*

PART IV

A WAY FORWARD?

9

CREATING A EUROZONE THAT WORKS

The euro can and should be saved—but not at any cost. Not at the costs of the recessions and depressions that have afflicted the eurozone, the high unemployment, the ruined lives, the destroyed aspirations. It doesn't have to be this way. One can create a eurozone that works, that promotes prosperity and advances the cause of European integration.

The halfway house in which Europe finds itself is unsustainable: there either has to be "more Europe" or "less"; there has to be either more economic and political integration or a dissolution of the eurozone in its current form.

Those who originally promoted the euro realized that in its original stage, it was incomplete, and that more would have to be done. A successful euro required—and would lead to—"more Europe." And more has been done. But what has been done so far is not nearly enough. What is required is not beyond the grasp of Europe—most of what is entailed has already been widely recognized. But it requires "more Europe" than the existing arrangement, and certainly "more Europe" than those who say that the eurozone is not a transfer union are willing to countenance.

The reforms in structure and policy that I describe will make the kinds of crises that have become a regular feature of the eurozone less frequent and less severe; but there still may be crises. I argue that a quite different set of emergency policies would be of benefit to the eurozone as a whole, but especially to the crisis countries. The depressions that have marked the euro crisis, with their long lasting effects, are avoidable.

REFORMING THE STRUCTURE OF THE EUROZONE

Reforms of the structure of the eurozone itself should aim at an economic system that can simultaneously achieve full employment and robust growth in *each* of the member countries with sustainable current account deficits in the *absence* of flexible exchange rates and independent monetary policies. There needs to be *a fundamental commitment of the eurozone to maintain the economies at full employment.* Markets do not on their own maintain full employment, and markets on their own are not in general stable. In the absence of government intervention, there can be persistent unemployment and high instability.

Most critics of the euro crisis policies have focused on austerity, and rightly so. But without appropriate reforms in the *structure* of the eurozone—the institutions, rules, and regulations that govern it—restoring the countries to full employment will lead to unmanageable current account deficits. We saw how the eurozone's current structure leads to divergence and actually creates current account deficits and crises. The eurozone needs to be reformed so that *all* countries within the eurozone can attain and maintain full employment. The current eurozone structure does not allow this. As we saw in the previous chapter, while the programs that have been imposed on the crisis countries are intended to eventually lead the country back to full employment, the path is extraordinarily costly with uncertain success. What is certain is that these programs will lower the crisis countries' potential growth for years to come. It is also certain that these programs have other effects, such as increasing divisiveness within and between countries and giving rise to unpalatable political dynamics.

Six structural changes—changes in the basic rules governing the eurozone and their shared economic frameworks—are essential.

STRUCTURAL REFORM #1:
A BANKING UNION

This reform is one on which the European leaders already agree. A common banking system—a banking union—entails more than common supervision; it entails common deposit insurance and common procedures for what should be done with banks that cannot meet their obligations (called common resolution).[1] Of these three, the most important is a common deposit insurance fund. Without it, money will flow from the banking system of "weak" countries to the banks in strong countries, weakening further those already having problems. But without a common regulatory system, there is the worry that a system with a common deposit insurance scheme could be open to abuse. But, as I explain below, a common regulatory system has to be *well designed*, so that it can encourage expansion in those countries that need it and constrain lending in overheated economies. Later, we will explain how this can be done.

Without such flexibility, broadening mandates and instruments, a common regulatory framework will act as an *automatic destabilizer*—that is, when the economy is weak, it makes the economy even weaker. Indeed, chapter 5 showed that under the current system, the *private austerity* arising from the contraction of bank lending was a key contributor to the depressions in the crisis countries. But inflexible implementation of banking regulations would exacerbate the already present downturn: In any economic downturn, there is an increase in nonperforming loans (defaults). If regulators respond rigidly,[2] banks will be forced to contract lending, and that will exacerbate the economic downturn. While rigid enforcement of standards makes sense for a bank in isolation, when weaknesses are a reflection of an economic downturn, it's counterproductive: the economic slowdown arising from decreased lending will lead to even more defaults, in a downward vicious spiral.[3]

The incongruence between the pace of markets and that of politics presents a problem for the euro's survival. Many European leaders recognize that *eventually* a single banking framework, with common regulations, deposit insurance, and resolution, will be necessary. But others argue that such a dramatic reform must be done carefully, in a step-by-step process. First, there must be common regulations, and when the regulatory system has been "proven," Europe can go on to the next stage(s).[4] Were there not an ongoing crisis, such an argument would have merit. But those with capital in, say, the Spanish banks will not wait: the benefits of waiting are nil, the risks are substantial. And so, while European leaders dither, the banking system will be weakened, and with the weakening of the banking system, there will be a weakening of the economies.[5] And there can be strong effects: once the capital has left the country, once the banking system has been weakened, it may take a long time to restore the banking system and the country to health.

STRUCTURAL REFORM #2: MUTUALIZATION OF DEBT

Just as creating a banking union is necessary if there is not to be divergent and destabilizing movements in capital, some form of mutualization of debt is necessary if there is not to be divergent movements in labor. *Place-based* debt makes little sense in a world in which individuals are mobile; individuals can simply walk away from debts incurred by their parents or by profligate politicians or by misguided decisions of the ECB. The movements in population are not only destabilizing, they are inefficient—undermining the very rationale for free mobility of labor.

Mutualization of debt could be accomplished through a number of institutional mechanisms, such as having the ECB issue a Eurobond underwritten by the eurozone as a whole with the revenues on-lent to different eurozone countries. There are already proposals on how to design such a system, in a way that won't lead to excessive borrowing.[6] The amount of mutualized debt could be limited, with safety valves for debt associated with cyclical fluctuations, recognizing that when a country goes into a recession it may be desirable to run a large deficit. The funds coming in from the new debt issues could be spent only on investments in, for example, infrastructure or education. There could be a requirement, too, that, except when the economy is in recession, any increase in debt over a certain level be subject to a referendum within the country.

The position of some in Europe against such mutualization—claiming that Europe is not a transfer union—is wrong on two counts:

1. It exaggerates the risk of default, at least the risks of default *if* debt is mutualized. At low interest rates, most of the crisis countries should have no trouble servicing their debts. Of course, in the absence of debt mutualization, there is a serious risk of partial default (which has already happened in the case of Greece). The irony is that existing arrangements may actually lead to larger losses on the part of creditor countries than a system of well-designed mutualization.
2. Any system of successful economic integration must involve some assistance from the stronger countries to the weaker. Recognizing this, Europe itself has provided substantial funds to new entrants. (These are called the Structural Funds and Cohesion Fund and include multiple programs.) One program, the European Regional Development Fund, provides €40.2 billion to Poland, the top recipient, from 2014 to 2020.[7]

The reforms just described are key to preventing divergence. Later in this chapter, I will describe further structural and policy reforms designed to promote convergence.

STRUCTURAL REFORM #3: A COMMON
FRAMEWORK FOR STABILITY

Europe faces two further paramount questions: (1) how to promote stability of the eurozone as a whole; and (2) how to ensure that *all* of the countries of the eurozone do well. As we have noted, for instance, the Maastricht restrictions on fiscal deficits can effectively be an automatic destabilizer. As tax revenues plummet, when the 3 percent deficit target is breached, there have to be cutbacks in expenditures, which lead to further declines in GDP.[8]

The current automatic destabilizers need to be replaced by automatic stabilizers at the eurozone level. We'll shortly provide examples.

Even with reforms that enabled the eurozone as a whole to have stable output and employment *on average*, there will remain significant differences among countries—some will be in recession, while others are in a boom. With the exchange rate and interest rate no longer in the tool kit, other tools will have to be found to ensure that *each* of the countries in the eurozone remains prosperous.

There are six parts of a stability reform agenda. The first involves a fundamental reform of the Maastricht convergence criteria. Second, a new growth pact supported by a European *solidarity fund for stabilization*—akin to earlier European solidarity funds provided for new entrants into the EU that we mentioned above. Third, a commitment to *progressive automatic stabilizers* that increase spending automatically when the country faces a downturn—and a corresponding ban on automatic destabilizers. Fourth, enhancing the flexibility with which monetary policy can respond to in an economic slowdown within any country. Fifth, in recognition of the fact that markets on their own may *create* instability, instituting regulations that try to control market-generated instability. And sixth, more active countercyclical fiscal policies, reducing the burden that has been imposed on monetary policies in recent years.

[1] A COMMON FISCAL FRAMEWORK— BEYOND A SUICIDE PACT

If the eurozone is to work—that is, if it is to provide a framework within which countries can prosper and countries can *persistently* attain full employment—the first necessary reform is a common fiscal framework. This reform will require more than, and fundamentally differs from, an austerity pact or even a strengthened version of the Stability and Growth Pact—the "reform" that Germany seems to have had in mind, as it calls for stricter enforcement of more stringent budgetary rules. The Germans have emphasized the need for *all* the countries of Europe to follow the rules—and in particular the budgetary constraints (the 3 percent limit on deficits). They worry that without such rules, strongly enforced, there will be economic chaos—the eurozone won't be able to function. Germany's stance is predicated on the belief that profligate government spending leads to crises—and that it led to the current eurozone crisis. That is simply wrong.

Better budget rules

One can still have fiscal discipline by focusing on the structural deficit—what the deficit would be if the economy were at full employment. Many of the crisis countries' deficits would appear in a markedly different light when looked at from this perspective.[9] The most important reform, however, involves creating a *capital budget*, distinguishing between government spending on consumption from that on investment, with constraints on spending centered on consumption. A government should behave not like the Swabian housewife but like the modern firm—which looks at its balance sheet and undertakes debt if the returns on the investments that it finances exceed the cost of capital.

[2] A SOLIDARITY FUND FOR STABILIZATION

Addressing the underlying problems of Europe is at its core a *collective action problem* for Europe, requiring European-wide resources—more resources than are currently available to the afflicted countries.

A year after the beginning of the Greek crisis, it was already apparent that the austerity measures imposed at the very beginning were not helping the economy recover. The leaders of Europe had committed themselves to helping Greece grow. They obviously didn't do that, and one of the reasons is that they lacked the tools. They had set aside funds to help rescue banks and countries that were in trouble, in the European Stability Mechanism.[10] But it was focused on the moment of crisis itself, when a bank was collapsing or a country was shut out of capital markets.

Even for the crisis countries that have done everything that they were told to do, the return to prosperity has been slow. What is needed is enough funding to help countries facing adverse shocks to maintain full employment and grow again. This means, for instance, common funding for unemployment insurance, especially the abnormal expenditures associated with a deep downturn.[11] The solidarity fund for stabilization could be used to fund unemployment and other cyclically related social expenditures and to support active labor market policies that help move people into new jobs in a restructured economy.

Even with a successful banking union and common deposit insurance, banks in crisis countries are likely to be weak. The contraction in bank lending is particularly hard on small and medium-size enterprises, which depend on banks for finance. As they are cut off from funding, they have to lay off workers—reinforcing the downward cycle.[12] What is thus needed is a European-wide *small and medium-size lending facility*, like the United States' Small Business Administration, which provides loans and/or partial guarantees for small business loans; and it should target its lending particularly to countries or regions within a country where there is a shortage of SME lending and/or the economy is showing particular weakness.[13]

Expanding existing European institutions

Some of the existing European institutions could make a contribution to stability, especially if this was seen as part of their mandate. The European Investment Bank is the largest multilateral lending institution,[14] a European-wide institution that has successfully financed infrastructure projects around the region. While it already sees itself as having a countercyclical role, that aspect of its mission could clearly be greatly strengthened.[15]

Mutual insurance

I have described a variety of forms of support that Europe as a whole could provide to countries with significant economic downturns. One country might be the recipient at one time, but be among the large contributors at another—a quick look at the history of rankings in growth rates in Europe demonstrates the large variability in standings. We have already noted that many of the crisis countries grew faster in the years before the crisis than the eurozone grew as a whole. So, too, for others—for example, from 1995 to 2000, not only did Ireland, Spain, and Greece grow much faster than Germany (with growth rates of 10.1 percent, 4.1 percent, and 3.6 percent, respectively), but so did France (2.9 percent) and Italy (2.0 percent). Germany grew at a rate of just 1.9 percent. Among those countries, Germany also placed second to last from 2000 to 2005 (when it averaged 0.5 percent).

(3) AUTOMATIC STABILIZERS

The third part of a fiscal pact for stability focuses on creating automatic stabilizers, so that when the economy faces a downturn, money is injected into the system *automatically*. Unemployment insurance is an example. Normally, as workers lose their jobs from a negative "shock"—for example, a decrease in the demand for exports—they cut back their spending, so that the effects get *multiplied*. But if workers are protected with unemployment insurance, this multiplier is short-circuited.

In countries with flexible exchange rates, the exchange rate can act as an automatic stabilizer; a country facing a problem will see its exchange rate decline, and that will encourage exports and discourage imports, increasing national income. But in joining the euro, countries gave up this automatic stabilizer, making it all the more important to strengthen other automatic stabilizers (like progressive taxation and good unemployment schemes and other forms of social insurance). Unfortunately, in recent years, these automatic stabilizers have been weakened. Indeed, the worry is that automatic amplifiers (destabilizers) have been or are being put in place. In particular, earlier, we noted that stringent enforcement of capital adequacy standards for banks would act as an automatic destabilizer, and even more so in the absence of a common deposit insurance system. These are among the reasons that Europe's current approach to creating a banking union—first having common regulation and supervision, and then, gradually, perhaps, common deposit insurance—is unlikely to work for the foreseeable future.

[4] FLEXIBILITY IN CREDIT CREATION

Previous chapters have described how the existing eurozone acts as an automatic destabilizer in so many ways. One of the worst is through credit: the current design leads to large *pro-cyclical* movements in credit, especially to small and medium-size enterprises. That is, credit declines when the country goes into trouble, increasing the depth of the downturn. Some such changes are natural: firms in a slowing economy will need less money to expand. But the problem in the eurozone is that those small businesses that do want to expand— they may have customers abroad, for instance—can't get the finance they need. Some can't even get the working capital they need to function. Lack of finance is part of the process of strangulation of the economy; chapter 5 noted that the failure to account adequately for the resulting private austerity may help explain why Troika predictions have so consistently been off the mark. If there is to be stability in the eurozone, this *has* to be reversed.

The eurozone took away two forms of flexibility: in the exchange rate and in the interest rate. But while it is inevitable that the ECB set a single interest rate for the eurozone as a whole, there doesn't have to be the same rigidity in the application of regulatory standards, especially when it comes to *macro-prudential regulations*—that is, regulations aimed at stabilizing the overall economy. There needs to be not just a broad mandate, to focus on employment, growth, and stability, but also more *flexibility* in the way that the eurozone's banking system is run. Capital requirements (the amount of capital banks have to hold, in relationship to their lending) can be tightened in those countries (regions) facing excess demand. This would force a reduction in lending, which in turn would dampen inflationary pressures there. Similarly, capital requirements could be loosened in those countries facing weak demand. This will strengthen lending, stimulating the economies that need it.

There are a host of other regulatory provisions that can be adjusted according to the macroeconomic circumstances of the particular country or region. As another example, lending standards for mortgages should, for instance, be tightened at a place or time where there appears to be the risk of a bubble forming.[16] The key is that there needs to be more *flexibility* in the way that the eurozone's banking system is run.

One of the major lessons of the 2008 crisis was that earlier notions of monetary policy were misconceived—they were not only excessively narrow in the mandates that they imposed on central banks but also in the instruments that they provided (suggesting, for instance, that the only instrument should be the short-term interest rate); and even when the need for more tools was recognized, the need for flexibility in their use was not. A key reform for creating a viable euro is creating an ECB and European financial regulatory authorities with broader mandates and more instruments, that are more flexibly managed.

[5] REGULATING THE ECONOMY TO PREVENT EXCESSES

As we've seen, in several eurozone countries recent downturns have been a result of real estate bubbles breaking—these bubbles were the result of private sector failures, of a kind that have repeatedly occurred. Excessive credit expansion and excessive risk-taking is frequently the source of economic volatility; financial markets on their own are simply not stable. In other words, an important part of preventing recessions and depressions is to prevent the excesses that give rise to them. Successful control of this excessive expansion needs to be a joint undertaking of the ECB, banking regulators and supervisors, and the broader regulators of the financial system. This won't be possible in the regime of "light" or "self"-regulation that prevailed prior to 2008. It won't be possible either if the ECB only focuses on inflation, as conventionally defined. There are tools that the ECB and financial regulators already have, or should have, that can prevent, or at least control the size of, these bubbles.[17]

[6] STABILIZING FISCAL POLICIES

While the proximate cause of so much of the economic volatility that has afflicted market economies is the excesses of the financial sector, in some cases central banks *condone*, if not instigate, this bad behavior. After the tech bubble broke in the early 2000s in the United States, aggregate demand slumped. Politics seemingly did not allow the construction of an effective fiscal surplus, putting the burden on monetary policy; and the United States resorted to the favorite instrument, lowering interest rates. The Bush administration was enthralled with deregulation, and the combination of low interest rates and deregulation was a toxic cocktail. Ben Bernanke and Alan Greenspan, both former chairs of the Federal Reserve, may have been pleased at the scorecard by which central bank governors are usually judged: inflation was low (largely the result of China's low and competitive prices along with its exchange-rate policy of stable and slow appreciation) and the economy was near full employment. But if one dug deeper, it was obvious that they had turned a blind eye to the excesses that were building up. The same can be said for Willem Frederik "Wim" Duisenberg and Jean-Claude Trichet, the first two governors of the ECB, during whose terms the imbalances that created the euro crisis occurred.

One cannot simply leave the burden of macro-adjustment on monetary policy, regardless of how much faith the neoliberals have in this instrument if it is used correctly (to stabilize inflation). Fiscal policy, directed at needed investments, needs to be put more in the center of macro-stabilization. The United States and the EU both need large amounts of investment for retrofitting their economies for global warming. Both need large investments in education and technology, if there are going to be continuing increases in standards of living. Reduced investments in basic research (as a percentage of GDP) may well result in a slower pace of innovation in the future. Recently, Robert Gordon[18] has suggested that we are moving into an era of a much slower pace of increase in standards of living. But this is at least in part a consequence of decisions being made, on both sides of the Atlantic, to invest less in basic research, technology, and education: it is from these that future increases in standards of living will largely come. This runs counter, of course, to conservative ideology focused on downsizing the government. Thus, on both sides of the Atlantic, in some countries, the downturn has been met by cutting taxes for corporations and rich individuals matched by cutbacks in government spending. This book has explained why these policies predictably led to lower output today; but when the cutbacks are in critical public investments, they also lead to lower output in the future.[19] The key point is that if fiscal authorities are doing their job well, there will be less pressure on the monetary authorities to create, or at least tolerate, the excesses of which they have so often been a part.[20]

STRUCTURAL REFORM #4: A TRUE CONVERGENCE POLICY—TOWARD STRUCTURAL REALIGNMENT

The absence of the exchange-rate mechanism in Europe means that *real* exchange rates can get out of alignment, as a result of differences in the rates of growth of productivity or prices across countries. This kind of misalignment occurred in the years before the crisis, partly caused by the euro. There are three parts of the strategy to respond, each reflecting part of the analysis of the underlying causes of the misalignment.[21]

(1) DISCOURAGING SURPLUSES

Generally, one would expect the exchange rate of the eurozone as a whole to be such that it achieves current account balance for the region as a whole. Any country or region maintaining large current account surpluses (or deficits) poses a risk for the entire global economic system. That is why the IMF and the international community have continually talked about global imbalances and tried to get countries not to have them. Surpluses pose a risk because for every surplus there *must* be a deficit (that is, if some country exports more than it imports, some other country has to import more than it exports), and deficits have to be financed. There can be a sudden stop, in which those supplying such finance suddenly take the view that there is a significant risk that the loan will not be repaid, and refuse to provide further finance or even to roll over existing loans. These sudden stops are a major source of crises.

But if the eurozone as a whole typically has a zero balance, that means if some country runs its economic policy in ways that result in a surplus, *necessarily* other countries have to have a deficit. The surplus country, in a sense, creates through its actions deficits elsewhere. The surplus countries impose costs on others, an externality, through, in effect, the creation of their deficits. Those trade deficits create, in turn, a risk of instability—for instance, the sudden changes in market moods can result in an abrupt stop in the flow of funds to finance these deficits, setting off a crisis. Even short of a crisis, trade deficits make it more difficult for the deficit countries to achieve full employment, because trade deficits *subtract* from *domestic* aggregate demand—on net, some of the demand is being met not by production at home but by imports—and weak domestic aggregate demand leads to unemployment.[22] To offset the effects of weak aggregate demand, governments in the post-Keynesian world typically resort to government (deficit) spending. Thus, the surplus countries—Germany in particular—can even be thought of as being a fundamental cause of the fiscal and trade deficits and the unsustainable credit expansion in other countries of the eurozone.

One can see this in another way: follow the money. A current account surplus means that a country has to be lending, just as a deficit means that a country has to be borrowing. If the current account of the eurozone as a whole is balanced, it means that the surplus countries (mainly Germany) are, in effect, lending to the deficit countries. If Germany had a surplus (and the eurozone as a whole was balanced), it was *necessary* that the other countries were borrowing. In some cases, it was the public sector that was borrowing, in others the private. But their deficits were just part of the *equilibrium* that followed from Germany's surplus. It was, of course, only a temporary and unstable equilibrium.

I have described how Germany's surpluses thus almost inevitably led to divergence among the countries of the eurozone. This had political as well as economic consequences. It was recognized early on that differences in countries would result in, say, different monetary policies being appropriate for each.[23] That was part of the rationale for policies to promote convergence. Differences in circumstances can also lead to large *political* differences; differences in economic circumstances led to differences in interests. As we noted earlier, no difference is more important than that between a creditor and debtor, and Germany's persistent surpluses converted the basis of the eurozone from solidarity to the conflicting relationship of creditor and debtor.[24]

Europe needs a *true convergence policy*, and such a policy needs to discourage surpluses. Keynes proposed a solution—a tax on surpluses. This tax would not only discourage countries from having a surplus, but the revenues from the tax could be used to help fund the solidarity fund for stabilization outlined earlier in this chapter.[25]

[2] EXPANSIONARY WAGE AND FISCAL POLICIES IN SURPLUS COUNTRIES

There are many policies that the surplus countries undertake that lead to the surpluses. In the case of China, for a long time two policies played a central role: it managed its exchange rate and it controlled wages—for instance, by restricting the scope for unionization. Low wages, in turn, lead to lower prices, and thus a lower *real* exchange rate.

The first tool is, of course, not available to Germany, but the second has been key. In advanced countries, there are a variety of tools for affecting wages, most importantly minimum wages and the legal framework affecting unionization and bargaining. Until recently, Germany did not have a minimum wage, and the absence of the minimum wage puts downward pressure on wages more generally. Under Chancellor Gerhard Schröeder, incomes at the bottom actually fell.[26] While this drop was lauded as making Germany more competitive, these actions are an invidious form of competitive devaluation and beggar-thy-neighbor policy. They gave Germany an advantage over its neighbors, because the social and economic structure of these countries would not tolerate similar inequitable wage reductions. Thus the lowering of Germany's real exchange rate came in part at the expense of its trading partners.[27]

Moreover, the current adjustment framework puts the burden of the adjustment on the deficit country, through what I described earlier as internal devaluation. It is a very costly and very asymmetric adjustment process.[28] It is, however, typically far easier for the surplus country to take actions to reduce its surplus than for the deficit countries to reduce their deficits. In the end, the global imbalance may be eliminated through either route—but the costs of achieving the eventual "balance" can be markedly different.

Not only should surplus countries raise their minimum wages, they should strengthen workers' bargaining rights[29] and engage in expansionary fiscal policies. They have easy access to funding for such expansionary policies. These policies will put some upward pressure on prices (though far from runaway inflation)—and that's exactly the point. There *has* to be an adjustment of the real exchange rate, and these policies achieve that at far lower cost than those of the current eurozone framework.

[3] REVERSING THE OTHER DIVERGENCE POLICIES

In chapter 5, I described several other policies that either create divergence or prevent convergence: for instance, Europe's strictures against industrial policies, which might enable the countries that are behind to catch up.

Rich countries have an advantage over poor ones in many ways. They can, for instance, provide a higher-quality education to their children. Europe can't correct for all these differences—though in the future, with greater solidarity, it can do a far better job. But there are some differences that Europe can and should address now, including differences in the quality of infrastructure. Good infrastructure (partially financed through the European Investment Bank) can help integrate Europe further. Public infrastructure increases the returns to the private sector and thus can have both supply-side and demand multiplier effects.

STRUCTURAL REFORM #5: A EUROZONE STRUCTURE THAT PROMOTES FULL EMPLOYMENT AND GROWTH FOR ALL OF EUROPE—MACROECONOMICS

Even if the eurozone were to manage all of these reforms and if the countries within it were finally to converge—or at least move closer together—full employment or high growth would not be guaranteed. Europe could have a stable economy beset by low growth and high unemployment. Indeed, that is the direction in which Europe seems to have been moving. It feels self-satisfied if it manages to prevent another crisis—even if a quarter of its young people are unemployed, and even if growth is mediocre at best. There are reforms in both the macroeconomic framework of the eurozone and in the eurozone structure itself that would facilitate full employment with sustainable growth. The key *macroeconomic reform* is changing the mandate of the ECB.

In the implementation of an expanded mandate to promote full employment, growth, and economic stability, and not just be fixated on inflation, the ECB should have a particular responsibility to make sure that the financial sector is working in the way it should—not only *not* exposing the economy to huge risks, not only *not* exploiting the rest of the economy, but actually serving society through the provision of credit for productive purposes, such as lending to small and medium-size enterprises.[30] The ECB, like the Fed, has greatly expanded liquidity, yet little of that has gone to create new jobs or make new *real* investments. Much of it has gone to finance investments in fixed assets, like land, providing no stimulus to the economy. Other lending has simply been part of a round-robin in which the central bank transfers money to the banks, which then hold money (reserves) in the central bank. Someone from the outside looking at this whole process would be as mystified by it, just as someone would when looking at the mining sector where large amounts of money and resources are spent digging up gold (with considerable risk to the environment) that is then, at great expense, buried back into the ground in vaults.

STRUCTURAL REFORM #6: STRUCTURAL REFORMS OF THE EUROZONE TO ENSURE FULL EMPLOYMENT AND GROWTH FOR ALL OF EUROPE

Here, I discuss four *common* structural reforms that can help ensure sustainable growth with full employment. Many of these reforms entail moving away from the policy framework of the past third of a century—during which neoliberalism dominated and it was presumed that the freer the market, the better—and recognizing the critical ways in which markets often fail to produce efficient and stable outcomes.

(1) MAKING THE FINANCIAL SYSTEM SERVE SOCIETY

Most of the discussion of financial sector reform (including that above, under Reform #2) has focused on preventing the financial sector from imposing harm on others—for instance, through the instability it has brought to the entire economy as a result of its excessive risk-taking.[31] Little has focused on ensuring that the financial system actually performs the important functions that must be performed if the economy is to function well. It is precisely this failure that is behind the alleged savings glut: Ben Bernanke attempted to blame the weakness in the global economy before the crisis on excessive global savings, especially in China. But even as he spoke about the savings glut, many firms and countries had high-return investment projects that were not being financed. It is not that there is a surfeit of savings. It is that the financial markets have failed in their basic task of recycling the savings, making sure that the savings are used productively. This function is referred

to as "intermediation"—intermediating between savings and investment. Financial systems in both Europe and America have failed to
perform this key role well. Indeed, in the United States, the financial
sector has been engaged in disintermediation, taking money *out* of the
corporate sector, resulting in fewer funds available for investment.
Huge amounts, for instance, are leaving firms in the form of share buybacks—in 2014, some 4 percent of GDP, and in 2015, 3.5 percent.

Moreover, much of the savings is being done by "long-term savers,"
those saving for their retirement or money put aside by countries in
their sovereign wealth funds. Many of the key investment opportunities (infrastructure and technology) are long-term investments.
It is perhaps not a surprise that shortsighted financial markets are
unable to intermediate well between long-term savers and long-term
investments.

There are reforms in the legal, regulatory, and tax frameworks of
Europe that would help focus the financial sector on the long-term—
and on doing what it should do, and not doing what it shouldn't.[32]

[2] REFORMING CORPORATE GOVERNANCE

Firms, too, have become increasingly shortsighted, focusing on quarterly returns. A firm focused on the next quarter won't make important long-term investments in research and technology, in plant and
equipment, and, most importantly, in its employees. A firm that pays
its CEOs and other executives excessively, and distributes too much
to its shareholders through dividends and share buybacks, won't have
enough money left over either to pay its workers decently or to invest
in the future.

While these changes have been less extreme in Europe than in the
United States, the differences are narrowing. Europe has to understand what led to America's short-termism, and to make sure that
it takes actions to ensure that the disease of short-termism doesn't
spread more to Europe.

It is perhaps not a surprise, given the importance of financial markets on both sides of the Atlantic, that the short-term myopia of the financial markets has spread to the rest of the economy. Some of Europe's institutions—like "social partners" stakeholder capitalism, where firms are not exclusively focused on the well-being of shareholders, narrowly defined—have successfully proven a bulwark against the extremes found in the United States, where CEO pay has now risen to be 300 times that of the typical worker.[33]

There are, however, other factors that have contributed to rampant short-termism—for instance, the growth of stock options within the compensation packages of executives. While corporate executives claim that they are an important part of their incentive system, there is in fact little relationship between pay and performance: the stock of an airline will go up, for instance, when the price of oil goes down. Stocks more generally go up when the interest rate decreases. The growth of stock options in turn is related to deficiencies in corporate governance and in the rules governing transparency and disclosure.[34] Many shareholders do not realize the extent to which CEO stock options have diluted the value of their holdings. Again, there is a rich and important agenda to reform the "rules of the game."[35] This rewriting of the rules in ways that might result in firms focusing on the long-term would lead to an economy with higher and more stable growth.

[3] A SUPER-CHAPTER 11 FOR BANKRUPTCY

A regular feature of capitalism is that firms and households get too indebted; they need a fresh start. That's why virtually every modern economy has a bankruptcy law, a procedure for the orderly discharge and restructuring of debt.

When, however, there is an economic downturn, such as has plagued Europe for the last several years, then *many* firms and households wind up overindebted. In the United States, there is an expedited procedure for firms to go through bankruptcy; their debt is written down quickly, so that the firm can continue producing and jobs are not lost. This is called Chapter 11. When many firms and households are simultaneously going bankrupt, it is even more important to have an expedited process—a super–Chapter 11. For in the absence of such an expedited process, there can be economic paralysis. Such a super–Chapter 11 is particularly important in the crisis countries right now.[36]

[4] PROMOTING ENVIRONMENTAL INVESTMENTS

A eurozone that works has to have not just high growth but sustainable growth, and sustainability entails not just economic sustainability but environmental sustainability. Once one recognizes the huge investments that are needed to retrofit the economy for climate change, one sees the foolishness of any claims that there is a "savings glut." But, as we have seen, it will be hard to incentivize firms to make "green investments" if there is no price of carbon—that is, if those who pollute are not forced to pay the consequences of their pollution. That is why it is important for there to be a high, European-wide price of carbon.[37]

STRUCTURAL REFORM #7: A COMMITMENT TO SHARED PROSPERITY

One of the central problems facing the advanced world today is the increase in inequality. As we have noted, inequality affects the performance of the economy in numerous ways. But the eurozone framework limits what can be done to address it.

Free mobility of capital and goods without tax harmonization not only can lead to an inefficient allocation of capital but it can also reduce the potential for redistributive taxation, leading to high levels of after-tax and transfer inequality and in some instances, even market income inequality. Competition among jurisdictions can be healthy, but there can also be a race to the bottom. Capital goes to the jurisdiction that taxes it at the lowest rate, not where its marginal productivity is the highest. To compete, other jurisdictions must lower the taxes they impose on capital. Thus, the scope for redistributive taxation is reduced. (A similar argument applies to skilled labor.)

The eurozone's structure has not only led to more money (after tax) at the top but also to more people in poverty at the bottom. As the crises in Spain, Greece, Portugal, and elsewhere illustrate, it is the poor who suffer the most from instability.[38] Moreover, one of the major factors contributing to increasing inequality is high unemployment, such as has arisen in all of the crisis countries. The failure of the eurozone to create a true *stability* framework has thus contributed to inequality.

The EU (and this analysis thus goes beyond the eurozone) must adopt two further sets of policies: First, it needs to limit the race to the bottom, the kind of tax competition that worked so well for a few countries like Luxembourg but at the expense of others. This is a real example of an externality—of an action by one country that imposes harms on others. And yet Europe has failed to take adequate action, partially because many in Europe are enamored of the idea of low taxes and a small state, and this kind of race to the bottom suits them fine.

Secondly, given the easy mobility around the European Union, the major responsibility for redistribution must lie at the EU level.[39] The EU should follow the United States in levying taxes based on citizenship, wherever individuals are domiciled or resident. And they should impose an EU level tax on all incomes over a certain threshold, say €250,000, at a modest rate like 15 percent. The funds could be used to bankroll efforts, such as resettlement of migrants or foreign assistance. This would perhaps do far more to create political integration in Europe than the euro itself.

A true *growth and stability* agenda interacts strongly with other elements of the reform agenda: the only sustainable prosperity is shared prosperity.

REFORMS IN "CRISIS POLICY"

These structural reforms are *necessary* for the long-run viability of the eurozone. But they will not be sufficient. Even with a well-designed eurozone structure, there will be shocks that lead some of the countries within the eurozone into a recession. It should be obvious from previous chapters that how Europe has responded has typically exacerbated the downturns rather than restored the afflicted countries quickly to full employment. Dismal policies lead to dismal results. It is imperative that there be a set of reforms in the policies for crisis countries. But as we noted earlier, even the best of policies won't work unless they are accompanied by (or preceded by) the structural reforms I've described.

THE IMPORTANCE OF DISCRETION AND FLEXIBILITY

There are two important aspects of the policy framework that I have noted briefly earlier. Germany has emphasized the importance of *obeying the rules*. Of course, obeying the *wrong* rules can lead to disaster—the wrong rules within the eurozone have led to its poor economic performance.

But it is hard to design a set of rules that is appropriate for all countries, in all circumstances. Indeed, we need to admit the limitations in our knowledge. And even if we had a policy framework that was ideal for the economy of 1990, that framework may not be appropriate in 2016.

In its response to the euro crisis, the Troika in fact exercised considerable discretion, but their choices have been frequently wrong—too frequently, in too many important areas. At the time that they imposed the programs, they exuded enormous confidence: they seemed to believe that they knew precisely the consequence of each policy. Afterward, the IMF has often owned up to the mistakes—but the other members of the Troika have been less forthcoming.

If the eurozone is to work, it has to recognize the large differences among the countries, and policy frameworks have to be sufficiently flexible to accommodate these differences. There has to be a greater ability to adapt to differences in economic circumstances and beliefs.[40]

Some countries, for instance, are more committed to equality than others. Some are more worried about the consequences of unemployment than others. Even within the United States, each state has wide discretion to pursue different policies. The basic principles are understood: those arenas that do not give rise to external effects on other countries should be reserved to the individual countries. (This principle is sometimes referred to within the European Union as subsidiarity.) Some aspects of harmonization may have some slight economic benefit, but there is still a social cost in reducing the country's own degree of discretion. Getting the right balance is difficult. But at least in some areas, the programs that have been imposed on the crisis countries have *excessively* reduced their economic sovereignty, with little justification in terms of reducing adverse externalities.

Below, I discuss two necessary changes in the policy frameworks for addressing countries in crisis.

CRISIS POLICY REFORM #1: FROM AUSTERITY TO GROWTH

European leaders have recognized that Europe's problems will not be solved without growth. But they have failed to explain how growth can be achieved with austerity. Instead, they assert that what is needed is a restoration of confidence. Austerity will not bring about either growth or confidence. Europe's sorry record of failed policies—after repeated attempts to fashion patchwork solutions for economic problems it was misdiagnosing—have undermined confidence.[41]

The reforms to the structure of the eurozone that I described earlier—including the mutualization of debt, the banking union, and the solidarity fund for stabilization—would provide space for a return to growth: there could be a mutually reinforcing expansion of government spending on, say, growth-enhancing public investments. This could be coupled with government assistance for private lending that would support private investments.

There are two further aspects of this policy reform.[42]

[1]RECOGNIZING THE LIMITS OF MONETARY POLICY: THE CONCERTED USE OF FISCAL POLICY

Europe, like the United States, has relied on monetary policy in its response to the recent economic crises. It has more than relied on monetary policy: both in the United States and Europe, there has been austerity. Monetary policy simply can't fill the void. And the reliance on monetary policy has resulted in even greater inequality: the big winners are the wealthy, who own stocks and other assets that have increased in value as a result of low interest rates and QE; the big losers are the elderly, who put their money into government bonds, only to see the interest rates generated virtually disappear. In Europe and America, there has been mediocre growth, stagnation, and the beginning of what I predicted in my book *Freefall* would be the "Great Malaise," now also called the "New Mediocre" by the IMF.

Indeed, the reliance on monetary policy is setting the economy up for future problems. Because the credit channel hasn't been fixed, too much of the liquidity that has been created has gone to creating bubbles, threatening future economic stability. For those firms that have access to capital at low interest rates, even though wages have stagnated, in some cases the cost of capital has fallen even more, inducing these firms to use more capital-intensive techniques of production, contributing, over the long run, to unemployment.

[2] RECOGNIZING THE PRINCIPLE OF THE BALANCED-BUDGET MULTIPLIER

Even with restrictions on the size of the deficit, the government can stimulate the economy: increases in spending matched by increases in taxes increases GDP, because the stimulative effect of the spending is greater than the contractionary effect of the (corresponding amount of) taxes. And if the spending and taxes are chosen carefully—say, welfare payments for the poor and inheritance taxes of the rich—then the multiplier can be large, that is, the increase in GDP can be a multiple of the increased spending. Public investments in infrastructure and technology may increase the returns on private investments, and thus stimulate it. Indeed, there are some taxes, like pollution taxes, that can even stimulate the economy even as they improve societal well-being by improving the environment: a tax on carbon emissions, for instance, will induce firms to spend money on emission-reducing investments. Other taxes, like those on luxury cars (all of which are imported into a country such as Greece) improve the country's current account by discouraging such imports; improve the distribution of income—since taxes on these goods are only paid by the rich; and may promote domestic employment, since they encourage shifting of spending from these imported goods to other goods, some of which are produced by the country itself.

Unfortunately, as we noted in chapter 7, the hidden (and in many cases, not so hidden) agenda of much of neoliberalism has been simply to reduce the size of government.

CRISIS POLICY REFORM #2: TOWARD DEBT RESTRUCTURING

For most eurozone economies, these reforms would, for now, suffice. But there may be some (like Greece) where the cumulative impact of past mistakes—their own and those forced upon them—is such that more is needed.

The high debt represents a stranglehold on the country's growth. In the past, there have been three ways that countries have dealt with high debt-to-GDP ratios. Many countries have engaged in inflation, so that the real value of the debt declines. This is particularly effective if the debt is long-term. A second way is to grow the economy: If GDP goes up, the debt-to-GDP ratio goes down. Debt becomes *relatively* unimportant.

But as we've seen, the eurozone has taken these two strategies out of the tool kit. The ECB won't allow inflation, and the Troika won't allow indebted governments to spend in order to invest in their country's future. (Indeed, as we've seen, the austerity programs have lowered GDP, thus making existing levels of debt less sustainable—explaining how debt-to-GDP ratios are consistently worse now than they were at the beginning of the crisis.)[43] That leaves only the third alternative, debt restructuring. Debt restructuring is an essential part of capitalism. As we have noted, typically, a country has a bankruptcy law that facilitates the restructuring of debts in an orderly way. After the Argentine crisis, there were calls for the creation of a sovereign-debt restructuring mechanism—one of President George W. Bush's many sins was to veto that initiative. In the subsequent years, when there were no sovereign-debt crises, there was little concern about the issue.[44]

If some country needs debt restructuring to enhance growth, it should be done quickly and deeply. It is important that the debt write-down be deep—otherwise, lingering uncertainty about the possibility of another debt restructuring will cast a pall over the recovery. By the same token, as we noted earlier, the costs to the economies doing the restructuring may be less than widely assumed and the benefits can be significant. Both theory and evidence suggest that countries which do such restructuring can later regain access to global financial markets, often quickly;[45] but even if, going forward, countries have to rely on themselves, rather than turning to foreigners for funds, any adverse consequences may be far less than the benefits they receive from immediate debt restructuring. A deep debt restructuring provides more fiscal space for expansionary policies, so long as the government does not have a primary deficit. Money that would have been sent abroad to service the debt stays at home.

Argentina has also shown that there is life after debt and that there are large benefits to the reform of monetary arrangements. With these changes, Argentines escaped a years-long death trap where unemployment had soared as high as 22.5 percent in 2002—levels approaching those in Greece today; after the changes, Argentina's GDP grew at an average of 8.7 percent from 2003 to 2007 until the global financial crisis and unemployment came down to an estimated 6.5 percent in 2015.

Because of the uncertainty about future growth, and therefore of whether a given level of debt is really sustainable, GDP-indexed bonds—which pay off more if the country does well—can be useful in a debt restructuring. Such bonds represent an effective form of risk-sharing between a country and its lenders. These can be thought of, at the sovereign level, as the equivalent of the conversion of debt into equity at the corporate level.[46] These bonds have a further advantage: they align the interests of creditors and debtors. With GDP-linked bonds, Greece's creditors do better if Greece does better. Under current arrangements, Greece bears all of the consequences of the mistaken policies imposed on it from outside. With GDP-linked bonds, creditors like Germany would have an incentive to think twice about these policies.

CONCLUDING COMMENTS

I have outlined a set of changes to the structure and policies of the eurozone that would enable the eurozone to work—to bring shared prosperity to this region. In one sense, they are modest. They fall far short of the degree of economic and political integration that defines the United States and other federal structures sharing a common currency. But what is required is far more than what exists today.

I have focused on *economic reforms* that would result in convergence among the European countries and create shared prosperity. These changes would at least hold open the promise of an increase in solidarity among European countries, rather than the divisiveness that has marked recent years. Especially the joint projects—such as infrastructure projects linking Europe closer together and the solidarity funds for stabilization—are likely to promote political integration. But more needs to be done.[47] The teaching of history in school, for example, should be broadened so that students learn not just about the legacy of strife in Europe, but also about the continent's joint battles to establish human rights and democracy.

The euro was supposed to set the stage for further political integration. Many thought it would speed up such integration. Today, we have noted, it is having just the opposite effect. Some suggested that Europe had put the cart before the horse. Closer political integration, with a broader consensus on what good policies look like, is more likely to make a common currency system viable. There are a host of political reforms, widely discussed within Europe, that would strengthen the EU and the eurozone—often, however, at the expense of the politicians who dominate today on the national stages. Not surprisingly, many of these reforms are resisted by politicians who prefer the security of being "a big fish in a small pond" to the prospect of playing an uncertain role in a politically more important EU/eurozone. It was simply naïve to believe that sharing a common currency would change these political dynamics.

SOME MAY LOOK at my list of reforms and argue that it is far from minimal. I believe that reforms that fall short of this comprehensive agenda will substantially increase the likelihood that the euro *fails*. And if it survives, it will survive without bringing the benefits that were promised. I have repeatedly emphasized that the euro was not an end in itself but a means to broader ends. So far, the euro not only has failed to achieve those broader ends but has had the *opposite* effects: poorer growth and more divisiveness.

These or similar reforms are necessary to prevent the divergence, instability, stagnation, growth in inequality, and increase in unemployment that have marked the euro. They are intended to cope with the consequences of the absence of exchange-rate flexibility and having a single interest rate prevailing over a diverse region, to make it more likely that the eurozone will perform well *in spite* of the inherent limitations on adjustment that follow.

The absence of these normal market mechanisms makes it all the more important that the eurozone economic system does not face *further* impediments, further sources of instability and/or stagnation.

Doctrines and policies that were fashionable a quarter century ago are ill suited for the 21st century. The reforms of this chapter are designed to free the eurozone from its unfortunate historical legacy, and to give it sufficient flexibility to address new problems and to incorporate new ideas as they evolve.

The ECB under Draghi has demonstrated more flexibility than many thought possible—and has done some critical things that many in Germany think is not within its mandate. Still, the ECB remains far more constrained, far less well adapted to the economic realities of today than the Federal Reserve.

Many in Europe would agree on the merits of many, if not most, of the reforms I have outlined. But, they would say, Europe is a democracy and democracies move slowly. Thus, the argument is put, be patient. But the timing and sequencing of reforms are critical, and this is especially so when there is a mismatch between economic and political integration. The creditor/debtor relationship between northern and southern Europe is corrosive. Unless the reforms I have suggested (or something else along a similar line) are made, this corrosion will only deepen. The damage that is being done will be hard to undo.

Markets are impatient, and they will not wait until, perhaps, further reforms are made. The fact that there might be a banking union with common deposit insurance in 2017 is no reason not to take out money from a Spanish or Greek bank now. The downward spiral has already been costly, and even if the decline is arrested, the slow recovery will exert its toll. Europe's future potential growth is being lowered as a result of the mistakes being made today. There are important *hysteresis* effects: the generation entering the labor force today will not be building up their skills, creating the human capital that would make them more productive in later years. The term *hysteresis* simply refers to asymmetries in time and adjustment costs: undoing the imbalances that the euro created in just a few years is taking years far longer than the time required for them to build up, and the costs of undoing these imbalances is far greater than the benefits received as they were built up. So, too, once capital or talented young people leave a country, it is often hard to get them back. Much of the economic debate is about which asymmetries are important. For example, the inflation hawks worry that once inflation increases, bringing it down is costly; the benefits of a short period of high inflation (if any) are far less than the costs of bringing it down. The evidence is that the asymmetries that we are focusing on are far more important.

From what I have seen, however, there is little likelihood of *sufficient* progress in undertaking the deep reforms in the structure of the eurozone at *sufficient* speed.[48] Delay is costly in another way: as Europe struggles with a flawed eurozone, which is bringing the economic travails that I have described, other crises emerge—most notably, the threat of a breakup of the nation-state in Spain, the threat of the departure of the UK, and the onslaught of migrants, especially from the Syrian conflict. The persistent euro crisis and the conflict over how it has been managed makes it more difficult to develop consensus policies in any of these areas, which would be extraordinarily difficult in any case.

That is why Europe needs urgently to begin thinking about alternatives to the single-currency arrangement—the alternatives that I outline in the next two chapters. Perhaps doing so will increase their resolve to do what it takes—to create a eurozone that works.

10

CAN THERE BE AN
AMICABLE DIVORCE?

The last chapter described an agenda to make the euro work, and I believe that making the reforms suggested is the first-best course. However, while I think it is eminently doable, there is more than a small probability that it will not be done. In that case, there are only three alternatives: First is the current strategy of muddling through—in other words, doing the minimum to keep the eurozone together but not enough to restore it to prosperity. Second is the creation of the "flexible euro," described in the next chapter. The third option is a divorce, which Europe should strive to be as amicable as possible.[1]

In this chapter we discuss what a friendly separation could look like, not necessarily into 19 different currencies, as existed prior to the eurozone, but into at least a few (two or three) different currency groupings. The central message of this chapter is simple: an amicable divorce is possible. In fact, some of the institutional innovations that would facilitate that divorce, making use of 21st-century technology, would also in time improve the overall performance of the economy.[2] And to demonstrate the argument that such a divorce can be done without high costs either to the country leaving or to the rest of the eurozone, I illustrate the analysis by looking at the case of Greece, but a similar analysis would apply to any other country contemplating leaving the eurozone. Is a Greek exit—or Grexit—possible without destroying Greece's economy or imposing high costs on the rest of the eurozone? If Greece could manage, presumably so could countries that are far better off. There will, of course, be costs. Monetary arrangements matter, and leaving the eurozone is a big change. But there are *huge* costs in the current strategy of muddling through—as shown in chapter 3. For the eurozone as a whole, we calculate them in the trillions of dollars. For Greece, in depression without end, the losses today give but a glimpse of the losses going forward. A rational calculus has to set these known and persistent costs against the risks of a divorce. At least with a divorce, even if there is a rocky start to the new life, there is the upside potential of an end to depression and the start of real growth.[3] This chapter suggests that in a reasonably well-managed amicable divorce Greece would do far better than it is doing under the current programs imposed upon it by the Troika.[4]

There are, of course, political dimensions that economic calculus ignores. And those political dimensions are multifaceted. The divorce would restore dignity to the Greek people, who have been treated shabbily by Germany and the Troika; it would restore democracy—Tsipras's acceptance of the Troika demands, after 62 percent of the population had voted in a referendum *against* the austerity program, removed all doubt that their economic sovereignty had been forfeited.

The final section of the chapter explains that if there is to be a limited breakup of the eurozone, it makes more sense for Germany to leave, instead of the countries around the periphery. We conclude with some remarks about why it is so important to have an *amicable* divorce.

HOW TO LEAVE THE EURO AND PROSPER

There are several difficulties in managing an exit: managing the fiscal deficit, the current account deficit, and the debt; creating and maintaining a stable banking system, with a stable supply of credit to finance new investments; and creating a new financial transactions system.

The 2008 global financial crisis and the subsequent discussion of financial sector reforms highlighted the failures of financial markets and the enormous consequences of these failures for the economic system. These included excessive volatility in credit creation, with a misallocation of capital and a mismanagement of risk; more credit going to the purchase of fixed assets rather than to the creation of productive assets; excessive and volatile cross-border flows of short-term capital, leading to volatility in exchange rates and trade flows; excessive charges for the running of the payments mechanisms; and an array of socially unproductive practices, from market manipulation to insider trading to predatory lending. I've described the macroeconomic consequences, where misguided credit flows to the periphery countries created the imbalances from which Europe is suffering still.

A monetary union is about *money* and, more generally, a country's financial system. It was dysfunctions in the eurozone's financial system that led to the crisis; it was restoration of financial stability upon which the ECB and the Troika focused—with seemingly little regard for the consequences of the lives of the people affected. Hence as, say, Greece departs a failed monetary/financial system, the relevant question is, what would replace it? The normal presumption has been that Greece would go back to the drachma, with all the problems associated with that. Those depicting this alternative typically ignore that in the last, say, two decades of the drachma, Greece grew far faster with lower unemployment than in the almost two decades since entering the eurozone.

But much has happened in the past four decades. Modern technology provides the basis of a *new* financial system. Greece doesn't need to go back to the past. It can create the financial system of the future—the kind of financial system that current special interests within the financial sector, wanting to preserve the huge rents that they garner for themselves, have prevented us from creating. The following sections describe briefly the key elements of such a system—a low-cost "medium of exchange" for facilitating transactions and a system of credit creation focused on the *real economy,* managed in a way far more conducive to macroeconomic stability than the current system.

CREATING A 21ST-CENTURY FINANCIAL TRANSACTIONS SYSTEM

Our banking and monetary system serves multiple purposes. One of them is as a medium of exchange. The world has several times made a change in the prevailing medium of exchange. Gold was once used; then, at least in the United States, there was a move to the bimetallic standard, where gold and silver were used, and finally we moved to paper (or "fiat") money. For years, it has been recognized that it would be far more efficient to move to e-money, away from currency. A Grexit could provide an opportunity for doing so—in a way that would facilitate the Grexit and strengthen the Greek economy.

As various pundits considered the potential Greek exit from the eurozone, articles in the press appeared about the logistics and whether it would be possible for Greece to get enough currency printed, how they would manage a switchover to the drachma—dealing with the conversion of bank accounts, designing, printing, and delivering a new banknote, and how to impart value to the new currency. Greece could not very well begin printing money before it leaves the eurozone, and it was not clear what would happen in the interim.[5]

People who ask these questions apparently have not noticed what has happened to our payments mechanism—the way we transact with each other. Currency, those funny pieces of paper, with faces of famous people or buildings on them, are mostly a relic, just as gold and silver were once the key part of the payments mechanism but are no longer. We now have a much more efficient electronic payments mechanism, and in most of the world we could have an even more efficient one, if it were taken out of the hands of the monopolistic financial system. Electronic transfers are extraordinarily cheap, but banks and credit card companies charge exorbitantly for the service, reaping monopoly profits as a result.[6]

Electronic money is more convenient for people on both sides of the transaction, which is why it has become the dominant form of payment. It saves the costs of printing money, which has increased as the sophistication of counterfeiters has increased. It has a further advantage, especially in countries like Greece where small businesses predominate—it significantly curtails the extent of tax avoidance.[7]

With electronic money, leaving the euro can, in principle, be done smoothly, assuming there is cooperation with other European authorities. Upon a Grexit, the Greek-euro would instantly come into being. It would be the money *inside* the Greek banking system. In effect, this money would be "locked in." But anybody could transfer the money in his bank account to that of anyone else. Thus everybody has, in effect, almost full use of his money.[8] The Greek-euro would be just like any other currency, with a well-defined value relative to the ordinary euro.

Most individuals today have accounts; only the very poor are "unbanked," and in recent years governments and NGOs, like the Gates Foundation, have been making great efforts to bank the unbanked. The government could quickly create new bank accounts for the few people who remain unbanked. In most countries, government pension payments are now transferred through bank accounts, partly to reduce the risk of stolen checks, partly to reduce the outrageous charges that are sometimes charged by check-cashing services.[9]

CREDIT: CREATING A BANKING SYSTEM THAT SERVES SOCIETY

Earlier in this chapter, we noted the successive changes in monetary arrangements, in the "medium of exchange." A big advantage of the use of fiat money was that one could regulate the supply. When gold was used as the medium of exchange, when there was a large discovery of gold—or when the gold supply increased as Spain conquered the new world—there would be inflation, as the price of gold would fall relative to other goods; if there were few gold discoveries, then there would be deflation. Both caused problems. Deflation, for instance, would redistribute income from debtors to creditors, increasing inequality and imposing hardship. America's election of 1896 was fought on the issue of the money supply. The debtors wanted to increase the money supply by moving from gold to gold and silver, a bimetallic standard.[10]

While the modern financial system based on fiat money didn't suffer from the vagaries of gold discoveries, it suffered from something even worse: volatility in the creation of money and credit by the banking system, without adequate regulation, giving rise to the booms and busts that have characterized the capitalist system.

Banks effectively increase the supply of money by increasing the supply of credit. In a modern economy, central banks regulate, typically indirectly, banks' creation of money and credit. They are supposed to do it *in just the right amount*, so there is a Goldilocks economy, neither under- or overheated but "just right."

TARGETED REGULATION OF CREDIT CREATION

There is a problem in this system: because the central banks' control mechanisms are typically very indirect, the economy is often over- or underheated. Sometimes there is too much credit creation, leading to an excess of aggregate demand, and prices rise; there is inflation. Sometimes there is a lack of demand, and prices fall; there is deflation.

Part of the reason for this failure is that while central banks can regulate the supply of credit reasonably well, they can't (or more accurately don't) regulate the *use* to which the credit is put. Much of the credit goes to buying preexisting assets, like land. What determines whether the economy is over- or underheated is the purchase of new goods and services (whether for consumption or investment). Thus, after the 2008 crisis, there was a massive increase in liquidity, as the Fed pumped money into the economy. But relatively little of this went to buy goods and services in the United States, so in spite of the huge expansion of the money supply as conventionally measured, the economy remained weak.[11]

In short, even with fiat money, there may still be a deficiency of domestic aggregate demand—a deficiency that could be easily corrected: there are individuals and firms who would like to spend but cannot get access to credit. As I have repeatedly noted, that is one of the central problems in Greece and Spain. The ECB, with its belief in markets and its misunderstandings of monetary policy, has devoted little attention to the flow of credit. A near-zero interest rate does not mean businesses can get access to credit at such a rate—or at any rate.

In spite of the single market, there is not a single lending rate. Indeed, the disparity in lending rates is part of the divergence built into the eurozone system. The individual countries, which have given up control over their own monetary system, have no way of trying to equalize the cost of capital, to firms, households, or even to government. This is the unlevel playing field that is inherent in the current euro system.

THE IMPACT OF "DIVORCE" ON THE FLOW OF BANK CREDIT

The banking system is central to the provision of credit. There is the worry: Won't leaving the euro lead to the crash of the banking system, and at minimum a severe heart attack for the economy? Indeed, from all accounts, it was the threat that this would happen which led the Greek government to give into the demands of the Troika in the summer of 2015.

But again, this is a false fear. The traditional view of banking was based on a primitive agriculture economy. Farmers with excess seed—with harvests greater than they wanted to consume or plant the next season—could bring the seed to the bank, which would lend, at interest, the seed to some farmer who wanted more seed than he had, either for consumption (say, because he had a bad harvest that year) or planting. The bank had to have seed deposits in order to lend. In effect, those worrying about where Greece would get the money necessary for running its banking system have in mind this corn economy: the Greeks have no corn to put into the new banking system, and why would any foreigner put his corn into the new Greek banks?[12]

But this reasoning again totally misses the nature of credit in the 21st century. In a modern economy, banks effectively create credit out of thin air, backed by general confidence in government, its ability and willingness to bail out the banks, which includes its power to tax and borrow. The euro, however, has limited those abilities, and in the absence of a banking union, has thus undermined national banking systems.

RESTORING DOMESTIC CONTROL
OVER CREDIT CREATION

Once we restore a country's economic sovereignty, as the country—say, Greece—leaves the eurozone, its ability to create credit is largely restored. Think of this most directly as occurring through a government bank. It can add "money" to the payments mechanism by lending money to a small enterprise with a proven reputation that wants to build a hotel on an island where the demand for hotel rooms has persistently exceeded supply.

The government simply puts more "money" into the bank account of the enterprise, which the enterprise can then use to pay contractors to build the hotel. Of course, in providing credit there is always a risk of nonrepayment, and standards have to be established for evaluating the likelihood of repayment.

In recent decades, faith in government's ability to make such evaluations has diminished, and confidence has been placed in the private financial system. The 2008 crisis, as well as other frequent crises that have marked the last third of a century, have shown that that confidence has been misplaced. Not only didn't the banks make good judgments—as evidenced by the massive, repeated bailouts—but they systematically failed to fulfill what they should have seen as their major responsibility, providing credit to businesses to create new jobs. By some accounts, their "real" lending amounts to just 3 percent of their activities; by others, to some 15 percent. But by any account, bank finance has been absorbed in other directions.[13]

There were always obvious problems in delegating the power of credit creation, backed by government, to private institutions: they could use their power to benefit their owners, through what we defined earlier as *connected lending*. Regulations circumscribed this, motivated by the experience of *bad* lending perhaps more than by the implicit corruption and inequality to which such lending gives rise. But circumscribing connected lending didn't address the key underlying problem: credit is scarce; giving private banks the right to create credit with government backing gave them enormous "economic rents." They could use this economic power to enrich themselves and their friends. Russia provides the quintessential example: those with banking licenses could use that power to buy enormously valuable state assets, especially in natural resources. It was through the banking system that the Russian oligarchs were largely created. In Western countries, matters are done more subtly—but creating enormous inequality (though not of the magnitude of Russia).

In many cases, they lend money to those whom they "trust" and judge creditworthy, with collateral that they value: in short, the bankers lend money to those who are similar to themselves. Even if Banker A can't lend to himself or his relatives, Banker A can lend to the relatives of Banker B, and Banker B can lend to the relatives of Banker A. The fallibility of their judgments has been demonstrated repeatedly: overlending to fiber optics at one moment, to fracking at another, to housing in a third.

There is a second danger to the delegation of the power of credit creation to private banks. Throughout history, moneylenders have had a bad reputation, because of the ruthlessness with which they exploit the poor, especially at moments of extreme need, where without money they, their children, or their parents might die. At such times, there is an enormous asymmetry in bargaining power, which the moneylenders sweep in to exploit. Virtually every religion has tried to proscribe such exploitation, prohibiting usury, and in some cases, even interest. Somehow, in the magic of neoliberalism, this long history was forgotten: bankers not only didn't suffer from the stigma of being called moneylenders, they were elevated to being the paragons of capitalism. In the enthusiasm over their new virtues, as linchpins in the workings of the capitalist system itself, it was simply assumed that such exploitation would not occur, perhaps in the belief that competition would ensure it *couldn't* happen, perhaps in the belief that with the new prosperity of workers, citizens wouldn't let it happen.

All of this was wishful thinking. Freed of constraints, bankers, our 21st-century moneylenders, have shown themselves every bit as ruthless as the moneylenders of the past; in fact, they are in some ways worse, because they have discovered new ways of exploiting both the poor and investors. They have been moving money from the bottom of the economic pyramid to the top.[14] The financial sector has enriched itself on the back of the government's credibility, without performing the societal functions that banks were supposed to perform. In doing so, the financial sector has become one of the major sources of the increased inequality in Europe and around the world.[15]

Even given this history, the government may want to delegate responsibility for making credit decisions to private enterprises, but it should develop strong systems of incentives and accountability, such that the financial system actually focuses on lending for job and enterprise creation and so that it does not make excessive profits as it performs these functions. This can be put another way: the government should be adequately compensated for its backing. In effect, in the current system all the "value" of the underlying government credit guarantee is captured by the private sector.[16]

CREDIT AUCTIONS

Here is one possibility for addressing this issue and providing for greater economic stability—one that a country leaving the eurozone and its strictures and legal frameworks could avail itself of. First, the central bank (government) auctions off the rights to issue new credit. The amounts would be added to the "money" that is within the financial system. The magnitude of net credit that it allows to be added each month will be determined by the country's central bank on the basis of its assessment of the macroeconomic situation—that is, if the economy is weaker, it will provide more credit to stimulate the economy. The winners of the credit auction then allocate this "money" to borrowers, on the basis of *their* judgments about repayment capacity, within the constraints that the central bank may impose (described below).[17]

Note that in this system, banks cannot create credit out of thin air, and the amount of money being created each month is known with considerable precision. The winners of the credit auction can only transfer money from their account to the borrowers' accounts.

Conditions would attach to selling the "rights to lend" to the banks. Minimum percentages of the loans would go to small and medium-size enterprises and to new enterprises; a maximum would go to real estate lending (perhaps apportioned by location, on the basis of local changes in prices), to purchases of other existing assets, or to those engaged in speculative activities, like hedge funds. None would be allocated to socially proscribed activities, like those contributing to global warming or associated with the promotion of death, such as cigarettes. In short, there would be minimum standards for social responsibility. There would be limits on the interest rates charged.

Discriminatory lending practices and other abusive practices by credit card companies would be proscribed. So, too, would connected lending. There would be further restrictions to ensure that the loan portfolio of the bank is safe and sound, and there would be strict supervision by government regulators to ensure compliance with the regulations governing any such program.

In a 21st-century banking system, a bank's ability to lend is, in a sense, given only temporarily. It is conditional on compliance with the rules and standards established. The government would allow for entry into the banking system; indeed, separating the depository and lending functions and the open auction of rights to issue credit should make entry easier, and thus competition more vigorous than under current arrangements.

Still, since lending is an information-based activity, and the gathering of information is a fixed cost, one would like stability in the new banking system, and this will require that banks not live on the edge— that is, they be sufficiently well capitalized and sufficiently profitable. By saying "sufficiently profitable," I do not mean the 25 percent return on equity that one of the European banks, Deutsche Bank, famously came to expect as normal. Hence, entry of enterprises with sufficient capital and who also satisfy other conditions that enhance the presumption that they would be responsible lenders, would be encouraged.[18] The system of auctioning of credit would ensure that banks not earn excessive returns; most of the value of the public's backing to the creation of money/credit would be captured by the public, rather than as now by the bankers. At the same time, the new system of credit creation ensures that the social functions of finance are more likely fulfilled, at least better than under current arrangements.

This is an example of how to create a 21st-century banking system, responding to the advantages of electronic technology, doing things that would have been far harder to accomplish in earlier decades—a banking system more likely to ensure responsible lending and macroeconomic stability than the current system, and without the huge rents and exploitation that have contributed so much to the inequality that has stalked advanced countries around the world.

But this reform is about more than curbing bankers' exploitation. It is about enhancing macroeconomic stability. One of the major contributors to macroeconomic instability is the instability in credit supply, and, in particular, to the supply of credit for the purchase of *produced* goods and services. The 2008 crisis demonstrated that all the advances in markets and our understanding of markets has *not* led to greater stability in this crucial variable—in fact, quite the opposite. Our system not only enhances stability in this critical variable, it provides the basis of a virtuous circle leading to an increase in overall stability of the economy. One of the most important reasons that small businesses don't repay loans is macroeconomic fluctuation: loans simply can't be repaid when an economy is in depression. Ensuring greater macro-stability (than under the current regime) would do more than anything else to ensure the viability of the banking system.

WHENCE BANK CAPITAL?

The beauty of the modern credit system is that it doesn't really require the same kind of capital as it did before. Recapitalizing a destroyed banking system in a eurozone country would not require gold or borrowing to buy seeds as it did in the old days. As we have seen, the government itself can simply create credit (through a government bank) or it can delegate credit creation through the auction mechanism just described.

The fact that the money created by the government can be used to pay the taxes that are owed to the government, and that the government has the power to levy taxes, ensures the value of the credit it has created. Indeed, because the credit that has been created is electronic money, the movement of which can easily be monitored, the government has not only the ability to levy taxes; it also enhances the ability to collect taxes.

The only reason for bank capital in this world is as a partial guarantee that the bank has the capacity to repay the credit—the bank's "purchases" from the government of the right to issue credit are only temporary, and the credit thus created has to be repaid to the government. (The fact that the bank will lose its own capital has, in addition, strong incentive effects, incentivizing the bank to make good decisions about to whom to give the credit and to monitor the loan well.) But if the government is doing an adequate job of bank supervision and has imposed appropriate regulations (for example, on connected and excessively risky lending), the amount of capital required will be limited. And that fact alone should lead to more competition in the market for the provision of credit—reducing the excessive returns currently received.

MANAGING THE CURRENT ACCOUNT DEFICIT IN AN AMICABLE DIVORCE

The euro crisis was brought on by Greece not being able to finance its trade and government deficit—or, more particularly, not being able to roll over the debt it owed. Greece has relied massively on eurozone help, though as we have noted, the vast majority of so-called aid actually went to European creditors, not to Greece. This is itself good news for Greece (or any other of the crisis countries) about the ability to manage on its own.

With an appropriate debt restructuring (discussed later in this chapter), the country would be little the worse off, even were its "partners" not to extend a helping hand in an amicable divorce. Indeed, freed from the conditions imposed as part of the "assistance," freed from austerity and counterproductive structural reforms, the country would actually be in better shape. At this juncture, some half decade after the onset of the euro crisis, there is even better news: Greece, the worst afflicted of the crisis countries, has virtually eliminated its trade and its (primary) fiscal deficit. If the elimination of those deficits had been the sole objective of the Troika programs, and one cared nothing about the costs of achieving these goals, then the Troika programs could be declared a success. But the goals were broader: it was to have Greece be able to stand on its own, at full employment, with growth, but, on the contrary, Greece is in a deep depression. And as this book has shown, the costs of achieving the reductions in the trade and fiscal deficits has been absolutely enormous.

Looking forward, on net, money will be flowing *the other way*. Money will be going not *from* Germany and others in Europe to Greece but from Greece *to* Germany and others in the Troika. This reverse flow is scheduled to go on *for decades*. Greece will not need help from outside—and won't be getting any.

Outside the eurozone, Greece (or any of the other crisis countries) would be able to use the flexibility of its exchange rate (the fact that the value of the Greek-euro may be less than that of the euro) to correct any trade imbalance and to strengthen the economy. As we've seen, the origins of the trade deficit largely arise from the inability to adjust the exchange rate. As the exchange rate falls, exports become more attractive and imports less so, and typically (though sometimes not right away), this enables the current account deficit to be brought to manageable levels, if not to actually be eliminated. Moving to a Greek-euro would accomplish this de facto devaluation.

Greek exports some commodities like olive oil, and its mining sector is large as well. But as in any modern economy, Greece sells not only goods but services—in fact, services account for 80 percent of GDP. Greek tourism alone makes up some 7 percent of GDP.[19] The effective devaluation would give Greece a competitive edge in this space, where consumers are price sensitive, and that edge would increase its foreign exchange revenues.[20]

Of course, over the long run, there are other things it could and should do. It could, as we've discussed, develop its renewable energy capacities. A devaluation would enable it to derive more Greek-euros from the sale of this energy to the rest of Europe. It also could develop itself as the Sunbelt of Europe (as Florida and Arizona have done in the United States), an attractive place for retirees (particularly if it strengthened its health care sector) and businesses, like American Express, that are electronically based and can locate essentially anywhere.

A further concern: Will those who export to Greece be willing to accept Greek-euros in payment? They almost surely would, particularly if financial markets developed to hedge against changes in the value of the Greek-euro and the ordinary euro. Of course there will be some fluctuations in the value, just as there are fluctuations in the value of the many currencies within the EU—the Swedish krona and the British pound. But modern financial markets know full well how to manage those risks.

MANAGING THE CURRENT ACCOUNT DEFICIT THROUGH TRADE CHITS

There is another reform that would simultaneously resolve any doubts about the acceptability of the Greek-euro and help the adjustment process, an idea that has been suggested even for the United States (which has had a persistent current account deficit, contributing to the weak US economy) by none other than Warren Buffett.[21] It would assure, too, the necessary flow of trade credit. In this proposal (alternatively called trade chits, or Buffett chits) government would provide to any exporter a chit, a "token" (in this case, electronically recorded), the number in proportion to the value of what was exported; to import a Greek-euro worth of goods, there would be a requirement to pay, in addition, a Greek-euro's worth of chits or "trade tokens." There would be a free market in chits, so the demand and supply of chits would be equal; and by equating the demand and supply of chits, one would automatically balance the current account.

In practice, the value of the chit might normally be very small. For instance, before the turmoil that hit the Greek economy beginning in early 2015, Greece had a current account surplus, in which case the value of the chit would be zero. But this system would be a way of managing the high level of volatility in market economies. With the free flow of capital, the exchange rate is determined by the vagaries of the market. And those capricious changes in exchange rate then drive exports, imports, the trade deficit, and borrowing, and in doing so, give rise to macroeconomic instability. With the system of trading chits, the trade deficit can be controlled, enhancing overall stability.[22]

In the analysis above, where every import needs a chit, there is either a trade surplus or trade balance. The government could use this system to limit the size of the deficit or surplus as well. For instance, if it wants to limit imports to be no more than 20 percent greater than exports, it can issue 1.2 import chits for every euro of exports. When there would be an excessive surplus, every import would be granted an "export" chit. Then every export would require a chit. This would automatically bring exports down to the level of imports. By issuing both import and export chits, the trade balance can be kept within any prespecified bounds.

The fact that the country could thus stabilize the size of the trade deficit or surplus has an enormous macroeconomic advantage: it facilitates macroeconomic stabilization itself. It means, for instance, that a small country doesn't have to suffer from the vagaries of its "external balance," its net export position. These fluctuations impose enormous costs on society, of which the market, in generating them, takes no account.

But deficit/surplus stability also engenders longer-term stability, for as we have seen, national indebtedness, built up over many years, can suddenly become unsustainable. The market sees the world through very myopic lenses. It is willing to lend year after year—until it suddenly changes its mind. By limiting the trade deficit, a country is in effect limiting national borrowing; this framework thus reduces a key source of instability.

The experience of Europe—and elsewhere—has shown that it is not so much government borrowing that gives rise to crises, but national borrowing. In some cases, the national borrowing was government borrowing (Greece), but in many other cases (Ireland and Spain) it was private borrowing. When a crisis hits, the debt quickly moves from the private balance sheet to the public's.

Moreover, we can see how this system would help strengthen the Greek-euro. In the absence of the chit system, an increase in the demand by Greeks for imports (that is, for, say, German-euros to buy German cars) would lead to a fall in the price of the Greek-euro. But now, with imports discouraged by the necessity of also paying to purchase a chit, the increased demand for imports would be reflected in an increased price of a chit, rather than a decrease in the value of the Greek-euro. The Greek-euro will be stronger than it otherwise would be. The dramatic fall in the value of the Greek-euro that might have otherwise been expected in the event of a Grexit is thus avoided.[23]

MANAGING THE FISCAL DEFICIT

Outside of the eurozone, Greece (or the other crisis countries) could not only manage its trade deficit without assistance, it could also manage its fiscal deficit. Higher growth would generate more tax revenues, and a debt restructuring (described below) would reduce the drain of the nation's resources abroad. Over the longer term, prudent use of trade chits would prevent the buildup of large external debts (whether public or private).

Interestingly, today, even *within* the eurozone, Greece does not have a significant problem financing its fiscal deficit. The country can easily survive without the funds from the IMF and the eurozone. Greece has done such a good job of adjusting its economy that, apart from what it's paying to service the debt, it had a surplus by 2014. The turmoil of the summer of 2015 strained finances somewhat, but by the beginning of 2016 it had returned to balance, and it is expected to have a large surplus by 2018.[24]

An amicable divorce would of course recognize that, nonetheless, assistance in the path towards creating an independent currency would be very helpful. There will be bumps and uncertainties in the process of leaving the eurozone. Europe should help with "adjustment assistance," in the transition. Solidarity would suggest that the money be in the form of grants.[25]

Even if such assistance were not forthcoming, the transitions could be managed with relative smoothness. Money is needed by the government for three purposes: to finance the purchase of domestic goods and services, to service the debt, and to finance the purchase of foreign goods and services. The first is at least conceptually easier to address. The government can, in effect, issue credit to itself (in the manner described earlier, in our discussion of how government can issue credit to other parties). The subsequent increase in aggregate demand would be beneficial to the economy. Critics will raise a concern about inflation. But the crisis countries have been facing deflation, a deficiency of aggregate demand.

If there is a need for government finance beyond the amount that would restore the economy to full employment, then the government will have to raise taxes. The information available through the electronic payment mechanism will, however, enable it to do a much better job of collecting the taxes already on the books, making the necessity of raising tax rates even less likely.

The need for funds for servicing the debt will be greatly reduced through debt restructuring, which should be an important part of any amicable divorce. This is discussed in the next section. The need for foreign exchange can also be easily addressed, if the other parts of the program (including the use of Buffett chits) are adopted. For then there will be no real "shortage" of foreign exchange.[26]

MANAGING DEBT RESTRUCTURING

Most of the crisis countries have a large debt, denominated in euros. As I discussed in the last chapter, in some cases such as Greece, it is already apparent that that debt has to be restructured. But that will be all the more so after the country leaves the eurozone. For it is likely that the currency (for simplicity, we will continue calling it the Greek-euro, rather than the drachma) will be worth less than the ordinary euro, which we will still refer to as just the euro.

I explained in chapter 7 that debt restructurings (bankruptcy) are a central feature of modern capitalism. Still, they are often contentious.

The Greek government could do a few things to smooth the process. First, the government should declare all euro-denominated debts payable in Greek-euros. Such redenominations have happened before. When the United States left the gold standard, debts denominated in gold were redenominated into dollars. Indeed, upon entry into the eurozone, debts that had been denominated in drachmas got converted into euros.[27]

If the Greek-euros trade at a discount relative to the ordinary euro, it would be tantamount to a debt restructuring, but one done smoothly, without recourse to the complexity involved in ordinary debt restructurings. Interestingly, the system of chits described earlier would reduce the extent of the decline in the exchange rate.[28]

In a few cases—Greece is one—there will have to be explicit debt write-offs. So, too, if there are debts owed under contracts issued under foreign laws, in which case the crisis country cannot simply redenominate. (With a truly amicable divorce, other EU countries should agree that debt issued under other EU jurisdictions could be redenominated.)

In the case of private debts, the government should pass a law providing for expedited restructuring.[29] The United States has recognized the importance of giving corporations a fresh start, and doing so quickly, in Chapter 11 of its bankruptcy code. When many companies are facing default—as may well be the case if their euro-denominated debt is not redenominated—this is all the more important. As we noted in the previous chapter, the crisis countries in Europe need to adopt some variant of this idea—and this is true whether they do or do not leave the eurozone.

This chapter is focused on an amicable divorce, and with most of Greece's debts owed to its European partners, one hopes that they would understand the importance of giving a fresh start, the importance and necessity of a deep debt write-off, and rather than confronting the country with a barrage of lawsuits, would use their own powers and influence to limit the scope for such suits from private creditors. With a backdrop of European solidarity, they could proceed with a debt restructuring that went well beyond the minimal set of principles adopted by the international community in 2015, enabling the debt restructuring process to be even smoother and more successful.[30]

THE ADVANTAGES OF A GERMAN DEPARTURE

The previous discussion described a number of institutional reforms and innovations that would lay the groundwork for a smooth transition of any one of the crisis countries out of the eurozone. Our analysis suggests, too, that simply having Greece leave will not resolve the problems of the eurozone, either now or over the long run. There are other countries in depression and recession, from which they will not emerge anytime soon. Rather than having each of the crisis countries leave, one by one, or the countries of the eurozone stick together, mired in an ill-fated near-stagnation, there is an alternative solution: Germany and perhaps some of the other northern European countries (say, Netherlands and Finland, should the country soon recover from its current problems) could leave. This would be an easier way to bring Europe back to health.[31]

The departure of some of the northern countries would allow an adjustment of the exchange rate of the remainder relative to that of the northern countries. That adjustment would help restore current account balance—without having to resort to recessions or stagnation to suppress imports. The lower exchange rate would increase exports and reduce imports, which would stimulate growth. The increased growth would provide more revenue to the government, bringing an end to austerity. The downward vicious circle that has been part of Europe since the onset of the crisis would be replaced by a virtuous circle of growth and prosperity.

The increased strength of the economies in southern Europe would enable them to service their debts, and even pay down some of the debt. With the departure of the northern countries, the currency in use by the southern countries would still be the euro (that of the northern countries we will refer to as the northern-euro). Because debts are owed in euros, and the countries in the south had retained the euro, there would not be an increase in leverage, as there would be if the southern countries left the eurozone—with all the adverse effects attendant to the increase in leverage.

Meanwhile, in northern Europe, the stronger northern-euro would work wonders to eliminate the persistent trade surplus, which has been problematic not only for their partners in the eurozone but for the global economy. Germany would then be forced to find other ways of stimulating its economy—doing some of the things suggested in the previous chapter, like increasing wages at the bottom, reducing inequality, and increasing government spending. In the current environment, monetary policy (even that of the northern countries) would be relatively ineffective, and so if Germany wishes to maintain full employment, it would have to rely on fiscal policy.

With firms, households, and even governments in the north owing money in euros, and the value of the northern-euro appreciating relative to the euro, there would be an automatic deleveraging of the economy, which would stimulate growth. This would partially offset the contractionary effects of the elimination of the trade surplus.

CONCLUDING COMMENTS

This chapter has described how one can manage an amicable divorce. We have shown how each of the central problems facing the crisis countries could be addressed in such a separation. Current account deficits could be eliminated or even turned into surpluses. Governments would be able to finance their expenditures. The economies could be returned to full employment—after years mired in recession and depression—with neither inflation nor deflation. I have described a system that would enable even the traditional "weak" economies from building up the foreign debts that have repeatedly precipitated crises. Even within this framework, there will be decisions to be made: at least in the early years of transition, I would suggest that they aim for a current account surplus, tilt public spending toward investment, run a small fiscal surplus, and, if necessary, use the balanced-budget multiplier to ensure aggregate demand.

Of course, matters seldom go so smoothly. As always, there are likely to be hurt feelings, some finger pointing: Who's to blame? Would the marriage have gone differently if only . . . ? If only Greece had behaved better? If only the Troika had not been so abusive? The Greeks will almost surely exhibit aspects of a person in an abusive relationship (sometimes referred to as the battered woman syndrome)—they will say, if only we had been more accommodating . . . If only we had . . .

The previous chapters have said, however, that what is at fault was the *structure* of the eurozone itself. I explained how it is unlikely that the outcome would have been much different if Greece's negotiators had been more accommodating—over the course of the crisis, Greece has had negotiators with a panoply of styles, and none have fared well. There really is no need for self-recrimination.

MANY WITHIN EUROPE will be saddened by the death of the euro. This is not the end of the world: currencies come and go. The euro is just a 17-year-old experiment, poorly designed and engineered not to work. There is so much more to the European project, the vision of an integrated Europe, than a monetary arrangement. The currency was supposed to promote solidarity, to further integration and prosperity. It has done none of these: as constructed, it has become an impediment to the achievement of each of these goals, and if the reforms to the eurozone discussed in the last chapter are beyond the reach of the eurozone today, it is better to abandon the euro to save Europe and the European project.

11

TOWARD A FLEXIBLE EURO

Looking at Europe today, we might say that it is in a pickle. It wants to preserve the euro, even though the euro has not been working. It would like to pretend that if only member countries had obeyed the rules, if only there had not been that American-made financial crisis, all would have been well. But in its heart of hearts, Europe must know that this is not true. Countries that obeyed the rules also went into crisis. It was not just countries of the southern periphery but also Ireland. Even virtuous Finland is having trouble adjusting, and has had unacceptably high unemployment—9.3 percent in early 2016.

The nature of the market economy is that "stuff happens." And the stuff that happens affects different countries differently, and requires large adjustments. The euro makes those difficult at best.

While northern Europe castigated the countries of the south for the fiscal profligacy of the so-called garlic belt, troubles in Finland showed that the problems were deeper and different. Finland had been one of the success cases of Europe. After having been a near-vassal of Russia, its GDP per capita in 1960 was but $10,500 (adjusted for inflation), 68 percent of that of the United States at the time. Then, through heavy investments in education, it grew to the point that by 2007 its per capita income was $42,300, or 93 percent of that of the United States. But then a series of problems befell the country: in the fast-changing world of hi-tech, its leading company, Nokia, lost out to competitors. Finland had close ties with Estonia, which was badly hit by the 2008 crisis. And after the fall of the Berlin Wall, Finland had profited by strong trade with Russia. But sanctions with that country hurt Finland as well as Russia, which also suffered from the decline in oil and gas prices.

Finland's GDP shrank by 8.3 percent in 2009, and in 2015 it was still some 5.5 percent below its 2008 peak. In the absence of the euro, Finland's exchange rate would have fallen, and the decrease in imports and increase in exports would have stimulated the economy. In the absence of the fiscal constraints imposed by eurozone membership, it might have borrowed to finance government expenditures that would stimulate the economy. Instead, it got caught up in the wave of austerity afflicting Europe. Divisive cuts in wages of public sector employees were somehow supposed to mysteriously increase the competitiveness of Finland's exports. Instead, the wage cuts decreased demand, deepening the downturn. In short, the euro-medicine worked little better in well-behaved Finland than it did in the more recalcitrant patients of the south.

The alternative entailing "more Europe," creating a eurozone that works, is almost surely the best path forward for Europe, but it appears too much for at least some of the countries in the eurozone to stomach. On the other hand, the alternative discussed in the last chapter, the amicable divorce, is equally unpalatable. For those who saw the euro as the next, and critical, stage in European integration, divorce would be a sign of giving up, of resignation. I argued that this view was misguided—sharing a common currency is not, or should not be, at the heart of the European project—but perception is, at least to some extent, reality: if significant numbers of people within Europe see even an amicable divorce as at least a temporary surrender, then it could set back the agenda for European integration.[1]

Here, I want briefly to discuss one last alternative, which I call the

"flexible euro." It entails recognizing that there has been some progress in creating eurozone institutions since the euro crisis broke out,
though not enough to make a single-currency system work. The flexible euro builds on these successes, in the hope that one could create
a system in which different countries (or groups of countries) could
each have their own euro. The value of the different euros would fluctuate, but within bounds that the policies of the eurozone itself would
affect. Over time, perhaps, with the evolution of sufficient solidarity,
those bounds could be reduced, and eventually, the goal of a single
currency set forth in the Maastricht Treaty of 1992 would be achieved.
But this time, with the requisite institutions in place, the single currency might actually achieve its goals of promoting prosperity, European solidarity, and political integration.

THE BASIC IDEA

The basic idea draws upon chapters 9 and 10: recognizing the gaps in
the eurozone structure that exist now and are likely to persist in coming years, we can use some of the tools that we would use in the case
of an amicable divorce to arrange for sufficient policy coordination so
that the fluctuations in the various euro-currencies would be limited.

We make use of the observation made in the last chapter that by
and large, in the 21st century, we have moved to a digital economy—
and accelerating that process would increase efficiency and facilitate
tax collection. Rather than a single currency for the entirety of what is
now the eurozone, there would be several groupings, each with their
own currency. Each country or country grouping would create an
electronic currency—along the lines described in chapter 10. Money
could be easily transferred from one person's account to another, for
instance, upon the purchase of goods and services. Firms would pay
into these accounts their workers' wages; they would similarly pay
their suppliers and be paid by their customers. I described in chapter
10 how money could be added to or subtracted from within the elec-

tronic system—for instance, through the creation of new credit or a decrease in the supply of credit.

I described, too, a system by which net payments to and from abroad could be kept balanced: exporters would receive chits in addition to payments in the local-euro into their account, and those who wanted to import would have to buy a corresponding number of chits, in addition to making payments out of their accounts. The system of marketable trading chits would ensure that the value of exports equaled the value of imports—there would be no net flow in or out of the payments system. As we saw in chapter 10, countries could decide to allow a trade deficit or insist on a trade surplus, simply by changing the ratio of chits one received for a euro of exports relative to those needed for imports.

In this system, the value of one country's euro could vary relative to that of another's (and even more, the value of that country's euro plus the associated value of a chit). This is the flexibility in exchange rates that the current system lacks. At the same time, I explained how the system of chits would likely limit the variability of the value of one euro-currency against another.

STABILIZING RELATIVE EXCHANGE RATES

There are many ways that Europe could, collectively, work to limit the extent of the movements in exchange rates in our system of flexible euros. I discussed these in chapter 9, so I shall be brief here.

LIMITING SURPLUSES

First, the countries (most especially Germany) that have traditionally run trade surpluses—imposing large external costs on their European neighbors and global economies through the resulting imbalances—could commit to reducing those surpluses. They would do this by the same chit system. Not only would this reduce global imbalances, but the same reasoning that suggested that the Greek-euro will be stronger than it otherwise would have been (with chits limiting trade deficits) implies the German-euro will be weaker than it otherwise would be with chits limiting the magnitude of the surplus.

Eurozone leaders, if they wished, could thus achieve close to parity among the different national or regional euros simply by adjusting the chit system.

MORE EFFICIENT SHARING OF
THE BURDEN OF ADJUSTMENT

Earlier chapters noted that trade imbalances were caused by the rigidity in real exchange rates that follows from the rigidity in nominal exchange rates. The eurozone approach of trying to achieve the desired real exchange rate adjustments through magical productivity adjustments (for example, in structural reform programs) or through internal devaluation simply has not worked—and has been very painful.

Part of the reason for the failure of adjustment is that Germany has insisted on an asymmetrical adjustment process, that the burden of adjustments be borne by the deficit countries (through lowering wages and prices)—this in spite of all the evidence and theory that downward adjustments are far more costly than the reverse. It would be far better if Europe could commit itself to an asymmetrical process, but this time, with the opposite bias: the surplus countries should follow policies (for example, fiscal and wage policies) that lead to upward adjustments of wages and prices.

PRODUCTIVITY CONVERGENCE

We have seen, too, in previous chapters how Europe has put in place a process of productivity divergence, as the sources of finance in weak countries sour and as public investments in infrastructure, education, and technology plunge.

Europe already has some institutions in place to do the opposite, and it says it is committed to doing more. For instance, the European Investment Bank can strengthen investment in weak countries. If the eurozone follows through quickly on its commitment to create a real banking union, with common deposit insurance, it would do much to prevent the extremes of divergence in access to private finance. But small and medium-size enterprises in weak countries would still almost surely be at a competitive disadvantage. Again, a eurozone SME lending facility, directed especially at weak countries, could help rectify these disadvantages. If Europe created a solidarity fund for stabilization or assumed more responsibility for social expenditures like unemployment in afflicted countries, it would free up the budgets of these countries to make more of these forward-looking investments.[2] So, too, if Europe were to encourage industrial policies, rather than proscribe them, the lagging countries would have a better chance of converging toward the leading ones.

THE ECONOMIC RATIONALE

Previous chapters have explained the problems with the single-currency system of the eurozone. Large trade imbalances on the part of the periphery countries built up in the years before the crisis—and the system did nothing to stop the buildup. It then imposed a painful and costly adjustment in the aftermath of the crisis—where the costs were typically borne by the deficit countries. If we look *inside* the countries, matters are even worse: workers and small businesses are paying the price of this asymmetric adjustment process; but it was others who benefited in the creation of the earlier imbalances—in the case of Spain, for instance, construction firms and real estate speculators. We are asking innocent bystanders to pay for the mistakes of others.

The system is rife with macroeconomic externalities—where the actions of some individuals and firms impose high costs on others. Whenever there are externalities, there is a need for public action.

That is obvious in the case of environmental externalities like pollution; public action in response has led to cleaner air and rivers. It has worked. But America's banks polluted the global economy with toxic mortgages: regulators should have done something about this, but they didn't. Within the eurozone, something similar occurred. In some cases (Ireland and Spain), there was a real estate bubble; in others, the excesses took different forms.

The system described here provides a simple framework within which macroeconomic externalities are better addressed. It is almost surely not a panacea. There will still be macroeconomic fluctuations; but if well managed, they will be less severe and so will their consequences. This system would enable Europe to emerge from stagnation.

Some might complain: Aren't we interfering with the market? The eurozone itself is a massive interference with the market. It fixes a critical price, the exchange rate. It says that there has to be a single interest rate for the entire region, set by a *public* body, the European Central Bank. The question is, with this government-imposed rigidity, how well does the rest of the market perform? Can it assure stability? There is now more than a decade of evidence, and the answer is a resounding no.

This proposal entails minimal intervention in the market, and even in doing so, uses market mechanisms. It corrects for a well-recognized externality, the market externality associated with external imbalances. Europe has gotten itself into the current mess partly by assuming that markets are more perfect than they are. Markets exhibit enormous volatility in both prices and quantities: interest rates demanded of borrowers from different countries have moved violently in different directions, and capital and credit flows have fluctuated in ways that are virtually uncontrollable under current arrangements.

Workers are told that they should simply accept being buffeted by these maelstroms that are not acts of nature but the creations of irrational and inefficient markets. Workers should accept wage cuts and the undercutting of social protections, in order for the capital markets to enjoy their "freedom." The flexible euro system is intended to bring a modicum of order to this chaos, which has not even produced the higher growth in GDP that was promised—let alone the social benefits that were supposed to accompany this higher GDP.

There are some fundamental philosophical differences between the flexible eurozone framework and that of today's euro. The latter assumes that if the ECB sets the interest rate correctly and individual countries adhere to their debt and deficit limits, all will be well. It hasn't been. There is an abstract theory (called the Arrow-Debreu competitive equilibrium theory) that explains when such a system of unrestrained competitive markets might work and lead to overall efficiency. It requires markets and information that are far more perfect than that which exists anywhere on this earth. And even then, these Nobel Prize–winning economists were unable to show that the economic system was dynamically stable. It was an *equilibrium* theory; there was no explanation of how the economy would get to that equilibrium.

In the real world in which we live, it is often better not to just rely on prices—to try, as our flexible-euro framework does, to control the *quantity* of credit and net exports, and to regulate the uses to which credit is put and the amount of foreign denominated debt. The management of the economy in our proposed framework relies, however, heavily on the use of prices, but not fully so; there is no micro-management, but more macro-management than exists today.

Decades ago, we learned that one could not let a market economy manage itself. That is why, for instance, every country has a central bank determining interest rates and regulatory authorities overseeing banking. Some arch-conservatives would like to roll back the clock, to a world without central banks and with free banking, with no restraints. Anyone who has read his economic history knows what a disaster that would likely be.

But anyone observing macroeconomic performance in recent years will see that things have not gone well. Chapter 3 showed the massive waste of resources. It would be wrong if we did not try to improve upon this sorry record. The framework provided here and in the previous chapters does this. These are modest reforms that would not upend the system. But they systematically address some of the major weaknesses of current economic arrangements, some of the major instabilities that have proven so costly to our economies and our societies.

There are, of course, a large number of details to be worked out. The system is surely not perfect. But almost as surely, it is better than the current system, which has imposed such high costs on so many within the eurozone. This framework of eurozone economic cooperation with the flexible euro could lead to greater economic stability and growth.[3]

THE NEED FOR EUROZONE COOPERATION

Just as European cooperation is required if there is to be an amicable divorce, European cooperation would be helpful to ensure smooth functioning of the flexible euro. Even if there is hesitancy on the part of some for this proposed alternative,[4] the system is such that it can be undertaken by a "coalition of the willing," any grouping within the eurozone could adopt the system; these countries could then work together to ensure the relative stability of movements in the local-euro exchange rates, in the manner that I described earlier in this chapter. Of course, if all, or even most, of the countries of the eurozone, with the exception of perhaps Germany, join this coalition of the willing, then de facto, Germany's exchange rate itself would become flexible, for it would then be variable with respect to all of the other local-euros. It would then be in the interests of Germany to join the overall system, to help ensure stability of its exchange rate relative to those of the others.

Given sufficient European solidarity and cooperation, the framework would result in exchange rates moving within increasingly narrow bands. With sufficient success in exchange-rate coordination, in narrowing the band, it might, someday, allow Europe to move forward, toward a single currency.

12

THE WAY FORWARD

This book has provided a bleak assessment of the state of the eurozone and the prospects going forward. I have described the underlying flaws in its construction, how they were the result in part of flaws in economic understanding but also in part of a lack of political will and solidarity. We have seen how that same lack of economic understanding and solidarity has led to the flawed response to the crisis.

It is not just Europe's present that is being sacrificed but also its future. The euro was supposed to "serve" the European people; now they are asked to accept lower wages, higher taxes, and lower social benefits, in order to save the euro. And it is not just Europe's economy that is being sacrificed but, in many ways, confidence in its democracy.

The Germans and other leaders in the eurozone have put forward the idea that *"there is no alternative"* (TINA) to their draconian policies. I have explained how there are—alternatives that would even make the creditors better off.

In this concluding chapter, I want to address three questions: Where is the eurozone likely to go? Why is it taking the course that it is—is there *something* else beneath the surface that is playing out? And why is the European project so important?

WHITHER THE EUROZONE?

I have outlined three alternatives to the current strategy of muddling through. I know which I would prefer if I were a European—the reforms described in chapter 9 that would make the eurozone work.

Economists have a poor record in forecasting—the Troika may have set new records in serially bad forecasting when it came to their programs around the eurozone—but political forecasting is even more difficult. I worry, though, that even the amicable divorce or the flexible euro will be put aside, as the current strategy of muddling through continues. The afflicted countries will be given just enough hope for the future to stay inside the eurozone. Germany and others in the eurozone will play on the strong support in Greece and elsewhere for the eurozone: the citizens in these countries irrationally see not being in the eurozone as being not in Europe or the EU, forgetting about Denmark, Sweden, and the UK, which are in the EU but not in the eurozone; or forgetting about Switzerland, Iceland, and Norway, which are not even in the EU but are very much part of Europe.

The political scenario going forward then is not pretty: with the centrist parties committed to the euro losing ground to parties more to the extreme; in the case of Spain, the continued growth of parties asking for regional independence. Throughout Europe, as the fears of unemployment spread, we are likely to see the growth of parties rejecting Europe's openness, wanting especially to close its borders to migrants. No one can be sure when the political will to stay in the euro will break in one country or another. But it is clear that there is a risk, even a significant probability that that will happen. One can already see it in the votes.

And when that break does happen, there is a risk of the floodgates crashing down: if any country exits smoothly, then almost surely others will join, unless before then the Troika has relented and/or these countries have recovered—and at present, both of these seem remote possibilities. That these dramatic events would have profound economic and political consequences not just for Europe but for the world is an understatement.

Europe's leaders viewed themselves as visionaries when they created the euro. They thought they were looking beyond the short-term demands that usually preoccupy political leaders. The future of Europe and the euro now depends on whether the current political leaders of the eurozone can combine a modicum of economic understanding with a visionary sense of, and concern for, European solidarity.

WHAT IS GOING ON? THE INTERPLAY BETWEEN POLITICS AND ECONOMICS

I have remarked several times that there is something strange about the policies imposed on the afflicted countries. Normally, lenders impose conditions on borrowers designed to enhance the likelihood that the loan will be repaid. By contrast, the conditions imposed by the Troika reduced those countries' capacity to repay, particularly in the case of Greece. As I write this, Greece is in a deep depression and has been so for years, with a 27 percent fall in GDP from its peak, a 24 percent unemployment rate, and a youth unemployment rate more than twice that: I can think of no depression, ever, that has been so deliberate and had such catastrophic consequences.

It is thus natural to ask, what is going on?

IDEOLOGY—ONCE AGAIN

One possibility—a real one—is that the architects of austerity truly believed in the economic doctrines that they espoused, in spite of the overwhelming evidence against them accumulated over more than three-quarters of a century.

Advances in behavioral economics and psychology provide some explanation for the persistence of such beliefs—the theory of *confirmation bias* holds that individuals discount information that is not consistent with their prior beliefs. And in our complex world, it is easy to do so. It is hard, of course, to deny the decrease in Greece's GDP. But it is possible to find alternative explanations—Greece didn't do everything that it should have done.

I had seen such rationalizing on the part of the IMF in the multiple failed programs in developing countries and emerging markets. The programs were well designed, it was argued; the failure was one of implementation on the part of the country. Such arguments, I believe, are disingenuous—an attempt to shift the blame for the failure of the program to the victim of the program.

BLAME THE VICTIM

As we've seen, in the case of the 2015 program imposed on Greece, there was an attempt to blame Greece for the poor performance, and even the poor design, of the program. If they had only bargained better . . . If they had only had a more conciliatory finance minister than Yanis Varoufakis, one who adhered better to conventions (finance ministers *always* wear ties, but Varoufakis refused), one who was not so aggressive. Even many Greeks blamed themselves.

I had watched Greece negotiate programs with the Troika over a half-decade, first with the mild-mannered, intelligent, conciliatory George Papandreou, then with his successor, Antonis Samaras, and finally with the Syriza government. It is hard to detect much, if any, difference in outcomes.

It is not surprising that Germany and others in the eurozone would blame Greece. They would rather hold on to their incoherent and discredited theories; to reconcile what happened with what their theories predicted meant they *had* to blame Greece: the patient wasn't following the doctor's orders. In fact, few if any democracies have been able to achieve the magnitude of "fiscal consolidation"—reduction in the size of the fiscal deficit—in the span of a few years that Greece achieved. They succeeded in transforming a large primary deficit into a surplus in five years.

Even the way the money was given had the effect of making Greece *look* more dependent on Germany and its other eurozone partners than it was. The short-term credit, with tranches being dribbled out, helped reinforce the unfavorable image of Greece. Compare a five-year $100 billion loan with a sequence of five one-year loans, where the debt keeps getting rolled over. In the latter case, Greece has had to borrow $500 billion—and it still hasn't gotten things in order. Of course, in terms of money, the two are identical. But to ordinary citizens, not used to the tricks of high finance, it makes a great deal of difference whether Greece has been lent $100 billion or $500 billion. The latter number seems to make it clear that Greece is on the dole.

As we've seen, Greece has gotten but a pittance of the money loaned—most of it went to private sector creditors—but it has paid a high price to preserve other countries' banking systems.

The scenario is eerily similar to the predatory lending now rampant in the United States. A poor American will buy a $500 couch, overpaying by two or three times in order to get credit. Credit is provided at a rate of 200 percent a year. If a payment is missed, fees are added. Within a couple of years, the poor individual owes $2,000. But it's not like he's been living high on credit. His only profligacy was the $500 couch. All the rest is interest, interest on interest, and interest on the interest on the interest. In the case of the predatory lender, it is about money—the banks and other predatory lenders have figured out how much they can fleece poor people within the law.

But here, something else is going on. The IMF and the other "official" creditors do not need the money that they are demanding. Nor are they in the business of making profits. Under a business-as-usual scenario, the money received from Greece would most likely just be lent out again to Greece (typically, almost immediately)—to be given back again to the lenders, in a grand charade, a shell game, but one with real consequences.

As each loan, as each tranche of each loan, gets discussed, the Troika puts in demands that Greece finds unacceptable. And of course, politically, it is unpalatable for any Greek politician who cares about his country to simply throw people out on the street, as one Troika demand implied. But, with Greece resisting the demands of the Troika time after time, the country looks increasingly like a recalcitrant and unrepentant borrower. At least back at home, Germany's case for treating Greece so tough is reinforced.

TINA

The German attitude discussed in chapter 1, referred to as TINA, set the tone for the negotiations: on the variable most critical for macroeconomic performance, the primary surplus, there was little if any give—in 2015, Syriza's government succeeded in postponing the pace of tightening a little bit, in recognition of the changed circumstances, but the 2018 primary surplus of 3.5 percent remained fixed. Germany wouldn't even negotiate with the IMF on the question of debt restructuring, which everyone knew had to occur. As we noted in chapter 7, Greece was made to sign up to a program that all parties knew was incoherent, the pretend and extend of no debt restructuring.

Some within Europe, with little background in economics, could fool themselves into believing that the program would work. When individuals come to a belief that is countered by evidence—beliefs that cannot and will not be shaken by evidence—we say that they are blinded by ideology. In recent years, we have seen ideologies shape behavior in a number of spheres of public and private life. In the arena of economics, so closely linked to politics and policies that shape society, it is no surprise that ideologies often play an important role.

FAILURE TO LEARN

Almost as surprising as the Troika's not learning from history—that such private and public austerity virtually always brings recession and depression—is that Europe's leaders have not even learned from the experiences within Europe.

The IMF should be complimented for at least recognizing that contractionary policies are contractionary, and at least it recognized some of the mistakes in the policies that had been imposed in the cases of Greece and Ireland.[1] Apparently, the other members of the Troika were unhappy with such honesty.[2]

The Troika, as we have noted, is *still* demanding that Greece achieve a primary budget surplus (excluding interest payments) of 3.5 percent of GDP by 2018 and beyond. That target is punitive. Ironically, not only have these policies cost Greece a depression, they have already cost the creditor countries substantial amounts and are likely to cost them still more in the future.

A LACK OF FAITH IN DEMOCRACY

Why would Europe act in this way? Why did European Union leaders resist Papandreou's first proposal of a referendum, or the Syriza government's 2015 referendum—refusing even to extend by a few days the June 30 deadline for Greece's next payment to the IMF? Isn't Europe all about democracy? Papandreou believed that he would win the referendum—that a majority would support his painful measures; and he believed that that support was necessary for the effective implementation of the program. The Syriza government wanted to ensure that there was democratic legitimacy in their accepting a program that was so at odds with what so many in Greece had asked for, so at odds with the elections of January 2015.

That concern for popular legitimacy was incompatible with the politics of the eurozone, *which was never a very democratic project.* Most of its members' governments did not directly seek their people's approval to turn over their monetary sovereignty to the ECB. Moreover, the political accountability of the ECB, the major eurozone institution itself, was limited. When Sweden and Denmark sought public approval to join the eurozone, their citizens said no. Perhaps these polities understood that unemployment would rise if the country's monetary policy were set by a central bank that focused single-mindedly on inflation. In the early 1990s, Scandinavians had painfully learned the consequences of paying insufficient attention to financial stability, as they experienced their worst economic downturn since the Great Depression.

Today, part of the popular resistance to the euro is the concern of excessive influence of Germany and the ideas and ideologies that prevail there. In this book, we have repeatedly noted the role that neoliberalism has played in shaping the eurozone's structure and policies. In many other countries, prevailing opinion agrees with those expressed by the research department of the IMF and by this book: austerity is contractionary and the Troika policies are counterproductive. But within the eurozone, such ideas have been given short shrift. It is not, of course, that Germany *runs* the ECB or the European Commission, the other two members of the Troika. Indeed, the ECB has never been headed by a German, and some of its policies, such as quantitative easing, have violated its orthodoxy. Yet, somehow, the old adage that "he who pays the piper calls the tune" has by and large played out. With the strongest economy in the eurozone, its dominance of policy is perhaps not a surprise.[3]

One might, accordingly, think that Germans would be enthusiastic about the euro. At the time the euro was created, many worried that, tethered with the profligate countries of southern Europe, the euro

would be a weak currency and the eurozone would be marked by inflation. They got what they wanted, and perhaps more: a strong currency
and a region bordering on deflation. But even in Germany, some polls
show that almost two-thirds of its citizens think their country would
be better off outside the eurozone[4]—though their reasons are different. They believe that they will eventually be forced to "share" with
their poorer neighbors to the south in some bailout.

Sure enough, what one saw unfold, 16 years after the start of the
eurozone, was the antithesis of democracy: Many European leaders
in Europe wanted to see the end of Prime Minister Alexis Tsipras's
leftist government. They seemed to believe that they could eventually bring down the Greek government by bullying it into accepting an
agreement that contravenes its mandate.

In the end, they failed to bring down the government—Tsipras was
given a new mandate in 2015 with an even larger majority. But he was
forced to accept conditions that were antithetical to what the vast
majority of Greece's people wanted. Greece had surrendered its economic sovereignty in order to stay in the eurozone. When I saw Tsipras returning from Brussels, having finally yielded to the demands of
the Troika, the image of President Suharto surrendering Indonesia's
economic sovereignty 18 years earlier to the IMF, with the IMF's managing director, Michel Camdessus, lording over the once-powerful
leader, came to mind.[5]

As bad as things may be now, there are proposals for further
"reform" of the eurozone that would make matters worse. Germany
has clung to the notion that countries must live within their budgets,
and if they only did so, then all would be well. And to enforce the rules,
Wolfgang Schäuble, Germany's finance minister, together with Karl
Lamers, the CDU (Germany's conservative party) former foreign
affairs chief, have proposed "a European budget commissioner with
powers to reject national budgets if they do not correspond to the
rules we jointly agreed."[6] In effect, an appointed commissioner would
have the ability to veto the actions of national parliaments.[7]

IDEOLOGY AND POWER

Though few would admit it, the debate—the struggle—over the euro is as much or more about power and democracy, about competing ideologies, visions of the world and the nature of society, than it is about money and economics.

This is not simply an academic debate between the left and the right. Some focus on the political battle: the harsh conditions imposed on the left-wing Syriza government should be a warning to any in Europe about what might happen to them should they push back.[8] Some focus on the economic battle: the opportunity to impose on Greece an economic framework that could not have been adopted in any other way.

It is striking how the Troika has failed to convince the citizens of Greece, Portugal, and Spain of the virtue of their policies. I believe strongly in democratic processes—that the way to achieve whatever framework one thinks is good for the economy is through persuasion. In the current case, Greek, Portuguese, and Spanish citizens seem to have a better grasp of economics than Germany's finance minister or the Troika.

Even if one weren't deeply committed to democracy and democratic processes, the success of the programs being foisted on the crisis countries depends in part on "ownership," on their believing that the medicine, as painful as it is, is the right medicine. The Troika has convinced some in the crisis countries that that is the case (more than I would have thought, given both the weight of theory and evidence against them). But the polls show convincingly that the majority have not been convinced.

Anyone engaged in public policy knows how important public perceptions are. If these public perceptions are wrong, then successful policy implementation requires countering them. For instance, in all countries, tax collections depend largely on voluntary compliance, but when the tax system is viewed as unfair and biased, one should not expect increased compliance—no matter how many lectures are given about the laziness and noncompliance of Greek citizens. So, too, programs that entail alienating and demoralizing the bureaucracy that is supposed to carry them out, and include cutbacks in their resources, predictably won't be carried out well.

In the days of the repeated crises in emerging markets, when IMF programs failed, the IMF would say that the programs were well designed. They wanted to shift blame for the failures to the countries: the problem was with the implementation. So, too, with the repeated failure of the Troika programs. It is an oxymoron to say programs are well designed when there are repeated and consistent failures in implementation. Programs must be designed so that ordinary mortals—bureaucrats constrained by resources, and political leaders constrained by electorates to whom they are responsible—can carry them out. And success requires the support of both the electorates and the bureaucracy. The Troika seems not to have recognized this; indeed, with their antidemocratic stances, for instance against referenda, they seemed openly hostile to these perspectives.

I am not so Pollyannaish to believe that democratic politics will necessarily lead to good economic or social policies. Americans who have seen economic policies pushed by conservatives in the United States, with strong support of electorates in certain states, have to recognize this: the result in some states has been austerity in an era of negative real interest rates when real returns to public investments are enormous. The repeated revival of supply-side economics, after its predictions have been strongly shown to be wrong just years earlier, provides another instance. But neither am I Pollyannaish about experts: it was the so-called experts in the financial sector who developed regulatory and macro-management models that led to the crisis of 2008. It was the experts who believed that the euro would lead to stronger economic performance.

In much of the world, there is a growing understanding that the ideology of the right has failed, and so, too, its economic doctrines of neoliberalism. As an American, I have seen and experienced this:

beginning around 1980, the country began a bold experiment, of lowering taxes on the top, allegedly to improve incentives, and "freeing the economy," deregulating, especially the financial sector. The results are now in: the bottom 90 percent have seen their incomes stagnate, large proportions have seen their incomes fall; only those at the very top have done well. And the economy as a whole has performed more poorly, with growth lower than that in the decades after World War II. The right rewrote the rules of the market economy in ways that benefited the few; that is why there is now a campaign to once again rewrite the rules, but this time to benefit the vast majority of Americans.[9]

The eurozone was another attempt to rewrite the rules—another attempt that has led to more inequality and economic stagnation. With these ideas now having failed on both sides of the Atlantic, it is no wonder that their devotees are on the defensive and have to rely on force (or in some cases, deception and unholy alliances with anti-immigrant groups) to achieve their political ends.

Austerity is contractionary; inclusive capitalism—the antithesis of what the Troika is creating—is the only way for creating shared and sustainable prosperity.[10] But austerity is only part of a grander strategy concerning the role of the state. For instance, Wolfgang Schäuble has argued "that under normal economic circumstances the rate of public expenditure should not rise faster than the nominal growth rate."[11] There is, however, no general theory—either in economics or in political philosophy—in support of such a conclusion. If, as is the case in most countries, government is responsible for health care, and as people become richer and live longer, they as a democratic society decide to devote more public spending to health care, why should that *not* be done?

The changing structure of our economy and society may well call for an increasing share of public expenditures: in an innovation economy, basic research becomes increasingly important, and only government can finance such research; with more and more individuals living in cities, there is a growing need for publicly provided urban amenities; with heightened inequality associated with the market economy, a stable and just society may wish to undertake more aggressive actions to combat it; with global warming and other environmental risks, the government may need to do more to protect the environment.

The issue here, however, is not who is right, or which view is right. What concerns me is that the economic framework of the eurozone is being used to push for a particular set of views concerning the economy and society—and these perspectives are effectively being imposed on the crisis countries.[12]

WHY THE EUROPEAN PROJECT IS SO IMPORTANT

It is not in the interest of Europe—or the world—to have a country on Europe's periphery alienated from its neighbors, especially now, when geopolitical instability is already so evident. The neighboring Middle East is in turmoil; the West is attempting to contain a newly aggressive Russia; and China, already the world's largest source of savings, the largest trading country, and the largest overall economy (in terms of purchasing power parity), is confronting the West with new economic and strategic realities. This is no time for European disunity and economic weakness.

I would argue even more strongly that all people have an interest in the success of the European project. Europe was the source of the Enlightenment, which resulted in the increases in living standards that have marked the last two centuries. The Enlightenment, in turn, gave rise to modern science and technology. We too often forget that for eons before, standards of living had changed little.[13]

In many parts of the world, and often even within the United States, while the fruits of the Enlightenment are readily enjoyed, its basic values are questioned. One of my friends in the Obama administration, exhausted from fighting to prevent global warming and climate change, has commented that he has to relitigate the Enlightenment every day. Europe has been in the forefront of the battle to save the planet; a more united Europe would be better able to wage that battle.

The Enlightenment was marked, too, by a new sense of tolerance, including of those who differed from oneself. The Enlightenment also gave birth to notions of basic human rights, to be enjoyed by all individuals. America was lucky to have been founded just as these ideas were percolating, and so one sees them strongly reflected both in its Declaration of Independence and its Bill of Rights. The struggle to create political and social systems fully reflecting these Enlightenment values is never-ending; there are constantly new frontiers, and in many of these areas, Europe, too, has led the way—from the fight for gender equality to the fight for the rights of privacy; from the struggle for transparency in government and the "right to know" to democratizing participation in all aspects of life.

The moment the world is in now calls out for these values. There is the existential fight to prevent unacceptable levels of climate change. While Obama has been a strong advocate for global cooperation, with so many climate deniers in the Republican Party and in the US Congress, Europe will have to play a pivotal role. Concerted action by Europe might enable the imposition of cross-border taxes on goods, from countries like the United States and China, that are made in a carbon-unfriendly way.

The world is engaged too in a war against ISIS and terrorism more generally. More immediately, the world faces a humanitarian migrant crisis—a crisis that Europe saw so vividly, as it flared in the summer of 2015. The imminent cause of that crisis was the war in Syria, itself part of a wider war against ISIS and terrorism. These crises pose multiple challenges both to Western values and to the European project. One is how to wage the wars against ISIS and terrorism without unduly sacrificing the very values we seek to protect. Europe will be central in ensuring a balanced and effective global response; a united Europe will be more effective in ensuring that the responses are consistent with our values.

While America has long celebrated its open doors for immigrants, the reality in recent years has been otherwise. The United States took a fraction of the number of refugees from Iraq—refugees created by America's war against Iraq—than much-smaller Sweden. Evidently, the Bush administration felt no moral responsibility for the millions of displaced persons that their war had created. The world needs a united Europe to formulate a humanitarian response to these migrant crisis.

But as our discussion in earlier chapters has highlighted, for Europe to have a consensus response with fair burden-sharing will require a functioning European economy. The migrants will not want to go to countries where there is massive unemployment, and countries in deep recession or even stagnation can ill afford to accept them. Both migrants and the host country know that without jobs, these new migrants will not be able to start the new life that they crave for; and if migrants have to compete with those who have long been unemployed for jobs, there will be resentment and hostility.

Ironically, the policies imposed on Greece helped to create and shape one aspect of the migrant crisis. For instance, Greece had been home to many from the Balkans. As Greece's economy plummeted, these migrants had to look elsewhere. With so many countries in the eurozone with high unemployment, the only place for them to go was Germany and the few other countries in the eurozone with full employment.[14]

The unbalanced flow of migrants is a predictable result of the economic imbalances the euro created within Europe. Chapter 5 highlighted how the current eurozone structure led to divergence; but the relatively few countries doing well will also resent having the burden of refugees placed on them. But as this book goes to press, the failure to resolve the migrant crisis poses an existential crisis for the EU: a fundamental principle of the EU is free mobility of labor, but that principle, in conjunction with the divergent eurozone, inevitably implies that the burden of migrants will lie with those like Germany that are *relatively* prospering. Without shared prosperity—at least more sharing that is likely to exist under the eurozone's divergent structure—it will be difficult for Europe to abide by both its humanitarian principles and its principle of free mobility. Something will have to give: but it would be far better to change the monetary arrangements along one of the ways we have suggested.

Economic divergence, especially when combined with a sense of unfairness and deep differences in views about values and economic principles, makes it difficult to forge a European consensus around other issues. Again, one sees this played out most dramatically in the migration crisis. Greece is at the frontier with Turkey and the Middle East, and after eurozone programs have led to a 27 percent decline in its GDP, it is in no position to deal with the large numbers of migrants arriving at its borders. The abuse that Greece received at the hands of its "partners" obviously made it less trusting in dealing with the migrant issue. Forcing Greece, already suffering from depression, to bear, by itself, so much of the brunt of the surge of migrants, especially those from Syria—has deepened the perception that European solidarity, or even a minimal sense of justice and fair play, have withered.

POLITICAL AND ECONOMIC INTEGRATION: LESSONS FROM THE EUROZONE

Globalization has meant that the world is more integrated than it ever was. It means that what one country does has effects on others, that what citizens do in one country can have effects on citizens in others. In many ways, we have become a global community—a community with a system of global governance without a global government.

There is an ongoing process of shaping that global community, and how it is shaped will reflect the values and concerns in different parts of the world. The voice of Europe, with the values that I have described in the previous paragraphs, needs to be heard, and it will be heard more clearly if the European project succeeds. It will not be heard if Europe is in disarray and if there is not shared prosperity.

The experiences of the eurozone have one further important lesson for the rest of the world: be careful not to let economic integration outpace political integration. Be skeptical of anyone who suggests that political integration will naturally follow from economic integration. And be especially skeptical of anyone who proposes a monetary union in the absence of adequate political integration. Perhaps the one silver lining in the European cloud is that this lesson has been learned: a variety of proposals for monetary unions elsewhere have quietly been put on the back burner.

Around the world, there are many efforts at advancing economic integration without commensurate moves toward political integration. The drivers of that integration—and the source of the flaws in the design—are often similar to those that we have seen in the creation of the euro. The euro was constructed on the simplistic premise that a single currency would facilitate the movement of capital and goods; the resulting economic integration would improve societal welfare *everywhere* within the eurozone. In the case of many economic changes, there are winners and losers; the changes are defended on the grounds that the benefits of the winners far exceed the losses of the losers and that in the long run, almost all will be winners. The argument for the eurozone too was that everyone, or almost everyone, would benefit. The reality, as we've seen, has been otherwise: Germany is the big winner; much of the rest of the eurozone, especially the crisis countries, are the big losers; and the eurozone as a whole has done poorly—the losses of the losers far outweigh the gains of the winner.[15] The lesson is that markets are complex institutions; simplistic tinkering, based on ideology rather than a more profound understanding of how markets actually work, without a deep appreciation of the complexities, can lead to disastrous outcomes.

The United States today is pushing a trade agenda across the Pacific and the Atlantic that is premised on the idea that the *freer* movement of goods across more borders would similarly increase the well-being of *all* the countries involved—indeed, would benefit all the countries of the world. But, again, with simplistic free market ideology and special interests working together, the trade agreements that are emerging—the Trans-Pacific Partnership and the Transatlantic Trade and Investment Partnership—are even more unlikely to deliver on its promises than the eurozone's. There will be winners—the big corporations, especially the pharmaceutical companies and coal and oil companies threatening the environment. But as in the eurozone (in its current form), the losses of the losers will outweigh the gains of the winners. The agreement would make access to generic prescription drugs more difficult, would almost surely lead to more inequality, and would make it more difficult for governments to regulate the environment, health, safety, or even the economy in the public interest.[16]

SAVING THE EUROPEAN PROJECT

The ongoing debate over the euro—its structure and the policies and programs imposed on the crisis countries—have raised deep questions about values and objectives. Too often, it seemed as if saving the banks, or even just the euro, was given precedence over human welfare. Success was measured in sovereign bond spreads—the difference between what the bonds of Greece or Italy were paying and those that Germany was paying. When those spreads came down, victory was declared.

So, too, as we have noted, programs were declared successful when unemployment started to fall or GDP started to grow—not when unemployment was restored to an acceptable level or when living standards were restored to what they would have been but for the crisis, or even more modestly, to what they had been before the crisis.

Remarkably, in assessing the success of the Troika programs—programs often motivated by worries about government debt and deficits—little attention was paid to the debt-to-GDP ratio, a measure of debt sustainability that had not improved. Indeed, as we've seen, the debt-to-GDP ratio rose in the crisis countries, in some cases to levels that would normally be viewed as unsustainable, because of the adverse effects on GDP.[17] The denominator of the ratio has been reduced by more than the numerator has been circumscribed.

There should be a single, simple measure of the success of any economic program, and that is the well-being of a country's citizens, and not just the 1 percent at the top. Well-being is *more* than just income, and there is more to the measurement of success than assessing what has happened to GDP, or even GDP per capita. For most individuals, meaningful and decent work is an important part of their life, and an economy that denies meaningful work for large fractions of its citizens—that denies employment for large fractions, let alone a majority, of its young—is a failed economy. An economic system or a set of economic arrangements that fails repeatedly to achieve well-being for large fractions of its people is a failed economic system, a failed set of economic arrangements. An economic system that leaves large fractions of the population facing high levels of insecurity, too, is a failure.

For young people, the prospect of living their dreams, a life with hope and aspirations, is critical to their well-being. For old people, a retirement with dignity and a modicum of security is essential to well-being. Many older people had planned *not* to retire, to continue working. But with high levels of unemployment and a major slowdown, these individual's jobs have disappeared. One might say: they should have planned for this. But how could one have expected that Europe's leaders would create such a dysfunctional system? Or would have imposed policies that have resulted in such dire outcomes? Advances in economic understanding were supposed to end the business cycle, or at least dampen it.

Research on individual and societal well-being has shown perhaps the obvious: individuals care about security and about jobs. The euro-

zone and the policies that have been imposed on the afflicted countries have increased insecurity and decreased jobs. A symptom of how
bad things have become in many of the crisis countries, as we have
noted, has been the dramatic rise in suicides.[18] In the most important
objective of economic policy, enhancing individual and societal well-
being, the eurozone has been a disappointment, to say the least.

Monetary systems come and go. Monetary arrangements, like the
Bretton Woods system that governed the world after 1944, was heralded at its onset as the replacement of the gold standard. It seemed to
work in the years after World War II, but in the end, it did not last even
three decades. The euro's moment of glory was even shorter; and as I
have argued, even in the brief time that it *seemed* to be working, the
imbalances that would eventually bring on the euro crisis were building up, and the euro (and the associated economic arrangements)
were largely to blame.

This book has shown that the euro can be saved, should be saved,
but saved in a way that creates the shared prosperity and solidarity
that was part of the promise of the euro. The euro was a means to an
end, not an end in itself. I have laid out an agenda of reform for the
structure of the eurozone and for the policies that the eurozone needs
to follow when one of its members faces a crisis. These reforms are not
economically difficult; they are not even institutionally difficult. But
they require European solidarity—a kind of solidarity fundamentally
different from the suicide pact that some leaders within Europe are
calling for.

For all the emotions that the euro has brought on, for all the commitments that have been made to preserve it, in the end, the euro is
just an artifice, a human creation, another fallible institution created
by fallible men. It was created with the best of intentions by visionary
leaders whose visions were clouded by an imperfect understanding of
what a monetary union entailed. This was perhaps understandable:
nothing like it had been tried. The real sin would be for Europe not to
learn from what has happened in the last almost two decades.

Three messages emerge clearly from my analysis. A common currency is threatening the future of Europe. Muddling through will not work. And the European project is too important to be sacrificed on the cross of the euro. Europe—the world—deserves better. I have shown that there are alternatives to the current system. Moving from where the eurozone is today to one of these alternatives will not be easy, but it can be done. For the sake of Europe, for the sake of the world, let us hope that Europe sets out to do so.

AFTERWORD: BREXIT AND ITS AFTERMATH

ritain's June 23, 2016 referendum on leaving the European
European—by a vote of 52 percent to 48 percent—set forth a
firestorm of political and economic upheaval on both sides of
the English Channel. Prime Minister David Cameron resigned; there
were calls for the leader of the opposition Labour Party, who, it was
felt, had not campaigned sufficiently vigorously for "Remain", to step
down. The pound fell 11 percent against the dollar in just four days to
a 30-year low—but only 8 percent against the euro. It became clear
that the advocates of "Leave" had no plan for what to do if they proved
victorious, and that there had been wild exaggerations, if not outright
lies, by those arguing for Brexit.

Europe's response to the UK's referendum was dominated by the
same harsh response that greeted Greece's June 2015 ballot-box
rejection of its bailout package. Herman Van Rompuy, former EU
Council[1] President, expressed a widespread feeling when he said that
Cameron's decision to hold a referendum "was the worst policy decision in decades." In so saying, he revealed a deep antipathy towards
democratic accountability. Understandably so: as we have noted, in
most of the cases in which voters have been directly turned to, they
have rejected the euro,[2] the European Union,[3] and the European

constitution.[4] Moreover, polls at the time of Brexit showed that a majority of those in many European countries besides the UK had an unfavorable view of the EU (including Greece, France, and Spain.[5])

The economic and political consequences of Brexit will, of course, depend a great deal on Europe's response. Most assume that Europe will not "cut off its nose to spite its face." It seems in the interests of everyone for there to be an "amicable divorce," to work out the best economic relationship consistent with the democratic wishes and concerns of those on both sides of the Channel. The benefits of trade and economic integration are mutual, and if the EU takes seriously its belief that the closer the economic integration the better, that implies an attempt to make the *closest* ties possible under the circumstances. Anything the EU does to the UK to try to punish it would have an "equal and opposite effect," hurting itself at least as much in the process. The fact that European stock markets were down markedly, and European banks were particularly hard hit at least suggests that Brexit was bad for Europe as well.[6]

But Jean-Claude Juncker, the proud architect of Luxembourg's massive corporate tax-avoidance schemes and now the head of the EU Commission, has taken a hard line—perhaps understandably, given that he may go down in history as the person on whose watch the dissolution of the EU began. His line is that Europe must be unrelenting in its punishment, and should offer little more than what the UK is guaranteed under normal global agreements, like the WTO, lest others join the rush to the exit.[7] What a response! According to Juncker, Europe is not to be held together because of the benefits that accrue, benefits which far exceed the costs, the economic prosperity, the sense of solidarity, the pride in being a European. No, Europe is to be held together by threats and fear—of what would happen if a country leaves.

It was a perfect storm—a confluence of untoward circumstances—that led to what the elites around the world (and 48 percent of UK voters) viewed as a great disaster, a rip tide going against the mainstream current of globalization and closer economic integration.

Historians will debate the *what if*—what if the leadership in Europe or the UK had done more to avoid the outcome which they almost all opposed? But that the referendum's outcome will reshape the future of the EU, the eurozone, and globalization seems indisputable.

As this book goes to press, the tensions over alternative courses are already evident: most politicians in the UK are arguing for a careful, judicious divorce; they are even hoping for an amicable one. Many in Europe (conspicuously François Hollande, the French President) just want a quick divorce. Uncertainty is costly, and the currently uneasy relationship between the UK and Europe may discourage investment in both Europe and the UK. And, as we have already noted, some like Juncker want a settlement so painful that no one should ever again think about exiting the Union.

Europe prides itself on its rule of law; and the legal treaties of the EU leave it to the country seeking a divorce to trigger the proceedings, and only set a two-year time limit from that date to their conclusion. But realpolitik does not always coincide with international law. Threats and counter-threats are a reality. At this juncture, even the best of crystal balls are cloudy.

The focus of this book has been narrower than the EU—our attention has been on the misconceived euro, the single currency shared by 19 of the 28 members of the EU, and the flawed institutions that have struggled to make it work, but from which have emerged a set of policies that have actually led to economic and political divergence. The UK was wise not to join the euro, but I will explain in what follows how the failures of the euro nonetheless reverberated in the UK referendum. And some of the same forces that were at play in leading to a failed euro have been at work in the EU more broadly, undermining popular support for it throughout the region. So, too, in laying out the way forward in chapters 9 and 12, many of the reforms I have proposed extend beyond the eurozone to the EU. Among them are reforms that are required to make the EU the success that its founders envisaged—a Union bounded by a sense of solidarity and common interest, not by the fear of the unknown, or, still worse, by the retribution that would be brought down upon them by those who still pretend to be their friends. In the final section of this Afterword, I discuss some of the additional reforms that are crucial. Neoliberalism and the perspectives of corporate elites provided the intellectual lodestar guiding not just the creation of the euro, but much of the evolution of the European Union.[8] This book has explained the failure of these ideas in the context of the monetary arrangement. But the failures have been broader, and if the Union is to succeed—if further messy divorces like that with the UK are to be avoided—the EU will instead have to disengage itself from this ideology and the interests that it serves.

THE PERFECT STORM

The UK has been, in part, caught up in the same maelstrom that has struck the US. Ordinary citizens on both sides of the Atlantic have had enough. A common theme contributed to the outcome of both the American Republican primaries and the British EU referendum: large portions of the population have not been doing well. The neoliberal agenda of the last third of a century might have been good for the 1 percent, but not for the rest. I have long predicted that this stagnation—actually, worse than stagnation for those who have not gone to college—would eventually have political consequences. That day now appears to have arrived.

For the US, the data reveal the dire straits in which we find ourselves: median household income, adjusted for inflation, is today less than 1 percent higher than it was in 1989.[9] Angry middle-aged, middle-class white men are among the strongest supporters of Donald Trump, again not surprisingly: real income of a typical full-time male worker is lower than it was more than four decades ago.[10] The stress created by stagnant wages, increased economic insecurity and reduced job protection—without unions to curb the abuses of bosses—has been too much for many: death rates have increased, including from social diseases like drug abuse and alcoholism, and suicide.[11] At the bottom, things are still worse: wages, adjusted for inflation, are at levels comparable to 60 years ago.

The data for the UK and Europe is only a little better.[12] Branko Milanović has strikingly shown how different groups around the world fared in the two decades from 1988 to 2008. The big winners were the global 1 percent—the very rich around the world—and the new middle classes in emerging markets such as China and India. The global middle has seen its incomes rise by 70–80 percent, while those of the top 1 percent have risen by 60 percent—and captured, alone, 27 percent of all the gains.

On the other hand, there were two categories which lost out in those decades, and continue to suffer or stagnate. Those at the very bottom, including poor farmers in the poorest countries, have been hard hit by trade agreements that allowed the rich countries to maintain their massive subsidies. So greedy were the special agricultural interests in the US and the EU that they got their governments to walk away from the Doha "development round" of trade negotiations, which finally died in December 2015, 14 years after it began. They preferred to see trade negotiations fail rather than give up their hefty subsidies; especially in the US, most of these went to rich farmers, often corporate farms, even as the resulting increased production drove down global prices, hurting the poorest of the poor in developing countries. Even when the US was found guilty of violating WTO rules with its massive cotton subsidies that hurt poor farmers in Africa, India, and Latin America, it refused to eliminate the subsidies.

But the group that did the *worst of all*—seeing virtually no growth in their incomes in a span of two decades—was the working class in Europe and America.[13] Things were not going well for them *before* the global financial crisis of 2008, but the crisis made matters worse, especially for the most vulnerable.[14] The banks were saved—in fact billions went to save the banks, the bankers who had caused the crisis, their shareholders and bondholders—but little went to the victims. They lost their jobs. In many countries, like the US, Ireland, Spain, and Greece, they lost their homes, with mass evictions. In the UK as well as the crisis countries upon which I have focused here, the victims suffered further as the ideology of austerity came to dominate. Massive and controversial cutbacks in the basic fiber of society—in health care and welfare—were required to make up for largesse to the banks. It all seemed so *unfair*—and it was.

THE GRAND EXPERIMENT

A third of a century ago, the bankers and others from the elite implicitly made a quite different set of promises, not dissimilar to those made at the time of the founding of the euro. Globalization, financialization, economic integration, the lowering of tax rates on corporations and high net worth individuals and liberalization more generally would all create a new economic order. Lower tax rates would incentivize the economy; liberalization would turbo-charge it. The two together would lead to a burst of economic energy from which all would benefit. True, there might be more inequality, but focusing on inequality was giving in to envy. If everyone was doing better, if the economic pie was bigger overall, who could complain if some did better than others—especially if those who were doing especially well were the job creators and innovators, the source of the growth of living standards for all the rest?

The one part of this narrative that turned out to be true is that these "reforms" did lead to more inequality—even more than the harshest critics feared. But in fact growth slowed, and the result was economic stagnation and increased insecurity for vast portions of society—in the US, for the bottom 90 percent. Most European countries (with the exception of Scandinavia) were not far behind.

The UK could pride itself on having lower unemployment than the rest of Europe—5 percent vs. 8.7 percent (and 10.2 percent for the eurozone) in March 2016.[15] But for those without jobs or job prospects, statistics are cold comfort. And those who had jobs weren't doing particularly well either: wages and productivity were stagnating, and the constant threat of government cuts to the social safety net upon which so many depended as a last resort made them feel ever more vulnerable.

On both sides of the Atlantic, many on the left bought into some of the neoliberal ideas. Their critique of the right was that it had a cold heart. It became increasingly difficult to distinguish between compassionate conservatives and the "new left." Bill Clinton in the US, Tony Blair in the UK, and Gerhard Schroeder in Germany all introduced reforms that those on the right had struggled to make for decades. In the US, for instance, Clinton lowered the tax rate on capital gains—the major source of income for the very rich—and engaged in massive financial market liberalization. In the UK, Blair and Gordon Brown, his successor, talked about "light" regulation—almost as much of an oxymoron as "self-regulation." There was a regulatory race to the bottom—with the banks the big winners, and our societies the big losers.

All of these leaders pushed trade deals, deals that not only lowered tariffs but also strengthened intellectual property rights, ensured financial market liberalization and integration, and advanced corporate interests in a variety of other ways, for instance making it more difficult to enact environmental, health, and economic regulations.

There was something very odd about the new politics that was emerging. Elites within both the left and the right seemed to have reached a broad consensus about many of the tenets of the economic order. Of course, there would be disagreements about details. The left, for instance, cared more about the environment and they at least talked about social justice and basic human rights. But there was broad support on the center-right and "new" left for an economic agenda which included liberalization and deregulation, globalization, and lower taxes (even if not quite as low as those sought by the right). In macroeconomics, this entailed fighting inflation and maintaining budget balance. In Europe, at the center of the new

consensus was the furtherance of the European project, and in most
of Europe that meant the euro. But this elite center-left/center-right
consensus wasn't really working for most citizens. The economic
and political order just wasn't delivering for most Americans or
Europeans.

The 2008 financial and economic crisis may have played a critical
role in precipitating the current political crisis. Politicians who promised changes didn't deliver what had been expected. Citizens knew
that the system was unfair and rigged, but after the crisis and lopsided
"recovery" they saw it as even more unfair, more rigged than they had
imagined; and they lost what little trust they had in the political process to correct it. They voted for politicians who promised to rectify
the situation. Barack Obama campaigned on a platform of "change
you can believe in." Even though Obama did deliver in some areas—
successfully pushing through a health care reform that Democrats had
been trying to achieve for decades—in areas of economics that were
crucial to individuals' well-being, somehow it didn't happen. No wonder: the new politicians—in the US, in the UK, and elsewhere—were, to
a large extent, of the same ilk, servants of the same ideology, accountable to the same special interests as those that had promised that
globalization would bring benefits for all.

EXPLAINING THE FAILURE: THE CENTER-RIGHT—DOUBLING DOWN

There has been a huge scrum of explanations and prescriptions for our
current ills, and a plethora of explanations for why the construction of
the "neoliberal order" over the past third of a century, which *promised*
such benefits to *all*, has failed so miserably, with such adverse effects on
so many. An upsetting of the balance among the social partners, labor,
employers, and government changed economic, social, and political
dynamics. Weakening bargaining positions of workers, for instance,
meant a declining share of labor and greater insecurity. It meant, too,

that there was no counterbalance to corporate political influence. Financialization, accompanied by short-termism, led to lower growth, so that workers were getting a smaller slice of a small pie.

The right (the Conservatives in Britain, like the Republicans in the US) said we simply needed to double down on our bet: more of the same would do the trick—more budget cuts, more trade agreements, more financial market liberalization and integration, lower tax rates for corporations and individuals. It was like medieval blood-letting: when the doctors saw the sick patient was not recovering, they demanded still more blood-letting—it was clear that the bad humors that were causing the disease were still present. George Osborne, the UK's Chancellor of the Exchequer at the time (equivalent to the Minister of Finance or the US Secretary of Treasury) was particularly disingenuous. While calling continually for austerity, he carefully lifted his foot from the brakes and put it on the accelerator in the run-up to the election of 2015, enabling him to claim that his policy of austerity was working.[16] But even his sleight of hand couldn't do anything about UK's stalling productivity and long-term unemployment, especially in the north of England; and his constant threats to cut the budget heightened economic and social anxiety.

EXPLAINING THE FAILURE: THE CENTER-LEFT GETS CO-OPTED

Within the eurozone, the center-left was defending the failed policies that have been shown to lead to stagnation or worse. They would campaign on promises of lifting austerity—their citizens grasped that austerity wasn't working—but Germany would have none of that. And so austerity continued, and citizens felt increasingly disempowered. What they cared most about—the decisions which affected their lives and livelihoods—were seemingly out of their hands, and in the hands of those without democratic accountability.

Those in the countries of the eurozone that are faring badly can rightly blame the euro for at least part of their plight, as we have seen.

But not so for the UK, or at least not so directly: the weakness in their major trading partners across the Channel has clearly hurt the UK. The UK, of its own accord, had imposed austerity on itself. The Tories were under the influence of the same mistaken economic doctrines, the same ideology that prevailed in Germany: they believed that the deficit was the source of UK's economic weakness; curing the deficit was necessary and almost sufficient for a return to robust growth. They believed, too, that through trickle-down economics, this growth would benefit all.

The center-left and center-right had two problems: they were unable either to adequately explain why what they had promised had not been delivered or to provide viable alternatives. More broadly, they had lost their credibility. Given the gap between what had been promised and what was delivered, why should they be trusted?

This has left an opening for those of more "extreme" positions of both the left and the right. Actually, what gets labeled now as the "far left" is what, in another era, would pass as moderate. The center, with its neoliberal ideology, has moved so far to the right that so-called moderates no longer seem so. These moderates, now viewed as extremists, have put forward an agenda which would actually lead to more growth with more equality. They have called for an end to austerity and recognition that *any* change in economic policy may have large distributive consequences which have to be taken into account. We will return to this agenda later in this Afterword.

The extreme right has focused on two themes (besides the excesses of the financial sector): trade and immigration. There is more than a grain of truth in the charges that trade liberalization and immigration have played important roles in the plight of the working class, as uncomfortable as that reality is to the center in politics. Of course, other forces (like changes in technology) have played a role too, and in many cases, an even bigger role. But changes in technology are largely out of our control, or at least they appear to be so. Trade and immigration are matters of policy: they reflect *choices*. Other policies might have led to better outcomes—more jobs with higher wages and better job protection. And even with the opening up of trade and immigration, there were alternative policies that could have done better at mitigating the adverse effects. Ironically, especially in the US, the proponents of trade liberalization actively opposed such policies.

By contrast, the UK's former Conservative Chancellor George Osborne actually did undertake some actions to help those at the bottom and to increase opportunity, but they were insufficient. The minimum wage for workers aged 25 and over was raised, from £6.70 to £7.20 per hour, and with further planned increases to about £9 an hour by 2020. It wasn't enough, but it was still something, especially when seen in comparison with the seemingly much richer US, where the minimum wage remained at $7.25 an hour, lower than it had been in the late 1950s in inflation-adjusted terms (at the pre-Brexit-vote exchange rate, equivalent to £4.83 per hour). The fact that the working classes have fared better in some countries, like France, Denmark and Sweden, than in others, like the UK and US, suggests that policies do matter.[17]

Osborne's income-contingent loan program (making the repayment of student loans contingent on the income that an individual earned) was designed to expand educational opportunity in the UK, directly addressing a problem that had come to the fore in the US presidential campaign—the burden of student debt (totaling in excess of one trillion dollars)—making higher education increasingly less affordable to ordinary Americans. But whether this fully offset the effects of the marked increase in tuition in England remained debatable.[18]

Ironically, the most important policy that would have led to more jobs, with the increased demand for labor resulting in higher wages, would have been an end to austerity. But the Conservatives, aided and abetted by the center-left (New Labour), had convinced the populace of the importance of bringing down the deficit. Osborne may not have been quite as successful as Merkel, with her constant reference to the responsible Swabian housewife (see chapter 7) in promoting deficit fetishism, but he was not far behind. So the national debate turned to the far more complex and even more controversial issues of trade and immigration.

TRADE

On both sides of the Atlantic, citizens seized upon trade agreements as a source of their woes. While this is an over-simplification, it is understandable. The trade agreements (including the most recent proposed ones such as the Trans-Pacific Partnership (TPP), bringing together 12 countries on both sides of the Pacific, and the Transatlantic Trade and Investment Partnership (TTIP) between the US and Europe) have been negotiated in secret, with corporate interests at the table—but not those of either ordinary citizens or workers. Not surprisingly, the outcome is one-sided. They have furthered the weakening of the bargaining position of workers, compounding the effects of other legislation weakening unions and workers' rights, as well as of changes in technology.

The objection to trade liberalization has not been directed at free trade *within* the EU, but at the trade deals that the EU (and the US) has made with the rest of the world. There is a simple idea—developed by Paul Samuelson, one of the greatest economists of the 20th century— that under the assumptions of perfect markets (which underlie most neoliberal economic analyses) free trade results in the equalization of wages of unskilled workers around the world. Trade in goods is a substitute for movement of people.[19] Importing goods from China—goods that require a lot of unskilled workers to produce—reduces the demand for unskilled workers in Europe and the US. And this force is so strong that if there were no transportation costs (and if the US and Europe had no other source of competitive advantage, such as in technology[20]), then eventually it would be *as if* there was free mobility of workers, *as if* Chinese workers continued to migrate to Europe and the US until there were no wage differences. Not surprisingly, the neoliberals never advertised this consequence of trade liberalization, as they claimed—one could say lied—that all would benefit. In the US, Congressional Republicans were even worse: they even opposed assistance to those that were directly hurt by such measures. Recent research has shown that those places in the US that produced goods which are close substitutes for those that were part of the surge of imports from China have lower wages and higher unemployment.[21] While such complex and detailed studies have not been conducted for Europe, it would be surprising if similar effects were not true there too.[22]

Neoliberal analysts who argued that trade would benefit all made two critical mistakes. First, they assumed the markets worked well, so that the economy was always at full employment. This is because, in neoliberal analyses, markets work perfectly and an increase in imports is offset by an increase in exports. Exports create jobs, imports destroy jobs, but in perfectly performing economies—with a central bank focusing on full employment and governments not constrained by austerity—macroeconomic policy ensures that there is always full employment. The shift to the more productive export sector raises living standards.

But the evidence is markedly to the contrary—in Europe, the unemployment rate has remained stubbornly high. And that means that the job-destroying effects of trade liberalization can more than offset the job-creating effects, especially in the short to medium term. The destruction of jobs in one sector does not automatically mean the creation of jobs in some other.

Secondly, they ignored the distributive consequences of trade agreements. Even if GDP increases, there are, as we have seen, big losers. All that the argument "trade is good" implies is that the winners *could* compensate the losers. And if trade is to benefit all, the winners *should* compensate the losers, but that doesn't mean that they *will*. Under neoliberal policies, they *didn't*. Even in countries like the US that have managed to keep the "official" unemployment rate low, the distributive effects have been overwhelming. If trade liberalization destroys jobs in textiles and apparel, but creates jobs in hi-tech, the textile workers have neither the abilities nor skills to make them productive in the expanding sectors. Besides, the new jobs are often created at a distance from the old jobs being destroyed, which means, at a minimum, that communities will be disrupted and families torn apart. Without generous compensation and active training policies, trade has hurt many people.[23] And those who have been hurt are angry, and feel they were lied to by the centrist politicians who said that the new trade agreements would make everyone better off. They feel even angrier as they are now told that they not only have to accept cuts in wages and job protections, but also in social programs upon which they rely—in order to "compete." The politicians who told them that these trade agreements would make them better off are now telling them that to "do well" under these trade agreements, they must accept a substantial lowering of their standards of living. No wonder they no longer trust these politicians or the political system.

IMMIGRATION

The subject of migration has become even more tinged with emotion than trade. Many of the refugees are victims of civil conflicts to which Western powers contributed, both by what they did and did not do. The colonial powers did less to inculcate democratic values than they should have—quite the opposite, they acted in an authoritarian way. The legacy still plagues many of the ex-colonies, and providing help to the refugees from this oppression is the moral responsibility of all, but especially of the ex-colonial countries.

From a sheer economic perspective, while many might deny it, standard laws have strong predictions: with downward-sloping demand curves (the usual case), an increase in supply *normally* leads to a lower equilibrium price. In labor markets this means that an influx of more unskilled workers leads to lower wages. And when wages can't or won't be lowered, greater unemployment results. This is especially of concern in places where economic mismanagement has been such that there already is a high level of overall unemployment.

There are exceptions to this general presumption: an influx of highly skilled workers could lead to an increase in the productivity (and thus wages) of unskilled workers. An influx of rich refugees could lead to an increase in demand for goods, with demand effects more than offsetting supply effects. But even here, there can be large distributive consequences: the rich immigrants may raise the price of real estate in certain places, like New York, Vancouver, and London, so much so that it makes living in these urban centers unaffordable for ordinary Americans or Canadians or Britons. The fact that the rich landowners in each of these places have become even richer is of little comfort.

Within Europe, places that have done a *better* job in reducing unemployment will predictably get more than their fair share of refugees. Workers in these countries bear the cost in depressed wages and unemployment that is higher than it otherwise would have been, while the corporations may celebrate the benefits of getting cheaper labor. The burden falls on those least able to absorb it.

The problem rose to the fore even earlier, as the much poorer countries of Eastern Europe were welcomed into the EU. It was striking that EU leaders didn't take more account of these basic laws of economics as they pushed for the expansion of the EU to include the eastern European and Baltic countries. It was an act of generosity with profound implications for those living in these countries. Most studies suggest that the most important variable determining success of the transition from communism to a market economy was incorporation into the EU. This helped create the legal and institutional framework necessary for a modern market economy.

But this generosity was largely borne on the back of ordinary workers—and among the beneficiaries were the corporations in Western Europe who could obtain labor at a lower cost. There are two competing interpretations: the leaders of Europe were criminally negligent in not taking into account the social and economic costs—and who would bear them; or the leaders of Europe were working at the behest of corporate interests—for whom the stress on workers was precisely what they wanted—to have a more pliant labor market, one where the power of unions could at last be broken. The neglect of the adverse effects on workers was totally consistent with the perspective of those who see so much of the EU's neoliberal agenda as working in service of corporations.

As in trade, the advocates of immigration liberalization overestimated the overall benefits, and underestimated the distributive effects and their consequences. There is much talk about the country receiving the immigrant *as a whole* benefiting. For a country providing low guaranteed benefits to all citizens—a poor system of social protection, a low safety net, poor education, poor health care, etc.—that may be the case. But to those providing a semblance of equalitarian social services, the opposite will be true. Even if the country as a whole benefits, as we have noted, certain groups of workers are likely to be hurt. If it was the case that the country as a whole benefited, the winners *could* compensate the losers, but such compensation is almost never made. It was never part of the EU framework.

So, too, it has been generally *assumed* that the countries sending the migrants will benefit. For the individuals migrating, this seems obvious: they would not migrate unless they felt sure they would be better off. But a societal analysis is more complicated. If the most talented individuals from Greece migrate out of the country, it can result in weaker job-creation and lower wages for the unskilled workers remaining behind.[24] In chapter 5, we noted how this would lead to lower tax collection and an increase in the public debt burden per capita on those remaining. In the case of Greece, cutbacks forced by Germany and the Troika in the health care system have allegedly led to 7,500 Greek doctors moving abroad, including to Germany.[25] Thus Germany and other European countries get improved health services, while the Greeks suffer from poorer access to doctors—after having invested millions of euros in their education.[26]

In the early days of the transition from Communism to the market economy, this out-migration of the most talented young people was so severe that it was referred to as a "hollowing out" of the economy. Those left behind were the old, the infirm, and those too young to travel. Though the country benefited from the remittances sent from the migrants back home, often those remittances dwindled over time, and in any case, they could not really make up for the consequences of the "hollowing out."[27]

Thus, as I explained in chapter 5, outside the unrealistic models of perfect markets with no taxes, no debts, no information imperfections, etc. free mobility of capital and labor could lead to *divergence* rather than convergence. The corollary is that free migration may result in a lowering of the welfare of both the country receiving the migrants *and* the country sending them. Even when the country as a whole benefits, there may be great distributive consequences, with large segments of the population—even a majority—worse off. The only sure winners are the migrants themselves and the corporations that get their cheaper labor.

While the neoliberal analysis of migration was clearly flawed, it was as wrong to focus on immigration as the source of the plight of workers as it was to focus on trade. Had European governments, including the UK, adopted other policies—a growth policy rather than austerity, stronger labor market policies, including higher minimum wages, better retraining programs, and reforms strengthening union bargaining power rather than weakening it—then more workers would have been better off.

Free migration was like the euro: an example of economic integration outpacing political integration. In the long run, it was inconceivable to have a single Europe without free migration. But as I have again repeatedly noted, a key lesson that I learned in my years as Chief Economist of the World Bank is that pacing and sequencing of reforms are critical. This book has shown how putting a single currency before the institutions that would make it work has been an economic and political disaster—*impeding* further economic and political integration. The same goes for free migration.

HOW THE FAILURES OF THE EUROZONE HAVE CONTRIBUTED TO DISILLUSIONMENT WITH THE EU

The UK was wise not to join the euro. One might have expected, especially upon reading this book, that it would be a country within the eurozone that would be the first to leave. But within the UK there was great skepticism about the EU at the time of joining, perhaps more skepticism than elsewhere in the region, and what has happened since has only made matters worse.

Europe, and especially the eurozone, has been badly mismanaged, to the point where average unemployment in recent years has been persistently above the American rate, and frequently in the double digits. Obviously this has undermined confidence in Europe. But there are several further consequences.

First, free migration within Europe has the obvious implication already noted: places that have done a better job in reducing unemployment will predictably get more than their fair share of refugees. In a Europe with free migration, the UK has a special place: it is a country that has already become multi-ethnic, multicultural. With English becoming the universal language, migrants find it particularly attractive. Not tied to the euro, it has also been able to achieve a high employment economy—making it very appealing to immigrants just happy to have a job.

Secondly, the dysfunction of the eurozone, the trampling of sovereignty in the crisis countries, has made Europe a "club" that seems less and less attractive—especially as Germany has seemed to dominate in a high-handed way that seems offensive to many. If those policies had been able to restore these countries quickly to full employment, that would have been one thing, but the abject failure of such policies—combined with the arrogance and unforgiving way with which they have been implemented—has only made things worse.

This, in turn, has reinforced a long-standing view of the EU— as a rule-bound, unthinking bureaucracy. The UK's Conservative Party had long played on this. It was a useful ploy, to blame the EU bureaucracy for whatever ills befell the country, and these views may also have reinforced existing stereotypes. In the "Leave" campaign, there was simply too much misleading exaggeration, for instance that the EU was going to require bananas to be straight. Such fallacies were common enough for them to gain their own term: the "euromyth."[28] There were plenty of false stories circulating, but some were based on a grain of truth. Everyone in the UK knew (or believed they knew) about some regulation or another with which they disagreed: for example, what could be sold under the heading of "ice cream" or that eggs could not be sold by the dozen but had to be priced by weight.

What was happening inside the eurozone fed another longstanding view of the EU: that there was a large democratic deficit. The views I have described here on this deficit, evident in the governance of its central institutions, like the ECB (discussed in chapter 6), and in the policies which emerged in response to the crisis, do not originate with me—they are views that are held throughout Europe. Rompuy's hostility towards asking the people their views is also widely shared among the elites that govern, as I have shown repeatedly. Thus, while the British did not suffer *directly* from the democratic deficit so evident in the euro crisis,[29] it played directly into their perceptions of the EU itself.

THE MIGRANT CRISIS

Attention since mid-2015 has shifted from the euro crisis to the migrant crisis—the hundreds of thousands of refugees, mainly from the war-torn Middle East, and especially Syria, but also from North Africa, sub-Saharan Africa, and farther afield.

As has been observed, Germany liked to label most of the latter as economic refugees, not deserving of the right to immigrate—though the distinction is less clear than their differential treatment might suggest, and the West may also have more than a little culpability for these economic migrants. We have a global economic system that leads to prices for cotton that are so low that a Mali farmer cannot support his family—and migration is the only way to stave off death for his children. One of the reasons that cotton prices are so low is the huge cotton subsidies of the advanced countries. Global warming—historically the result of the carbon emissions of the advanced countries—has contributed to the desertification of the Sahel, again increasing the numbers of economic migrants.

Whatever the moral responsibility of Europe towards the migrants, whatever its responsibilities under international law and Europe's own laws towards accepting the migrants, there is a broad consensus that Europe managed the migrant crisis poorly. The divergences across Europe to which the euro contributed made this almost inevitable: it was hard to construct an equitable burden-sharing arrangement. From an economic perspective, it made sense for those countries with near full employment to accept the lion's share of the immigrants, and for the wealthier countries to help the poorer countries with the social costs of immigration. But Germany repeatedly stated that "Europe is not a transfer union," blocking this just and reasonable approach. What inevitably followed was stalemate, with the migrant camps in Calais, the closest place in France to the UK for those waiting to cross the Channel, serving as a daily reminder of these failures.

THE CONSEQUENCES OF BREXIT

The immediate aftermath of the referendum was as bad, or worse, than those arguing for "remaining" had claimed. As noted, the pound fell almost 11 percent in four days, to a 30-year low. The stock market fell dramatically. The rating agencies downgraded British debt.[30] But consonant with the view that trade and economic integration is *mutually* beneficial, the euro also fell against the dollar, and Europe's stock markets fell. As in 2008, there was a "flight to safety," with German and US interest rates falling to a five-year low.[31]

We are, however, used to markets over-reacting—and reacting negatively to increased uncertainty. Within a few days of the referendum result, the Financial Times Stock Exchange (FTSE) 100 was higher than it had been 10 months earlier. But that index consists largely of multinationals. UK real estate funds were hammered, with so many so worried about further declines that they demanded to cash in, resulting in a number telling investors that they could not, at least for the time being, get their money back. The only certainty was that the future had become even more uncertain. And uncertainty discourages investment. What would happen depended on the new economic (and political) relationship that would be forged. Pundits laid out a variety of scenarios.

In one, the UK would delay invoking Article 50 of the Treaty of Rome, which sets off the two-year clock for the finalization of the divorce. In the meantime, negotiations would succeed in putting a brake on immigration and other democratic reforms would be pushed through, sufficient to justify asking the British people once again for their views. In this scenario, "Reform and Remain" wins—and Brexit never happens.[32]

The other extreme entails a real Brexit with a hardline Europe refusing initially to grant the UK any special status. It might even threaten a worse and worse "deal" the longer that the UK delays invoking Article 50.[33] This is the scenario of "cutting off the nose to spite the face"—to discourage anyone else from leaving an EU so democratically unpopular that it can be held together only through such threats.

The reality is that UK is not likely to be much worse off—and potentially even better off—so long as the divorce is not too unpleasant, and so long as Europe doesn't violate its obligations under the WTO rules (including the critical "most-favored-nation" provision, which requires that one treats every nation, outside a common market, no worse than any other, so that the UK could not be treated any worse than the US).

Much noise has been made about economic integration, and almost certainly the world has benefited as tariffs have come down. The WTO created the beginning of an international rule of law—I say only "the beginning" because powerful countries essentially flout the rulings when it seems desirable to do so for reasons of domestic politics. But recent agreements—even those that are called "trade" agreements—are more about "harmonizing" regulations, protecting intellectual property, and liberalizing financial markets than about trade itself. While corporate interests have been well served, the benefits to society are more questionable. As an example, the "closer" economic integration brought about by the massive regional trade agreement, the Trans-Pacific Partnership, has been variously estimated to affect US GDP by minuscule amounts varying from slightly negative to 0.15 percent—and then only after a long period, and under unrealistically optimistic assumptions.[34] Even the IMF has come to question the benefits of taking down all barriers to the free flow of capital—in the aftermath of the global financial crisis, its new "institutional view" called for the selective use of capital controls, for what has come to be called "capital account management."[35] In the absence of such capital controls, destabilizing "hot money" flows can exacerbate instability.

We should note that the United States and Canada have both prospered—indeed, they have been doing far better than the eurozone (see chapter 3)—without free migration between them, without being a single market, and without full economic integration. In fact Canada is thankful that its economic integration with the US has been limited; otherwise, it would have suffered the full calamity of the 2008 crisis, as its financial sector would have been forced to adopt the flawed neoliberal ideas governing its financial system. (The world, too, is thankful that there was some "diversity" in economic frameworks: otherwise the global financial crisis would have been a multitude of times worse than it was.)

Earlier in this book I talked about the benefits and costs of economic and political integration. The world has suffered greatly from warring countries and some degree of global cooperation is clearly beneficial. The UN has been of enormous benefit, even though it is a far from perfect institution. But even as the United States was formed, large areas of governance were reserved for the individual states. It was a federal structure, not a unitary government. Figuring out how much and what powers should be devolved and how many should be central is complicated, and there is indeed no "right" answer. There are many possible solutions. The principle of subsidiarity is crucial: that those activities which are local in nature, which have limited externalities on others, should remain to be decided at a lower level of government. The issue is identifying what those decisions are which cannot or should not be devolved, and recognizing which combinations between devolved and undevolved are unlikely to work.

I noted earlier how the eurozone got it wrong: it was thought that limited *fiscal* deficits and public debts were critical to making a single currency work. In so thinking, the founders of the eurozone created a divergent system that has contributed strongly to the eurozone's stagnation and growing lack of political solidarity. But there were similar mistakes made by the European Union, both in what they did and what they didn't do.

I have already commented on two of these: fearing unfair competition, and under the influence of neoliberal ideology, they prohibited the kinds of industrial policies that would have enabled those countries entering the Union from behind to catch up, to converge. A narrow interpretation of unfair "state aid" has thrown doubts over whether Italy can come to the assistance of its ailing banks—but without such assistance, credit from small- and medium-sized enterprises will be limited, and Italy's growth will continue to be stymied.

I noted too how the failure to harmonize tax policies and enact a European-wide progressive tax has contributed to destructive tax competition and to Europe's growing inequality. Each country finds itself in an impossible position if it wants to impose a progressive tax within its borders: its wealthiest citizens threaten to move elsewhere, in the full knowledge that they can do so while continuing to run their businesses. The current President of the European Commission, Jean-Claude Juncker, in his role of Prime Minister of Luxembourg, was the master of this race to the bottom. Of course, this race—the competitive lowering of individual and corporate tax rates—served corporate interests well.[36]

There were other mistakes. It is fairly clear that the EU has imposed more regulatory harmonization than is necessary—and that this excessive enthusiasm for regulatory harmonization is one of the things that has gotten the EU into trouble with the British. The costs of the excessive zeal are obvious, the benefits less so—except perhaps to the Brussels bureaucrats who seem to derive pleasure from enunciating regulations: why should everyone everywhere in Europe have exactly the same standards for ice cream (whether those regulations are too lax or too tough) or car windscreens? The United States and Canada have a joint sphere of co-prosperity with extensive trade across the border without such tight common regulations at every turn.

Underlying EU policy there should have been a simple principle: where the lack of harmonization has significant *cross-border* effects, then there may be a need for harmonization. It might seem "unfair" competition if English ice cream wasn't required to have cream, but Italian ice cream was. The costs of production of ice cream in England would be lower. Ironically, in the ideal world of neoliberalism, where perfect information reigned, this wouldn't be a problem. English ice cream—or particular brands of English ice cream that lacked cream—would suffer a reputation loss. Well-informed consumers would make a decision whether the benefits of ice cream with cream were worth the cost; if they thought so, they would choose the Italian product; if not, the English. In reality, consumers are far from well informed, but there is a much simpler solution than requiring all ice cream to have a certain cream content: adequate disclosure of the cream content. Provide the relevant information, and let consumers make the choice for themselves.

Car windscreens provide a slightly more complex example. It may be slightly cheaper to force all cars to have the same glass standard—but by a small margin. The US and Europe have had trade in cars with varying standards without difficulty. It is obvious that one doesn't need to standardize colors. It might be a little cheaper if all car manufacturers could paint all cars black —but different consumers want different colors, and the benefit of product variety far exceeds the average cost reduction of having a single color. So, too, there are negligible costs to adapting a car to differences in windscreens—whether tinted or not, or whether shatter-resistant or not.[37]

Having a standard on GMOs for seeds is a different matter. Genetically modified seeds can blow across a border, fertilizing a GMO-free field. Many Europeans care deeply about whether their food is genetically modified, and are willing to pay extra for GMO-free food. Thus, having a neighboring field in another country growing GM seeds imposes an *externality*, a cross-border cost. This is an area where a uniform regulation may be necessary.

But even here there can be trade without uniform regulation. The US and Europe can have different regulations. Of course, if consumers care, they should have the right to know about them. In trade negotiations between the US and Europe, the US has demanded that consumers *not* have the right to know—that there be *no* labeling, because such labeling puts American GMO products at a disadvantage. But it makes sense for Europe to require such labeling, and not to give into the pressure from US trade negotiators: forcing US products to label increases Europe's well-being; to deny them the ability to do so, reduces it. So far, *in this case*, EU trade negotiators have not given in.

In adopting regulations, this careful balancing of the benefits and costs too often seems missing. Sometimes, though not always, it seems as if corporate interests prevail. We saw the same problem in the context of so-called structural reforms in the crisis countries. There was no reason that Greece should have been forced to declare ten-day-old milk fresh—except that doing so would benefit big milk producers in the Netherlands and elsewhere.

LINKING FREE TRADE, FINANCIAL MARKET LIBERALIZATION, HUMAN RIGHTS, AND FREE MIGRATION

Many—including Prime Minister David Cameron during the referendum campaign—have suggested that the pre-Brexit UK had "the best of all possible worlds." It was not saddled with the dysfunctional euro, but had all the other economic benefits of economic integration of the EU. It is hard to quantify those benefits persuasively, and the discussion above has suggested that those benefits have been accompanied by costs.

Many in Europe argue that if the UK is to be given any special benefits (benefits that go beyond those to which they are entitled under WTO rules), the UK must accept the principle of free migration. In doing so, they are attempting to link trade and financial market integration with labor market integration.

This kind of linkage makes little sense. It is not as if the UK's stance on migration gives its banks or its car manufacturers a competitive advantage—quite the contrary, if one is to believe Europe's rhetoric about the economic benefits of migration. Clearly, if one were to worry about "unfair" competitive advantages in labor markets, one should worry about the lack of an adequate minimum wage or adequate job protection, or a structure of bargaining which helps push wages down. But Europe has been silent on these issues, reinforcing the view that the EU's economic agenda seems more aligned with promoting corporate interests than in promoting "fair trade."

At the same time, Europe has had an active human rights agenda, and in some instances these human rights have been broadened to include workers' rights, with certain safeguards and minimum standards. Interestingly, these were the grounds on which many from the Labour Party, including its leader, Jeremy Corbyn, who was otherwise unenthusiastic about the EU, supported remaining in the EU—and some Conservatives advocated leaving.

Some in the financial sector have argued that without the single market, without free migration between the UK and the EU, with different regulatory systems in the EU and the UK, they would have to leave London and relocate elsewhere in the EU. This too makes little sense. As we noted earlier, global banks operate globally. Much of the US derivatives business is conducted via London. Virtually all of the financial activities operating in offshore centers like the Cayman Islands actually occur in London and New York: in these offshore centers, there is often little more than a mailbox or postal address. All the real work is done elsewhere. Banks and other financial firms have learned how to operate under a multiplicity of jurisdictions (in the US, there are 50 different insurance regulators). Of course, they would prefer a single system—provided it is the system with the lightest regulation. And that perhaps may provide a hint at the real motive: the UK has been the strongest advocate within the EU for "light" regulation, both under Labour and the Conservatives. The financial sector may be worried that without the pressure from the British, the demand for stronger regulation from so many European quarters will prevail.

THE REAL COSTS—OR BENEFITS—MAY BE POLITICAL

While in the immediate aftermath of the Brexit referendum, attention has centered on the economic consequences, the political consequences, both for the UK and Europe, may be far more significant. A trend of more than a hundred years standing towards more integration has been reversed. Some worry that it will lead to the separation of Scotland, which voted overwhelmingly to remain, from the UK. Some worry that it will provide further impetus for separatist movements in Spain and elsewhere.

Others worry that, especially if the UK does reasonably well economically, it will provide an impetus for voters in Italy, Greece, Spain, or Portugal to leave the eurozone. The reality, though, is that the unrelenting commitment to austerity by the European Commission—as it threatens to impose penalties on Spain and Portugal because of their failure to get their deficits down *enough* even after years of very painful austerity—will probably do more to encourage the exit from the eurozone than anything the UK does. It is the failure of the eurozone—not Brexit— that will in the end undo the eurozone.

Hopefully, the Brexit referendum will be a wake-up call to the EU's leaders: unless they make the EU more democratic, more democratically accountable, and more economically successful, the likelihood of further integration, political or economic, could be nil. The failure of the EU to deliver economically for large parts of its citizenry is not because of inexorable economic forces; it is the result of economic policies, too often shaped by neoliberal ideology and corporate and financial interests.

THE WAY FORWARD

The refrain of those in the UK who wanted to stay in was "Remain and Reform." There will have to be reforms if the EU is to survive and prosper—and by prosperity I mean not just an increase in GDP but a shared prosperity, in which democratic values are honored and respected. The citizens should *want* to be in the EU because of the prosperity it brings, not because they fear the wrath that will be brought down upon them by their friends and neighbors if they leave.

The debate following the Brexit referendum about these reforms across Europe has been almost as bitter as the referendum itself in Britain. The gap between political and economic integration that seems so obviously at the root of the problems of both the EU and the euro has been widely recognized. I have argued here that if the euro is to work, there has to be *more* Europe—not necessarily like the federal structure in the US, where two thirds of public expenditure are at the national level—but still far more than exists today. The alternative is *less*, including the abandonment of the single currency. This book has argued that the current halfway house is not sustainable. A similar argument holds for the EU more broadly. If there is to be a single set of regulations applying across Europe, there must be confidence that they are being set to reflect the interests of its citizens as a whole, not just corporate interests. If there is to be free migration, the economic system has to be better designed—to ensure that more countries have full employment and that there are adequate systems of social protection. There has to be a better system of burden-sharing within and across countries, including for the system of social protection of migrants. One cannot have an *economic* union without some sharing of risks and burdens. To abide by the refrain "Europe is not a transfer union" means the European Union cannot work.

Many of Europe's leaders have been quick to dismiss any moves towards "more Europe." Europe is not ready for it, so they claim. But if that is the case, neither is Europe ready for a single currency or free migration or the single market. The thesis of this book is that a single currency requires *more* Europe. The thesis of this Afterword is that a single market and free migration also require *more* Europe. What is required, from an economic perspective, is not a lot. It is clearly within the reach of Europe. Whether it is *politically* attainable, given the current politics of Europe, is another matter.

The last chapter of this book set out an agenda for what needs to be done if the euro is to work. Several items in this agenda also apply to the EU more broadly: tax harmonization and a progressive Europe-wide tax system and social safety net; and industrial policies to help those countries that are behind to catch up.

This Afterword has called attention to several more necessary reforms: a more sensible trade and migration policy, which recognizes the national and distributive costs of migration, the uneven burdens that trade liberalization and migration impose, and the provision of EU-wide help for the countries and groups disproportionately bearing those burdens. As is the case with the euro, problems that are collectively created must be collective addressed.

It takes time and resources to integrate migrants into communities, and without such integration, the risks of adverse effects are even greater. This means that countries should have the right to impose some restrictions. The countries which the individuals leave should also receive some compensation for the loss of the human capital in which they have invested. Of course, the magnitude of these restrictions will depend on the extent of European solidarity itself and the success of the broader European project. If more of the countries within Europe succeed in attaining full employment, that will automatically result in a better sharing of the burden, and enhance the willingness to accept new migrants.

But if Europe continues with changes in labor legislation that weaken workers' bargaining rights, and if, as expected (partly as a result) wages do not rise much, that will increase the resistance to accepting migrants. If the EU increases its budget, and allocates more of the budget to help pave the way for migration, rather than subsidizing corporate agriculture or bailing out financial institutions, then one would expect more openness to migration.

Most importantly, the EU has to wake up to what has been happening in Europe: just as there is in the United States, there is a growing divide, a political elite out of touch, economic stagnation experienced by large portions of the population, and an economic system that has not delivered for many—in some places, even for the majority.

The evisceration of the middle classes and its consequences is much the same on both sides of the Atlantic. There is anger—understandable anger. But voting in anger—which at least some did in the British referendum, enough to have swung the result—does not solve the problem. It may lead to politicians in power and a political and economic situation that is even worse for those who have voted in that way. The response should not be a round of recriminations and further anger, directed at those who voted "wrongly" or at those political leaders who arguably might have done a better job at convincing the electorate to once again "trust them" that there would, in fact, be the reforms that were promised and that a new, reinvigorated EU would at last deliver on its promises. In the UK, the establishment parties *together* were seen as the culprits; among those that have felt betrayed by the politics of the last third of a century, their working together to oppose Brexit may have even reinforced the image of a bi-partisan establishment in London once again pushing establishment policies.

The European project was a project intended to bring the peoples and the countries of Europe closer together. In some ways it has worked. Young people all over Europe now identify themselves as Europeans. Even in the UK, some three-quarters of the young voted to remain.[38] They were *hopeful* about the future of Europe, hopeful that the EU could and would be reformed. Perhaps it was simply naive youthful enthusiasm. Their elders had lost hope, and for good reason. They had seen a project intended to promote solidarity and well-being do just the opposite; it seemed held hostage by corporate interests and neoliberal ideology. Though the UK was spared the worst effects because their leaders had wisely chosen not to join the eurozone, those without jobs and the even larger number with jobs that were paying poorly *knew* that they were not doing well, they *knew* that the system was unfair, they *knew* that the political leaders who had promised a new prosperity had lied to them. Too many in the UK had lost not just hope but trust. They voted accordingly.

As I listen to the post-Brexit discussions on both sides of the Channel, I become alternatively hopeful and despondent. Despondent that so many on both sides have not understood what has been happening. Despondent at the hard line taken by some of the leaders who have so faithfully served the corporate interests—and are themselves so much the source of Europe's problems. Despondent at the inability to make these leaders understand basic principles of economics, to make the reforms in the structure of the eurozone which would enable Europe to return to shared prosperity. If they cannot make the seemingly obvious reforms, in relatively short order, how will they make the deeper reforms necessary to make the EU work, both economically and politically?

A basic principle in economics is to let bygones be bygones. On both sides of the Channel, politics should be directed at understanding the underlying sources of anger; how, in a democracy, the political establishment could have done so little to address the concerns of so many citizens, and figuring out how to do that *now*: to create within each country, and through cross-border arrangements, a new, more democratic Europe, which sees its goal as improving the well-being of ordinary citizens. This can't be done with the neoliberal ideology that has prevailed for a third of a century. And it won't be done if we confuse ends with means—the euro is not an end in itself, but a means, which, if well managed, *might* bring greater shared prosperity, but if not well managed *will* lead to lower standards of living for many, possibly the majority of citizens. The fact that so few of the leaders on either side of the Channel understand this also makes me despondent.

But perhaps more important than all of these reasons for pessimism are the reasons for hope: that so many throughout Europe have held on to their faith in the European Project, that even in countries where there is every reason for despair there is still hope—hope that the EU can and will be reformed. There are political leaders throughout Europe who understand the ideas I have outlined here, who have become politicians because they still believe that democratic politics can bring about changes that will deliver shared prosperity to ordinary citizens. And throughout Europe, there are especially young people who have marched, by the tens of thousands, for a different Europe, one, for instance, in which new trade agreements serve not just corporate interests but broader societal interests.

Fortunately, there are alternatives to the current arrangements that can create a true shared prosperity: the challenge is to learn from the past to create this new economics and politics of the future. The Brexit referendum was a shock. My hope is that the shock will set off waves on both sides of the Channel that will lead to this new, reformed European Union.

NOTES

Preface

1 More precisely, around 45 percent at the start of 2016, according to Eurostat.

2 The address was published as Robert E. Lucas Jr., "Macroeconomic Priorities," *American Economic Review* 93, no. 1 (2003): 1–14; the quote appears on p. 1.

3 With every country's currency pegged to gold, the value of each currency *relative* to the other was also fixed.

4 Bryan uttered this phrase in his July 9, 1896, speech at the Democratic National Convention in Chicago.

5 See Barry Eichengreen, *Golden Fetters: The Gold Standard and the Great Depression, 1919–1939* (New York: Oxford University Press, 1992).

6 The equivalent value for US and China GDPs are $17.9 trillion and $11.0 trillion, respectively. (In purchasing power parity, PPP, a standard way of making cross-country comparisons, the EU was about 1.0 percent smaller than China, but 7.0 percent larger than the United States.) Because of varying exchange rates (the value of the euro relative to the dollar varied during 2015 alone from 1.06 to 1.13), the relative size (at current exchange rates) varies. In 2014, the EU was actually the largest economic block—the fall largely reflects the changing exchange rate, which fell by some 17 percent.

7 Formally known as the Treaty on European Union.

8 Not surprisingly, many other economists and political scientists have found the euro crisis similarly fascinating, and a large literature has grown up trying to understand it, approaching the subject from many different perspectives— as a financial crisis, a political crisis, and an economic crisis. The distinctive

approach taken by this book is to focus on those aspects of the structure of the eurozone itself—its rules, regulations, and governance—that essentially made the crisis and its overall poor economic performance virtually inevitable. For an early survey of the crisis, see Philip R. Lane, "The European Sovereign Debt Crisis," *Journal of Economic Perspectives* 26, no. 3 (Summer 2012): 49–68. For a thoughtful European perspective written in the early years of the monetary union, see Tommaso Padoa-Schioppa, *The Euro and Its Central Bank: Getting United After the Union* (Cambridge, MA: MIT Press,2004); and for a view of the next steps, see Henrik Enderlein et al., "Completing the Euro: A Roadmap Towards Fiscal Union in Europe, Report of the 'Tommaso Padoa-Schioppa Group,'" Notre Europe, 2012, available at http://www.notre-europe .eu/media/completingtheeuroreportpadoa-schioppagroupnejune2012 .pdf?pdf=ok. For a somewhat more up-to-date survey, see Enrico Spolaore, "What Is European Integration Really About? A Political Guide for Economists," Tufts University and NBER Working Paper, June 2013, and a special volume of the *Journal of Macroeconomics* dedicated to the euro crisis, "The Crisis in the Euro Area. Papers Presented at a Bank of Greece Conference," 39, part B (March 2014). The volume includes papers by (in order of appearance in the journal) Heather D. Gibson, Theodore Palivos, George S. Tavlas, George A. Provopoulos, Vítor Constâncio, Seppo Honkapohja, Michael Bordo, Harold James, Barry Eichengreen, Naeun Jung, Stephen Moch, Ashoka Mody, John Geanakoplos, Costas Azariadis, Paul De Grauwe, Yuemei Ji, Vito Polito, Michael Wickens, C. A. E. Goodhart, Lucrezia Reichlin, Stephen G. Hall, Karl Whelan, Anabela Carneiro, Pedro Portugal, and José Varejão, among others.

9 In *Globalization and Its Discontents* (New York: W. W. Norton, 2002), I describe these failures and my interpretation of the politics, interests, and ideologies behind them.

10 See *Globalization and Its Discontents*.

11 See, in particular, *The Price of Inequality: How Today's Divided Society Endangers Our Future* (2012), *The Great Divide: Unequal Societies and What We Can Do About Them* (2014), and *Rewriting the Rules of the American Economy: An Agenda for Growth and Shared Prosperity* (2015) (with Nell Abernathy, Adam Hersh, Susan Holmberg, and Mike Konczal), all from W. W. Norton. These recent books are built on my earlier work—such as "Distribution of Income and Wealth Among Individuals," *Econometrica* 37, no. 3 (July 1969): 382–97— and on "Dynastic Inequality, Mobility and Equality of Opportunity," written with Ravi Kanbur, Centre for Economic Policy Research Discussion Paper No. 10542, April 2015, to be published in *Journal of Economic Inequality* in 2016. Kanbur served as one of my principle advisers at the World Bank.

12 Robert E. Lucas Jr., "The Industrial Revolution: Past and Future," *The Region*

(May 2004), Federal Reserve Bank of Minneapolis, pp. 5–20, available at https://www.minneapolisfed.org/publications/the-region/the-industrial-revolution-past-and-future. He went on to say, "The potential for improving the lives of poor people by finding different ways of distributing current production is nothing compared to the apparently limitless potential of increasing production." While the *potential* for improving the lives of the poor may be enormous, all too often this has not actually happened. Both Europe and the United States today provide living examples.

13 See, for example, Stiglitz, *Price of Inequality* and the references cited there; OECD, "In It Together: Why Less Inequality Benefits All," May 21, 2015, available at http://www.oecd-ilibrary.org/employment/in-it-together-why-less-inequality-benefits-all_9789264235120-en; Andrew G. Berg and Jonathon D. Ostry, "Inequality and Unsustainable Growth: Two Sides of the Same Coin?," IMF Staff Discussion Note 11/08, April 8, 2011, available at https://www.imf.org/external/pubs/ft/sdn/2011/sdn1108.pdf; and Jonathan D. Ostry, Andrew Berg, and Charalambos G. Tsangarides, "Redistribution, Inequality, and Growth," IMF Staff Discussion Note 14/02, February 2014, available at https://www.imf.org/external/pubs/ft/sdn/2014/sdn1402.pdf.

14 Bruce C. Greenwald and Joseph E. Stiglitz, "Externalities in Economies with Imperfect Information and Incomplete Markets," *Quarterly Journal of Economics* 101, no. 2 (1986): 229–64.

15 I became particularly engaged in "the economics of crises" during my time at the World Bank and wrote extensively on the subject, both alone and with my colleagues at the World Bank. A popular account is provided in *Globalization and Its Discontents*. See also my articles "Lessons from the Global Financial Crisis," in *Global Financial Crises: Lessons from Recent Events*, ed. Joseph R. Bisignano, William C. Hunter, and George G. Kaufman (Boston: Kluwer Academic Publishers, 2000), pp. 89–109 (originally presented at the Conference on Global Financial Crises, Bank for International Settlements and Federal Reserve Bank of Chicago, May 6, 1999); "Financial Market Stability and Monetary Policy," *Pacific Economic Review* 7, no. 1 (February 2002): 13–30; "Lessons from East Asia," *Journal of Policy Modeling* 21, no. 3 (May 1999): 311–30 (paper presented at the American Economic Association Annual Meetings, New York, January 4, 1999); "Responding to Economic Crises: Policy Alternatives for Equitable Recovery and Development," *Manchester School* 67, no. 5 (September 1999): 409–27 (paper presented to North-South Institute, Ottawa, Canada, September 29, 1998); "The Procyclical Role of Rating Agencies: Evidence from the East Asian Crisis," with G. Ferri and L.-G. Liu, *Economic Notes* 28, no. 3 (November 1999): 335–55; "Must Financial Crises Be This Frequent and This Painful?," *Policy Options* 20, no. 5 (June 1999): 23–32 (paper originally given on September 23, 1998, as University of Pittsburgh McKay Lecture); "Knowledge

for Development: Economic Science, Economic Policy, and Economic Advice," in *Annual World Bank Conference on Development Economics,* ed. Boris Pleskovic and Joseph E. Stiglitz (Washington, DC: World Bank, 1998), pp. 9–58.

I wrote several papers addressing what kinds of reforms in financial systems—both nationally and globally—would lead to greater stability: "Reforming the Global Economic Architecture: Lessons from Recent Crises." *Journal of Finance* 54, no. 4 (August 1999): 1508–21; "The Underpinnings of a Stable and Equitable Global Financial System: From Old Debates to New Paradigm," with Amar Bhattacharya, in *Annual World Bank Conference on Development Economics 1999,* ed. Boris Pleskovic and Joseph E. Stiglitz (Washington, DC: World Bank, 2000), pp. 91–130; "Robust Financial Restraint," with Patrick Honohan (who later went on to be head of Ireland's Central Bank, and with whom I had the opportunity to discuss many aspects of the Irish crisis—some of which are discussed below), in *Financial Liberalization: How Far, How Fast?,* ed. Gerard Caprio, Patrick Honohan and Joseph E. Stiglitz (Cambridge, UK: Cambridge University Press, 2001), pp. 31–63.

With Jason Furman, who would later go on to be the chairman of President Obama's Council of Economic Advisers, I wrote a paper trying to understand the factors contributing not only to the East Asia crisis but to crises more generally: "Economic Crises: Evidence and Insights from East Asia," Brookings Papers on Economic Activity No. 2, September 1998, pp. 1–114 (presented at Brookings Panel on Economic Activity, Washington, DC, September 3, 1998).

And also with three World Bank colleagues—Daniel Lederman, Ana María Menéndez, and Guillermo Perry—I wrote a couple of papers trying to understand the Mexican crisis of 1994–1995: "Mexican Investment after the Tequila Crisis: Basic Economics, 'Confidence' Effect or Market Imperfection?," *Journal of International Money and Finance* 22, no. 1 (February 2003): 131–51; and "Mexico—Five Years After the Crisis," in *Annual Bank Conference on Development Economics 2000* (Washington, DC: World Bank, 2001), pp. 263–82. Finally, with two other World Bank colleagues—William R. Easterly and Roumeen Islam—I wrote two papers trying to understand the forces underlying economic volatility: "Shaken and Stirred: Explaining Growth Volatility," in *Annual Bank Conference on Development Economics 2000* (Washington, DC: World Bank, 2001), pp. 191–212; and "Shaken and Stirred: Volatility and Macroeconomic Paradigms for Rich and Poor Countries," in *Advances in Macroeconomic Theory,* ed. Jacques Dreze, IEA Conference Volume 133 (Houndsmills, UK: Palgrave, 2001), pp. 353–72 (speech given for Michael Bruno Memorial Lecture, 12th World Congress of IEA, Buenos Aires, August 27, 1999).

Importantly, my engagement with these crises helped me understand what was wrong with conventional monetary economics, as I explain in *Towards a New Paradigm in Monetary Economics,* with Bruce Greenwald (Cambridge: Cambridge University Press, 2003), to which I shall make reference often below.

16 The standard model is called the Dynamic Stochastic Equilibrium model. It does not even explain how this "equilibrium" is attained. It simply assumes that it is.

17 See, for instance, Stiglitz and Greenwald, *Towards a New Paradigm in Monetary Economics*; and my book *Freefall: America, Free Markets, and the Sinking of the World Economy* (New York: W. W. Norton, 2010).

Chapter 1. The Euro Crisis

1 For consistency, where possible, the IMF was the source of data, unless otherwise noted. (At the time of writing, some 2014 and 2015 figures were IMF staff estimates.) Different data sources will yield different figures, but the overarching story remains the same.

There are 28 countries in the European Union: Bulgaria, Croatia, the Czech Republic, Denmark, Hungary, Poland, Romania, Sweden, and the UK belong to the EU but do not use the euro. The UK and Sweden have made it clear that they are unlikely to do so anytime soon. There are currently 19 countries in the eurozone, though as recently as 2007 there were only 13— Austria, Belgium, Finland, France, Germany, Greece, Ireland, Italy, Luxembourg, Netherlands, Portugal, Slovenia, and Spain. (Cyprus, Estonia, Latvia, Lithuania, Malta, and Slovakia joined between 2008 and 2015.) As we discuss later in chapter 2, there are many other economic groupings within Europe.

Throughout this book, when making comparisons between the present and the time before the financial crisis, I have generally used only data from the 13 countries that were in the eurozone as of January 1, 2007. In discussions of data from later years, I generally use the definition of the eurozone at that moment in time. Whenever possible, I have made a note about which countries are included for a particular discussion—when doing so would not unduly disrupt the narrative.

2 Having fallen from €30,294 (gross domestic product per capita, constant prices, 2010) in 2007 to an estimated €29,752 in 2015.

3 There is no generally accepted definition among economists of "depression." I employ the term as in common usage, a severe economic downturn, with high levels of unemployment and GDP below its previous peak.

4 The Eurostat database was used throughout the book for unemployment, poverty, inequality, labor cost, and emigration data, unless otherwise noted. (Eurostat is the official statistical agency of the EU.) Eurozone's unemployment rate was 10.2 percent in March 2016, after peaking above 12 percent in 2013. The rate has generally been stuck in double digits since the end of 2009. In contrast, the US rate briefly peaked above 10 percent in October of 2009 and has been in nearly smooth decline since 2010, reaching 5.0 percent in April 2016. I will delve more deeply into these statistics in chapter 3.

5 The March 2016 youth unemployment rate for the eurozone was 21 percent. For Greece and Spain, the worst-hit countries, 52 percent (in January, the last reported month) and 46 percent, respectively.

6 Or in the case of Spain, at 5.9 percent in 2012. The usual way of measuring how bad things are is to look at the *spread*, the excess of the interest rate that a country has to pay over, say, that paid by Germany. The spread reached 21 percent for Greece in 2012 and 4.4 percent for Spain in 2012. Source: OECD data on long-term interest rates (rates for government bonds with 10-year maturity), available at https://data.oecd.org/interest/long-term-interest-rates.htm.

7 Even so, much responsibility for setting public policy is not actually devolved in practice—it flows from the Council of Ministers. And subsidiarity is a principle more honored in the breach than in the observance.

8 European Union data.

9 Congressional Budget Office, "Summary of the Budget and Economic Outlook: 2016 to 2026," January 19, 2016, available at https://www.cbo.gov/publication/51129.

10 It is important to realize that this is true even for countries not under a "program," where they have borrowed money from their partners, and with the loan come *conditions* that they have to satisfy. The European Commission (EC) has the power to veto a budget that it believes does not satisfy certain conditions.

In October 2015, 62 percent of Portuguese voters supported parties opposed to austerity. This was the main issue in the election. When the newly elected government of António Costa proposed a *less* austere budget, the European Commission threatened to veto it. In the end, there was a compromise, with Costa agreeing to a €135 million cut, illustrating the fine-tuning to which the EC would go (€135 million represented less than 0.01 percent of Portugal's GDP). Peter Spiegel and Peter Wise, "Portugal Agrees Extra 135m Euro Budget Cuts to Avoid Brussel Veto," *Financial Times*, February 7, 2016, p. 4.

11 The UK *now* looks at stability as well—having learned the lessons of the crisis. One of the key problems with the eurozone is that it lacks the flexibility to incorporate the "lessons of history" as they occur.

12 As we noted earlier, this book cannot provide a history of the euro. Pivotal in its creation was the work of the head of the European Commission, Jacques Delors, formerly France's finance minister, and his 1989 report (called the Delors report), which set the stage for the Maastricht Treaty three years later.

13 I will use the terms *market fundamentalism* and *neoliberalism* interchangeably and somewhat loosely. Of course, not everyone adheres to these theories to the same extent. Some might, for instance, believe that *normally* markets allocate resources efficiently and can be relied upon, and still believe in the need for bank regulation, recognizing that there are in that sector specifically

large market failures. Most European neoliberals never went as far as those in some countries in advocating the privatization of virtually every aspect of what the government undertakes, including the judicial system.

14 The widespread skepticism about the EU should have made European leaders even more cautious about going forward with an "incomplete" project. In the next chapter, I'll describe the magnitude of "euro-skepticism," as reflected in both polls and referenda.

15 Throughout this book, I make reference to "real GDP," "real wages," etc. In these situations, we are adjusting current GDP or wages for inflation.

16 As noted earlier, when I refer to the eurozone GDP here, we mean the 13 eurozone member countries as of January 1, 2007. (See note 1 in this chapter.)

17 Throughout the book, average growth rate means the average annualized growth rate, the growth rate that would have achieved the observed increase over the period.

18 And as we note in chapter 3, Germany's performance was markedly weaker than even Japan's.

19 See Oxfam, "The True Cost of Austerity and Inequality: Germany Case Study," September 2013. According to Oxfam, real wages in Germany fell an average of 1.6 percent a year from 2002 to 2012. OECD data show the large decline in wages of the ninth decile relative to the fifth, and the share of low-paid workers (full-time workers earning less than two-thirds of gross median earnings of all full-time workers) increasing from under 16 percent to almost 20 percent. While Germany did a far better job than the United States in "correcting" the large increase in market income inequality, the increase in poverty suggests that it was far from fully successful.

20 The euro is usually dated to January 1, 1999, when the exchange rates between the countries became fixed, though the euro itself did not come into circulation until 2002.

21 I discuss the East Asia crisis in my book *Globalization and Its Discontents*.

22 The seminal work in this area is that of Robert Mundell. See his "A Theory of Optimum Currency Areas," *American Economic Review* 51, no. 4 (1961): 657–65.

23 A 2013 study in the *British Medical Journal* and a 2014 study in the *British Journal of Psychiatry* found that suicide increased especially in Europe in the wake of the Great Recession. A study in the journal *BMJ Open* found that suicides had increased by 35 percent in Greece between 2010 and 2012. Yet another study in the journal *Social Science & Medicine* in 2014 demonstrated that the increase in Greek suicides could be closely tied to fiscal austerity. See Nikolaos Antonakakis and Alan Collins, "The Impact of Fiscal Austerity on Suicide: On the Empirics of a Modern Greek Tragedy" 112 (2014): 39–50.

24 The current account is the balance of trade, net primary income or factor income (earnings on foreign investments minus payments made to foreign

investors), and net cash transfers, that have taken place over a given period of time.

25 As Keynes once wrote, "In the long run we are all dead." *A Tract on Monetary Reform* (London: Macmillan, 1923), p. 80.

26 For instance, they do not build in, or build in in a fully adequate way, essential market imperfections—for example, the irrationality of financial markets, as emphasized by the research of Nobel Prize–winning economist Rob Shiller (see, for instance, his book *Irrational Exuberance* [Princeton, NJ: Princeton University Press, 2000]) or the pervasive imperfections of information (as emphasized by Nobel Prize–winning economists Michael Spence, George Akerlof, and myself).

For a more extensive discussion of the failures of the standard macroeconomic models, see, for instance, Stiglitz, "Rethinking Macroeconomics: What Failed and How to Repair It," *Journal of the European Economic Association* 9, no. 4 (2011): 591–645; and Stiglitz, "Stable Growth in an Era of Crises: Learning from Economic Theory and History," *Ekonomi-tek* 2, no. 1 (2013): 1–38 (originally delivered as keynote lecture to the Turkish Economic Association, Izmir, November, 2012). See also Olivier J. Blanchard, David Romer, Michael Spence, and Joseph E. Stiglitz, eds., *In the Wake of the Crisis: Leading Economists Reassess Economic Policy* (Cambridge, MA: MIT Press, 2012).

27 Some observers have pointed out that even Germany domestically follows a social model at odds in many ways with the conditions imposed on Greece and elsewhere. But, as I note below, such economic and social arrangements arise out of a sense of solidarity; Germany's internal solidarity appears quite different from the solidarity that it expresses outside its boundaries.

Current debates demonstrate the complexity of the politics: while Germany has recently for the first time imposed a minimum wage, it has also imposed constraints on spending (called a debt brake), a mild form of austerity that risks slowing Germany's growth below its recent anemic performance.

The migrant crisis that gained unprecedented attention since the summer of 2015 also illustrates the complexity of these issues. Germany was, at least initially, enormously generous. Some 1 million migrants arrived in the country over the course of 2015, and Germany announced intentions to accept 500,000 refugees a year for the next several years. Germany has, however, distinguished strongly between refugees and those wishing to move to Germany simply to escape economic suffering. And toward the end of the year, it became unclear whether the country would grant long-term protection to those fleeing war.

By early 2016, conditions among migrants in Germany were sufficiently bad that many chose to return to the war-afflicted areas than to remain in Germany, and Germany has facilitated the return flow by paying for their transport back. In 2015, 37,000 signed up for its voluntary repatriation program, triple the 2014 number. Guy Chazan, "Frustrated Iraqis Head Home as German Services Struggle," *Financial Times,* February 7, 2016, p. 4.

28 There are many variants of the European social model. Some involve unions and employers working with government (the social partners) to solve societal problems. Some have country-wide labor bargaining; others, sectoral bargaining. Some have stronger systems of social protection than others.

29 There is, however, a large literature in behavioral economics suggesting that individuals do not exhibit this kind of rationality.

30 This is called confirmatory bias. There is a large literature showing the importance of this phenomenon.

31 Bonds are the way that countries, companies, and other institutions borrow through *capital markets,* rather than through banks. They are nothing more than an IOU, a promise to pay, with interest, which can be bought and sold.

32 My earlier book *Freefall* explained how the neoliberal ideology that underpinned the eurozone led to the financial crisis, and in *Globalization and Its Discontents*, I explained how the same ideology has resulted in globalization not living up to its promise. Later in this book, I describe some of the basic economic research that overturned the premises of market fundamentalism/neoliberalism.

33 The pathbreaking work was that of Kenneth Arrow and Gerard Debreu (for which both received the Nobel Prize). (Kenneth J. Arrow, "An Extension of the Basic Theorems of Classical Welfare Economics," in *Proceedings of the Second Berkeley Symposium on Mathematical Statistics and Probability*, ed. J. Neyman [Berkeley: University of California Press, 1951], pp. 507–32; and Gerard Debreu, "Valuation Equilibrium and Pareto Optimum," *Proceedings of the National Academy of Sciences* 40, no. 7 [1954]: 588–92; and Debreu, *The Theory of Value* [New Haven, CT: Yale University Press, 1959.]) The circumstances that they identified where markets did not lead to efficiency were called *market failures.* Subsequently, Greenwald and Stiglitz showed that whenever information was imperfect and markets incomplete—essentially always—markets were not efficient ("Externalities in Economies with Imperfect Information and Incomplete Markets"). Of course, even earlier, Keynes had emphasized that markets do not by themselves maintain full employment.

34 See James Edward Meade, *The Theory of International Economic Policy*, vol. 2, *Trade and Welfare* (London: Oxford University Press, 1955); and Richard G. Lipsey and Kelvin Lancaster, "The General Theory of Second Best," *Review of Economic Studies* 24, no. 1 (1956): 11–32.

35 See David Newbery and J. E. Stiglitz, "Pareto Inferior Trade," *Review of Economic Studies* 51, no. 1 (1984): 1–12.

36 The ERM was effectively broken in 1992 with the attack on the British pound, followed by attacks on Sweden and Spain's currency. Since the start of the

euro, it continues as what is sometimes called ERM II, a band linking the Danish krone to the euro.

37 Though the basic idea of full employment is clear—that everyone who would like a job can get one at the prevailing wages for those with the individual's skills and talents—there is some controversy over the precise definition of full employment. The general notion is that the labor market is just sufficiently loose—with job seekers matching employers looking for employees—that there is no inflationary pressure. Because of labor market frictions—it takes time to find a good match between employers and employees—this "natural rate" is greater than zero, normally around 2 to 3 percent. Unemployment might also exist because of rigidities in the adjustment of relative wages—the labor market for skilled labor might be so tight that wages are rising, but there may still be unemployment of unskilled workers. This level of unemployment is sometimes referred to as structural unemployment. "Full employment" simply indicates that what unemployment that exists isn't the result of weak demand in the economy. (For further discussion of the concept and problems in ascertaining the rate of unemployment below which inflation starts to increase, see chapter 9, note 9.)

Chapter 2. The Euro: The Hope and the Reality

1 With the United States, as measured by exchange rates, with the precise ranking depending on the fluctuations in the exchange rate.

2 See my book with Linda Bilmes, *The Three Trillion Dollar War: The True Cost of the Iraq Conflict* (New York: W. W. Norton, 2008).

3 The fact that it was willing to support strong economic sanctions is testimony to the importance of noneconomic considerations.

4 Indeed, in the design of the programs for Greece and the other crisis countries we are seeing the questionable "benefits" of Europe acting together—policies dragging one country after another into depression. Even in this case, unity is not arrived at as a result of a consensus of perspectives. There are, of course, many countries who agree with Germany and the "consensus." Eurozone consensus is arrived at least partly through fear of Germany. Italy and France have loudly expressed unhappiness with austerity. They *know* that austerity does not work, especially in the extremes to which it has been carried out. So, too, for some of the other crisis countries. But countries dependent on German assistance—or potentially so—do not want to offend Germany. In still other countries, the question is not about whether austerity will or will not work. It is simply that their voters will not countenance providing assistance to countries whose citizens are better off than they are. In this sense, the consensus in support of the crisis policies is really a reflection of the lack of solidarity within Europe.

5 There are, of course, other arenas besides military interventionism where if Europe spoke with a single voice, it might have more influence—at the UN, at the World Bank, at the IMF, and in international negotiations more broadly.

6 It is necessary here to draw something of a distinction between the hopes and expectations Europe's leaders had for the European Union and the euro in particular—it was the former that they more prominently promoted as an effort to bring together the continent. However, it is undeniable that many considered the realization of a common currency to be an integral part of that vision. When German chancellor Helmut Kohl proclaimed in 1995 that the stakes of European integration were "war and peace in the 21st century," he was promoting not only the idea of the European Union—which though nascent, had already successfully been established—but also Europe's full economic and monetary integration. According to his biography, "Kohl's ultimate goal was . . . [to] make sure that peace prevails. 'We are determined to make this process irreversible,' he says. In his view, the means to do so [was] the common currency, which will create a strong bond between the European economies." Henrik Bering, *Helmut Kohl: The Man Who Reunited Germany, Rebuilt Europe, and Thwarted the Soviet Empire* (Washington, DC: Regnery, 1999), p. 164. The fact that his goal was to make the process of integration irreversible underlines how important it was for the euro's founders to get all the details right—something that, unfortunately, they did not accomplish. See chapter 1 for a longer discussion of the euro's founding, and see, as well, Alan Cowell, "Kohl Casts Europe's Economic Union as War and Peace Issue," *New York Times*, October 17, 1995. There is, of course, the notion that economic interdependence increases the costs of war, and therefore makes war less likely. The EU brought about extensive economic integration. The question is, whether the additional economic integration (if any) resulting from a monetary union would have any significant incremental effect.

7 Adam Smith's classic work was *The Wealth of Nations* (1776).

8 Ricardo (1772–1823) was the father of the theory of comparative advantage.

9 The existence of which can actually strengthen arguments for economic integration.

10 Joseph E. Stiglitz, "Devolution, Independence, and the Optimal Provision of Public Goods," *Economics of Transportation* 4, nos. 1–2 (March–June 2015): 82–94.

11 See my book with Bruce C. Greenwald, *Creating a Learning Society: A New Approach to Growth, Development, and Social Progress* (New York: Columbia University Press, 2014; abridged reader's edition, 2015).

12 Economists use the term *public goods*, or *pure public goods*, in a technical sense, to refer to goods that are *inherently* public—that is, there are no costs associated with an additional individual enjoying those goods. Many publicly provided goods are not public goods in this sense. Knowledge is an example

of such a public good: when one more individual knows something, it doesn't subtract from what others know.

13 Germany's obsession with inflation, in turn, is usually attributed to its inter-war experience and the rise of Hitler. But we should be clear: Hitler arose as Germany faced high unemployment. It was not inflation but unemployment that gave rise to the Nazis. (See Robert Skidelsky, *John Maynard Keynes: The Economist as Saviour 1920–1937* [London: Macmillan, 1992].) Those who claim otherwise are rewriting history. Knowing the political and social costs of high unemployment, one would accordingly have thought that ensuring that high unemployment did *not* occur would be at the center of their atten-tion. But as we will explain in chapter 7, it has been just the opposite: the poli-cies that they have demanded in Greece and Spain predictably have generated *very* high unemployment rates; and we are already beginning to see the worri-some political consequences.

14 Citizens of, for instance, Romania have the right to *migrate* to the UK (since they are both in the EU), but because UK is not in Schengen, they still have to go through passport controls.

15 Croatia, Hungary, and Romania are candidates but not yet participating.

16 The EU's controversial Common Agricultural Policy accounts for some 40 per-cent of the budget. See European Commission, *The European Union Explained: Agriculture*, Luxembourg: Publications Office of the European Union, 2014, avail-able at http://europa.eu/pol/pdf/flipbook/en/agriculture_en.pdf; and European Commission, "European Budget for 2016 Adopted," November 25, 2015, available at http://ec.europa.eu/budget/news/article_en.cfm?id=201511251641.

17 Though as recent events in Greece have demonstrated, not even that risk has been fully eliminated. Moving to a currency union may change the nature of risk—from frequent small realignments to large episodic and cataclysmic changes. In a fundamental sense, the latter may entail even greater risk.

18 Advocates of fixed exchange rates suggest that wages and prices could, instead, adjust. In later chapters, we will explain why wage and price adjustments typi-cally fail as a substitute.

19 The default was, at that time, the largest in history. Of course, the high com-modity prices, largely a result of China's rapid growth, played an important role in Argentina's success during the period after devaluation.

20 Elsewhere, I have explained why especially in such circumstances, GDP is not a good measure of overall economic performance. See Joseph E. Stiglitz, Amartya K. Sen, and Jean-Paul Fitoussi, *Mismeasuring Our Lives: Why GDP Doesn't Add Up* (New York: The New Press, 2010).

21 Similar observations hold within countries: when there is too much inequal-ity, it is often hard to support the kinds of collective action necessary to ensure the overall performance of the society. This is one reason that there is such a high price to inequality. See Stiglitz, *Price of Inequality*.

22 See Scott J. Wallsten, "An Econometric Analysis of Telecom Competition, Privatization, and Regulation in Africa and Latin America" *Journal of Industrial Economics* 49, no. 1 (2001): 1–19; Anzhela Knyazeva, Diana Knyazeva, and Joseph E. Stiglitz, "Ownership Change, Institutional Development and Performance," *Journal of Banking and Finance* 37, no. 7 (2013): 2605–27.

23 See David E. Sappington, and Joseph E. Stiglitz, "Privatization, Information and Incentives," *Journal of Policy Analysis and Management* 6, no. 4 (1987): 567–82; Herbert A. Simon, "Organizations and Markets," *Journal of Economic Perspectives* 5, no. 2 (Spring 1991): 25–44.

24 Using Eurostat data on labor cost index (LCI) on wages and salaries, the LCI was 108.7 for Greece in 2007, and in 2014 (latest year data available), it was 91.5, a 15.8 percent decline. Other measures of labor costs generate somewhat smaller reductions.

25 For instance, see the detailed discussion in chapter 8 of the agreement that Greece's prime minister Alexis Tsipras made with the Troika on July 12, 2015 (widely viewed as Greece's "terms of surrender").

26 These labor issues are discussed more extensively in chapter 8.

27 See Robert N. Mefford, "The Effect of Unions on Productivity in a Multinational Manufacturing Firm," *Industrial and Labor Relations Review* 40, no. 1 (1986): 105–14; and Kim B. Clark, "The Impact of Unionization on Productivity: A Case Study," *Industrial and Labor Relations Review* 33, no. 4 (1980): 451–69.

28 Economists also emphasize that no rule can fully contemplate all the relevant contingencies. Thus, one of the reasons that I and others in the Clinton administration so strongly opposed an amendment to the US Constitution that would have forbidden deficits (i.e., required balanced budgets) is that we knew that there would be circumstances like the Great Recession of 2008. One can, of course, write more complicated rules, anticipating some contingencies. But it is impossible to anticipate all. Conservatives like Milton Friedman argued, similarly, that monetary authorities use simple rules, like expanding money supply at a fixed rate. It turned out that the underlying model, as well as it may have worked in earlier decades, broke down beginning in the 1970s. Governments that adopted his simplistic rule found that their economies did not perform well.

29 Interestingly, while the eastern and central European countries that joined the EU did far better than those that did not, the growth of most of these countries has been disappointing, with the exception of Poland.

30 The turnout in the referenda rejecting the euro was impressively high: in Denmark, 53 percent voted against, with a turnout of 87.6 percent on September 28, 2000, and in Sweden, 56 percent voted against, with a turnout of 81 percent, on September 14, 2003. Some 69 percent of Irish voters voted yes on the Maastricht Treaty in 1992, but following the rejection of the constitu-

tion by voters in France and Netherlands, the planned Irish referendum on the euro was never held. The UK decided not to join the eurozone but did not put the matter to a vote. A 2015 poll showed that 70 percent of voters in the UK opposed joining the euro (*Daily Mail*, December 30, 2015). A 2009 poll showed similar opposition (71 percent). (*Guardian*, January 1, 2009). Remarkably, a 2012 poll showed that even 65 percent of Germans thought they would be better off without the euro and 64 percent of French would reject the Maastricht Treaty (creating the euro) if they were to have voted then (Reuters, September 17, 2012).

31 These and other details of the program can be found in the document "Memorandum of Understanding between the European Commission Acting on Behalf of the European Stability Mechanism and the Hellenic Republic and the Bank of Greece," August 19, 2015, available at http://ec.europa.eu/economy_finance/assistance_eu_ms/greek_loan_facility/pdf/01_mou_20150811_en.pdf. Contemporaneous news accounts describe the bargaining that went into the agreements, though of course the official documents do not refer to differences of stances of various parties.

Chapter 3. Europe's Dismal Performance

1 The IMF reports that Ireland grew 7.8 percent in 2015, a rate exceeding the second-fastest-growing economy, Malta, about 1.5 percentage points. In the rest of Europe, only Malta grew faster than 5 percent for the year.

Throughout this chapter (and the book), I look at the increase in real GDP—that is, I correct for inflation. In making such comparisons, one has to choose a base year and express, say, GDP in each year in terms of the value in dollars or euros in that year. In looking at growth, the choice of base years makes little difference; but of course, GDP in, say, 2015, using 2010 as a base, will be different than using 2009 as a base. In most instances, I have adjusted GDP to use 2010 as the base, because that is the base used by most of the official sources. In cases where other bases have been used, I have had to adjust the data to the 2010 base. (For US data, for instance, because the US price level—as calculated for GDP, called the GDP deflator—has increased by 8.4 percent between 2015 and 2010, to convert 2010 GDP numbers into 2015 dollars, one simply multiplies the 2010 numbers by 1.084.)

There is a technical issue in making comparisons over time. There may be changes in the market basket of goods, and the rate of inflation may depend on the market basket of goods. Thus, there can be slight differences in estimated rates of real growth depending on which year is chosen as a base. Economists have "solved" this problem by constantly adjusting the base (called chain-weighted GDP). Because we are looking at growth over a relatively short span of time, these technical issues, by and large, are of second-order importance.

There is one more technical issue: a lag in the production of data. One wants numbers to be as up to date as possible. All data are subject to revision. Such revisions occur sometimes years after the initial release, and sometimes even give a slightly different picture of what happened.

2　As I will note later in this chapter, the International Commission on the Measurement of Economic Performance and Social Progress (the Stiglitz-Sen-Fitoussi Commission) explained why GDP is not a good measure of economic performance. (See Stiglitz, Sen, and Fitoussi, *Mismeasuring our Lives: Why GDP Doesn't Add Up.*)

3　GDP is adjusted throughout for inflation, but because inflation rates differ across countries, important technical issues arise in the analysis of aggregates, such as eurozone GDP. Still more complicated issues arise when comparing GDP across countries, because the market basket of goods consumed in different countries differs and different goods cost different amounts in different countries. In this book, we focus on the effect of the euro on growth, and we assess growth by using each country's own price deflator. When comparing levels of GDP to take account of differences in prices of different goods in different countries, a standard approach is to calculate real PPP (purchasing power parity) GDP, discussed briefly in note 6 in the preface. It compares incomes using a standardized basket of goods.

4　GDP in 2015 for the 13 countries that had adopted the euro as of January 1, 2007, was merely 0.6 percent above that in 2007. Figures were actual, with the exception of Belgium and Luxembourg, as reported by the IMF.

5　Graph shows the largest contractions over 2007–2015. For countries with multiple contractions within 2007–2015, I took the time-weighted average. See Social Democracy for the 21st Century: A Post Keynesian Perspective, "The Great Depression in Europe: Real GDP Data for 22 Nations," July 7, 2013, available at http://socialdemocracy21stcentury.blogspot.com/2013/07/the-great-depression-in-europe-real-gdp.html.

6　Throughout this chapter, non-eurozone Europe refers to Norway, Sweden, Switzerland, and the UK.

7　This is the 2007 GDP–weighted average of the growth rates of real GDP of the non-eurozone countries. Though eurozone real GDP increased in 2015, real GDP per capita declined, as we will note in more detail below. The key point, that non-eurozone Europe has performed far better than eurozone Europe, remains.

8　Emigration data from Eurostat. The latest reported is 2013, and data was not reported for Greece for 2007.

9　By more than 1 percent from 2008 to 2013, according to data from the World Bank. If 2014 is included (the latest available year), the decrease in population is about 2 percent. This likely changed, of course, as Greece became the main recipient of refugees from Syria and elsewhere in the last couple of years, though this is a different kind of migration altogether—refugees choose Greece as a gateway to Europe and not because it is the most attractive destination for settlement.

10 Greece's working-age population as percentage of total population fell from 66.7 percent in 2007 to 64.6 percent in 2015. Thus, the share of the declining population that was of working-age population decreased by more than 2 percentage points. Even if the unemployment rate had been unchanged and even if productivity had remained the same, GDP on this account alone would have fallen by more than 4 percent, reducing the country's ability to pay back its debts.

11 Government expenditure converted to real terms using GDP deflator using IMF data.

12 World Bank data.

13 Eurostat data.

14 And well below that of the much maligned Japan, whose real GDP per working age population exceeds by a considerable amount both Europe and the United States. Source: Economic Report of the President, 2015, based on World Bank data, available at https://www.whitehouse.gov/blog/2015/02/19/2015-economic-report-president.

15 These productivity numbers are based on real output per worker. But the crisis has not only increased unemployment but also decreased hours worked per worker—implying that productivity, as measured by output *per hour worked*, has performed somewhat better than these numbers would suggest. In Greece, for instance, before the crisis, workers worked, on average, 17 percent more hours than did Americans. The crisis had hardly any effect on hours worked per employee in the United States (less than 0.5 percent as of 2014), but hours worked per Greek worker fell by about 3.3 percent, implying a decline in output per hour of just 2.1 percent; Germany, meanwhile, had a decline in hours worked per employee of 3.7 percent, resulting in a slight increase in output per hour. Source: hours worked are from OECD database.

16 From 26.3 percent in 2013 to 20.5 percent in Spain at the beginning of 2016, and from 27.9 percent to 24.4 percent in Greece at the end of 2015 (the most recent data). Source: Eurostat.

17 There is a large body of economic research showing that young people entering the labor force in a year of high unemployment have substantially lower lifetime incomes than their peers who entered just a few years earlier or later when the unemployment was lower. T. von Wachter, Oreopoulos, and A. Heisz, "Short- and Long-Term Career Effects of Graduating in a Recession," *American Economic Journal: Applied Economics* 4, no. 1 (January 2012): 1–29.

18 Source: OECD data. Note that once account is taken of the decline in hours worked, productivity, as measured by output per hour, looks better. At the same time, the fact that hours worked is so much higher in Greece than in Germany means that productivity per hour worked is so much lower.

19 From Oxfam, "The True Cost of Austerity and Inequality: Greece Case Study," September 2013, available at https://www.oxfam.org/sites/www.oxfam.org/files/cs-true-cost-austerity-inequality-greece-120913-en.pdf; and Hellenic Statistical Authority, "Living Conditions in Greece, 2013," available at http://www.statistics.gr/documents/20181/1216584/LivingConditionsInGreece_0413.pdf/991e648b-e175-4be0-8d2b-1bf70d297966

20 See UNICEF, "Children of the Recession," September 2014, available at http://www.unicef-irc.org/publications/pdf/rc12-eng-web.pdf. See also Yekaterina Chzhen, "Child Poverty and Material Deprivation in the European Union During the Great Recession," Innocenti Working Paper No. 2014-06, UNICEF Office of Research, Florence, 2014, available at http://www.unicef-irc.org/publications/pdf/wp_2014_yc.pdf.

21 Euro area here includes Austria, Belgium, Finland, France, Germany, Greece, Ireland, Italy, Luxembourg, Netherlands, Portugal, and Spain. Slovenia is not included in this analysis due to data unavailability in the 1980s. Euro area GDP is obtained from aggregating GDP (in national currency, constant prices) of these countries using IMF WEO data available accessed on May 4, 2016. Also used was the GDP deflator (index) of the involved countries from IMF WEO data available at the same source (accessed on May 4, 2016) to make all GDP (in national currency, constant prices) data series in our aggregation have the same base year of 2010. The GDP (in national currency, constant prices) of Belgium and Luxembourg in 2015 are IMF estimates instead of the actual outputs. Projection (i.e., trend fitting) was based on data from 1980 to 1998.

22 Future dollars are valued at less than present dollars. To reflect this, economists use the concept of "present discounted value." The present discounted value depends on the (real) interest rate. The €200 trillion loss is based on a real discount rate of 1 percent (somewhat higher than the current real interest rate).

23 Economists call the relationship between inputs and output the production function. It seems as if the production function has shifted down—certainly down from where it otherwise would have been, given the nature of progress of technology.

24 Kenneth J. Arrow, "The Economic Implications of Learning by Doing," *Review of Economic Studies* 29, no. 3 (June 1962): 155–73. The general theory described here is developed at greater length in my book with Bruce C. Greenwald, *Creating a Learning Society.*

25 See *Rewriting the Rules of the American Economy* for some of the underlying forces contributing to this shortsighted behavior.

26 For a longer discussion of these trends, see Kai Daniel Schmid and Ulrike Stein, "Explaining Rising Income Inequality in Germany, 1991–2010," Macroeconomic Policy Institute, Dusseldorf, Germany, 2013. By one measure used there, the income share of the bottom 10 percent of Germans decreased by 11.2 percent from 1991 to 2010.

    Moreover, to repeat the important point raised earlier: as in most countries, the standard of living of ordinary workers may be hurt even more than the conventional statistics indicate, as they face more insecurity and cutbacks in public programs that are essential to their well-being.

27 The income share of the German top 1 percent, including capital gains, increased from about 10.6 percent in 1992 to about 13.1 percent in 2010. Latest data from the World Wealth and Income Database, available at http://www.wid.world/#Database.

28 See OECD, "Country Note: Germany," 2008, from the OECD's 2008 publication *Divided We Stand*, available at http://www.oecd.org/els/soc/41525346.pdf.

29 This is illustrated by the more recent OECD study, which notes that "low-educated persons in Germany own 60% less than those with upper/post-secondary education, while persons with a tertiary degree own 120% more. This is the widest gap after that recorded in the United States." Moreover, "In Germany, the lower 60% of the population own a mere 6% of all household wealth." OECD, "In It Together."

30 The issues are obviously more complex than I can do justice to in this short summary. Supporters of the euro might also point out that the devaluation could set off an inflationary spiral, and as wages and prices increase, the benefits of the lower nominal exchange rate would be diminished. Typically, however, wages and prices do not rise when there is significant unemployment and excess capacity—the situation being discussed here.

31 In addition to the studies I referred to in chapter 1, an Oxfam study notes a 26.5 percent increase in the suicide rate of Greece from 2010 to 2011 alone. Based on data from the Hellenic Statistical Authority and the nongovernmental organization Klimaka. See Oxfam, "The True Cost of Austerity and Inequality: Greece Case Study," September 2013, available at https://www.oxfam.org/sites/www.oxfam.org/files/cs-true-cost-austerity-inequality-greece-120913-en.pdf.

Chapter 4. When Can a Single Currency *Ever* Work?

1 At its inception, there were 11 countries.

2 It used to be that most countries fixed the value of the exchange rate in terms

of gold; and with each specifying the amount of gold to which they were equivalent, relative exchange rates—the exchange rate between, say, the US dollar
and the British pound—were fixed. But since the early 1970s, exchange rates
have not been so fixed. In some cases, they are market determined—that is,
the value of the dollar relative to the pound is determined by the laws of supply and demand. But it is oversimplified to say that they are *just* market determined, since among the most important determinants of demand are those
set by government policies. In some cases, governments intervene directly
into the foreign exchange market to affect the value of their currency; in these
instances, the country is said to have a managed exchange rate. In a few cases,
countries peg the value of their currency relative to another; to maintain the
peg, they have to adjust the interest rate and buy and sell foreign exchange.
Often, eventually they find it impossible to maintain the peg—this is what
happened in the case of Argentina in 2001.

3 There is considerable controversy over the relative importance of the different channels by which monetary policy affects the economy. While many
economists believe that lower interests directly affects consumption and
investment, others believe that it is really the greater availability of credit
associated with the loosening of monetary policy (lowering interest rates)
that really matters. See, for instance, my book with Bruce Greenwald, *Towards
a New Paradigm in Monetary Economics.*

4 An area that could easily share a common currency came to be referred to
as an *optimal currency area*: big enough that the currency would be taken as
a *serious* currency, but not so big that the differences among the countries
would impede macroeconomic stability and impose excessive costs. The
debate surrounding the eurozone has, however, not been about whether it
was an "optimal" grouping. It is about whether it is a grouping that can be
made to work. As the discussion that will follow of the United States illustrates, the amount of diversity compatible with sharing a currency depends
on political arrangements and a variety of social and economic factors. The
challenge is, how, with a single currency, can a diverse region maintain full
employment in all of its parts? If there is easy migration, then people can
easily move from areas where there is a shortage of jobs to one where there
is a surplus. If the government has active policies for creating jobs in places
where there is high unemployment, then that can substitute for exchange-
rate and interest-rate flexibility. If, of course, all parts of the region are
similar, the *same* interest-rate policy and exchange rate would enable all to
experience full employment simultaneously. The following discussion will
make clear that these conditions are not satisfied within the eurozone. See
Robert Mundell, "A Theory of Optimum Currency Areas," *American Economic Review* 51, no. 4 (1961): 657–65.

5 I have not seen any persuasive analysis justifying these particular numbers. Almost surely, they were partly politically driven: one wanted the toughest numbers that were realistically achievable by the countries planning to join the eurozone. In fact, the numbers proved sufficiently tough that France and Germany missed the targets in the early years of the euro. Further conditions were imposed on a country wishing to join the euro in the years *before* joining the euro—for example, stipulations concerning stability of its exchange rate and its long-term interest rates.

6 The obligations go beyond the deficit and debt levels to "medium-term budgetary objectives," designed to ensure fiscal sustainability over a longer horizon. The details of the requirements and procedures are complicated and need not derail us here.

7 South Dakotans may care, of course, though surely not with the same passion that Greece does.

8 Although it is worth observing that even in the United States, free migration has not eliminated large differences in standards of living across states.

9 In a purely agrarian economy, as more people leave, there is more land per worker, so incomes rise. This limits the extent of migration. In a modern industrial economy, there may be economies of scale. As more people leave, the ability to sustain the basis of a modern knowledge-based economy weakens. Productivity may actually decline.

10 Actually, it wouldn't have been quite that bad—Washington Mutual's assets were about the size of Washington's GDP. But still, if Washington had had to bail out WaMu, it, too, would have faced a fiscal crisis.

11 Data for Portugal, Germany, and Latvia are from IMF, comparing gross domestic product per capita, constant prices; for Connecticut and Mississippi, from the US Bureau of Economic Analysis and the Census. The Portugal-Germany divide was the largest at the time of the euro's establishment.

12 Eurostat data. Estonia also did not exceed the deficit limit, but it did not join the eurozone until 2011.

13 See "Will It Hurt? Macroeconomic Effects of Fiscal Consolidation," chapter 3 of International Monetary Fund, *World Economic Outlook: Recovery Risk and Rebalancing* (Washington, DC: International Monetary Fund, 2010), pp. 93–124. See also the excellent earlier studies cited in chapter 7, note 57.

14 Of course, if at the same time the euro *appreciates,* then in spite of the fact that it has become more competitive relative to other countries in the eurozone, it will be less competitive relative to other countries.

The value of the UK currency, the pound sterling, relative to the dollar, is called the *nominal* exchange rate. Even if it does not change, if UK inflation is lower than that of the United States, then we say that the *real* exchange rate has decreased.

15

COUNTRIES	AVERAGE INFLATION RATE 2010–2015 (%)
Portugal	1.41
Spain	1.36
Greece	0.89
Ireland	0.38
Austria	2.03
Luxembourg	1.97
Finland	1.90
Belgium	1.77
Italy	1.57
Netherlands	1.55
Germany	1.38
France	1.32
Slovenia	1.28

16 The 2010–2015 average growth rate for volume of exports of goods and services: Cyprus, 1.75 percent; Greece, 1.18 percent; Ireland, 6.40 percent; Portugal, 4.68 percent; and Spain, 5.42 percent.

17 Based on Eurostat data.

18 I think that goes too far. The confusion these scholars make is that they
observe that those countries that went off the gold standard did better, some
recovering quite strongly. But that was in part because others remained on
the gold standard, so that they could benefit from a competitive devaluation.
If all had gone off the gold standard, then that would not have been true. Even
then, in a world in which monetary authorities feel constrained in expanding the money supply by their reserves of gold, going off the gold standard can
lead to a monetary expansion, which can have significant beneficial effects on
aggregate demand.

   See Barry J. Eichengreen, *Golden Fetters: The Gold Standard and the
Great Depression, 1919–1939* (New York: Oxford University Press, 1992); Ben
Bernanke and Harold James, "The Gold Standard, Deflation, and Financial
Crisis in the Great Depression: An International Comparison," in *Financial
Markets and Financial Crises*, ed. R. Glenn Hubbard (Chicago: University of
Chicago Press, 1991), pp. 33–68; Peter Temin, *Lessons from the Great Depres-
sion* (Cambridge, MA: MIT Press, 1989); Barry Eichengreen and Jeffrey Sachs,

"Exchange Rates and Economic Recovery in the 1930s," *Journal of Economic History* 45, no. 4 (1985): 925–46.

19 Even from a social point of view, some government restrictions on firing (requiring severance pay) may be desirable. See Carl Shapiro and Joseph E. Stiglitz, "Equilibrium Unemployment as a Worker Discipline Device," *American Economic Review* 74, no. 3 (1984): 433–44; and Patrick Rey and Joseph E. Stiglitz, "Moral Hazard and Unemployment in Competitive Equilibrium," 1993 working paper.

20 These theories arguing that lowering wages lowers workers' productivity were first developed in the context of developing countries, where it was observed that low nutrition resulting from low wages hurt productivity. See Harvey Leibenstein, *Economic Backwardness and Economic Growth* (New York: Wiley, 1957). In a series of papers, I then extended the idea to advanced countries, focusing on the fact that lower wages lead to more labor turnover, and that increases training costs, beginning with Joseph E. Stiglitz, "Alternative Theories of Wage Determination and Unemployment in L.D.C.'s: The Labor Turnover Model," *Quarterly Journal of Economics* 88, no. 2 (1974): 194–227. I then showed that similar effects arise as a result of imperfect information: lowering wages leads to a lower quality and less motivated labor force. This research was part of the work that provided the basis of the Nobel Prize that was awarded to me. There is now a huge literature on the subject, providing empirical verification as well. See, for instance, George A. Akerlof and Janet L. Yellen, eds., *Efficiency Wage Models of the Labor Market* (New York: Cambridge University Press, 1986); and Jeremy Bulow and Laurence Summers, "A Theory of Dual Labor Markets with Application to Industrial Policy, Discrimination, and Keynesian Unemployment," *Journal of Labor Economics* 4, no. 3 (1986): 376–414.

21 The combination of austerity and poorly thought-out structural reforms associated with the IMF/Troika programs simply increased this uncertainty. In Europe, with the free flow of capital, money left the banks in the crisis countries, further compounding the problems, as I explain in the next chapter.

22 And that's why it's so difficult parsing out each of the effects separately. In East Asia, where bankruptcy and debt default rates reached 50 percent or more, the adverse effects on demand of the increased risk of delivery was palpable. The quantitative importance of this effect in different European countries has not been assessed.

23 Source: Eurostat data for 2015. Percentage of EU member states exports in value with other EU members was 63.2 percent.

24 The fact that a few countries and the ECB have "broken" the bound by having slightly negative interest rates does not change the analysis. The real point is that when economies are very weak, monetary policy is typically relatively ineffective. Though economists argue about the reason for this, there is a

broad consensus over the limitations of monetary policy—emphasized, for instance, even by successive chairs of the Federal Reserve. (Elsewhere, I have argued that the zero lower bound is not the critical reason for the ineffectiveness of monetary policy. Even if real interest rates could be lowered from, say, minus 2 percent to minus 4 percent, there would be little effect on investment. The high level of economic uncertainty predominates, and businesses won't respond much to these changes in interest rates.)

25 See Joseph E. Stiglitz and Bruce C. Greenwald, "A Modest Proposal for International Monetary Reform," in *Time for a Visible Hand: Lessons from the 2008 World Financial Crisis*, ed. S. Griffith-Jones, J. A. Ocampo, and J. E. Stiglitz, Initiative for Policy Dialogue Series (Oxford, UK: Oxford University Press, 2010), pp. 314–44.

26 By my former student, Columbia colleague, and former chief economist of the Inter-American Development Bank, Guillermo A. Calvo. See, for instance, "Capital Flows and Capital-Market Crises: The Simple Economics of Sudden Stops," *Journal of Applied Economics* 1, no. 1 (1998): 35–54.

27 Many countries attempt to postpone the day of reckoning, finding some high-cost way of raising short-term funds accompanied by severe budget cutbacks. These usually turn out to be only short-term palliatives.

28 Typically, too, the loan is denominated in foreign currency. As the flow of money coming into the country diminishes, there is a shortage of dollars (or other "hard" currencies). This leads to a *currency crisis*.

29 This is the reverse causality discussed in the previous section: it is not that the fiscal deficit *caused* the trade deficit; it is the other way around.

30 In the case of countries with a flexible exchange rate, facing the situation just described, the value of the dollar soars—the value of the local currency plummets. (Sometimes governments try to postpone the day of reckoning by using their scarce foreign exchange reserves to prevent the exchange rate from plummeting. But these interventions, too, are typically short-term palliatives.) The currency crisis interacts with the debt crisis. Those in the country who have borrowed in foreign exchange but make their income in local currency now are even harder pressed to repay—their income doesn't buy as much foreign exchange as it used to. The currency crisis exacerbates both the debt and financial crises. (These results should be contrasted with what happens in the absence of debt—the fall in the exchange rate would just stimulate demand.)

When the country turns to the IMF for help, the IMF sometimes intervenes to prevent the exchange rate from falling. The money the IMF lends to the country is used to support the currency. In addition, it typically forces the country to raise interest rates and taxes, and cut spending. That sometimes works—by killing the economy enough that consumers stop importing and demand for foreign exchange becomes aligned with the supply. But the price of saving the currency is high.

31 Economists refer to these as "political economy problems."

32 The particular form that the "haircut" took in Cyprus was a tax on deposits. Selfishness on the part of Cyprus's partners was perhaps the dominant motive, but many of the depositors seemed to be Russians engaged in trying to move money out of their country, in not always totally aboveboard means. Cyprus had achieved a reputation as one of the offshore venues of choice for Russians. Not surprisingly, many in the eurozone felt reluctant to engage in what they saw as a subsidy for these Russians. However motivated, even the widespread discussions that there might be a haircut had serious consequences.

   In the end, small depositors were not forced to take a haircut. And European leaders typically shift blame for what is now viewed as the hare-brained proposal to make them do so onto the Cyprus government. As we note below, whoever was responsible matters little: the result is a loss in confidence in the banking system in weak countries.

33 Just as the IMF's announcement in 1998, after shutting down 16 private banks in Indonesia, that more banks would be shut down and depositors would be left unprotected induced a run on the banking system. For a more extensive discussion of these ideas and how they applied in the East Asia crisis, see my book *Globalization and Its Discontents*.

34 According to OECD data on long-term interest rates (rates for government bonds with 10-year maturity).

35 According to data aggregated by the St. Louis Fed.

36 One of the rating agencies, S&P, seemed unaware of this, as it downgraded US debt in 2011. The value of those dollars might diminish were it to resort to such measures, but there was no evidence that government borrowing had any effect on inflationary expectations; indeed, at the time that S&P downgraded US debt, inflationary expectations were so low that the United States could borrow even long-term at unprecedentedly low rates.

37 There is overwhelming evidence, however, that the markets do not work well in this respect.

38 For instance, by insisting the banks' foreign exchange liabilities and assets be matched.

39 Such a mechanism, called the European Stability Mechanism (ESM), was set up in 2012.

40 Not surprisingly, the creditor countries have done all they can to prevent the creation of an international rule of law to deal with such defaults. A UN resolution calling for such a framework was passed on September 9, 2014. A set of principles was overwhelmingly adopted—over the opposition of the creditor countries—on September 10, 2015.

41 In 2014, China's trade surplus was 3.7 percent of GDP, while Germany's was 6.7 percent. Source: World Bank data.

42 Some in Germany like to make a distinction between their surplus, which

they think of as a virtue, and that of China's. China's surplus is a result of its "manipulation of the exchange rate," it is claimed. But exchange rates and trade surpluses are a result of a wide gamut of policies. If China removed restrictions on its citizens investing abroad, the exchange rate would almost surely fall, and its trade surplus would increase. So, too, if it followed Europe's and America's lead in lowering its interest rate. Germany's wage and public expenditure policies are among the factors that contribute to Germany's surplus. Indeed, in early 2016, it was only because of direct government intervention in the exchange rate that China's currency did not experience a substantial devaluation. By contrast, the IMF, in its regular review of the German economy (called the Article 4 consultation) for 2014 estimated that Germany's exchange rate was *undervalued* by some 5 to 15 percent.

43 See John Maynard Keynes, *General Theory of Employment, Interest and Money* (London: Macmillan, 1936), chapter 23, "Notes on Mercantilism, the Usury Laws, Stamped Money and Theories of Under-Consumption."

44 Macroeconomics focuses on *net* capital flows. Behind these net flows there can be complicated patterns: Germany need not lend directly, say, to Spain. A German bank may lend to a party in a third country, and some (possibly other) party in that third country lends to Spain.

45 ILO data for 2015. See ILO, *World Employment Social Outlook—Trends 2016*, available at http://www.ilo.org/global/research/global-reports/weso/2016/ WCMS_443480/lang--en/index.htm. This situation, where there has been a deficiency of aggregate demand, has persisted for a long time. Indeed, one of the reasons that the Fed encouraged the reckless lending that led to the housing crisis was to make up for what would otherwise have been a weak aggregate demand within the United States.

Ben Bernanke, former chairman of the Federal Reserve, referred to the situation as a "savings glut." See "The Global Saving Glut and the U.S. Current Account Deficit," Remarks by Governor Ben S. Bernanke at the Sandridge Lecture, Virginia Association of Economists, Richmond, Virginia, March 10, 2005, available at http://www.federalreserve.gov/boardDocs/Speeches/2005/200503102/ default.htm.

Of course, there are many good investment opportunities, but the world's financial system wasn't then—and isn't now—capable of intermediating effectively between the savers and these investments.

46 This number is higher than the US minimum wage but much lower than the $15 an hour that is being adopted in some American cities, and even lower than the $10.10 an hour required for enterprises doing business with the US government.

47 Thus, the eurozone's surplus was substantially larger than China's, which stood at $293.2 billion. Germany's surplus alone was estimated to be $285.2 billion in 2015. In 2014, Germany's surplus of $286 billion alone exceeded

China's $220 billion, and if we add those of Italy and Netherlands, the surpluses exceeded that of China by more than 50 percent.

48 Keynes suggested a tax on surpluses, and more recently, I and my coauthor Bruce C. Greenwald have proposed a new system of global reserves that would include strong incentives for countries not to run surpluses. See Joseph E. Stiglitz and Bruce C. Greenwald, "Towards a New Global Reserves System," *Journal of Globalization and Development* 1, no. 2 (2010), Article 10. The idea behind such a system has been promoted by the international Commission of Experts of the President of the UN General Assembly on Reforms of the International Monetary and Financial System, which released its report in September 2009, which in turn was published as *The Stiglitz Report* (New York: The New Press, 2010). See also John Maynard Keynes, "The Keynes Plan," 1942–43, reproduced in J. Keith Horsefield, ed., *The International Monetary Fund 1945–1965: Twenty Years of International Monetary Cooperation*, vol. 3, *Documents* (Washington, DC: International Monetary Fund, 1969), pp. 3–36; and Martin Wolf, *Fixing Global Finance* (Baltimore: Johns Hopkins University Press, 2010).

Chapter 5. The Euro: A Divergent System

1 A quite different antigravity force has been at play elsewhere in the world, as money has moved from developing and emerging markets to the developed countries. In *Making Globalization Work* (New York: W. W. Norton, 2006), I explain how this is a result, in part, of the global reserve system.

2 For instance, in 2000 the GDP per capita in southern Italy was 55 percent of the wealthy northwestern region, a figure that remained unchanged in 2014. And GDP per capita in the south actually decreased slightly as compared to the northeast between 2007 and 2014. Comparisons made using Eurostat data.

3 The fate of history was that many of these countries were faced with an external situation that would, in any case, make matters difficult. China's rise led to an increase in the demand for Germany's sophisticated manufactured goods. At the same time, there's less Chinese demand for some of the less sophisticated goods produced elsewhere in Europe—China provides low-cost substitutes for such goods. For a discussion of some of these trends, see Stephan Danninger and Fred Joutz, "What Explains Germany's Rebounding Export Market Share?," *CESifo Economic Studies* 54, no. 4 (2008): 681–714; and Christoph Schnellbach and Joyce Man, "Germany and China: Embracing a Different Kind of Partnership?," Center for Applied Policy at the University of Munich Research Working Paper, September 2015, available at http://www.cap-lmu.de/download/2015/CAP-WP_German-China-Policy-Sep2015.pdf.

4 Each number is the percentage decrease, from the precrisis peak, of new loans to

nonfinancial corporations of €1 million or less, as reported by those countries' national banks. The precrisis peak varies depending on the country but is generally 2007 or 2008. Data for Greece is from Institute of International Finance, "Restoring Financing and Growth to Greek SMEs," June 18, 2014, available at https://www.iif.com/publication/research-note/restoring-financing-and-growth-greek-smes. See also Institute of International Finance, "Addressing SME Financing Impediments in Europe: A Review of Recent Initiatives," January 12, 2015, available at https://www.iif.com/publication/research-note/addressing-sme-financing-impediments-europe-review-recent-initiatives. The source of the figures for Portugal, Spain, Ireland, and Italy is a report from Bain and the Institute of International Finance, "Restoring Financing and Growth to Europe's SMEs," 2013, available at http://www.bain.com/Images/REPORT_Restoring_financing_and_growth_to_Europe's_SMEs.pdf.

5 See European Commission, "Annual Report on European SMEs 2014/2015," November 2015.

6 See Helmut Kraemer-Eis, Frank Lang, and Salome Gvetadze, "European Small Business Finance Outlook," European Investment Fund, June 2015, available at http://www.eif.org/news_centre/publications/eif_wp_28.pdf.

7 Later, I'll discuss other reasons that returns to capital in the crisis countries may be lower than elsewhere in the eurozone.

8 Similarly, there is a high correlation between the insurance premiums that each has to pay to insure against the risks of default. See V. V. Acharya, I. Drechsler, and P. Schnabl, "A Pyrrhic Victory? Bank Bailouts and Sovereign Credit Risk," *Journal of Finance* 69, no. 6 (December 2014): 2689–2739.

There are many other aspects of the link between sovereign risk and the banks within its jurisdiction. Banks typically hold significant amounts of the country's bonds in their portfolio. Thus, a weakening of the sovereign results in a weakening of its banks, and their ability and willingness to lend. See Nicola Gennaioli, Alberto Martin, and Stefano Rossi, "Banks, Government Bonds, and Default: What Do the Data Say?," IMF Working Paper, July 2014. (Obviously, a bank whose balance sheet has worsened is likely to lend less. See Stiglitz and Greenwald, *Towards a New Paradigm in Monetary Economics*.)

At the same time, given the fact that governments do in fact bail out banks, weaker banks lead to an increase in government's implicit liabilities, increasing sovereign risk.

For further discussions, see, for instance, Adrian Alter and Yves Schueler, "Credit Spread Interdependencies of European States and Banks during the Financial Crisis," *Journal of Banking and Finance* 36, no. 12 (December 2011): 3444–68; and Patrick Bolton and Olivier Jeanne, "Sovereign Default Risk and Bank Fragility in Financially Integrated Economies," *IMF Economic Review* 59, no. 2 (2011): 162–94.

9   See, for instance, the discussion in my book *Freefall* or in Simon Johnson's *13 Bankers* (New York: Pantheon Books, 2010).

10 The exit from Spanish banks, while significant—and leading to a credit crunch—has been slower than some had anticipated. Some refer to it as a "capital jog" rather than capital flight. This, in turn, is a consequence of institutional and market imperfections (for example, rules about knowing your customer, designed to curb money laundering), which, interestingly, the neoclassical model underlying much of Europe's policy agenda ignored. There is far less of a single market than is widely thought to exist.

11 There are similar distortions *within* countries. Because the likelihood of a government bailout is greater for big banks—especially the banks that are viewed to be too big to fail—such banks can acquire funds at a lower rate than small banks. They can thus expand, not based on their relative competency or efficiency, but on the basis of the relative size of the implicit subsidy that they receive from the government. But the system is again divergent: as the large banks get larger, the likelihood of a bailout increases, and thus the difference in the implicit subsidy gets larger.

12 This would not *fully* fix the problem: given that banks in weak countries would, in any case be weaker and perceive the risks they face as higher, lenders to these banks would demand higher interest rates, and the banks in turn would charge higher interest rates, putting firms in their country at a disadvantage. Thus, there would still not be a level playing field. But it would be *more* level than the current system. See Stiglitz and Greenwald, *Towards a New Paradigm in Monetary Economics*.

13 Central banks are supposed to lend to banks that are facing liquidity problems and can't get access to funds, but not to banks that are insolvent and have a negative net worth. In fact, if everyone knew that the bank was solvent, then presumably, if markets worked well, there would be no problem of access to funds. Of course, the bankers always believe that they are fundamentally solvent; it is only the temporary irrationality of markets that has created their problem. Evidently, while the bankers are among those who most consistently preach the religion of free market fundamentalism, when "markets" rate them less highly than they believe they deserve, their faith in markets vanishes, and as suddenly, there is a surge in the belief in government—at least that government should bail out deserving institutions such as themselves.

14 While before the crisis, London and New York competed vigorously against each other in reducing regulations, perhaps the real winner—or I should say loser—was Iceland, which garnered for itself a banking system with assets that were at least ten times the size of its GDP. Iceland also showed the consequences: British and Netherlands depositors in its banks lost their money. Not only had they (wrongly) assumed that the Icelandic banks were effec-

tively regulated; they assumed that the deposit insurance actually would pay off. They typically did not turn to their lawyers before putting money into Icelandic accounts, to find out whether the deposit insurance scheme was adequately capitalized and what the Icelandic government's obligations would be if it were not. The widely held assumption was that the deposit insurance was adequately capitalized (it was not), and the obligations of Icelandic government if the deposit insurance fund went broke were unlimited—but as it turned out, the deposit insurance funds were insufficient to cover the losses and the relevant European court held that the Icelandic government was not responsible for making up for the deficiencies. Depositors experienced large losses.

15 Many other major banks paid billions in fines or made settlements related to the Libor scandal. These include Citigroup, Deutsche Bank, JPMorgan, Rabobank, Royal Bank of Scotland, and UBS. As this book goes to press, traders convicted in the scandal were appealing their verdicts. Meanwhile, some banks were still under investigation. In another case of massive market manipulation, Citigroup, JPMorgan, Barclays, Royal Bank of Scotland, and UBS agreed to plead guilty to a felony of market manipulation.

16 George A. Akerlof and Robert A. Shiller, *Phishing for Phools: The Economics of Manipulation and Deception* (Princeton, NJ: Princeton University Press, 2015).

17 In the United States almost unbounded campaign contributions are made to the individual and the party that comes the closest to leaving the sector unregulated, with significant amounts given to the opposition for good measure. This diversified portfolio approach to campaign giving has worked well for the banks, generating large bailouts under both Democratic and Republic administrations. These investments in America's political process paid off far better than the financial investments that were supposed to be their expertise, but episodically turned out to be disastrous.

18 See later discussion of Chile's experience with stripping away virtually all regulations.

19 In December 2014, the US Congress put a provision undoing one of the key parts of the Dodd-Frank Wall Street Reform and Consumer Protection Act regulating banks—a provision intended to ensure that government-insured institutions do not engage in risky trading in derivatives—in a budget bill that the president had to sign to keep the government open.

20 As one example: it would have the right to ban insurance products where the buyer of the insurance has no insurable risk—that is, I cannot buy a life insurance product on someone whose death would have no consequence for me. I can't, in short, take out such bets. This is a well-known principle, because it creates perverse incentives—to have the insured-against person die. But modern financial markets have not recognized this principle: a bank could place a

bet that company X will collapse and then subtly take actions that might affect X's collapse. It would have an incentive to do so. A good regulatory regime would ban such financial products.

21 That is debt undertaken by a particular country within the eurozone.

22 The result is more general: it applies to any mobile factor of production.

23 See the discussion in chapter 7 on how the ECB *secretly* forced Ireland to do so.

24 Interestingly, this problem has long been recognized in the theory of fiscal federalism/local public goods. See, for instance, J. E. Stiglitz, "Theory of Local Public Goods," in *The Economics of Public Services*, ed. M. S. Feldstein and R. P. Inman, (London: Macmillan, 1977), pp. 274–333; J. E. Stiglitz, "Public Goods in Open Economies with Heterogeneous Individuals," in *Locational Analysis of Public Facilities*, ed. J. F. Thisse and H. G. Zoller (Amsterdam: North-Holland, 1983), pp. 55–78; and J. E. Stiglitz, "The Theory of Local Public Goods Twenty-Five Years after Tiebout: A Perspective," in *Local Provision of Public Services: The Tiebout Model After Twenty-Five Years*, ed. G. R. Zodrow (New York: Academic Press, 1983), pp. 17–53.

The magnitude of the distortion (instability) is related to the elasticity of the demand for labor. If the marginal product of labor does not rise much as labor moves out, and, say, the debt burden rests totally on workers, then after-tax wages can fall as labor migrates out. Then there exists a corner "solution" where no one lives in the country. Alternatively, there can exist an inefficient equilibrium, where the number of people living in Ireland has diminished so much that the wage after tax is the same as in, say, the UK.

More generally, this literature has shown that free migration into and out of a country does not result in the efficient allocation of labor, once again demonstrating that those relying on elementary textbook economics can easily be led astray.

25 Whether these "benefits" to migration outweigh the long-run adverse effects noted above is an empirical question.

26 By the same token, if some of the burden of taxation is imposed on capital, it will induce capital to move out of the country.

27 As I make clear later in the book, there are alternative institutional arrangements for achieving much the same result. And there are many details in the institutional design, ensuring that countries do not get overindebted and/or that the Eurobond debts incurred are for productivity-increasing capital expenditures.

28 Recall from the last chapter that deficits cannot exceed 3 percent of GDP.

29 See Joseph E. Stiglitz, "Economic Organization, Information, and Development," in *Handbook of Development Economics*, ed. H. Chenery and T. N. Srinivasan (Amsterdam: Elsevier Science Publishers, 1988), pp. 93–160; and Robert J. Lucas, "On the Mechanics of Economic Development," *Journal of Monetary Economics* 22, no. 1 (1988): 3–42.

30 CAF (Corporacion Andina de Fomento), the Development Bank of Latin America, is an example.

31 This is sometimes referred to as a capital budget. One worry is that it will result in certain types of investment (for example, in infrastructure) being given preference over others (such as in the health of young people, which is typically not treated as "investment").

32 See, for instance, J. E. Stiglitz, "Leaders and Followers: Perspectives on the Nordic Model and the Economics of Information," *Journal of Public Economics* 127 (2015): 3–16.

33 See World Bank, *The East Asian Miracle* (New York: Oxford University Press, 1993); and *World Development Report 1988–89: Knowledge for Development* (New York: Oxford University Press, 1998).

34 See my book with Bruce C. Greenwald, *Creating a Learning Society*.

35 Even the World Bank has changed its views on industrial policies; yet views about industrial policies are to a large extent enshrined in the eurozone's basic economic framework. See Joseph E. Stiglitz and Justin Yifu Lin, eds., *The Industrial Policy Revolution I: The Role of Government Beyond Ideology* (Houndmills, UK, and New York: Palgrave Macmillan, 2013); Joseph E. Stiglitz, Justin Yifu Lin, and Ebrahim Patel, eds., *The Industrial Policy Revolution II: Africa in the 21st Century* (Houndmills, UK, and New York: Palgrave Macmillan, 2013). For a more general theoretical discussion, see Stiglitz and Greenwald, *Creating a Learning Society*, 2014.

36 Trade agreements often purport to similarly create a level playing field. A closer look at these agreements raises questions. While industrial subsidies that might help those lagging behind to catch up are circumscribed, massive agriculture subsidies—a result of a powerful lobby group in Europe and America—are allowed.

37 Called the European Stability Mechanism. Countries drawing upon the funds must have signed the Fiscal Compact (discussed later) and agree to a "program." Later chapters will discuss how the programs so far have been counterproductive.

38 Increases in government spending to pay for the greater unemployment and decreases in government revenue as the economy slows down (for example, as a result of progressive taxes) are called *automatic stabilizers*. They help prevent downturns from getting worse. Automatic stabilizers, built into the economy in the years since World War II under the influence of Keynesian analysis, are one of the reasons that economies have been much more stable since then than they were, say, before World War I.

39 Poorly designed bank regulation and enforcement also often act as automatic destabilizers: as the economy gets weaker, bank losses mount, and a rigid bank enforcer, insensitive to the concerns of forbearance discussed earlier, will force the bank to cut back on lending, and that reinforces the economic

downturn *automatically.* Earlier in this chapter we discussed proposals for tighter uniform regulation across the eurozone in which forbearance would play little or no role. The worry is that the eurozone will have created a powerful automatic destabilizer.

40 The EU subsequently ruled that some of what they were doing circumvented European rules.

41 See OECD, "Crisis Squeezes Income and Puts Pressure on Inequality and Poverty," briefing from May 2013, available at http://www.oecd.org/els/soc/OECD2013-Inequality-and-Poverty-8p.pdf. See also the OECD series of inequality reports, including "In It Together."

Chapter 6. Monetary Policy and the European Central Bank

1 In his July 26, 2012, speech in London: "Within our mandate, the ECB is ready to do whatever it takes to preserve the euro. And believe me, it will be enough."

2 While it is authorized to pursue more general purposes: to "support the general economic policies in the Union with a view to contributing to the achievement of the objectives of the Union," these objectives are secondary. See "On the Statute of the European System of Central Banks and of the European Central Bank," *Official Journal of the European Union,* May 9, 2008.

3 Germany's obsession with inflation was central. As we noted earlier, Germans had rewritten history to believe that it was inflation, not high unemployment, which had brought on Hitler and fascism. But however untethered belief systems are to reality, once established, they are part of the reality that has to be dealt with. With Germany becoming the dominant power within the eurozone, its beliefs, its conviction that the central problem was inflation, became embedded into the "constitution" of ECB.

4 "On the Statute of the European System of Central Banks and of the European Central Bank."

5 From Article 127 of the Treaty on the Functioning of the European Union.

6 Of course, the gold standard of more recent times was different from that in earlier centuries, before the widespread adoption of paper money. Around the time of the European discovery of the New World, actual gold specie (along with other precious metals) was circulated on the continent. It was the medium of exchange. Later, cumbersome coins were replaced by cloth or paper bills that were backed with specific amounts of gold. But for our purposes in this particular discussion, the effect is similar: the value of money was tied to the oscillations of gold's value, and not to policy that government could tweak.

7 The act also created the Council of Economic Advisers, to advise government on how to achieve those goals. I served as chairman of that council under President Clinton.

8 See Charles P. Kindleberger, *Manias, Panics, and Crashes: A History of Financial Crises* (New York: John Wiley & Sons, 1978).

9 A term used by Alan Greenspan in a famous speech delivered in Washington at the American Enterprise Institute on December 5, 1996, titled "The Challenge of Central Banking in a Democratic Society." I was there when he delivered the speech, and was interested in the reaction of the audience and the media to it. They were reading the speech to see what it portended for short-run monetary policy (and as he explained to me, he was aware that that was what they would be looking at). The bigger implications for the conduct of monetary policy—including his argument that monetary authorities should not direct their policies toward asset price inflation—were largely ignored. His remarks were partially directed at what many saw as the bubble in Japanese stock markets and led to an almost immediate decrease in the Tokyo stock market by 3 percent, with follow-on effects around the world. The phrase "irrational exuberance" has now entered into the standard lexicon, and though widely attributed to Greenspan, he may have gotten the term from Nobel Prize–winning economist Robert Shiller in a private conversation. See the blog post at http://ritholtz.com/2013/01/did-greenspan-steal-the-phrase-irrational-exuberance/. See also my more extensive discussion in my book *The Roaring Nineties: A New History of the World's Most Prosperous Decade* (New York: W. W. Norton, 2003).

10 Compensation was typically not based on long-term results. Particularly harmful were stock options, which encouraged them to report results and to take actions which increased stock prices in the short run, with little regard for the long-run consequences. See my book *The Roaring Nineties* and Stiglitz et al. *Rewriting the Rules of the American Economy*.

11 There is no general theory that argues the optimal response to the higher oil price should be that the demand for all nontraded goods should be lowered so that a particular index, the weighted average price, should be unchanged.

12 Indeed, as we have noted elsewhere, the ECB, worried about inflation, actually increased interest rates twice in 2011.

13 See chapter 4 for a discussion of competitive devaluation.

14 See Milton Friedman and Anna J. Schwartz, *A Monetary History of the United States, 1867–1960* (Princeton, NJ: Princeton University Press, 1963).

15 The rate itself was determined mechanically—the rate of growth of the *real* economy.

16 Japan began its quantitative easing in earnest in 2011, buying hundreds of billions of dollars' worth of bonds since then. The United States' quantitative easing, which was even larger (though not relative to the size of its economy), began in 2008 and eventually entailed buying trillions of dollars' worth of bonds. The Bank of England's somewhat smaller program ran from 2009 to

2012. The theory behind QE is discussed at greater length at the end of this chapter.

17 This presumes that the local banks have the *capacity* to lend. As we noted in the last chapter, one of the problems of the eurozone construction was that it facilitated the flight of capital out of the banks of weak countries, undermining their ability to lend. In practice, there is a risk that Europe would tilt the playing field even more: if they treated lending to weak countries as riskier, it would discourage even stronger banks in stronger countries from engaging in cross-border lending into the weaker countries. For a discussion of the general principles at play, see Stiglitz and Greenwald, *Towards a New Paradigm in Monetary Economics.*

18 Even more ambitiously, the US CRA (Community Reinvestment Act) requirements have successfully induced banks to provide more credit to underserved communities.

19 Defenders of these policies claim that the government was repaid. But whether that is so is not the point: the government lent money to the banks at far below the market interest rate, and that in itself is a major gift. There were many other ways that central banks (sometimes working in conjunction with government, sometimes seemingly independently) provided hidden subsidies to the banks. They perpetuated the prevalence of too-big-to-fail (too-correlated-to-fail, and too-interconnected-to-fail) banks; indeed, on both sides of the Atlantic, governments encouraged mergers, exacerbating the problem. The lower interest rates that such banks can obtain acts as a hidden subsidy. Quantitative easing itself represented in part a hidden recapitalization of the banks, much as the policies pursued in the Clinton administration had done after the savings and loan (S&L) crisis. Long-term bonds went up in value, and banks that held these were in effect given a major transfer of wealth. In the case of the United States in the S&L crisis, banks had been encouraged to hold these bonds through regulatory accounting that treated these bonds as zero risk, though it was obvious that there was considerable variability in their price, and the returns they received reflected this volatility. (See my book *The Roaring Nineties.*) In the aftermath of the 2008 crisis, such hidden recapitalizations (sometimes referred to as stealth recapitalization) became even larger, and began to be talked about by market analysts. For instance, Meredith Whitney in a discussion with *Bloomberg*'s Jonathan Weil, estimated that "$100 billion in capital was replenished just through what she calls the Federal Reserve's 'Great Agency Trade.' . . . (As quoted by Edward Harrison, "Q1 Bank Earnings Due to Marking Up Assets, Not Fundamentals—Meredith Whitney," *Seeking Alpha*, May 6, 2010, available at http://seekingalpha.com/article/203263-q1-bank-earnings-due-to-marking-up-assets-not-fundamentals-meredith-whitney.)

In the eurozone, the "bootstrap" operation described in chapter 7 provided the conditions for a similar hidden recapitalization. The ECB's LTRO (Long-Term Refinancing Operation) program beginning in late 2011 lent money to the banks at low interest rates. Many used the funds to purchase long-term government bonds. Nine months later, the ECB's OMT (Outright Monetary Transactions) program, authorized government bonds to be purchased from the market. Though the program was never used, the seeming confidence it gave helped drive up their prices, recapitalizing the banks. QE continued the recapitalizations, which the economist Markus K. Brunnermeier of Princeton University and his coauthors have referred to as stealth recapitalizations (see his presentation at the G7 Conference in Frankfurt, March 27, 2015, available at https://scholar.princeton.edu/sites/default/files/markus/files/diabolicloop_ sovereignbankingrisk.pdf).

20 In the World Economic Forum's 2012 and 2013 *Global Risk* reports, "severe income disparity" was ranked number one.

21 See Jonathan D. Ostry, Andrew Berg, and Charalambos G. Tsangarides, "Redistribution, Inequality, and Growth," *IMF Staff Discussion Note*, SDN/14/02, 2014, available at https://www.imf.org/external/pubs/ft/sdn/2014/sdn1402 .pdf; and Federico Cingano, "Trends in Income Inequality and its Impact on Economic Growth," OECD Social, Employment and Migration Working Papers No. 163, 2014, available at http://www.oecd.org/els/soc/trends-in-income-inequality-and-its-impact-on-economic-growth-SEM-WP163.pdf.

22 In countries with big ethnic and racial divides (such as the United States and France), there can be further dimensions to this growth in inequality. When the economy goes into a slump, it is the workers from these groups that are first laid off. When there is a heated economy (as in the late 1990s in the United States), these divides narrow markedly.

23 *El Dilema* (Barcelona: Planeta, 2013). Translation obtained from http:// openeuropeblog.blogspot.com/2013/11/whats-best-place-to-publish-ecb-letter.html.

24 The demands were remarkably specific and far reaching. There was a demand to eliminate the linking of wages with prices, important if workers are to be protected against inflation but clearly of no concern at the moment, since prices were, if anything, falling. ("We are enormously concerned about the fact that the government has not adopted any measure to abolish inflation-indexing clauses. Such clauses are not an appropriate element for the labour markets in a monetary union, as they represent a structural obstacle to the adjustment of labour costs.") There was a demand to virtually eliminate job protections, at least temporarily. ("We see important advantages in the adoption of a new exceptional work contract that is applied for a limited period of time, and where compensation for dismissal is very low.") There was a "suggestion" that the government figure out how to stifle wage increases (described as "exceptional measures to promote wage moderation in the private sector").

Of course, the ECB also focused on fiscal policies, but here it was far more stringent than the eurozone's official rules. ("The government should prove in a clear manner, by action, its unconditional commitment to the achievement of its fiscal policy targets, *irrespective of the economic situation* [italics added].)" And the ECB showed no hesitation in intruding into an area of enormous sensitivity in Spain, the fiscal relations between the central government and the regions—the central government needed to ensure "control over regional and local budgets (including the authorisation for debt emissions by regional governments)".

25 Interestingly, these and similar labor market reforms remain at the center of political tensions in Spain as this book goes to press.

26 As we noted earlier, in most cases, the reason that the central bank has to act as a lender of last resort—providing liquidity when others are unwilling to do so, or at least unwilling to do so at any "reasonable" interest rate—is that the "market" has made a judgment that there is a high risk that they will not be repaid because the institution may be insolvent. Though central banks are only supposed to lend to *solvent but illiquid* institutions, necessarily, in doing so, they are putting their judgment against that of the market.

27 In the United States, almost all of the hundreds of billions of bailout dollars went to help the banks and their bondholders and shareholders. A negligible amount went to help homeowners, even though the crisis had begun as a housing crisis. The administration and the Fed believed in trickle-down economics: throw enough money at the banks, and the whole economy will benefit. It would have been far better for the economy had they tried a larger dose of trickle-up economics: help the homeowners, and everyone will benefit.

28 The Troika, in effect, threatened to bankrupt Ireland if the government tried to make bondholders bear some of the costs of bank restructuring. The threats were kept secret and only revealed later by the central bank governor, Patrick Honohan. See Brendan Keenan, "Revealed—the Troika Threats to Bankrupt Ireland," *Independent,* September 28, 2014.

29 As in the case of the United States, it was necessary and desirable to save the depositors, but not to save the bankers, the bondholders and shareholders. For a broader discussion of these issues, see my book *Freefall.*

30 The problems of governance are worse because of the inclination of bankers for secrecy and lack of transparency. (We have already seen two instances: the secret letter to Zapatero and the secret demand by the ECB that Ireland bail out its banks.) Bankers, almost by their very nature, are inclined to secrecy. Bankers realize that even more than knowledge being linked to power is that knowledge is linked to profits: differential information is the source of economic rents. Though central banks are public institutions, central bank culture is too often contaminated by the culture of *private* banks.

31 As quoted in William Greider's *Secrets of the Temple* (New York: Simon and Schuster, 1987), p. 473.

32 They don't typically represent the interests of all of those in the financial market; they are much more attuned, for instance, to the concerns of the banks than they are to the hedge funds or the venture capitalists.

33 Nonetheless, there are other sources of expertise (academia), and the expertise that is of critical importance for a central bank—understanding macroeconomics and the behavior of the financial sector as a *system*—is markedly different from that of the typical participant from the financial sector. (Draghi, with a PhD in economics from MIT, is an exception, combining the real world experience with the appropriate intellectual training that other central banks should strive for.) Some central banks proscribe those from the financial sector from even serving on their board, recognizing the conflicts of interest and the dangers of "cognitive capture."

34 In the United States and in many other countries, the massive bailouts, as the banks virtually demanded government money, revealed that the battles they had been fighting to get government out of the way were not about principles but about money. They demanded, too, that the government suspend the normal rules of capitalism, where shareholders and bondholders are responsible for the losses of a firm.

35 In the case of the United States, at least Alan Greenspan, the chairman of the Fed in the run-up to the crisis, made a *mea culpa*, as he admitted to the flaw in his reasoning, his belief in self-regulation. "I have found a flaw," he told Congress in October 2008. "I don't know how significant or permanent it is. But I have been very distressed by that fact." (See "The Financial Crisis and the Role of Federal Regulators: Hearing before the Committee on Government and Oversight Reform," October 23, 2008, available at https://www.gpo.gov/fdsys/pkg/CHRG-110hhrg55764/pdf/CHRG-110hhrg55764.pdf.) But even then, he failed to note the perverse incentives facing the banks and bankers, *of which he should have been aware*. But interestingly, Ben Bernanke, who assumed chairmanship of the Fed on February 1, 2006, never gave a similar *mea culpa*, and the worst abuses in the banking system actually occurred after he assumed office. Similarly, no such admission has come from those responsible for European banking.

36 Typically, though, the market has realized that the old bonds will never be repaid, so the market price of these bonds is much below the face value. The market price of the new bonds is often closely related to the market price of the old bonds.

37 Even then, if the banks in, say, Germany had had a problem, it would have been an easy matter for the German government to bail them out—a relatively light burden on a very rich country compared to the relatively huge burden

imposed on a small and relatively poor country. The power relations within Europe were again manifested and reflected in the policy of the ECB.

38 By contrast, in the East Asia crisis, the IMF demanded that the Indonesian government not bail out its banks, or even its depositors.

39 See Sebastian Gechert, Katja Rietzler and Silke Tober, "The European Commission's New NAIRU: Does It Deliver?" Institut für Makroökonomieund Konjunkturforschung (Macroeconomic Policy Institute), January 2015, available at https://ideas.repec.org/p/imk/wpaper/142-2014.html. For a more extensive discussion of this issue, see chapter 9, note 9.

40 See Stiglitz et al., *Rewriting the Rules of the American Economy.*

41 In the past, some governments may have tried to manipulate the economy before elections through monetary policy. But there are long and uncertain lags, making monetary policy not a very good tool for these purposes. Fiscal policy is, in fact, more effective. Some have suggested that, in the past, some central banks that were not independent at least attempted this kind of manipulation. Even if that is the case, the cure—making central banks so independent that they can easily be captured by the financial sector—is worse than the disease. There is, in fact, a wide range of institutional arrangements between full independence and being just another department of government. The governance of the ECB goes too far in the former direction.

42 The heyday of monetarism at central banks was in the 1980s and '90s; inflation targeting was first explicitly adopted by New Zealand in 1984, and subsequently spread around the world. After the 2008 financial crisis, most central banks revised their policy frameworks toward a more flexible framework, with more mandates (including financial stability) and a more nuanced view of inflation—with their responses depending on the source of inflation. See Luis Jácome and Tommaso Mancini-Griffoli, "A Broader Mandate," *Finance and Development* 51, no. 2 (2014): 47–50.

43 Moreover, because the administration and the Fed had done so little to address the underlying problems in the real estate and mortgage markets, real estate prices remained low; real estate was a major source of collateral for loans to small and medium-size enterprises, and this, too, inhibited lending to them.

44 See Milton Friedman, "The Role of Monetary Policy," *American Economic Review* 58, no. 1 (1968): 1–17; Milton Friedman, "Inflation and Unemployment," *Journal of Political Economy* 85, no. 3 (1977): 451–72; Edmund S. Phelps, "Money-Wage Dynamics and Labor-Market Equilibrium," *Journal of Political Economy* 76, no. 4 part 2 (1968): 678–711.

45 See, for instance, Roger E. A. Farmer, "The Natural Rate Hypothesis: An Idea Past Its Sell-By Date," NBER Working Paper No. 19267, 2013, available at http://www.bankofengland.co.uk/publications/Documents/quarterlybulletin/2013/qb130306.pdf.

Chapter 7. Crises Policies: How Troika Policies Compounded the Flawed Eurozone Structure, Ensuring Depression

1 See, for instance, Suzanne Daly, "Hunger on the Rise in Spain," *New York Times*, September 25, 2012.

2 See European Commission Directorate-General for Economic and Financial Affairs, "The Economic Adjustment Programme for Ireland," February 2011, available at http://ec.europa.eu/economy_finance/publications/occasional_paper/2011/pdf/ocp76_en.pdf.

3 See IMF, "Letter of Intent of the Government of Portugal," May 17, 2011, available at http://ec.europa.eu/economy_finance/publications/occasional_paper/2014/pdf/ocp202_en.pdf, p. 71. The rate actually peaked above 13 percent in 2012 before decreasing.

4 See European Commission, "The Economic Adjustment Programme for Portugal 2011–2014," October 2014, available at https://www.imf.org/external/np/loi/2011/prt/051711.pdf.

5 See Ricardo Reis, "Looking for a Success: The Euro Crisis Adjustment Programs," Brookings Papers on Economic Activity, BPEA Conference Draft, September 10-11, 2015, available at http://www.brookings.edu/~/media/projects/bpea/fall-2015_embargoed/conferencedraft_reis_eurocrisis.pdf. See also http://ec.europa.eu/economy_finance/publications/occasional_paper/2014/pdf/ocp202_en.pdf.

6 The austerity consisted of both that imposed by the Troika and that which the conservative government adopted itself, in an effort to conform to the prevailing ideology.

7 The German Council of Economic Experts wrote, in a July 28, 2015, press release for a longer report: "The economic turnarounds in Ireland, Portugal, Spain and—until the end of last year—also in Greece show that the principle 'loans against reforms' can lead to success. For the new program to work, Greece has to show more ownership for deep structural reforms. And it should make use of the technical expertise offered by its European partners." See German Council of Economic Experts, "German Council of Economic Experts Discusses Reform Needs to Make the Euro Area More Stable and Proposes Sovereign Insolvency Mechanism," July 28, 2015, available at http://www.sachverstaendigenrat-wirtschaft.de/fileadmin/dateiablage/download/pressemitteilungen/gcee_press_release_07_15.pdf and German Council of Economic Experts, "Executive Summary," July 2015, available at http://www.sachverstaendigenrat-wirtschaft.de/fileadmin/dateiablage/download/sondergutachten/executive_summary_special_report07-2015.pdf.)

Chapter 3 has documented some of the reasons that this perspective seems unpersuasive. For other critiques, see Suzanne Daly, "For Many in Spain, a

Heralded Economic Recovery Feels Like a Bust," *New York Times*, August 10, 2015 available at http://www.nytimes.com/2015/08/11/world/europe/for-many-in-spain-a-heralded-economic-recovery-feels-like-a-bust.html?_r=0; and Zero Hedge, "Sorry Troika, Spain's Economic Recovery Is 'One Big Lie,'" August 12, 2015, available at http://www.zerohedge.com/news/2015-08-12/sorry-troika-spains-economic-recovery-one-big-lie.

8 The ban was on foreclosures of homes where €200,000 or less was owed on the mortgage.

9 This is a drama that has played out through much of the United States: empty homes quickly deteriorate. The banks will only be able to resell them for a pittance. Communities, as well as families, get destroyed. There is a downward vicious circle, since homes that are not well maintained decrease the value of neighboring homes, leading to even more defaults.

10 See Kerin Hope, "Athens Backs Reforms to Unlock Bailout Funds," *Financial Times*, November 19, 2015.

11 In 2007, Greece had to pay only 0.3 percent more interest than Germany did. In 2010, that number had risen to 6.4 percent. Source: OECD data on long-term interest rates (rates for government bonds with 10-year maturity).

12 Two years after the program started, they expected the economy to be well on the road to recovery. But in fact, the downturn just continued. The Troika could not ignore the evidence. But rather than rethinking the program, or even rethinking their model, they took the same model, predicting a quick recovery, now from a lower base. Again, it didn't happen. And they repeated the same thing over and over again. The same story could be told for each of the crisis countries—for instance, in Spain or Portugal.

13 Projections from IMF's World Economic Outlook (WEO) September 2011, available at https://www.imf.org/external/pubs/ft/weo/2011/02/pdf/text.pdf.

14 Papandreou became prime minister in 2009. As we comment below, his term ended in 2011 after he proposed a referendum on the program being imposed on his country—a proposal that his eurozone colleagues viewed almost with horror. His father, Andreas Papandreou, had been prime minister from 1981 to 1989 and from 1993 to 1996, and was largely responsible for the creation of the left-of-center party PASOK. His grandfather, Georgios Papandreou, served as prime minister in 1944–1945, in 1963, and in 1964–1965. He was arrested during a military coup in 1967 that was widely believed to have been supported by the United States (or at least the CIA). The fight against Germany's cruel occupation of Greece, with forced loans to Germany that were never repaid, color not just Greece's history but attitudes toward more recent events.

15 Some of the budget chicanery had begun earlier, as Greece struggled to satisfy the conditions required for it to join the eurozone. In this, a critical and dishonorable role was played by Goldman Sachs, which constructed a nontransparent derivative that helped Greece hide its true situation. See Louise Story,

Landon Thomas Jr., and Nelson D. Schwartz, "Wall St. Helped to Mask Debt Fueling Europe's Crisis," *New York Times*, February 13, 2010; and Beat Balzli, "Greek Debt Crisis: How Goldman Sachs Helped Greece to Mask Its True Debt," *Spiegel*, February 8, 2010.

16 Still, the focus on deficits was not surprising, given the fixation on deficits and debt built into the construction of the eurozone noted in chapter 4.

17 At one time, it had demanded a primary surplus of 6 percent by 2014! By 2015, it was insisting on a surplus of 3.5 percent by 2018.

18 I saw a similar process at work when I was chief economist of the World Bank. Essentially, whenever there was a debt restructuring on the table, the forecasts would be rosy—the rosier the forecast, the less need for debt write-offs, which was, of course, what the creditors wanted. What struck me as particularly strange was the way the forecasts were often arrived at: they were as much the result of a negotiation as of an economic model.

19 Even an increase in investment, if it is not the right kind and if the government has not set in motion the right policies, may have an adverse effect on the unemployment rate. There is a positive supply-side effect, which *in the presence of a deficiency of aggregate demand in the future* will lead to an increase in unemployment. This effect will be especially large if the investments replace labor, for instance, self-checkout machines in groceries and drugstores replacing unskilled labor.

20 Other actions by the Troika contributed to tax evasion. One of the important ways to reduce the scope for tax evasion is to ensure that transactions go through the banking system. Cash transactions are hard to tax in any economy. But the closure of the banks in Greece for an extended period surrounding the referendum in the summer of 2015 and the proposal to force even small depositors to take a haircut in the Cyprus crisis (even though that provision was not adopted) encouraged individuals not to rely on banks.

21 See, for instance, Tariq Ali, "Diary," *London Review of Books* 37, no. 15 (July 30, 2015): 38–39. While Hochtief, the German company in question that built the airport, owned only 45 percent of the shares of the airport, it had full management rights. A Greek court ruled that Hochtief owed substantial amounts in value-added taxes on the services it had provided (which, according to some news reports, it collected but didn't turn over and which amounted to €0.5 billion). Other outstanding payments, such as to social security funds, could bring the amount owed to €1 billion. Some news reports also suggest no value-added taxes were paid on the construction of the airport. The case is mired in controversy; indeed, even what the court ruled is a matter of contention. What is clear is that the court ruled against Hochtief. Hochtief evidently argues that the company owning the airport pay *only* €167 million in fines and taxes, not the higher amounts reported in the media, and that the judicial process is not over. Hochtief also evidently claims that it didn't have to make

tax payments until it made a profit, but others say that it cooked the books by deducting the full cost of the investment in the first year, rather than following the conventional procedure of depreciating the investment over time—a long-term investment, lasting, say, 50 years, would entail only 2 percent of the costs of the construction being deducted. Subsequently, Hochtief was taken over by a Spanish company, and that company sold its interests to others. Where this leaves Greece in getting the taxes that courts have ruled it is owed is not clear.

22 Almost surely, there are tax and possibly other legal disputes between the Hellenic government and some foreigners refusing to pay taxes; and the bargaining power of each party depends on who holds the money. In the United States, for instance, when there are very large tax disputes, typically, the taxpayer has to pay the tax that has been imposed, and then he sues in the Federal Court to get back the money that he believes is owed back to him.

23 See chapter 5. If there was any doubt about the risk of having money in the banking system, it was resolved when the ECB stopped acting as a lender of last resort to Greek banks, leading to paralysis in the Greek banking system, with small limits on the amounts that could be withdrawn every day. As we have also previously noted, the proposed "bail-in" of depositors in Cyprus had a similar effect.

24 In this respect, it may not even matter whether the perceptions are accurate. For instance, see the discussion of the German-owned company responsible for the running of the Athens airport, which allegedly owed hundreds of millions of euros in taxes, as we discussed in an earlier note. Although the details of the case are controversial, the story has struck such a chord that it has circulated on the Internet and gained the weight of indisputable fact. The fact that the airport had the reputation of not being among one of the better-run airports around the world (even within the limited domain of southern Europe, it ranks fourth in the Skytrax World Airport Awards) may have made matters worse. (As we noted earlier, the airport and the company, of course, deny the allegations.) So, too, for the Troika demands that there not be withholding on taxes on foreign corporations—a demand that was never adequately explained.

25 See Henry George, *Progress and Poverty: An Inquiry into the Cause of Industrial Depressions and of Increase of Want with Increase of Wealth* (San Francisco, W. M. Hinton & Company, printers, 1879).

26 Some taxes can actually stimulate the economy. A high tax on inheritance can induce those about to die to spend more. Unfortunately, within the EU, easy mobility may constrain the ability to impose an inheritance tax that is much different from that imposed elsewhere. So, too, a tax on carbon can induce the private sector to invest in carbon-friendly technologies—replacing old carbon-intensive technologies.

27 The balance sheet looks at the assets and the liabilities. The difference is the net worth. A privatization entails the sale of an asset for cash. Thus, a privatization at a fair market value has *no* effect on the balance sheet. It simply shifts the composition of assets, from "real assets" to "cash." But, as I explain below, the Troika's demands for a fast privatization risked a sale at below true (long-run) market value in a fire sale, in which case the balance sheet would be worsened.

28 As chief economist of the World Bank, I repeatedly saw the adverse effects of privatizations done poorly: Mexico's privatization of Telmex led to high telecom prices; such high prices impose significant barriers to countries moving into the digital age. (See Organization for Economic Co-operation and Development, *OECD Review of Telecommunications Policy and Regulation in Mexico*, 2011, available at https://www.oecd.org/sti/broadband/50550219.pdf.)

In my book *Globalization and Its Discontents*, I pointed out that these problems with privatization were evidenced repeatedly. Even by 2015, the Troika had not yet absorbed these lessons.

29 Matters can be even worse when the foreign purchaser is protected by a bilateral investment agreement, which gives private parties the right to sue governments whenever there is a disadvantageous change in regulations, even if the change is desirable from the perspective of health and safety and implemented in a nondiscriminatory manner. This is relevant for the privatizations that are part of the eurozone program, because the winning bidder may be a foreign enterprise, incorporated in a jurisdiction with which there is a bilateral investment agreement. *So far*, however, this has not been a problem in any of the eurozone privatizations.

30 See Niki Kitsantonis, "14 Airports in Greece to Be Privatized in $1.3 Billion Deal," *New York Times*, December 14, 2015. There are ample opportunities to abuse the monopoly power associated with the control of a regional airport. The worry is that attempts to regulate, to prevent such abuses, will now become a cross-border dispute, with the German government (and therefore the Troika) taking the side of the oligarch/German partnership against the public interest.

31 In the case of Greece, the historically tense relationship with Turkey makes cutbacks in military spending especially difficult, even though when Georges Papandreou was foreign minister, there was a serious rapprochement.

32 See John Henley, " 'Making Us Poorer Won't Save Greece': How Pension Crisis is Hurting Its People," *Guardian*, June 17, 2015.

33 Matthew Dalton, "Greece's Pension System Isn't That Generous After All," *Wall Street Journal*, February 27, 2015.

34 Whether part of the formal or implied contract is of secondary concern.

35 There is an exception: when pensions have been gratuitously increased *after* the work has been done. In that case, the worker has been given a "gift," which

was not part of the contract. Reducing, or even eliminating, the gift, in the presence of extreme budgetary stringency, may then make sense.

36 In February 2014.

37 There are other anomalous aspects of the demands for pension reform. Part of the problem that the pension system finds itself in is because it held Greek government bonds, which experienced significant write-downs as part of debt restructuring. Had the restructuring been done earlier (in 2010) and had the Troika not imposed such contractionary policies, the size of the write-downs would have been markedly less. Thus, the Troika itself is partly to blame for the problems in the pension system.

38 As we noted earlier in the book, part of what was going on was a hidden recapitalization of the banking system.

39 According to OECD data on long-term interest rates (rates for government bonds with 10-year maturity).

40 Whether the ECB would be willing and able to do whatever it takes when put to the test has been put into question by the constant haggling with its German board members—for example, over whether buying the bonds of a country in crisis is desirable, or even permissible.

41 Moreover, the bailout provides an opportunity for the short-term private creditors to take out their funds, leaving an even greater burden on the rest.

42 There are a few exceptions, which are worth noting. Brazil in 1998 faced a crisis. It seemed that it was possible that there were two equilibria—a high interest-rate, high-default scenario and another low interest-rate, low-default scenario—and the IMF program provided the confidence that enabled it to move to the "good" equilibrium.

43 According to data from the IMF, Institute for Fiscal Studies, Federal Reserve Bank of St. Louis, and US Bureau of Fiscal Services (Bureau of Public Debt).

44 And in most of the European countries, the financial sector is even more concentrated than it is in the United States.

45 In other words, when the government recapitalizes a bank and does it properly, taking full value of shares corresponding to the money it is providing, there is no real expenditure. It is an asset transaction. Troika (and IMF) accounting treats these capital/investment expenditures much the same way they would a consumption binge; but from an economic perspective, they are totally different. No household (not even the proverbial Swabian housewife), let alone any firm, would treat an investment in the same way that it would other forms of spending. Accounting matters. Wrong accounting frameworks lead to wrong policies. In this case, the crisis countries are forced to engage in excessive austerity.

By the same token, the revenue from the sale of a national asset in a privatization should not be treated in the same way that tax revenues are. Again, with the flawed Troika accounting, they are. During my tenure as chief economist of the World Bank, this was a matter of repeated contention with the IMF.

46 Of course, one might argue that the interest rate only reflected a reasonable risk premium. But the charade that Germany and others in the Troika were playing said that with the program, Greece would recover and would repay the loan. So under the program, Germany claimed to be making a large profit off of its poorer neighbor.

47 See Phillip Inman, "Where Did the Greek Bailout Money Go?," *Guardian*, June 29, 2015. What happened is similar to what occurs in American predatory lending; the pattern is familiar: a poor individual borrows $100, but within a few years, he has paid thousands of dollars to the bank and still owes well in excess of $100. All the money that he has paid (and borrowed) simply goes to pay the bank's interest and fees.

48 That is, in paying interest and making its principal payments.

49 When the money was owed to private creditors, the creditors put enormous pressure on their governments to force the debtor countries to assume the private debts and to make sure that the creditors will be fully repaid, whoever owed them money.

50 There is some evidence that, on average, they are more than compensated for such risks.

51 Luis María Drago, Argentine's foreign minister at the time of Venezuela's debt crisis at the beginning of the last century, said (in what has come to be called the Drago Doctrine) that lenders to sovereigns should know that they are at risk of not being repaid. He argued, moreover, that "the public debt cannot bring about a military intervention or give merit to the material occupation of the soil of the American nations by a European power." See my book *Making Globalization Work* for a discussion.

52 Another reflection of the highly political actions of the Troika was the attempt of European authorities to suppress the release of the IMF findings concerning the unsustainability of Greece's debt until after the referendum on whether to accept the Troika program. Evidently, they didn't want voters to know about the true state of Greece's situation as they went to the polls. And they even tried to keep their actions to delay the release of the IMF findings secret. See "Exclusive: Greece Needs Debt Relief Far Beyond EU Plans: Secret IMF Report," Reuters, July 14, 2015, available at http://www.reuters.com/article/us-eurozone-greece-imf-report-idUSKCN0PO1CB20150714.

53 Debt structuring often entails extensive litigation, as Argentina's experience illustrates. On net, even taking into account these litigation costs, few would doubt that Argentina benefited from its debt restructuring. Moreover, there may be ways of going about debt restructuring that lower the risks of litigation. We discuss some of these in later chapters.

54 Some argue that in fact, debt restructuring is by far the most important, especially for Greece, because the increase in exports and decreases in imports from a change in exchange rates is limited. Such assertions remain controversial and are partially based on failing to take account that Greece's main foreign exchange earner is tourism, and tourism is price sensitive.

55 "Fiscal Consolidation Targets, Plans and Measures in OECD Countries," OECD, 2012, available at http://www.oecd.org/eco/public-finance/4.3%20 Blondal%20Klepsvik.pdf.

56 See Alberto Alesina and Roberto Perotti, "Fiscal Expansions and Fiscal Adjustments in OECD Countries," NBER Working Paper No. 5214, 1995; and Alberto Alesina and Silvia Ardagna "Large Changes in Fiscal Policy: Taxes versus Spending," in *Tax Policy and the Economy*, vol. 24, ed. J. R. Brown (Chicago: University of Chicago Press, 2010), pp. 35–68.

57 See, for example, Dean Baker, "The Myth of Expansionary Fiscal Austerity," Center for Economic and Policy Research, October 2010, available at http://cepr.net/documents/publications/austerity-myth-2010-10.pdf; and Arjun Jayadev and Mike Konczal, "The Boom Not The Slump: The Right Time For Austerity," Roosevelt Institute, 2010, available at http://scholarworks.umb .edu/cgi/viewcontent.cgi?article=1026&context=econ_faculty_pubs.

58 See, for example, International Monetary Fund, "Will It Hurt? Macroeconomic Effects of Fiscal Consolidation," chapter 3 in 2010 *World Economic Outlook*.

59 Eurostat figures for the eurozone for March 2016.

60 See, for example, International Monetary Fund, "Will It Hurt?"

62 Carmen M. Reinhart and Kenneth S. Rogoff, "Growth in a Time of Debt," *American Economic Review* 100, no. 2 (May 2010): 573–78.

62 By now, there is a large literature on the subject. See, for example, Thomas Herndon, Michael Ash, and Robert Pollin, "Does High Public Debt Consistently Stifle Economic Growth? A Critique of Reinhart and Rogoff," *Cambridge Journal of Economics* 38, no. 2 (2014): 257–79; Ugo Panizza and Andrea F. Presbitero, "Public Debt and Economic Growth: Is There a Causal Effect?," *Journal of Macroeconomics* 41 (2014):21–41; and Andrea Pescatori, Damiano Sandri, and John Simon, "Debt and Growth: Is There a Magic Threshold?," International Monetary Fund Working Paper No. 14/34, February 2014, available at https://www.imf.org/external/pubs/ft/wp/2014/wp1434.pdf.

63 Subsequently, a large literature has developed explaining why the standard models did so badly. See Joseph E. Stiglitz, "Rethinking Macroeconomics: What Failed and How to Repair It," *Journal of the European Economic Association* 9, no. 4 (2011): 591–645; and Joseph E. Stiglitz, "Rethinking Macroeconomics: What Went Wrong and How to Fix It," *Journal of Global Policy* 2, no. 2(2011): 165–75. See also Blanchard et al., eds., *In the Wake of the Crisis*.

64 As we noted in the preface, this view was forcefully articulated by Nobel economist Robert Lucas.

65 See our earlier discussions (chapter 6 and elsewhere) for the multiple reasons that this is so.

Chapter 8. Structural Reforms That Further Compounded Failure

1 There can, however, be characteristics of an economy that impede adjustment to a changed situation. We will consider that possibility below.

2 Chapter 5 highlighted the role that the irrational exuberance brought on by the euro had played. European solidarity funds also contributed to this growth. Still, the earlier high growth rates showed that these could grow strongly, so long as there was enough demand. Indeed, these statistics put to the lie the argument that it was widespread corruption that prevented Greece from growing. There is no evidence that corruption increased after 2008; if anything, the government of George Papandreou had, in some ways, circumscribed it.

3 Some may have taken their own rhetoric so seriously that they may actually have come to believe it, in spite of all the evidence to the contrary. In a sense, though, the eurozone leaders had no choice: One can imagine the response of these countries if they were told that their standards of living were being sacrificed so that this poorly designed monetary arrangement could be saved and that their citizens—including the poorest—had to suffer so that the German and French banks could get repaid.

4 Indeed, the lower prices in these sectors, if the demand elasticity is relatively low, could actually lead to an increase in expenditure on imported goods, worsening the current account balance.

The reforms attempting to increase competition had complex distributive effects. In some cases, some of the local monopolists were (at least in the case of Greece) "oligarchs," but in others, the beneficiaries of protection were ordinary individuals—taxicab drivers who owned their own cars or mom-and-pop owners of the local pharmacy. If the reforms "worked," these individuals would be hurt, while their customers might be better off. (In the case of the pharmacy reforms, even that turned out to be questionable.)

5 The Troika drew many of its demands from a massive 2013 OECD "Competition Assessment Review" on supposedly problematic areas of Greek regulation. See *OECD Competition Assessment Reviews: Greece*, OECD Publishing, 2014, available at http://www.oecd.org/daf/competition/Greece-Competition-Assessment-2013.pdf. The Euro Summit Statement of July 12, 2015, makes reference to this report and specifically calls for adoption of "OECD toolkit I recommendations, including Sunday trade, sales periods, pharmacy own-

ership, milk and bakeries, except over-the-counter pharmaceutical products, which will be implemented in a next step, as well as for the opening of
macro-critical closed professions (e.g. ferry transportation.)" among many
other demands. The full details of the existing regulations and the changes
demanded can be found in the OECD report.

6 See my *New York Times* op-ed "Greece, the Sacrificial Lamb," July 25, 2015,
for more details of some of these reforms, especially that on fresh milk. After
publishing the article, I had expected to hear a detailed explanation from the
Troika of what they were up to. I did not.

7 Of course, it is important that the kilo loaf actually weighs a kilo, and in all
countries, in the absence of government inspections, there is a tendency to
cheat.

8 When one needs a prescription quickly, having a nearby pharmacy may have a
particularly high social value. The Troika seems not to have considered such
benefits in its calculus.

9 Greek law contained a variety of other restrictions. Some of the restrictions
were outdated, some plainly devices to restrict competition in an unhealthy
way. See *OECD Competition Assessment Reviews: Greece.* A Greek who read up
on the issue could be justified in concluding that the welfare the Troika really
cared about was that of big companies, including the multinationals—not Greek
consumers, and certainly not the local pharmacists. The OECD report that
underpinned the pharmacy reform specifically called for removing restrictions
on pharmacy chains.

10 Harriet Torry, "Germany Yet to Swallow Some Economic Medicine Prescribed for Greece: Overhauls Demanded by Greece's Creditors Go Beyond
Those Enacted Earlier in Germany," *Wall Street Journal*, updated July 14,
2015.

11 "The Euro-Summit 'Agreement' on Greece—annotated by Yanis Varoufakis,"
July 15, 2015, posted on his blog at http://yanisvaroufakis.eu/author/yanisv/.

12 And when the profits went to a European country already at full employment, the net effect for Europe as a whole could be significantly negative:
while Greece would contract, Germany, already at full employment, could not
expand.

13 This is especially likely to be the case under Greece's new program, where
when government revenues fall, taxes *must* be raised or other expenditure
must be cut back.

14 There were other aspects of the reform agenda that were also counterproductive, as we noted in the last chapter. The demand that even small businesses
pay their taxes a year ahead of time not only encourages noncompliance, but it
also has an adverse supply-side effect: it creates a large barrier to entry. Only
someone with enough capital to pay their taxes a year ahead of time can enter,

or stay, in business. While seemingly neutral toward small and large businesses, it actually is strongly biased against small businesses, which make up more than 80 percent of the Greek economy—for big businesses typically have easy access to funds; they can borrow. (Very large businesses can borrow in the international market, and so aren't even bothered by the weaknesses in Greek banks.) We noted other examples in the last chapter: the demand that even remote islands pay a high value-added tax.

15 See my article "The Book of Jobs" in *Vanity Fair*, January 2012.

16 Indeed, in a knowledge and learning economy Adam Smith's presumption that markets are efficient is reversed: in general, markets are not efficient; there will be an underinvestment in knowledge. I elaborated on these themes in my book with Bruce C. Greenwald, *Creating a Learning Society*.

17 Contrary to the neoclassical model, there is no natural convergence. See Stiglitz, "Leaders and Followers."

18 See Maria Mazzucato, *The Entrepreneurial State* (London: Anthem Press, 2014). More recently, ideological perspectives of the right have argued for the curtailment of these policies in the United States, to the point where today as a percentage of GDP, the proportion of the federal government's budget allocated for research and development is more than 70 percent lower than it was 50 years ago (according to data from SSTI and the American Association for the Advancement of Science).

19 For a sample of the large literature that has developed on the subject in recent years, see Ha-Joon Chang, *Kicking Away the Ladder* (London: Anthem Press, 2002); Justin Yifu Lin, *New Structural Economics* (Washington, DC: World Bank, 2012); Stiglitz and Lin, eds., *The Industrial Policy Revolution I*.

20 See Joseph E. Stiglitz, "The Origins of Inequality, and Policies to Contain It," *National Tax Journal* 68, no. 2 (2015): 425–48.

21 See Stiglitz et al., *Rewriting the Rules of the American Economy*; Stiglitz, *Price of Inequality*; Jacob S. Hacker and Paul Pierson, "Winner Take All Politics: Public Policy, Political Organization, and the Precipitous Rise of Top Incomes in the United States," *Politics and Society* 38, no. 2 (2010): 152–204.

22 As we have discussed, the structure of the eurozone and the EU itself has put impediments in the ability of European countries to deal with this; for any country that imposed too progressive of a tax system would see the very rich leave, even as they continued to have their firms conduct business in the country—as France discovered to its chagrin.

23 See the September 2015 Oxfam report "A Europe for the Many, Not the Few," available at https://www.oxfam.org/sites/www.oxfam.org/files/file_attachments/bp206-europe-for-many-not-few-090915-en.pdf; and OECD, "Crisis Squeezes Income and Puts Pressure on Inequality and Poverty," 2013, available at http://www.oecd.org/els/soc/OECD2013-Inequality-and-Poverty-8p.pdf.

24 See European Commission, "The Economic Adjustment Programme for Greece," Occasional Paper No. 61, May 2010, p. 28, available at http://ec.europa.eu/economy_finance/publications/occasional_paper/2010/pdf/ocp61_en.pdf.

25 The source for this data is Eurostat. Interestingly, news reports highlighted a study from a Greek labor union in 2014 that, using different methodology, found a far more dramatic increase in poverty. According to the report, the poverty rate doubled from 2009 to 2012—to the point that four in ten Greeks were living below the poverty line. For some category of Greeks—like the increasingly large number who could only find part-time employment—the poverty rate exceeded 50 percent. Even for full-time employees, wages had fallen so much that almost a fifth were in poverty—a threefold increase from 7.6 percent in 2009 to 19.7 percent in 2012. Ioanna Zikakou, "Four in Ten Greeks Live in Poverty," *Greek Reporter*, July 29, 2015, available at http://greece.greekreporter.com/2015/07/29/four-in-ten-greeks-live-in-poverty/.

26 See 2015 Oxfam report "A Europe for the Many, Not the Few"; Anthony B. Atkinson, *Inequality: What Can Be Done?* (Cambridge, MA: Harvard University Press, 2015); and references cited above in notes 20 and 21.

27 See Joseph E. Stiglitz, "New Theoretical Perspectives on the Distribution of Income and Wealth Among Individuals: Part I. The Wealth Residual," NBER Working Paper No. 21189, May 2015; and Stiglitz, *Price of Inequality*, and the references cited there.

28 There were evidently problems arising from some oligarchs attempting to take advantage of the special provision for shipping to shift profits of other sectors to shipping. Such profit shifting is a major problem throughout the corporate sector, with a recent major OECD effort attempting to limit the scope. The Troika could and should have focused its attention on this.

29 Thus Apple, the largest firm by capitalization in the world, has claimed that a very large part of its profits originated in a subsidiary in Ireland. Multinationals can easily claim that their profits are earned in a low-tax jurisdiction. The mechanics by which this is done need not detain us here. In today's globalized world, production of a final good entails multiple steps, and firms have considerable discretion in determining where, along the production line, true value added occurs. The system is called the "transfer price system," because companies pretend that they buy and sell partially completed goods from one country to another. The prices are supposed to be arm's-length prices; the problem is that in the case of most of these partially completed goods, there does not exist a true market to determine the value.

30 An international commission of which I was a member, the Independent Commission for the Reform of International Corporate Taxation, proposed an alternative, and at a major UN conference on Finance for Development meeting in Addis Abba in July 2015, the developing and emerging markets, led by India, virtually unanimously supported beginning a UN process to look at

these alternatives. Unfortunately, none of the eurozone countries supported the initiative, and with the strong opposition of the United States, it died.

31 We noted, too, in the last chapter the privatization of the regional airports, to a partnership between a German company (with significant public ownership—in that sense, simply a shift from ownership by the Greek public to the German public) and a Greek oligarch. The Syriza government opposed this privatization, undertaken earlier by the oligarchic-linked New Democracy Party, but the Troika insisted on it going forward. Not only would this strengthen the power of the oligarchs, but it set the stage for conflicts down the line: regional airports are local monopolies, able to exert enormous influence on the development of the surrounding region. How they are run can benefit some at the expense of others. Such "natural" monopolies need to be very strongly regulated, but one can be sure that even if the oligarchic partnership engages in abusive practices enriching its coffers at the expense of others in the region, any attempts to regulate the airport for the public good will be strongly resisted; and one suspects the Troika will then come down on the side of the German-oligarchy partnership.

32 As we noted earlier, his successor, Antonis Samaras, was from the New Democracy Party, itself widely viewed as closely connected to and supported by the oligarchs. When such connected-lending resumed—even to media companies that on strictly commercial terms should not have gotten loans—the Troika turned a blind eye. The *Financial Times*'s coverage of the election in January 2015 represents this widespread perception. In describing the potential electoral victory of Syriza, after observing that "analysts said politicians have been reluctant to loosen the tycoons' grip on the economy, since they rely on their handouts to finance election campaigns and pay party workers," the paper went on to observe: "Among the criticisms of prime minister Antonis Samaras' handling of the bailout by troika officials has been his reluctance to go after the vested interests of his centre-right New Democracy party." Indeed, the article notes that even some "in the troika feel that there has been too little burden sharing of Greece's austerity programme, with the working classes bearing the brunt of spending cuts and tax rises while wealthier citizens and politically connected businesses were shielded by New Democracy." (Kerin Hope, "Taming Greek Oligarchs Is Priority for Syriza," *Financial Times*, January 6, 2015.) George Pleios, head of the Department of Communication and Media Studies at the National and Kapodestrian University of Athens, in an article in *AnalyzeGreece!* ("The Greek Media, the Oligarchs, and the New Media Law," February 11, 2016) describes the links between the oligarchic vested interests and the media. Of course, the links between New Democracy and the oligarchs are viewed especially critically by opposition parties. Upon the defeat of New Democracy in the second election of 2015 and the election of Kyriakos Mitsotakis, the 47-year-old son of former New

Democracy leader and prime minister Constantine Mitsotakis as head of the party, one of the opposing parties issued a statement saying, "New Democracy will now become a hardline neo-liberal party that will only do the bidding of the oligarchs, losing any connection with the people." (Quoted in Demetris Nellas, "Reformist Lawmaker Elected Greek Opposition Leader," Associated Press, January 10, 2016.)

33 There would have been, in addition, obvious benefits to Europe's security, as a result of less dependence on Russian gas. It would have put Europe in a better position to push for its principles and values, say, in Ukraine.

34 In Indonesia, in the East Asia crisis, the IMF closed down 16 banks, and announced that more would be shut down but that depositors wouldn't be covered by deposit insurance—instigating a predictable run on the banking system. (For a fuller telling of this story, see my book *Globalization and Its Discontents*.)

35 Bank of Greece data for credit institutions.

Chapter 9. Creating a Eurozone That Works

1 Because one doesn't want to *risk* banks not being able to meet their obligations, banks are shut down or otherwise constrained when their net worth becomes too small. When you go to the ATM to get cash, and it says, "insufficient funds," it should be because there are insufficient funds in your account, not insufficient funds in the bank itself.

2 Bank regulations require that banks have adequate capital relative to loans outstanding. An increase in losses reduces bank capital. Raising capital in the midst of a downturn is difficult and expensive at best, impossible in some cases; hence, typically, banks respond by contracting lending.

3 Macro-prudential regulations are designed to avoid this pitfall: in good times, banks are required to have *much* more capital than is needed, recognizing that in bad times, capital will fall. So far, such regulations have not been put into force. Doing so is an important aspect of making the eurozone work.

4 Although, as we noted in chapter 5 recently many in Germany have expressed some misgivings about whether there should be a system of common deposit insurance.

5 The slow pace of reforms has led to other problems: Ireland, one of the first countries to receive assistance, became concerned that later countries would get a better deal.

6 See Stijn Claessens, Ashoka Mody, and Shahin Vallée, "Paths to Eurobonds," IMF Working Paper No. 12/172, July 2012; Guy Verhofstadt, "Mutualizing Europe's Debt," *New Perspectives Quarterly* 29, no. 3 (2012): 26–28; Jörg Bibow, "Making the Euro Viable," Levy Economics Institute Working Paper No. 842, July 2015; Paul De Grauwe and Wim Moesen, "Gains for All: A Proposal for a

Common Euro Bond," CEPS Commentary, April 3, 2009, available at https://
www.ceps.eu/system/files/article/2009/06/Forum.pdf; Peter Bofinger et al.,
"A European Redemption Pact," Vox, November 2011, available at http://voxeu
.org/article/european-redemption-pact; Markus Brunnermeier et al., "European Safe Bonds (ESBies)," Working Paper, September 30, 2011, available at
http://www.columbia.edu/~rr2572/papers/11-ESBies.pdf; Jacques Delpla and
Jakob von Weizsäcker, "The Blue Bond Proposal," Bruegel Policy Brief,
May 2010, available at http://bruegel.org/wp-content/uploads/imported/
publications/1005-PB-Blue_Bonds.pdf; European Commission, "Green Paper
on the Feasibility of Introducing Stability Bonds," Green Paper, November 23,
2011, available at http://ec.europa.eu/europe2020/pdf/green_paper_en.pdf;
Carlo Ambrogio Favero and Alessandro Missale, "EU Public Debt Management and Eurobonds," European Parliament, Directorate General for Internal Policies, Note, September 2010, available at http://www.europarl.europa
.eu/document/activities/cont/201106/20110607ATT20897/20110607ATT20
897EN.pdf; Christian Hellwig, and Thomas Philippon, "Eurobills, not Eurobonds," Vox, September 2, 2011, available at http://voxeu.org/article/eurobills-
not-euro-bonds; and Daniel Gros and Stefano Micossi, "A Bond-Issuing EU
Stability Fund Could Rescue Europe," *Europe's World*, February 1, 2009, available at http://europesworld.org/2009/02/01/a-bond-issuing-eu-stability-fund-
could-rescue-europe/#.VxUArfkrJD8). Reform proposals have to deal both
with the legacy of past debt as well as future borrowing. There are many details
of such proposals, including the maturity of the debt—that is, as Hellwig and
Philippon point out, whether the debt should be long-term or short-term (bonds
versus bills).

7 Source: European Commission data available at https://cohesiondata.ec
   .europa.eu/funds/erdf. Note that these funds are *transfers*, unlike the funds
   provided in the Troika programs, which are just loans. To some, this might
   suggest that Europe has shown less generosity to its old partners facing a
   period of distress than to the new entrants.

8 The eurozone has attempted to deal with this problem by ensuring that in
   normal times, countries have a large enough fiscal surplus (small enough deficit) that when there is an economic downturn, the 3 percent limit will not be
   breached.

9 Of course, that would not be the case if something has supposedly changed
   about these economies so that, say, an 18 or 25 percent unemployment rate
   represents "full employment." A standard definition of "full employment"
   is the rate such that when unemployment falls below that rate, price or wage
   inflation starts to increase. This is the concept of the natural rate introduced
   earlier, and it corresponds to the notion that economists refer to as "NAIRU"—
   the nonaccelerating inflation rate of unemployment—or "NAWRU," the nonaccelerating wage rate of unemployment. That level of unemployment is

sometimes called the "structural unemployment rate": there is something about the structure of the economy that prevents unemployment from going below that level. As nonsensical as that might seem, the European Commission has claimed that Spain has a structural unemployment rate that is of such magnitude. See my earlier discussion in chapter 6.

Also, rather than focusing on the actual deficit, one should focus on the primary deficit—what the deficit would have been in the absence of interest payments—which can be highly volatile. Europe has been doing that in the case of the crisis countries, but the convergence criteria remain focused on the overall deficit.

10 Which replaced the earlier temporary European Financial Stability Facility. See the discussion in chapter 1.

11 As we have noted that the United States provides.

12 Cross-border lending stimulated by the eurozone was supposed to offset this, but it has not worked, and mostly for an obvious reason: the information necessary to make the judgments required to ascertain which small business is a good risk is very local in nature. (See Stiglitz and Greenwald, *Towards a New Paradigm in Monetary Economics*.)

13 The Solidarity Fund for Stabilization could work with the lending facility to provide loans and partial guarantees targeting the risks generated by the uncertain macroeconomic environment.

14 The ECB lends to banks and buys government bonds. But for the most part, it does not lend to the *real* sector, to businesses or for the construction of roads, ports, or other infrastructure. According to their website, the EIB focuses on lending for infrastructure, environment, and climate; access to finance for smaller businesses; and innovation and skills, and it attempts to make their lending countercyclical. They describe themselves as "the largest multilateral borrower and lender by volume," providing "finance and expertise for sound and sustainable investment projects which contribute to furthering EU policy objectives, ... projects that make a significant contribution to growth and employment in Europe." See European Investment Bank, "EIB at a Glance," available at http://www.eib.org/about/.

15 To fulfill this expanded mission, it would need further recapitalization.

16 My book with Bruce C. Greenwald, *Towards a New Paradigm in Monetary Economics*, emphasized the importance of these tools, which have macroeconomic consequences, though traditionally regulators have focused solely on the safety and soundness of *individual* institutions. The implementation of these regulatory standards, with appropriate care and flexibility, should be conducted jointly between European and national authorities. I explained earlier how a system of a single European-wide regulatory/supervisory authority, without adequate flexibility and without common deposit insurance, could actually make matters worse.

17 In the United States, the Federal Reserve was given some of these tools in 1994 (the ability to regulate the mortgage market), but it studiously refused to use them, even as one of the members of its board warned of the consequences. See, for example, my book *Freefall* (New York: W. W. Norton, 2010).

18 Robert J. Gordon, *The Rise and Fall of American Growth* (Princeton, NJ: Princeton University Press, 2016).

19 And this is especially so because much of this public investment is complementary with private investment—that is, it raises its productivity, thus inducing *more* private investment. The noted economic historian Alexander Field shows how in the earlier era of the Great Depression, government infrastructure investments had precisely these effects. See Alexander J. Field, *The Great Leap Forward* (New Haven, CT: Yale University Press, 2011).

20 Central bank authorities in the United States have been perhaps the most articulate in espousing the neoliberal ideology: one can't tell a bubble until after it breaks, and it would be far cheaper to clean up any mess created by the bubble than to interfere in the wonders of the market, in its efficient allocation of resources. While the IMF, which plays such a central role in managing the global financial market, seems to have taken onboard the lessons of the crisis, even after the crisis I heard Ben Bernanke and US Treasury officials espouse views that seemed remarkably little altered. See, for example, Joseph E. Stiglitz, "Macroeconomics, Monetary Policy, and the Crisis," in *In the Wake of the Crisis*, ed. Blanchard et al., pp. 31–42; Joseph E. Stiglitz, "The Lessons of the North Atlantic Crisis for Economic Theory and Policy," in *What Have We Learned?: Macroeconomic Policy after the Crisis*, ed. George Akerlof, Olivier Blanchard, David Romer, and Joseph E. Stiglitz (Cambridge, MA: MIT Press, 2014), pp. 335–47.

21 Three other parts of the convergence strategy have already been discussed in the first three items of the reform agenda.

22 Though as we noted in chapter 4, sometimes, in an era of exuberance, the weakness in aggregate demand is offset by unsustainable investment.

23 It meant, too, that shocks from the outside would affect each differently.

24 It is thus natural to ask: Is it a coincidence that there is such a similarity between the harsh policies imposed on Africa and East Asia by Western creditors and those being imposed on Greece, in spite of a supposed deep underlying *solidarity* relationship in the latter that was not present in the former cases? Or are the policies really being driven by the same underlying ideologies and interests, including the interests of a creditor? I wrote about these extensively in *Globalization and Its Discontents*.

25 The logic of such a tax follows naturally from the logic of the current fines on violating fiscal rules. Such rules were imposed in the (partially misguided) view that having a deficit imposes costs (externalities) on others. We have shown that it is surpluses, especially of a large country like Germany, that

really impose costs on others. A tax discourages such behavior and helps align the narrow interests of the country with the broader interests of the eurozone.

26 And the share of low-wage jobs in the economy (those paying less than €9 an hour) increased substantially. See Fabian Lindner, "Following Germany's Lead to Economic Disaster," Social Europe (website), December 16, 2011, available at https://www.socialeurope.eu/2011/12/following-germanys-lead-to-economic-disaster/.

27 Of course, more was going on, as we have already noted. The rush of money into some of the periphery countries, based on the euro-euphoria, given the market's remarkable failure to note the long-standing risks of real estate bubbles and the newly created risks of a European sovereign debt default, had fueled an increase in prices and wages in these countries, especially relative to the declining levels in Germany. But these countries basically had no tools within the euro framework to curb these private sector excesses. Monetary policy was aimed at inflation across the eurozone, not at individual countries, and with the euro, they had given up all control of their own monetary policy. The dictums of the time, the neoliberal policies, proscribed interfering with the real estate bubbles. And in some of the other countries, the fight to maintain full employment, without other tools or assistance from the eurozone as a whole, led to fiscal deficits.

28 There are, as we noted in chapter 4, two ways that real exchange rates can be realigned: internal devaluation for the "overvalued" currencies and inflation for the undervalued currencies. At an abstract level, these two adjustment mechanisms look similar. In practice, they are markedly different. First, internal devaluation represents an increase in leverage, in the real value of the debts in these countries, and thus the hoped-for expansionary benefits may not be realized. By contrast, inflation is a form of deleveraging in the countries with an undervalued currency and thus has an expansionary effect.

Moreover, there is ample evidence of "downward rigidities" in wages and prices, so in practice, engineering an internal devaluation is far harder than managing limited increases in wages and prices.

29 Such policies might, at the same time, address the problems that Germany has been facing at the bottom of its income distribution.

30 There are many ways in which the ECB could accomplish this. It could, for instance, give preferential terms to banks that lend to small and medium-size enterprises. It could give preferential terms to countries where SME lending is constrained—for example, because of weaknesses in their banking systems. In the United States, CRA (Community Reinvestment Act) requirements have encouraged high-quality lending to underserved communities. (Contrary to conservative complaints that such lending was responsible for the financial crisis, repayment rates on such loans were comparable or superior to non-CRA lending and had *nothing* to do with the financial crisis. See National Commission on the Causes of the Financial and Economic Crisis in the

United States, *The Financial Crisis Inquiry Report*, 2011, available at https://www.gpo.gov/fdsys/pkg/GPO-FCIC/pdf/GPO-FCIC.pdf; and Stiglitz, *Freefall*.) Still another mechanism that the ECB could use to encourage productive lending is making access to the ECB window (i.e., the ability to borrow from the ECB) conditional on banks making loans for the productive sector, especially to SMEs, and restricting nonproductive lending. What may be required is a combination of carrots and sticks, incentives to behave well (specifically, to lend to SMEs) and punishments for not doing so.

31 Or through its socially destructive practices of predatory lending, market manipulation, or abusing its market power.

32 Many of the problems can be traced to the rules and regulations governing the financial system, others to tax laws that encourage speculation, still others to bankruptcy laws that encourage excessive risk-taking through derivatives and excessive consumer lending, and yet others to deficiencies in corporate governance. For the United States, see Stiglitz et al., *Rewriting the Rules of the American Economy*; and National Commission on the Causes of the Financial and Economic Crisis in the United States, *Financial Crisis Inquiry Report*. My book *Freefall* describes some of the general principles.

33 The Economic Policy Institute (EPI) reports that the average annual CEO compensation of the largest 350 firms in America was $16.3 million in 2014—303 times larger than that of the typical worker ("average compensation of production/nonsupervisory workers in the key industries of the firms included in the sample"). Average inflation-adjusted CEO compensation has grown nearly 997 percent since 1978. See the EPI's online report "Top CEOs Make 300 Times More than Typical Workers," June 21, 2015, available at http://www.ecgi.org/ceo/2012/documents/unrestricted/Bolton.pdf.

34 In the United States, provisions of the tax code have provided further encouragement to stock options.

35 See, in particular, Stiglitz et al., *Rewriting the Rules of the American Economy*. An example of changes in the rules that might encourage long-term thinking on the part of firms includes loyalty shares, which give more voting rights to long-term investors than to short-term investors. See Patrick Bolton and Frédéric Samama, "L-Shares: Rewarding Long-Term Investors," ECGI—Finance Working Paper No. 342/20132012, January 2012, available at http://www.ecgi.org/ceo/2012/documents/unrestricted/Bolton.pdf.

36 I helped develop this idea when I was at the World Bank in the midst of the East Asia crisis, when some 70 percent of Indonesian firms were in or approaching default, as were nearly 50 percent of firms in Thailand and Korea. See Marcus Miller and Joseph E. Stiglitz, "Bankruptcy Protection against Macroeconomic Shocks: The Case for a 'Super Chapter 11,' " World Bank Conference on Capital Flows, Financial Crises, and Policies, April 15, 1999, available at http://www2.warwick.ac.uk/fac/soc/pais/research/researchcentres/csgr/research/

keytopic/global/milrstig.pdf; and Marcus Miller and Joseph E.Stiglitz, "Leverage and Asset Bubbles: Averting Armageddon with Chapter 11?," *Economic Journal* 120, no. 544 (May 2010), pp. 500–518.

37 There is an easy answer for those who worry that this will put European firms at a competitive disadvantage: Europe needs to impose a cross-border tax on goods from countries that do not put a correspondingly high price on carbon. Such a charge would, I believe, be WTO-compliant. See my book *Making Globalization Work.*

38 It is perhaps obvious: the least skilled are those who are let go first when there is an economic downturn; and the cutbacks in government spending associated with economic downturns are particularly costly to those at the bottom, who depend on government social spending. While many governments say that they will "protect" such social spending, in many cases, the cutbacks are in fact regressive. See, for example, Jason Furman and Joseph E. Stiglitz, "Economic Consequences of Income Inequality," in *Symposium Proceedings—Income Inequality: Issues and Policy Options* (Jackson Hole, WY: Federal Reserve Bank of Kansas City, 1998), pp. 221–63; and Stiglitz, *Price of Inequality.*

39 This was an early insight in the literature in the theory of local public goods, where individuals could move freely from one local community to another. See, for example, Joseph E. Stiglitz, "Theory of Local Public Goods," in *The Economics of Public Services,* ed. M. S. Feldstein and R. P. Inman (London: Macmillan, 1977), pp. 274–333. (Paper presented to IEA Conference, Turin, 1974.)

40 One of the central themes of my book *Globalization and Its Discontents* is that one-size-fits-all policies are doomed to failure.

41 As we noted in chapter 4, there is a persistent view that confidence can be restored if governments cut deficits (spending), and with the restoration of confidence, investment and the economy will grow. No standard econometric model has confirmed these beliefs. On the contrary, the first-order effect of the deficit reduction is a slowdown in the economy, and the slowdown destroys confidence.

42 In chapter 8, in the section entitled "Reforms That Would Have Mattered," I describe a number of structural reforms in crisis countries, such as Greece, which would have helped restore growth and prosperity.

43 See the data presented in the previous chapter.

44 More recently, with several countries facing the possibility of such crises, and with US courts (who have jurisdiction over bonds issued in the United States) taking peculiar views, essentially making such restructurings impossible, there is a renewed demand for creating a sovereign debt-restructuring framework. The UN General Assembly, with the support of the vast majority of countries, adopted a resolution to begin creating such a framework

in September 2014, and a year later, with even more support, they adopted a set of principles to guide the design of the framework. Elsewhere, I have described what such a framework might look like. See Joseph E. Stiglitz, "Sovereign Debt: Notes on Theoretical Frameworks and Policy Analyses," in *Overcoming Developing Country Debt Crises*, ed. Barry Herman, Josè Antonio Ocampo, and Shari Spiegel (Oxford, UK: Oxford University Press, 2010), pp. 35–69.

45 Russia regained access to international capital markets less than two years after its 1998 default.

46 For a broader discussion of the role of debt restructurings in dealing with debt crises, see Joseph E. Stiglitz and Daniel Heymann, "Introduction," in *Life After Debt: The Origins and Resolutions of Debt Crisis*, ed. Joseph E. Stiglitz and Daniel Heymann (Houndmills, UK, and New York: Palgrave Macmillan, 2014), pp. 1–39; and the other papers in that volume.

47 As we noted in chapter 2, the Erasmus program, where European students study in each other's countries, is an example.

48 As we noted in the case of the provision of deposit insurance within a banking union.

Chapter 10. Can There Be an Amicable Divorce?

1 Martin Wolf, in his very thoughtful writing about the euro and the euro crisis, has come to much the same conclusions, and has often used the marriage metaphor, suggesting that the breakup of the eurozone, including the exit of Greece, would be a messy divorce. This chapter shows how it might be somewhat less messy—though it may be stretching it to suggest it could ever be truly amicable. See Martin Wolf, *The Shifts and Shocks: What We've Learned—and Have Still to Learn—from the Financial Crisis* (New York: Penguin Press, 2014).

2 I won't discuss here the optimal groupings but instead will focus on how such a divorce can be managed.

3 Those in finance describe the divorce as providing an in-the-money option.

4 Of course, this logic implies that for countries that have managed to grow reasonably well within the confines of the eurozone, the benefit to leaving would be less than the cost.

5 See, for instance, Matthew Yglesias, "How Greece Leaving the Euro Would Actually Work," Vox, July 16, 2015, available at http://www.vox.com/2015/7/6/8901303/greek-crisis-grexit-how-it-works; and Jack Ewing, "Weighing the Fallout of a Greek Exit from the Euro," *New York Times*, July 9, 2015.

6 Regulators, legislatures, and courts in antitrust actions have finally begun intervening to curtail the high fees and abusive practices, but the fees remain far higher than what they should be.

7 As we noted in chapter 7, among the foolish mistakes of the Troika were its policies that effectively discouraged the use of the banking system and thus almost encouraged tax avoidance.

There are problems of scams in any monetary arrangement, and cyber security is one of the key problems faced in modern electronic payments mechanisms. The advantages of electronic transactions are, nonetheless, overwhelming, which is why even with monopoly pricing, there has been a shift toward this system.

8 The major exception, for the purchase of goods and services from abroad, is discussed later in this chapter.

9 Indeed, European authorities effectively encouraged the creation of such a system when they imposed restrictions on how much money people in Greece and Cyprus could take out of their accounts. This system goes just a little further: rather than limiting the amount that can be taken out of one's bank account to a very little amount—say, €50 a day—it puts the limit at zero, forcing the economy to move to a cashless electronic economy.

10 In the preface, we noted the role that this issue played in America's election in 1896.

11 There are several other "slips between the cup and the lips." Central banks in Europe, the United States, and Japan have increased their own balance sheet, providing more liquidity to their banks; but their banks have simply put much of the money back in deposit at the central bank, not even creating more private credit. When credit is created, in a world of globalization, it doesn't have to stay within the borders of the country creating it. In the early days of US QE, much of the money went abroad to the booming emerging markets. Finally, even when it stays at home, it can not only be used for buying existing assets but also to provide "margin" for speculative gambles.

12 The evolution of the banking system from the primitive corn economy toward its modern form is interesting and informative. Early banks were really based more on gold deposits than on corn deposits. Those with more gold than they wanted to spend put it in the bank, and the bank lent it out to others. Soon, banks discovered that they could create pieces of paper, claims on gold, that others would accept, and that they could produce more of such pieces of paper than they had gold, in the knowledge that not all holders of these pieces of paper would ask for their money simultaneously. As it gave gold to some who asked for it, it would receive gold from others.

Occasionally, there would be a panic when holders of these pieces of paper worried whether the bank could fulfill its promises, and, of course, when they panicked and all went to the bank to demand their gold, there was not enough to satisfy their demands. The banks would go bankrupt, and the economy could be thrown into a depression.

Deposit insurance was invented to prevent these panics: the government explicitly stood behind the banks' promises. This gave greater faith that the promises would be honored (so long as there was faith in the government), and this in turn reduced the likelihood of a panic. But if the government was to provide these guarantees, this insurance, it had to make sure that the bank was acting responsibly—for example, lending out money to people who could actually pay it back, and not lending to the owners of the bank and his friends. Gerry Caprio, with whom I worked at the World Bank and who studied government rescues around the world, was fond of saying that there are two kinds of countries—those who have deposit insurance and know it, and those who have deposit insurance and don't know it. Sweden, before its financial crisis in the 1990s, had no deposit insurance, but it rescued its banks nonetheless. In the 2008 crisis, around the world suddenly deposit insurance was extended to accounts that had not been fully insured before.

One can understand government taking on this new role, partially as a result of the magnitude and frequency of the panics and downturns in the market economy in the 19th and early 20th centuries. Moreover, as advanced countries, like the United States, transformed themselves from agricultural economies to industrial economies, with an increasing fraction of the population dependent on manufacturing and other nonagricultural jobs, these economic fluctuations took a toll. So long as ordinary citizens had little voice in what government did, so what if so many suffered so much? But with the extension of the franchise and increasing democratic engagement, it became increasingly difficult for government to ignore these mega-failures of the market.

13 See, for example, John Kay, *Other People's Money: The Real Business of Finance* (New York: Public Affairs, 2015); and Adair Turner, *Between Debt and the Devil: Money, Credit, and Fixing Global Finance* (Princeton, NJ: Princeton University Press, 2015).

14 More broadly, it has been shown that much of the increase in inequality in the advanced countries in recent decades is related to finance. See, in particular, James K. Galbraith, *Inequality and Instability: A Study of the World Economy Just before the Great Crisis* (New York: Oxford University Press, 2012); and Stiglitz, *Price of Inequality*.

15 For a further development of this critique, see my book *Freefall*.

16 This is especially so, through the privatization of gains and the socialization of losses that has become a regular feature in economies with too-big-to-fail banks. (See *Freefall*.)

17 The system is symmetric. The central bank may decide that there is too much money in the economic system—that is, the banks are lending too much, using "money" that they receive in repayment. In that case, the government can buy back rights to issue credit: they buy back the money that they have allowed the banks to effectively manage on their behalf. Again, there can be an open auc-

tion for those most willing to give up rights to issue credit. This would literally drain money out of the banking system.

18 Entry would presumably occur to the point where the before-tax return to capital (measured over the business cycle) would be slightly in excess of the normal return to capital. Some excess return may be necessary to induce more responsible social behavior on the part of bankers.

19 According to the World Travel & Tourism Council, which also estimates that tourism's total, secondary contribution to the Greek economy is about 17 percent of GDP. See the group's report "Travel & Tourism: Economic Income 2015: Greece," available at https://www.wttc.org/-/media/files/reports/eco nomic%20impact%20research/countries%202015/greece2015.pdf.

20 Earlier, we argued that an internal devaluation was likely to have limited benefits and significant costs, because it would simultaneously hurt the non-traded sector, even as the traded-goods sector was (slightly) helped. To accomplish a real devaluation required large declines in wages and that these wage decreases would get translated into price decreases for traded goods. A change in the nominal exchange rate *immediately* translates into an improvement in the real exchange rate. The main risks are (a) that an increase in inflation makes these benefits only temporary, and (b) as with internal devaluation, the increased real leverage when debts are denominated in foreign currency would lead to decreased demand for nontraded goods. Later in the chapter, I describe reforms that mitigate these effects.

21 See Warren Buffet, "America's Growing Trade Deficit Is Selling the Nation out from Under Us. Here's a Way to Fix the Problem—And We Need to Do It Now," *Fortune*, November 10, 2003.

22 To prevent the buildup of chits—speculators might buy them on the bet that a chit is more valuable some years into the future—the chits should be date-stamped; they would have to be used, for example, within a period of one year. (It's possible that some international rules, such as those currently stipulated by the WTO, would need to be changed to accommodate the system of chits. At least in the context of a transition of the kind being contemplated here, where a country faces a current account problem, existing rules provide sufficient flexibility that there should be no problem.)

23 Actually, as we have already noted, the current account had already turned into surplus by early 2015, and during 2015, it moved in different months between positive and negative. Given this, even without the system of chits, the magnitude of devaluation might have been limited. The system of chits, by ensuring the market that there would not be large trade deficits, would add further stability to the market.

It should be obvious that we have not had space to describe in detail the full workings of our electronic money/credit/chit system. The basic principles, however, should be clear. For instance, when a Greek firm exports olives to the

United States, it would deposit the dollars it receives into the electronic banking system, receiving a credit to its Greek-euro account of an amount equal to the Greek-euro value of those dollars. (It would also receive a corresponding number of chits, which it could freely sell to others.) The amount of "money" in the banking system would increase as a result of the deposit. The central bank would take this into account in deciding on the magnitude of credit to auction off. The system is designed to discourage circumvention—for example, through underinvoicing. Any such underinvoicing (besides being against the law) would result in the exporter not receiving the trade chits that he would otherwise be entitled to. There is no incentive for the creation of a black market.

24 Even now, it has surpassed prior expectations of a small primary deficit up until July 2015 by actually achieving a relatively large surplus, which it has maintained in the first quarter of 2016. See Silvia Merler, "Greek Budget Update—August," August 17, 2015, blog post on the website of the European think tank Bruegel, available at http://bruegel.org/2015/08/greece-budget-update-august/.

25 Indeed, one might argue that the counterproductive conditionality imposed on the crisis countries, which so undermined their economies, provides a moral obligation on the part of the eurozone. But I suspect that many of the eurozone members would not recognize this moral obligation and place the onus on the failure of the programs on the crisis countries themselves. In the absence of a grant, the eurozone could provide loans, with senior creditor status. (In effect, "lending in arrears." See the discussion below.)

26 That is, the chit rate could be set to generate trade balance, or even, as we noted, a surplus.

27 They got converted at the exchange rate defined in the entry into the euro. Still, the "switch" in currencies had far from trivial consequences, both for credit and debtor, since the risk properties of the two currencies could be quite different. A longer-term bond issued, say, in 1991 in drachmas would have paid an interest rate reflecting the exchange-rate risk. With the conversion into a euro, that risk was markedly reduced, handing the creditor, in effect, a large gift.

28 The government should treat the payment of a foreign debt in euros like an import. The foreign claimant would be given a claim on Greek-euros, which could be used to purchase goods from others inside Greece. However, if the creditor wanted to convert the Greek-euros into ordinary or German euros, he would have to purchase the foreign exchange, using chits.

Alternatively, the country could impose capital controls, paying the creditor in euros but not allowing the euros to leave the country. For instance, it could set up euro-bank accounts within the country, with money being able to move smoothly from one euro-bank account to another but not being able to be converted into currency or euros in a foreign euro account.

Capital controls have been used in the context of crises in Iceland, Greece, and Cyprus. This proposal is, in effect, a more efficient and simplified way of implementing such constraints.

29 We may have underestimated the costs of bankruptcy: with many of the debts contracted under foreign law, as we have noted, redenomination may not be possible. There might be litigation over whether payment in a "constrained euro"—a euro constrained to be spent in Greece, with a fee to take it out (the price of the chit)—is the same as a payment in an unconstrained euro and therefore fulfills the debt contract. If there is not redenomination, there would be adverse effects on balance sheets—but no worse than those associated with internal devaluation. A super–Chapter 11 might enable firms with excessive debts issued in foreign denomination under foreign jurisdiction to have a quick and fresh start. This might be facilitated by laws allowing easy asset restructurings—for example, a family with a foreign-denominated mortgage on its home issued in a foreign jurisdiction could treat its home as if it were a separate incorporated subsidiary, converting the mortgage debt into equity in the home but without forcing the individual into full bankruptcy. Similarly, this could be done for corporations. Given the increasing litigious nature of Western society, all of this is likely to be messy, but it is still less onerous than the current depression.

30 In any debt restructuring/bankruptcy, there is a provision called "lending in arrears," which allows those who lend to the entity after the restructuring process begins to get paid back in full, before other claimants are paid back in part. This should also be part of any amicable divorce.

31 George Soros forcefully and eloquently put this idea forward in his article "The Tragedy of the European Union and How to Resolve It," *New York Review of Books*, September 7, 2012. Indeed, the view that Germany should leave is widely shared among economists. Mervyn King, former head of the Bank of England, commented on CNBC: "That would be the best way forward, and I would hope that many of my American friends would stop pushing the Europeans to throw money at the problem and say we must make the euro successful." Tom DiChristopher, "Germany Should Leave Euro Zone: Mervyn King," CNBC, March 21, 2016, available at http://www.cnbc.com/2016/03/21/germany-should-leave-eurozone-mervyn-king.html.

Chapter 11. Toward a Flexible Euro

1 At least relative to the *hopes*, though not perhaps relative to the reality of the situation.

2 These are both ideas discussed at greater length in chapter 9 for creating a eurozone that works. This chapter argues that by adopting *some* of these ideas, Europe could gradually move toward such a regime.

3 There are, in addition, a host of legal issues: Would it be possible to settle a euro-denominated debt with a payment in a Greek- or German-euro? The functioning of the system would obviously be greatly facilitated if that were the case, as we noted in the previous chapter.

4 The system might not, in fact, be in the interests of all those in Europe: Germany has gained enormously from the current system, which has made it easier for it to run huge trade surpluses, which have contributed to its economic strength, even as they have contributed to instabilities in the global economy. The system of the flexible euro would almost surely lead to a stronger German-euro. As we have noted, Germany might even be unable to sustain its surpluses. It would thus not be a surprise were it to oppose this system.

Chapter 12. The Way Forward

1 See IMF, "Greece: Ex Post Evaluation of Exceptional Access under the 2010 Stand-By Arrangement," IMF Country Report No. 13/156, June 2013, available at https://www.imf.org/external/pubs/ft/scr/2013/cr13156.pdf; and IMF, "Ireland: Ex Post Evaluation of Exceptional Access under the 2010 Stand-By Arrangement," IMF Country Report No. 15/20, January 2015, available at https://www.imf.org/external/pubs/ft/scr/2015/cr1520.pdf.

2 See Richard Koo, "EU Refuses to Acknowledge Mistakes Made in Greek Bailout," Nomura Research Institute, July 14, 2015, available at http://ineteconomics.org/ideas-papers/blog/eu-refuses-to-acknowledge-mistakes-made-in-greek-bailout.

3 There are many possible reasons for this dominance. One is that many of the other countries in the eurozone, not yet in a crisis, worry that they, too, may need a bailout sometime in the future. They don't want to get on the bad side of Germany. At home, their leaders talked tough about how they would stand up to Germany. Somehow, the outcome of the meetings reflected their views at most in the margins.

Bailouts typically required the unanimous agreement of all countries, and in the case of Germany, the bailout has to be submitted to the parliament. The strong antibailout sentiment in Germany means that it could exercise effective veto power: if the bailout agreement does not accord sufficiently with what German leaders think and want, the chances of passing the parliament are slim.

The actions of the ECB have on several occasions been brought before German courts on the grounds that they violated the German constitution. The German courts have so far deferred to higher European courts—in January 2015, for example, the European Court of Justice ruled in favor of an ECB government bond-buying scheme, in a suit originally brought to the German Constitutional Court by several German plaintiffs. But the constant threat of a suit casts a pallor over the actions of the ECB.

4 According to a 2012 poll conducted by TNS Emnid. See "Most Germans Oppose Euro, French Also Losing Faith: Polls," Reuters, September 17, 2012, available at http://www.reuters.com/article/us-eurozone-germany-poll-idUSBRE 88G0Y720120917.

5 See Seth Mydans, "Crisis Aside, What Pains Indonesia Is the Humiliation," *New York Times*, March 10, 1998. The actual photo of the two men is widely available on the Internet: Camdessus standing sternly with folded arms over a stooped Suharto as the latter signs the agreement.

6 See Karl Lamers and Wolfgang Schäuble, "More Integration Is Still the Right Goal for Europe," *Financial Times*, August 31, 2014.

7 See Yanis Varoufakis, "Greek Debt Denial: A Modest Debt Restructuring Proposal and Why It Was Ignored," in *Too Little, Too Late: The Quest to Resolve Sovereign Debt Crises*, ed. Martin Guzman, José Antonio Ocampo, and Joseph E. Stiglitz (New York: Columbia University Press, 2016).

8 When 62 percent of Portugal's voters expressed opposition to austerity (a number remarkably similar to that in Greece), Portugal's conservative president publicly expressed his reluctance to install the antiausterity coalition that had won overwhelmingly. (The pro-austerity Portugal Ahead coalition—an alliance between the the CDS [People's Party] and the PSD [Social Democratic Party]—had won a plurality of votes, because the antiausterity votes were divided among several parties. But there was no way that it could form a coalition to continue the depression-inducing austerity policies.) It may have been partly that, in an antidemocratic way, he didn't want the country to change course. But it may have been partly out of genuine concern: What would happen if the government actually tried to implement policies that were consistent with the election promises? Perhaps he feared Europe's vengeance. For Portugal, the good news was that they were out of their Troika program, so the Troika's stranglehold over Portugal was much less. But many in Portugal realized the vagaries of the market: even if it did everything right, market sentiments can be very volatile, and if it again got closed out of capital markets, what options would it have?

Interpreting election results is always difficult: they are often influenced not just by policies and political sentiments but by personalities and events of the moment. Thus, in a subsequent election for the presidency of Portugal, the center-right party candidate won with 52 percent of the vote in January 2016. Meanwhile, in February 2016, the Irish, who seemed to have been most accepting of the austerity policies imposed on them, turned out the government that had imposed them, though eventually, after months of haggling, Prime Minister Enda Kenny was able to form a fragile minority government and maintain leadership.

9 Stiglitz et al., *Rewriting the Rules of the American Economy*.

10 Eurozone leaders often show their compassion by espousing a commitment to

a safety net. The question is, though, how low is the safety net? I would argue that a safety net that leaves large fractions of the population and an even larger fraction of children in poverty is an inadequate safety net, and is a far cry from inclusive growth. The safety net provided as part of the Greek program is not an adequate safety net.

11 See "Europe: The Current Situation and the Way Forward," Leaders in Global Economy Lecture, Columbia University, April 15, 2015, available at http://www.bundesfinanzministerium.de/Content/EN/Reden/2015/2015-04-15-columbia-university.html. In that same lecture, he revealed something about broader social attitudes. As he sought to explain the Great Recession, he repeated a view popular in extremely conservative circles around the world: "US policymakers tried to promote home ownership of poorly skilled workers by having less stringent lending practices." This view has been forcefully rejected by the bipartisan Financial Crisis Inquiry Commission. Indeed, it has become increasingly clear that not just bad judgments by those in the private sector were to blame, but fraudulent practices. See National Commission on the Causes of the Financial and Economic Crisis in the United States, *Financial Crisis Inquiry Report*, 2011.

12 As we discussed in chapter 2, what is at stake is not just a matter of views about how the economy works; it is also a matter of *values*. For instance, elsewhere in this book we have referred to the theory and evidence in support of the thesis that economies with less inequality and more equality of opportunity perform better. They grow faster and their growth is more sustainable. But *shared* prosperity is also a matter of values. The commitment at the UN to sustainable development goals on September 25, 2015, can be seen as a broad global consensus behind the ideas of inclusive growth. (See "Transforming Our World: The 2030 Agenda for Sustainable Development," available at https://sustainabledevelopment.un.org/post2015/transformingourworld.)

13 Indeed, the life of a peasant in 1700 was little better than it would have been two millennia earlier. See Stiglitz and Greenwald, *Creating a Learning Society*.

14 Germany labels these migrants as economic migrants, differentiating them from the humanitarian migrants, including those fleeing the war in Syria. But an "economic migrant" who sees as the alternative to migration watching his family starve sees things through a very different lens.

15 In this sense, the monetary union is different from trade integration. There, most economists believe that earlier trade agreements have generated small overall gains, though the distributive effects often overwhelm these gains, so that large proportions of the population are worse off. (As we will note, the newer proposed trade agreements, like the monetary union, may not even generate overall benefits.)

16 The so-called ISDS (investor state dispute settlement) allows corporations to sue governments for the passage of any regulation that lowers their expected

profits—no matter the extent to which those profits originate by imposing harms on others. See my column with Adam Hersh, "The Trans-Pacific Free-Trade Charade," Project Syndicate, October 2, 2015, available at https://www .project-syndicate.org/commentary/trans-pacific-partnership-charade-by-joseph-e--stiglitz-and-adam-s--hersh-2015-10.

17 See chapter 8.

18 See the discussion in chapter 1.

Afterword: Brexit and its Aftermath

1 The EU Council is the ultimate decision-making body in the EU. It consists of the heads of government of the constituent countries. The EU Commission manages the EU on a day-to-day basis. The Commissioners are appointed by the Council. Each Commissioner has a set of responsibilities analogous to a minister, e.g. there is a Competition Commissioner, a Commissioner for the Environment, etc. In practice, each country in the EU gets to appoint one Commissioner. The one direct link between voters and the EU is through the elections to the European Parliament, which divides its time between Brussels and Strasbourg. Historically, the European Parliament had very limited powers, but has strived to increase those powers over time.

2 As we noted, in the case of Denmark and Sweden.

3 As we have noted, in the case of Norway.

4 In the case of France and the Netherlands.

5 Pew Research Center, "Euroskepticism Beyond Brexit" (June 2016); available at: http://www.pewglobal.org/2016/06/07/euroskepticism-beyond-brexit/.

6 In fact, the Euro fell by more than 4 percent against the dollar in the first several hours after the Brexit vote, though it has since rebounded slightly.

7 "The United Kingdom will have to accept being regarded as a third country, which won't be handled with kid gloves," Juncker reportedly said, in a comment representative of his views, about a month before the referendum. "If the British leave Europe, people will have to face the consequences." See Alastair MacDonald, "Juncker says on Brexit: British 'deserters' to get no EU favour," Reuters, May 20, 2016; available at: http://www.reuters.com/article/us-britain-eu-juncker-idUSKCN0YB1O3.

8 There were other forces at work as well, such as a commitment to human rights. Sometimes, the two can come into conflict, especially in the area of labor, where neoliberalism has led to a weakening of worker protections, and the concern for human rights has pushed in the opposite direction. See the discussion below.

9 US Census Historical Income Tables H-6: http://www.census.gov/data/tables/time-series/demo/income-poverty/historical-income-households.html. The most recent median household income data is from 2014. The $53,657 median

income for that year is in between the figures for 1996 ($53,345) and 1997 ($54,443). In 1989, median household income was $53,306. (All these figures are in inflation-adjusted dollars based on 2014 values.)

10 US Census Historical Income Tables P-36: http://www.census.gov/data/ tables/time-series/demo/income-poverty/historical-income-people.html.

11 Anne Case and Angus Deaton, "Rising morbidity and mortality in midlife among white non-Hispanic Americans in the 21st century," *Proceedings of the National Academy of Sciences* 112, no. 49 (2015): 15078–15083.

12 In the UK, median income for working-age adult workers is lower than a decade ago, but 30 percent higher than two decades ago (UK National Statistics, Households below average income 1994/1995 to 2014/2015).

13 Located at the 80th percentile in the global income scale. In the UK, this group is typically referred to as the working class, while in the US it is the middle class. Branko Milanović has highlighted these findings in several presentations and papers, and most recently in *Global Inequality: A New Approach for the Age of Globalization* (Cambridge, Mass.: Belknap Press, 2016).

14 The effects would have been particularly hard had it not been that most of the advanced countries have had a system of social protection. In the US, for instance, 91 percent of the gains in the first three years of the "recovery" went to the upper 1 percent. More broadly, the OECD concluded that "excluding the mitigating effects of the welfare state, via taxes and transfers on income, inequality has increased by more over the past three years to the end of 2010 than in the previous twelve." See OECD, "Crisis squeezes income and puts pressure on inequality and poverty," May 2013; available at http://www.oecd.org/els/ soc/OECD2013-Inequality-and-Poverty-8p.pdf.

15 Eurostat. The latest comparable data at time of writing.

16 Of course, he benefited from the lower oil prices as well.

17 This is the central theme of my books *The Price of Inequality* and *The Great Divide*.

18 England's tuition policy was in marked contrast to that of Scotland, which had kept tuition fees much lower. England's income-contingent loans followed the very successful model that had long been used in Australia.

19 See Paul Samuelson, "International Trade and the Equalisation of Factor Prices," *Economic Journal* 58, no. 230 (June 1948): 163–84, and Wolfgang F. Stolper and Paul A. Samuelson, "Protection and Real Wages," *Review of Economic Studies* 9, no. 1(1941): 58–73. For a broader discussion, see Chapter 3 of *Making Globalization Work*.

20 Many economists argue that the West has other "institutional" advantages, such as those associated with the rule of law and the protection of property rights.

21 David H. Autor, David Dorn, Gordon H. Hanson, "The China Syndrome: Local Labor Market Effects of Import Competition in the United States," *American Economic Review* 103, no. 6 (2013): 2121–68.

22 Indeed, one would expect the effects to be even stronger, given the higher over-all unemployment rate.

23 Indeed, in a world with imperfect risk markets—the world we actually live in—free trade and trade liberalization can actually make almost everyone worse off. Trade liberalization exposes individuals to a multitude of new risks. See David Newbery and J. E. Stiglitz, "Pareto Inferior Trade," *Review of Economic Studies* 51, no. 1 (1984): 1–12. (The term "Pareto inferior" simply means *everyone* is worse off.)

24 This will be true if skilled and unskilled workers are complements, with more skilled workers increasing the productivity of unskilled workers.

25 See http://greece.greekreporter.com/2014/08/03/7500-doctors-have-left-greece-in-six-years/.

26 Mahathir Mohamad, the former prime minister of Malaysia, described to me how this was the *real* theft of intellectual property.

27 In some cases, the magnitude of the migration was enormous. In Bulgaria, for instance, a country with a population of some 9 million in 1985, more than 800,000 emigrated after the beginning of the transition to a market econ-omy; today, the population is just 7.2 million. Source: United Nations World Population Prospects 2015 database; available at https://esa.un.org/unpd/wpp/.

28 With a dedicated Wikipedia page: see https://en.wikipedia.org/wiki/Euromyth. But at the same time, there does appear to be a problem. A BBC report claimed that "Marketing standards for 26 types of produce were scrapped in November 2008," following information that "a fifth of produce had been rejected by shops across the EU for failing to meet the requirements." (BBC News, "Attempt at EU-wide 'wonky fruit and veg' ban fails," March 25, 2010.) In some cases, such as ice cream, it appears that recent EU standards represent a weakening of regulations. Thus, a report in *Eat Out* magazine argued that "The future of tra-ditional ice cream in the UK is under threat after the removal of long standing quality standards by the EU." (December 16, 2014.)

29 At least in the ways that we have seen it manifest itself in the eurozone. But the UK did feel the consequences of a host of EU-wide regulations, and many felt that there was a democratic deficit in the way these were promulgated and enforced.

30 But not too much store should be put on this: the rating agencies' record in anticipating problems is dismal, and their ratings often simply follow the con-ventional wisdom.

31 This is the 10-year yield rate on German and US Government bonds.

32 Given that the new Prime Minister Theresa May has repeatedly said that "Brexit means Brexit" this scenario seems increasingly unlikely.

33 Many in the UK seem to believe that the UK alone will determine when the clock starts ticking. It should be clear that the EU has more than a little power

to induce UK to move more quickly, and as this book goes to press, there is increasing evidence that the UK will be put under enormous pressure to invoke Article 50 quickly.

34 The United States International Trade Commission (USITC) has estimated an increase to annual GDP of 0.15% by 2032, as compared to baseline scenario. See USITC, "Trans-Pacific Partnership Agreement: Likely Impact on the U.S. Economy and on Specific Industry Sectors," Publication Number 4607 (May 2016). Other studies have shown even lower or more ambiguous gains to GDP. See, for example, Peter A. Petri and Michael G. Plummer, "The Economic Effects of the Trans-Pacific Partnership: New Estimates," Peterson Institute Working Paper 16-2 (January 2016); available at http://piie. com/publications/wp/wp16-2.pdf; World Bank, "Potential Macroeconomic Implications of the Trans-Pacific Partnership," Chapter 4 in *Global Economic Prospects* (January 2016): 219–55; available at http://pubdocs.worldbank. org/en/847071452034669879/Global-Economic-Prospects-January-2016- Implications-Trans-Pacific-Partnership-Agreement.pdf; and Mary E. Burfisher et al. "Agriculture in the Trans-Pacific Partnership," ERR-176, U.S. Department of Agriculture, Economic Research Service (October 2014); available at http:// www.ers.usda.gov/media/1692509/err176.pdf. The latter report estimated no real effect on GDP at all by 2025. On the other hand, a study from Tufts University predicted a loss to GDP. See Jeronim Capaldo and Alex Izurieta, with Jomo Kwame Sundaram, "Trading Down: Unemployment, Inequality and Other Risks of the Trans-Pacific Partnership Agreement," Global Development and Environment Institute Working Paper No. 16-01 (January 2016); available at http://www.ase.tufts.edu/gdae/Pubs/wp/16-01Capaldo-IzurietaTPP. pdf. As Adam Hersh and I explained in briefs we compiled for the Roosevelt Institute, the most credible calculations are those that suggest the net effect is likely negative. See "Tricks of the Trade Deal: Six Big Problems with the Trans-Pacific Partnership," March 28, 2016; available at http://rooseveltinstitute.org/ tricks-trade-deal-six-big-problems-trans-pacific-partnership/.

35 International Monetary Fund, "The Liberalization and Management of Capital Flows – An Institutional View" (November 14, 2012).

36 Many of these problems have been extensively researched earlier in the vast literature on fiscal federalism and the theory of local public goods. The "practical" men (and they were almost all men) creating the European Union seemed to have paid less attention to this literature and its insights than they perhaps should have done.

The effect of lowering the corporate income tax rate on investment illustrates the contrast between neoliberal ideology (which suggested that the lower the tax rate the better) and economic science. Since most investment is debt-financed, and in virtually all countries interest payments are tax-deductible, the corporate tax rate lowers the marginal return and marginal cost of investment proportionally, and so does not affect investment, at least in the "perfect world" of neoliberalism where firms are not cash-constrained. Indeed, with conventional depreciation allowances, where firms are allowed to deduct from their profits an amount for the depreciation of their plant and equipment which is greater than the true depreciation (that is, to depreciate their investments faster than true depreciation), lowering tax rates may actually lead to lower investment. See, for instance, J. E. Stiglitz, "Taxation, Corporate Financial Policy and the Cost of Capital," *Journal of Public Economics* 2, no. 1 (1973): 1–34.

37 The basic principles of the benefits vs. costs of product diversity have also been extensively examined within the economics literature. Individuals themselves value diversity, and different individuals have preferences for different commodities. But there can be significant costs to such product diversity. It is not clear either that markets or the EU have struck the right balance. See, for example, Avinash Dixit and J. E. Stiglitz, "Monopolistic Competition and Optimum Product Diversity," *American Economic Review* 67, no. 3 (June 1977): 297–308; and J. E. Stiglitz, "Toward a More General Theory of Monopolistic Competition," in M. Peston and R. Quandt (eds), *Prices, Competition, & Equilibrium* (Oxford: Philip Allan/Barnes & Noble Books, 1986), pp. 22–69.

38 There is some controversy about youth voter turnout. Early reports suggested it was very low, but a later study showed that that was not the case; but that much older individuals voted even more strongly for Brexit.

INDEX

Page numbers beginning with 361 refer to endnotes;
page numbers in *italics* refer to graphs.